The 1549 Rebellions and the Making of Early Modern England

This is a major new study of the 1549 rebellions, the largest and most important risings in Tudor England. Based upon extensive new archival evidence, the book sheds fresh light on the causes, course and long-term consequences of the insurrections. Andy Wood focuses on key themes in the new social history of politics, concerning the end of medieval popular rebellion; the Reformation and popular politics; popular political language; early modern state formation; speech, silence and social relations; and social memory and the historical representation of the rebellions. He examines the long-term significance of the rebellions for the development of English society, arguing that they represent an important moment of discontinuity between the late medieval and the early modern periods. This compelling new history of Tudor politics from the bottom up will be essential reading for late medieval and early modern historians as well as early modern literary critics.

ANDY WOOD is Professor of Social History at the School of History, University of East Anglia. His first book, *The Politics of Social Conflict: The Peak Country, 1520–1770* (1999), was declared *Proxime Accessit* in 1999 for the Royal Historical Society's Whitfield Prize.

Cambridge Studies in Early Modern British History

Series editors

ANTHONY FLETCHER
Emeritus Professor of English Social History, University of London

JOHN GUY
Fellow, Clare College, Cambridge

JOHN MORRILL
*Professor of British and Irish History, University of Cambridge,
and Fellow, Selwyn College*

This is a series of monographs and studies covering many aspects of the history of the British Isles between the late fifteenth century and the early eighteenth century. It includes the work of established scholars and pioneering work by a new generation of scholars. It includes both reviews and revisions of major topics and books which open up new historical terrain or which reveal startling new perspectives on familiar subjects. All the volumes set detailed research into our broader perspectives, and the books are intended for the use of students as well as of their teachers.

For a list of titles in the series, see end of book.

THE 1549 REBELLIONS AND THE MAKING OF EARLY MODERN ENGLAND

ANDY WOOD

University of East Anglia

CAMBRIDGE
UNIVERSITY PRESS

CAMBRIDGE UNIVERSITY PRESS
Cambridge, New York, Melbourne, Madrid, Cape Town, Singapore, São Paulo, Delhi

Cambridge University Press
The Edinburgh Building, Cambridge CB2 8RU, UK

Published in the United States of America by Cambridge University Press, New York

www.cambridge.org
Information on this title: www.cambridge.org/9780521832069

First published 2007
Reprinted 2009

Printed in the United Kingdom at the University Press, Cambridge

A catalogue record for this publication is available from the British Library

ISBN 978-0-521-83206-9 hardback

For Max and Rosa

CONTENTS

ACKNOWLEDGEMENTS

In 1938, Norwich gained a new City Hall. The entrance to the building is graced by impressive brass doors, decorated with eighteen plaques depicting the working lives of the people of the interwar city. Shoe production is represented, as is the then-new industry of aircraft manufacture; engineering is present, alongside the much older textile industry. The apparent intention was to project an image of industrial, urban modernity, suitable to an ancient city that looked to the future. Appropriately enough, Norwich's past also featured in some of the plaques. One of these depicted a tortured image of a man, dressed in mid-sixteenth-century clothing, twisting on a noose. Meaningless to most outsiders, the image was likely to be recognisable to most local people. It alluded to the most famous event in the history of the city: Kett's rebellion of 1549. In the course of this rising, three battles had been fought within Norwich, climaxing in a bloody encounter between the rebels and a royal army. Following his defeat, Robert Kett had been hanged in chains from the walls of Norwich Castle. It was the execution of this rebel leader that the plaque on the doors of Norwich City Hall commemorated. The image presents Kett's rebellion as a notable event in the history of Norwich. But the 1549 insurrections have a larger significance. The risings of that year reflect important changes both in popular politics and in the fabric of society, while the rebellions also represent a key moment in English history: the end of the tradition of late medieval popular protest.

This book seeks to recapture something of the causes, course, horrors, excitements, consequences and meanings of the 1549 rebellions. In writing the book, I have incurred a great many debts. First of all, it is a particular pleasure to be able to thank all three of the original editors of the series in which this book appears – John Morrill, John Guy and Anthony Fletcher – for providing encouragement at different stages of the book's production. I am also enormously grateful to Ethan Shagan for some characteristically perceptive and intelligent criticisms. Many other individuals have provided references, proposed lines of inquiry or suggested interpretive avenues. I would like to thank the following for suggestions, references, support and all sorts of other help: Nigel Amies, Ian Archer, John Arnold, Lloyd Bowen, Mike Braddick, Anne Carter, Matthew Champion, Lance Dawson, Dennis Glover, Paul Griffiths, Steve Hindle, Jim Holstun, Andy Hopper, Pat Hudson, Ronald Hutton, Mark Knights, Diarmaid MacCulloch, Neil MacMaster, Ellie Phillips, Jan Pitman, Carole Rawcliffe, Elizabeth and Paul Rutledge, James C. Scott, Alex Shepard, Alison Smith, John Walter, Jane Whittle, Nicola Whyte, Tom Williamson, Richard Wilson and Phil Withington. Keith Wrightson, Ethan Shagan and Dave Rollison read and commented upon the whole manuscript. The Arts and Humanities Research Council, the British Academy and the University of East Anglia all contributed vital funding. A visit to Oxburgh Hall proved especially memorable.

It seems a long time ago since I first came to Norfolk and heard the story of Robert Kett's rising. Way back in 1986, Sarah Bracking, appalled to learn that I didn't know the story, introduced me to the subject. I can only plead, as a Mancunian, that she hadn't heard of Peterloo either. One of the many wonderful things about my adopted county is the long-established tradition of local history writing, from which I have learnt so much. I hope that this book repays that community with some new knowledge.

The years during which this book was written were not always the easiest. There have been times when I have leaned perhaps too heavily on friends and family. I am therefore especially grateful to my parents, Jim and Joyce Wood, and to my friends for being there for me: John Arnold, Cathie Carmichael, John Morrill, Deb Riozzie, Dave Rollison, Lucy Simpson, Garthine Walker and Keith Wrightson.

Like many historians, I spend too much time in the past. As to the present and the future, I am immensely proud to be able to dedicate this book to my children, Max and Rosa. They have enriched my life in ways that, before they came into it, I could never have imagined.

ABBREVIATIONS

APC	J. R. Dasent *et al.* (eds.), *Acts of the Privy Council, 1542–1631*, new ser., 46 vols. (London, 1890–1964)
BL	British Library
Blomefield	F. Blomefield, *An essay towards a topographical history of the county of Norfolk* (1739–75; 2nd edn, London, 1805–10, 11 vols.)
CCCC	Parker Library, Corpus Christi College, Cambridge
CLRO	Corporation of London Records Office
CPR	*Calendar of Patent Rolls*
Crowley, *Select works*	J. Meadows Cowper (ed.), *The select works of Robert Crowley* (Early English Text Society, extra ser., 15, London, 1872)
CSP, Span	M. A. S. Hume (ed.), *Calendar of letters and state papers relating to English affairs, preserved principally in the Archives of Simancas*, 4 vols. (London, 1892–9)
ERO	Essex Record Office
HMC	Historical Manuscripts Commission
Holinshed	R. Holinshed, *Chronicles of England, Scotland and Ireland*, 6 vols. (1577 & 1586; new edn, London, 1808), III
Hooker	W. J. Harte, J. W. Schopp and H. Tapley-Soker (eds.), *The description of the citie of Excester by John Vowell alias Hoker*, 3 vols. (Exeter, 1919), II
L&P	*Letters and papers, foreign and domestic, of the reign of Henry VIII: preserved in the Public Record Office, the British Museum and elsewhere in England*, 21 vols. (London, 1880–91)

Latimer, *Sermons*	G. E. Corrie (ed.), *Sermons of Hugh Latimer, sometime Bishop of Worcester, Martyr, 1555,* Parker Society, 22 (Cambridge, 1844)
More/Robynson	T. More, *Utopia* (Eng. trans., 1551; London, 1910 edn)
Neville/Woods	R. Woods, *Norfolke furies and their foyle* (London, 1615)
NRO	Norfolk Record Office
P&P	*Past and Present*
PRO	National Archives, Public Record Office
Sotherton	B. L. Beer (ed.), 'The commosyon in Norfolk, 1549', *Journal of Medieval and Renaissance Studies*, 6, 1 (1976), 73–99
TRP	P. L. Hughes and J. F. Larkin (eds.), *Tudor Royal Proclamations*, 3 vols. (New Haven, CT, 1964–9)
VCH	Victoria County History

All dates have been modernised.
All place names are from Norfolk, unless otherwise indicated.

PREFACE

This book tells the story of the 1549 rebellions. It does so for three reasons: it is a story that is worth telling; the story illuminates key themes in late medieval and early modern history; and the story highlights fundamental changes in mid-sixteenth-century society and popular politics. Perhaps most of all, this book aims to dispel the notion that the 'masses of the Tudor period' were 'inarticulate'. In place of the characterisation of the rebels of 1549 as 'simple men and boys', it is here argued that popular political culture in Tudor England was rich, sophisticated and vibrant and that it deserves to occupy an important place in the historical interpretation of the period.[1] It is my intention, then, not only to add to the stock of knowledge about 1549, but also to suggest new ways in which a fuller appreciation of the lives of early modern labouring people might change historical interpretations of the period as a whole.

This book straddles two genres of historical writing: that of political history and social history. Its claim to occupy this interpretive high ground is based upon, firstly, the emergence of a post-revisionist history of politics and religion in sixteenth-century England; secondly, the development of new approaches to popular politics in late medieval England; and lastly, the emergence of a new social history of politics. Moreover, the book aims to break down some key historiographical boundaries: that which divides the late medieval from the early modern; and that which separates political history from social, cultural and economic history.

Over the past decade, the political history of Tudor England has gone through some significant changes. Just over ten years ago, the editor of an important collection of essays raised the possibility that a study might be written of the 'symbols, rituals and mentalities of popular political culture'; yet the essays that comprised that collection remained resolutely focused

---

[1] Quoting B. L. Beer, *Rebellion and riot: popular disorder in England during the reign of Edward VI* (Kent, OH, 1982), 63, 82.

xiii

upon high political culture.[2] Nowadays, it would be unthinkable too that such a volume did not deal with popular politics.[3] Just as recent work in social history has emphasised the ways in which early modern working people negotiated an otherwise unequal social order, so Ethan Shagan has argued that 'the English Reformation was not done *to* people, it was done *with* them'.[4] Shagan ends with the proposition that it is only 'by exploring popular politics that we can begin to understand the English Reformation'.[5] Elsewhere, a similarly nuanced picture of the relationship between Crown and people is beginning to emerge. In John Cooper's recent monograph, the parish church is presented as a key site in the organisation of political allegiance, persuasion and propaganda. In this account, the authority of the Tudors is shown to depend not only upon powerful magnates but also upon village and town elites.[6] After a long period in which Tudor political historians were almost ostentatiously uninterested in the political beliefs of the commons, popular politics seems suddenly to be everywhere.[7]

In a brilliant essay, Shagan has deployed the correspondence between Protector Somerset and the rebellious commons of 1549 as a way of exploring the 'relationship between Tudor court politics and "politics out-of-doors"'. For Shagan, this correspondence suggests the possibility of writing 'a post-revisionist interpretation of mid-Tudor politics' which 'might usefully spend less time examining the minutiae of government administration and more time analysing the government attempts at self-representation and the "feedback networks" that existed between government policy and public response'. Writing in 1999, it seemed to Shagan that this new history of the mid-Tudor polity should focus upon 'the period's unusually dynamic interplay between rulers and ruled'. At the heart of this analysis is Protector Somerset, whose populism appealed 'downward for support from those outside the political establishment, creating a power-base independent of either the court or local affinities'. Addressing the creative interplay between

---

[2] D. Hoak (ed.), *Tudor political culture* (Cambridge, 1995), xix.

[3] For a survey of recent developments, see S. Alford, 'Politics and political history in the Tudor century', *Historical Journal*, 42, 2 (1999), 535–48; on the recent literature in urban political history, see P. Withington, 'Two renaissances: urban political culture in post-Reformation England reconsidered', *Historical Journal*, 44, 1 (2001), 239–67.

[4] E. Shagan, *Popular politics and the English Reformation* (Cambridge, 2003), 25; M. J. Braddick and J. Walter (eds.), *Negotiating power in early modern society: order, hierarchy and subordination in Britain and Ireland* (Cambridge, 2001).

[5] Shagan, *Popular politics*, 310.

[6] J. P. D. Cooper, *Propaganda and the Tudor state: political culture in the Westcountry* (Oxford, 2003), 3, 8, 14, 26.

[7] See, for instance, Richard Hoyle's observation that petitions reveal 'the existence of popular political movements and a much richer political culture in the early sixteenth century than [historians] have hitherto assumed'. R. Hoyle, 'Petitioning as popular politics in early sixteenth-century England', *Historical Research*, 75, 190 (2002), 389.

the rebels and the Protector, Shagan argues that 'the Somerset regime announced to the nation its support for the rebels' programme and its willingness to accept the commons as contributors in the formation of policy'. All this amounted to 'an elaborate courting of public opinion' and a willingness 'to commit the regime to fundamental changes in policy at the initiation of the commons.' This illustrates, in Shagan's terms, 'the extraordinarily promiscuous relationship between "popular" and "elite" politics. Thus, the summer of 1549 witnessed a remarkable convergence of rhetoric between government and commons'. We are left with clear evidence that in the mid-Tudor period, 'the politics of the court was inseparable from the politics of village greens and provincial protest; each fed off the other's rhetoric, constantly interpreting the other's position to their own advantage'.[8]

A similarly dynamic picture of late medieval popular politics has started to emerge over the past few years. R. B. Goheen has argued that 'English peasants participated in the Crown's provincial politics partly at least on their own terms and for their own ends, and in the process they influenced both the form and contents of these politics'. In particular, Goheen emphasises 'the effectiveness of peasant politics'. Goheen's work leaves the strong impression that office-holding villagers were able to 'speak unmistakably of clearly perceived political interests' articulating a 'political will' which enabled them to maintain 'an active political discourse with the Crown that influenced the politics of the countryside'. I. M. W. Harvey has gone further, claiming that 'popular politics not only existed but grew in importance in the fifteenth century ... common people ... began to act as if they thought they mattered in politics, as if they were part of the political commonweal'. Harvey observes that, even if their rebellions were 'temporarily crushed ... [the commons] were never permanently deterred from talking and behaving as if they had a stake in the country's political life'.[9] Very similar to Shagan's notion of 'feedback', John Watts has discussed the dynamic interplay between elite and popular politics in the crisis of 1450–2.[10] Most recently, David Rollison has made a case for the existence

---

[8] E. Shagan, 'Protector Somerset and the 1549 rebellions: new sources and new perspectives', *English Historical Review*, 114, 455 (1999), 36, 37, 41, 46, 47, 50, 51.

[9] R. B. Goheen, 'Peasant politics? Village community and the Crown in fifteenth-century England', *American Historical Review* 96, 1 (1991), 42–3, 56; I. M. W. Harvey, 'Was there popular politics in fifteenth-century England?', in R. H. Britnell and A. J. Pollard (eds.), *The McFarlane legacy: studies in late medieval politics and society* (Stroud, 1995), 156, 164. See also two recent essays: C. Dyer, 'The political life of the fifteenth-century English village', in L. Clark and C. Carpenter (eds.), *The fifteenth century*, IV: *Political culture in late medieval Britain* (Woodbridge, 2004), 135–58; J. Watts, 'The pressure of the public on later medieval politics', in Clark and Carpenter (eds.), *The fifteenth century*, 159–80.

[10] J. Watts, *Henry VI and the politics of kingship* (Cambridge, 1996), 266–82.

of a popular political culture that spanned the period 1381–1649.[11] These historiographical developments may well mark a lasting change in approaches to the political history of late medieval and Tudor England.

In reconceptualising politics, however, it is not enough to note that the commons occasionally intervened in the world of their governors. As Heide Wunder has observed, it is too often the case that 'peasants . . . only turn up in political history when they attempt rebellions or peasant wars'.[12] Instead, a fuller appreciation of the subject requires a close focus upon the micro-politics of small communities, coupled with the radical redefinition of what is meant by 'politics'. In 1996, Keith Wrightson published an influential essay which laid the basis for the rewriting of popular politics. In this piece, Wrightson argued that early modern plebeian political life comprised five dimensions. In his analysis, these comprised the politics of patriarchy; of neighbourhood; of custom; of reformation and state formation; and of subordination and meaning.[13] Wrightson's insights, combined with Patrick Collinson's call for 'a new political history, which is social history with the politics put back in, or an account of political processes which is also social', has inspired recent attempts to reconnect social and political history.[14] Over the past few years, there has emerged what Steve Hindle has called the 'new social history of politics', a history of power relations built not only upon a new dialogue between social and political history, but also upon a broad definition of politics. Thus, for Hindle, politics comprises 'the pursuit, main-tenance and control of power'. The renewed interest amongst early modern social historians in the material basis of politics – oddly, at the same time that historians of the modern epoch are retreating from materialist analyses – has entailed a close study of the micro-politics of local communities: as Hindle puts it, 'the most ubiquitous and therefore perhaps the most significant politics in early modern England were the politics of the parish'.[15] In his investigation of state formation, Mike Braddick has likewise been drawn to micro-politics, arguing that 'by concentrating on the everyday use of political power through the whole network of . . . agents [of the state] a larger range of

---

[11] D. Rollison, 'Conceits and capacities of the vulgar sort: the social history of English as a language of politics', *Cultural and Social History*, 2, 2 (2005), 141–64; D. Rollison, 'The specter of the commonalty: class struggle and the commonweal in England before the Atlantic World', *William and Mary Quarterly*, 3rd ser., 63, 2 (2006), 221–52.

[12] R. W. Scribner and G. Benecke (eds.), *The German Peasant War of 1525, new viewpoints* (London, 1979), 144.

[13] K. E. Wrightson, 'The politics of the parish in early modern England', in P. Griffiths, A. Fox and S. Hindle (eds.), *The experience of authority in early modern England* (Basingstoke, 1996), 10–46.

[14] P. Collinson, *Elizabethan essays* (London, 1994), 11.

[15] S. Hindle, *The state and social change in early modern England, c. 1550–1640* (Basingstoke, 2000), 205, 237.

functional uses emerges. This [approach] tends ... to give ... prominence ... to problems of social order and the importance of vested social interests.' Hence, Braddick emphasises 'the ways in which ... [the state] impinged on ordinary lives'.[16] Throughout, the organising assumption of this new social history of politics is that early modern political life comprised more than the affairs of the central state, internal debates within ruling circles or the deeds of great men (or, rather less often, of great women). Instead, this rather gritty historical work has been preoccupied with conflicts over the distribution of power and resources.[17]

This book aims to link together these historiographical shifts. It is divided into three parts, each containing two chapters. Chapter One begins by defining the mid-Tudor crisis as a crisis of legitimation which affected both politics and social relations. The mid-sixteenth-century crisis is shown to stem both from the short-term context of the Duke of Somerset's protectorship and from longer-term, deeper-rooted social conflicts. This crisis climaxed in the rebellions of the spring and summer of 1549 and in the Earl of Warwick's subsequent coup against the Duke of Somerset in the autumn of that year. Much of Chapter One is dedicated to exploring the course of the 'commotion time' of 1549. Chapter Two looks at the bloody aftermath of the insurrections, at later attempts to organise popular rebellion and at plebeian involvement in state politics during the latter part of the reign of Edward VI. The central purpose of Part I is to lay out a narrative of the 1549 rebellions and of their immediate aftermath. The intention is to provide a context within which the more interpretive Parts II and III are to be set.

Part II, comprising Chapters Three and Four, is concerned with the politics of language. In this, it owes something to the 'linguistic turn' which preoccupied social historians of modern Britain during the 1980s and 1990s. Materialist historians have tended to dismiss the historical focus upon language as a 'retreat' from the analysis of class conflict. But as James Epstein has suggested, 'the turn to language cannot be viewed simply as a retreat; new openings and possibilities have emerged'.[18] In Part II, we therefore concentrate upon struggles over speech and meaning. One way in which an appreciation of language might enrich the social history of early modern England concerns the meanings given to speech and silence. It is significant, for instance, that the early modern gentry and nobility conceived of popular politics in auditory terms, as a 'commotion' or a 'hurly-burly'. This was

---

[16] M. J. Braddick, *State formation in early modern England, c. 1550–1700* (Cambridge, 2000), 94, 97.

[17] For my attempt to survey this literature, see A. Wood, *Riot, rebellion and popular politics in early modern England* (Basingstoke, 2002).

[18] J. Epstein, *In practice: studies in the language and culture of popular politics in modern Britain* (Stanford, CA, 2003), 3.

because speech represented a highly sensitive point in both everyday social relations and in political practice. Labouring people were meant to keep silent in the presence of the gentry and nobility; where they did not, and in particular where they discussed political matters, they were often felt to have trespassed upon the territory of their rulers.

Chapter Three deals with how labouring people achieved the right to speak, with the ways in which the state monitored and regulated plebeian political speech, and with how the gentry and nobility attempted to impose silence upon their subordinates. Chapter Four is concerned with *what* labouring people had to say about politics. In 1997, John Guy recognised that language represented an important element of political life in Tudor England.[19] Chapter Four extends this perspective further down the social scale, looking at popular political language. This chapter is especially concerned with struggles over the meanings of political keywords. It also looks at the ways in which the commons understood the Reformation; at the significance of ideas of order and disorder within rebel politics; and at how plebeians interpreted power relations in the period. Throughout Part II, we are concerned with the politics of rumour. As Shagan has recognised, 'What made rumours so important was that they were *unofficial*, spreading and changing along channels that were not only independent of the royal government but were uncontrolled and uncontrollable. It was exactly this freedom of movement that made rumours "political", since every person spreading them was implicated in the creation of their meaning.'[20]

Part III focuses on the long-term significance of 1549. Chapter Five looks at the causes of the decline of the late medieval tradition of popular rebellion. It is especially concerned with the relationship between state formation and social change and argues that in the later Tudor and early Stuart period, the wealthier villagers and townspeople who had hitherto led popular rebellion were increasingly drawn into state structures. The result was a broader, more stable polity which, while inclusive of the 'better sort of people', excluded poorer social groups. Chapter Six is concerned with the memory and historical representation of the 1549 rebellions. It looks at immediate popular recollections of the commotion time; at the politics that underlay later sixteenth-century historical accounts of 1549; at the role played by polemical accounts of the rebellions in sustaining the social order; and at the ways in which the commotion time became embedded within popular memory. Finally, the book concludes by looking at how the meanings given to Kett's

---

[19] J. Guy, *The Tudor monarchy* (London, 1997), 1–8.
[20] E. Shagan, 'Rumours and popular politics in the reign of Henry VIII', in T. Harris (ed.), *The politics of the excluded, c. 1500–1850* (Basingstoke, 2001), 32.

rebellion underwent fundamental change in the later nineteenth and twentieth centuries.

The book privileges the story of the Norfolk rebellion led by Robert Kett. The intention is not to downplay the significance of the insurrections elsewhere in England. There was, of course, large-scale rebellion in other parts of East Anglia, in the East Riding of Yorkshire, in south-eastern and southern England, in the Midlands and in the western counties. The book pays attention to those insurrections. In Chapter One, we map out the broad geography of the commotion time. Similarly, in Chapter Two, we look at attempted rebellion across England after 1549. Chapters Three and Four draw on a wide array of evidence, concerning both the 1549 rebellions and earlier insurrections, together with a bulk of evidence taken from the 1530s. Nonetheless, in all the chapters, and in Chapters Five and Six in particular, special attention is given to Kett's rebellion. There are good reasons for this. Most obviously, and most importantly, the archival evidence for Kett's rebellion is much richer than that for the other insurrections. Moreover, in the later sixteenth century Kett's rebellion became the subject of a number of important narrative accounts. Empirically, therefore, it is possible to describe Kett's rebellion in much greater detail than is the case for the other insurrections. But there is another reason for this focus upon Norfolk. This county was one of the most socially divided and economically precocious of all those in mid-Tudor England. The intensity of the violence within Norfolk in 1549 contrasted with the relative restraint exercised by rebels in many other parts of England in that year. The reason for this, it is argued, is to be found in the particular sharpness of social relations in Norfolk which in 1549, in a clash of arms and ideas, pitted the 'poor commons' against the gentry.

This book, then, takes a set of events that have traditionally been regarded as the territory of political history and subjects them to social-historical analysis. All through the book, we seek to contextualise the events of 1549 within the inherent politics of everyday life. We go on to look at the 1549 insurrections as a key moment in longer-term processes of social and economic change. Throughout, the intention is to do more than merely insert the commons into a predetermined, elite-centred, high-political narrative, but instead to look at the Tudor polity from the bottom up.

Introduction

Although historians usually situate the 1549 rebellions within the early modern period, the long-term significance of the risings lies in their place at the end of a long tradition of medieval popular revolt. This tradition stretched back to the Peasants' Revolt of 1381 and included insurrections in 1450, 1469, 1489, 1497, 1525 and 1536–7. Diverse though they were in other respects, these risings had five unifying characteristics. Firstly, there was a remarkable consistency in popular political language, hinting at a shared tradition of popular protest. Secondly, the causes of rebellion were often similar. Thirdly, there were clear continuities in their leadership and organisation. Fourthly, some communities and regions were repeatedly involved in insurrections. Lastly, there is the possibility that rebels were conscious of these continuities: that is, that a red thread bound one rebellion to another, producing an ideology of popular protest.[1]

Nonetheless, the rebellions of 1549 differ in two important respects from this tradition. Firstly, the early Reformation strongly influenced the politics of the commotion time of 1549. Secondly, 1549 saw the climax of a longer-term social conflict which pitched the gentry and nobility against the working people of southern and eastern England. Although fissured by significant social divisions, yeomen, poorer farmers, labourers, artisans and urban workers united in 1549 against their rulers. In some respects, the confrontation of 1549 had similarities with the conflicts that had generated the 1381 rising. But whereas in 1381 peasants, artisans and urban workers had risen against the constrictions of feudalism, the social conflicts that generated rebellion in 1549 were different. These conflicts were the result of the complicated, uneven emergence of early agrarian capitalism. The year 1549 therefore stands at the junction of two epochs: the medieval and the

---

[1] Rollison, 'Specter', makes a strong case for this latter point.

1

early modern. As such, it represents a good point from which to view not only the short-term crisis of the mid-Tudor period but also longer-term, more fundamental transformations in economic and social structures; in social relations; in religious practice; and in popular political culture.

Economic and social change often occurs more swiftly than do ways of conceptualising society. Certainly, mid-sixteenth-century visions of the social order had more in common with medieval norms than they did with those of the later sixteenth and early seventeenth centuries. One way of describing the late medieval social order was in terms of the mutual inter-dependence of those who worked (the commons); those who fought (the armigerous classes); and those who prayed (the clergy and monastic orders).[2] Another mode of conceptualising society was also built upon this notion of mutual interdependence but made space for the state. This defined the social hierarchy as a society of orders comprised of four collectivities: the Crown; the gentry and nobility; the Church; and the commons.[3] A common way of representing the late medieval social order was in bodily terms. As Carole Rawcliffe has put it, 'Medical theory ... inspired people to envisage the "body politic" in terms of class and rank because it recognised certain "noble," "principal," and "spiritual" organs, whose exalted function placed them in a position of authority over the rest.'[4] Sir John Fortescue emphasised the reciprocal relationship between Crown and people and drew attention to the limits of royal authority, arguing that where monarchs sought to rule outside established laws they became tyrants. In his discussion of the Crown's fiscal powers, Fortescue highlighted the conditional nature of the Crown's powers and suggested that illegal taxation led to popular insurrec-tion. Importantly for mid-Tudor fiscal strategies, G. L. Harriss has observed that in the late medieval period, 'financial rectitude was the paradigm of good kingship, for both profligacy and avarice would impel a King to tyranny as he sought to live at the expense of his people'. Throughout Fortescue's work, it was assumed that the Crown's powers were limited; that the Crown was but one order within a mixed polity; and that where one

---

[2] G. Duby, *The three orders: feudal society imagined* (1978; Eng. trans., Chicago, 1980).
[3] P. Zagorin, *Rebels and rulers 1500–1660*, vol. I: *Society, states and early modern revolution: agrarian and urban rebellions* (Cambridge, 1982), 61–86; M. L. Bush, 'The risings of the commons, 1381–1549', in J. H. Denton (ed.), *Orders and hierarchies in late medieval and renaissance Europe* (London, 1999), 114–16. R. Mousnier, *Social hierarchies* (1969; Eng. trans., London, 1973), takes the society of orders as reflective of social reality, rather than as an elite ideal. For an important critique of the concept, see A. Arriaza, 'Mousnier and Barber: the theoretical underpinning of the "society of orders" in early modern Europe', *P&P*, 89 (1980), 39–57.
[4] C. Rawcliffe, *Sources for the history of medicine in late medieval England* (Kalamazoo, MI, 1995), 31.

order trespassed upon another, the consequence was an imbalance within the polity as a whole.[5]

Relationships between the four orders were supposed to be negotiated through the law. Summarising late medieval attitudes to justice, Harriss writes that monarchs were expected to meet their 'obligations to uphold and govern by law, since "for fawte of law the commons rise"'.[6] Thus, one essential role of the Crown was that of the neutral dispensation of justice; where the Crown failed in this duty, or where it was prevented from so doing, the commons might rebel. As Michael Bush has put it, late medieval popular rebellions assumed 'a principle of answerability to the commons'. In his analysis, 'The essential purpose of a rising of the commons was to denote that the body politic was out of joint.' The disturbance of the polity released the commons 'from their duty of obedience, not permanently, but as a temporary emergency measure, in order to put things to right'. Hence, for Bush, 'risings of the commons were a defence of the society of orders'.[7]

In such accounts, popular rebellion is presented as performing a function, restoring balance to the polity and recalling rulers to their proper roles. There is certainly some evidence to support this view. Rebels did indeed present themselves as seeking the restoration of justice and order: one ballad behind which the rebels of 1536 marched proposed that 'Then no marvell / thoght it thus befell / Commons to mell / To make redresse'.[8] Other evidence, however, suggests that rebels had a more proactive vision of their political role. The articles of Robin of Redesdale, the leading figure in the 1469 rising, denounced the 'covetous rule' of '[s]edicious persones' and called for 'reformacion'. The stated object of the rebellion was to protect the 'comonwele of this lond' against the 'singuler loucour' of its rulers, and the articles denounced new taxes. Similarly, the corrupt administration of justice was held up as a target; the rebel articles claimed that this maladministration allowed 'gret murdres, roberyes, rapes, oppressions, and extortions'. All this was to the detriment of the interests of the 'trewe comons'. Therefore, 'the Kyngis true and feithfulle Commons' requested that for the 'gret wele' of the Crown and the 'common-wele of others his true subje[c]ttes and Commons' that taxation should not be levied upon them.[9]

---

[5] J. Fortescue, *On the laws and governance of England*, ed. S. Lockwood (Cambridge, 1997); G. L. Harriss, 'Introduction: the exemplar of kingship', in G. L. Harriss (ed.), *Henry V: the practice of kingship* (Oxford, 1985), 8, 15.
[6] Harriss, 'Introduction', 8. [7] Bush, 'The risings of the commons', 113.
[8] M. Bateson, 'Ballad on the Pilgrimage of Grace', *English Historical Review*, 5 (1890), 344.
[9] J. O. Halliwell (ed.), *A chronicle of the first thirteen years of the reign of King Edward the fourth* (Camden Society, 1st ser., X, London, 1839), 46, 48, 50.

The rebel articles of 1469 present the 'trewe comons' as a legitimate interest group that had been offended by corruption, taxation and 'oppressions'. We will see that in 1549, rebels applied a very similar interpretation. To suggest that popular rebellion was a 'corrective mechanism', therefore carries more than a tinge of functionalism.[10] Far from forming such a mechanism, it will be argued here that popular rebellion was reflective of a deeper, active popular politics. This plebeian politics was capable of mounting fundamental attacks on social inequality. As Rodney Hilton has put it, the 1381 rebels aimed at the 'distribution of all lordship (except the King's lordship) amongst all – in effect the abolition of lordship ... the establishment of popular policing ... the end of the control of labour; the division of church property amongst the commons; the clergy to have no property but only their subsistence'.[11] This programme amounts not to the *reassertion* of the society of orders, but to a radical *reconstruction* of society from the bottom up. As such, it implies that the commons were capable of articulating an entirely different vision than that of their rulers of the distribution of wealth and power.

The Norfolk rebels of 1549 demanded a polity based upon a combination of monarchic lordship and popular sovereignty in which small communities formed autonomous entities, linked to the state in a dispersed network. We will see in Chapter Four that this had important similarities to the politics of the 1381 rebels. Both the 1381 rebels and those of 1549 demanded the abolition of serfdom; the commotioners of 1549 also demanded the limitation of seigneurial power and the separation of lords from the village community. Moreover, the 1549 rebels sought to exclude the clergy from the economic life of the village.[12] Nor should we assume that popular politics was ideologically homogeneous; it is perfectly possible that the 'radical Christian tradition' which Hilton says existed amongst the 1381 rebels could endure alongside a static belief in the society of orders.[13]

The idea of the society of orders therefore represented one ideological resource upon which rebels could draw. As an ideal, it exercised a partial influence upon popular politics, inflecting political language while at times running alongside more radical discourses. This was very obvious in the 1530s and 1540s. Thanks to the Henrician Reformation, the Crown was popularly felt to be trespassing upon the territory of the Church and the

---

[10] Quoting Bush, 'The risings of the commons', 116.

[11] R. Hilton, *Class conflict and the crisis of feudalism: essays in medieval social history* (London, 1985), 149.

[12] C. Dyer, 'The rising of 1381 in Suffolk: its origins and participants', in C. Dyer, *Everyday life in medieval England* (London, 1994), 232; Hilton, *Class conflict*, 59; D. MacCulloch, 'Kett's rebellion in context', *P&P*, 84 (1979), 47.

[13] Hilton, *Class conflict*, 148.

commons. At the same time, lordly exactions led the commons to perceive of the gentry and nobility as venal, corrupt and oppressive. These two threats were experienced as linked; in the rebellions of 1536 and 1549, as in the reported seditious speech of that period, the commons interpreted the Reformation in terms of the dispossession of the parish community at the hands of greedy, avaricious and corrupt gentry, backed by the Crown. In these circumstances, the idea of the society of orders, with its neat separation of corporate bodies and social responsibilities, presented itself as an available discourse within which popular politics could be articulated. Thus, in July 1538 the Yorkshireman James Prestwich presented a strikingly assertive description of the separation of powers between Church and Crown, explaining that he had 'spoke[n] according to my co[n]cynions [that] I thought and yet do thynk that the kyng or mayster colde not be supreme hedd of this church of england [believing] . . . that yff he might the[n] yt shulde be aswell for other foreign princ[e]s to take the same in there domynyons and thus thynkyng I trust yt be farr fro[m] treson'.[14]

If the Crown was felt to be undermining the Church, so in some disturbing rumours it was also said to intend the destruction of another one of the orders – this time, that of the commons. In 1536, for example, Adam Fermour reported to the people of Walden (Essex) that there was 'evell newes for the kynge will make suche lawes that if a man dye, his wiff[e] and his child[r]en shall go a beggyng'.[15] We shall see later in this book that Fermour's fears were not isolated; rather, between the 1530s and the 1550s, labouring people frequently articulated such anxieties. While the idea of the society of orders continued to exercise a normative force, the everyday experience of social conflict undermined plebeian belief in the organic, hierarchical constitution of society. In John Heywood's poem *The spider and the fly*, the commons were personified as a Fly and the gentry as a Spider. The Fly recollected how the dangerous Spider had once 'kept your estate: and we . . . stood with our degre . . . / Dweld ech by other in welth and unit[i]e'. Now, Heywood suggested, those days were long gone.[16]

This book locates the 1549 rebellions at the juncture of late medieval and early modern popular political cultures. As such, it occasionally looks back to earlier insurrections. Sometimes it does so in order to highlight similarities and continuities; sometimes it does so in order to demonstrate important breaking points. At other times, it draws attention to the ways in which the 1549 rebellions shed light upon popular political culture in the later sixteenth and early seventeenth centuries. Both empirically and chronologically, the

---

[14] PRO, SP1/134, fol. 217v. [15] PRO, SP1/136, fol. 109r–v.
[16] J. Holstun, 'The spider, the fly and the commonwealth: merrie John Heywood and the agrarian class struggle', *English Literary History*, 71 (2004), 65.

book therefore ranges well beyond the commotion time of 1549. In particular, the book exploits the rich material concerning the 1536 and 1537 rebellions, together with the evidence of seditious speech and attempted insurrection in the later 1530s. This material is employed for two reasons. Firstly, in contrast to the state papers for the 1530s, those for the reign of Edward VI are scanty. Where we deal with issues such as the surveillance of popular political opinion, material from the later years of the reign of Henry VIII is utilised alongside that of the reign of Edward VI. Secondly, it is suggested that there are important continuities in popular protest between 1536–7 and 1549. These continuities are most obvious concerning the Western rebellion in Devon and Cornwall in 1549, whose conservative religious grievances bore some similarities to those of the Pilgrimage of Grace of 1536. But there are also less frequently acknowledged similarities between the rebellions of 1536–7 and the Norfolk commotion time of 1549. It is significant, for instance, that during the crisis of 1536–7, Thomas Cromwell and the Duke of Norfolk both feared that East Anglia – and Norfolk in particular – would rise in support of the northern rebels.[17] Such fears had some basis in reality. One of the plotters amongst the commons of Fincham, where the would-be rebels intended to kill the local gentry, spoke of how he wished that the 'Yorkshyer men myght a cume forthe ... that than the halydays that were putte down wuld a been restoryed ageyn'.[18] Geoffrey Elton has noted that of all the counties that were not directly involved in the Pilgrimage of Grace, it was in Norfolk that the largest and most serious attempted risings were mounted.[19]

Most significant of the attempted Norfolk risings was that in Walsingham in 1537, where the conspirators intended to slaughter the local gentry.[20] There were a number of organisational similarities between the intended insurrection in Walsingham in 1537 and the Norfolk rebellion of 1549. The Walsingham rebels planned to spread the rising under cover of archery matches into Suffolk; fairs were to provide the cover for rebel organisation; the town of Wymondham was cited as a centre for rebel organisation; and the rebels intended to seize King's Lynn.[21] But the most important continuities between the attempted risings of 1537 and Kett's rebellion of 1549 lay in

---

[17] BL, Cotton MS, Cleopatra F VI, fol. 257r–v; PRO, SP1/106, fols. 118r–v, 256r.

[18] PRO, SP1/121, fol. 173v.

[19] Thus, for instance, Mousehold Heath, which was to be the location of Kett's rebel camp in 1549, was mentioned in a prophecy of 1537 as the site where 'the prowdest p[ri]nce in Chrystendome shuld be ... subdyt'. G. R. Elton, *Policy and police: the enforcement of the Reformation in the age of Thomas Cromwell* (Cambridge, 1972), 135–51; PRO, SP1/120, fol. 103r.

[20] C. E. Moreton, 'The Walsingham conspiracy of 1537', *Historical Research*, 63 (1990), 29–43.

[21] PRO, SP1/119, fols. 33r, 36r, 141v.

language and ideology. Raphe Rogerson, one of the leading Walsingham plotters, observed to his neighbour William Guisborough that 'the gentle men buye upp all the grayn, kepe all the catal in their handes and hold all the farmes that poor men cann have no living'. Likewise, George Guisborough remarked to John Semble that 'ther was moche penery and scarcenes among the Comons and poor folks for remedy therof he thought it were very well don that ther might be an insurrection'.[22] A similar set of instincts drove the rebels in 1549. It is also possible to find similar organisational and ideological continuities between the commotion time of 1549 and the popular rebellions of the fourteenth, fifteenth and early sixteenth centuries. These continuities enable us to talk meaningfully of a popular political culture that spanned the period between 1381 and 1549.[23]

One enduring continuity concerned popular attitudes to law, order and state formation. Far from seeing the state as the coercive arm of the ruling class, late medieval rebels were more likely to perceive of it as an agency that needed to be strengthened against gentry violence and corruption. Since the state was (at least theoretically) the guarantor of legality and order, late medieval labouring people often contrasted the disorderly behaviour of their gentry opponents with their own orderliness and legalism. This legalism – later to be a defining characteristic of early modern popular politics – originated in the years before the Black Death. The peasants and townspeople of the early fourteenth century preferred to submit cases to royal courts out of a belief that their landlords influenced local courts. Thus, Rodney Hilton finds 'the earliest signs of ... [peasant] resistance to manorialism in the records of the royal courts'. By the late fourteenth century, Hilton discerns a 'peasant habit of litigation'. This use of the courts was more than merely tactical. Popular litigation also conditioned peasant self-organisation. In 1327, the tenants of Great and Little Ogbourne (Wiltshire) 'not only formed a conspiracy [against their lord] ... but supported it by a common purse'.[24] By the early fifteenth century, there were many manors upon which wealthier villagers had liberated themselves from the restrictions of serfdom. Such individuals became used to administering the law as village officers, as jurors and as litigants in central courts. In Goheen's analysis, this alliance with the law enabled the richer peasants to build 'their own communities according to their own rules'.[25]

In their conflicts with their rulers, labouring people sometimes developed comparisons between their own orderliness and the violence and oppressions of their opponents. Thus, the petition of the town of Swaffham to parliament

---

[22] PRO, SP1/119, fols. 36r, 38r.

[23] For perceptive assessments of these continuities, see Bush, 'The risings of the commons'; Rollison, 'Specter'.

[24] Hilton, *Class conflict*, 55, 56, 59, 62.   [25] Goheen, 'Peasant politics?', 43, 59.

in 1451 described Sir Thomas Tuddenham of Oxburgh as a dangerous figure who committed 'trespasez, offencez, wronges, extorcyons ... oppressions and per[j]uryes'. They compared him to a 'comon theef', observing that his oppressions had resulted in the 'sub[v]ercyon of the lawe and of the polityk governaunce of the land'.[26] Popular criticism of the gentry's brutality and venality therefore offered ethical and political arguments for state forma-tion.[27] This popular legal-mindedness influenced rebel behaviour. In 1381, rebels in St Albans (Hertfordshire) organised themselves as though they were setting a watch; elsewhere, in executing their leading opponents the rebels appropriated the state's rituals of execution and thereby asserted 'their judicial authority'. The rebels' legalism also influenced the care with which they worked through those estate archives which fell into their hands, pre-serving the documents which legitimated their rights while destroying those that prejudiced them. In demonstration of their claim to stand for the King, the 1381 rebels marched behind royal standards. Like Kett's rebels in 1549, who dispatched warrants in the King's name, the 1381 rebels appropriated 'the documentary forms of royal government'. Perhaps most notably, like Robert Kett in 1549, the leader of the 1381 Norfolk rebels, Geoffrey Lister, held lawcourts at which opponents of popular rights were punished.[28]

Such similarities can also be found in many of the causes of rebellion. Taxation featured, for instance, as an important cause of insurrection in 1381, 1450, 1469, 1489, 1497, 1525, 1536 and 1549. As suggested in Robin of Redesdale's complaints, taxation was conceived of as more than a simple financial burden, but was also regarded as an extension of the Crown's power and hence as a destabilising force.[29] In 1381, 1537 and 1549 the authority of the landlord class came under direct rebel assault. The venality of gentry office-holders fed into popular protest in 1450 and 1549. Likewise, the failings of the gentry and the claim that they were 'traitors' lay at the heart of popular rebellion in 1381, 1450 and 1536 and strongly influenced

---

[26] N. Davis (ed.), *Paston letters and papers of the fifteenth century*, 3 vols. (Oxford, 1976), II, 528–30. For fears in the same year that Tuddenham's conduct would cause the Norfolk commons to rise, see *ibid.*, 60. For other important examples of popular petitioning to parliament, see Harvey, 'Was there popular politics', 157–8.

[27] I. M. W. Harvey, *Jack Cade's rebellion of 1450* (Oxford, 1991), 42, 189; Bush, 'The risings of the commons', 110; Goheen, 'Peasant politics?', 55.

[28] S. Justice, *Writing and rebellion: England in 1381* (Berkeley, 1994), 28–9, 68, 69, 171; H. Eiden, 'Joint action against "bad" lordship: the peasants' revolt in Essex and Norfolk', *History*, 83, 269 (1998), 20.

[29] Harvey, 'Was there popular politics', 167; Harvey, *Jack Cade's rebellion*, 42. For a general discussion, see M. L. Bush, 'Tax reform and rebellion in early Tudor England', *History*, 76 (1991), 379–400. For popular criticism of taxation, or attempts to organise anti-fiscal rebellion during the reign of Henry VIII, see PRO, SP1/106, fol. 183r–v; NRO, NCR/16A/3, pp. 9–10; NRO, NCR/16A/2, fol. 3r–v, pp. 16–18, p. 173. Popular opposition to taxation in the reigns of Henry VII and Henry VIII deserves closer study.

rebel politics in 1549. Rebel violence in all these insurrections was not indiscriminate, but was instead directed against unpopular gentlemen, corrupt local officeholders or hated government ministers.[30]

Rather than acting out the gentry's nightmare of a murderous jacquerie, rebels often took out their frustrations upon the material fabric of lordship: they stole deer, rabbits, sheep and cattle from gentry land and broke into their rulers' mansions to plunder wine and food and to rifle through estate papers. It should not be a surprise, therefore, to find that rebellion often broke out in what the Norfolk rebels of 1549 called the 'camping time': that is, seasonal periods of festivity.[31] Between 1381 and 1549, the organisation of popular insurrection displayed very similar characteristics. In 1381, 1450, 1536–7 and 1549, initial support for insurrection was spread by anonymous letters, bills and libels, and (even more importantly) by rumour.[32] Rebels were so often summoned by the ringing of church bells that 'to ring awake' had, by the mid-sixteenth century, become a euphemism for popular rebellion.[33] If the auditory landscape of rebellion was defined by the sound of church bells, its administrative topography was built upon rebel leaders' prior experience of local government and law enforcement. In particular, the governmental machinery of the manor, parish and hundred (an administrative body comprising a group of perhaps ten or so parishes) was exploited by rebel leaders. Many of these leaders were used to holding office as constables, churchwardens, bailiffs or court jurors and were therefore able to draw upon the organisational networks that they deployed in those capacities.[34] Militia muster grounds, each pertaining to a particular hundred, were used as the location for rebel gatherings.[35]

---

[30] Harvey, *Jack Cade's rebellion*, 63, 64, 89, 90, 91, 92, 93, 117, 120, 123, 190; Justice, *Writing and rebellion*, 2, 23, 51, 91; Eiden, 'Joint action', 19, 29.

[31] Harvey, *Jack Cade's rebellion*, 94, 113, 126, 165–6; Justice, *Writing and rebellion*, 42, 156; Hilton, *Class conflict*, 58; Dyer, 'The rising of 1381', 224, 233; for the 'camping time', see MacCulloch, 'Kett's rebellion', 41; D. Dymond, 'A lost social institution : the camping close', *Rural History*, 1 (1990), 165–92.

[32] Harvey, *Jack Cade's rebellion*, 26, 49, 70, 77, 79, 80, 117, 183; Justice, *Writing and rebellion*, 24, 29, 77; W. Scase, '"Strange and wonderful bills": bill-casting and political discourse in late medieval England', *New Medieval Literatures*, 2 (1998), 231, 237–9, 240.

[33] For references to 'ringing awake', see J. S. Cockburn (ed.), *Calendar of assize records: Essex indictments, Elizabeth I* (London, 1978), nos. 288–91; *CPR, Elizabeth I*, V, 1569–72, no. 1818; PRO, SP1/160, fol. 157r. For the use of church bells in 1536, see PRO, SP1/110, fols. 137r–144r, 163r–173r, 191r–v; PRO, SP1/107, fol. 116r.

[34] For church bells and the 'auditory landscape', see A. Corbin, *Village bells: sound and meaning in the nineteenth-century French countryside* (New York, 1998), xi. For leadership, see Harvey, *Jack Cade's rebellion*, 7, 9, 105–6, 111, 185; Bush, 'The risings of the commons', 113; Eiden, 'Joint action', 26; Dyer, 'The rising of 1381', 225.

[35] For two examples from 1536, see PRO, SP1/110, fol. 89r; PRO, SP1/107, fol. 116r. For examples from 1450, see Harvey, *Jack Cade's rebellion*, 74, 75, 77, 103, 109, 124, 139, 161. For the role of military organisation in the 1450 risings, see M. Bohna, 'Armed force and civic legitimacy in Jack Cade's revolt, 1450', *English Historical Review*, 118, 477 (2003), 563–82.

Perhaps the most important – and yet also the most difficult – question in the history of late medieval popular rebellion is that of how far rebels were conscious of these centuries-long continuities. The politics of popular memory is more fully discussed in Chapter Six, but the question is worth pausing over here. I. M. W. Harvey has marshalled important evidence which suggests that the political culture of the fifteenth-century commons stemmed at least in part from just such a conscious link. Harvey refers to the 'psychological benefit of oral tradition', in particular to 'the inherited memory of the events of 1381' in organising and motivating rebels. In 1407, Warwickshire dissidents posted up bills criticising the Church in the name of 'Jack Straw and his companions'. In 1485, northern rebels named three of their captains 'Master Mendall' (a reference to John Amendall, the *nom de guerre* of Jack Cade), 'Jack Straw' and 'Robin of Riddesdale', 'thereby saluting the memories of the risings of 1381, 1450 and [1469]'.[36] There are, therefore, good reasons to think that a deep social memory of popular rebellion endured, conditioning protest and legitimating its ideology. Certainly, it is possible to demonstrate clear continuities in the sites of large-scale protest. All of the counties cited by Hilton as especially affected by 1381 – Middlesex, Kent, Essex, Surrey, Hertfordshire, Suffolk, Norfolk and Cambridgeshire – were caught up in the 1549 rebellions.[37] Textile-producing regions – the Kentish Weald, the Stour Valley, central Norfolk – seem to have been especially prone to rebellion.[38] As to individual communities, Bury St Edmunds (Suffolk) was involved in risings in 1381, 1450, 1525 and 1549. Melton (Suffolk) was the site of trouble in 1450 and 1549. St Albans, Norwich and Cambridge were all caught up in large-scale trouble in 1381 and 1549. Lavenham (Suffolk) fell into rebel hands in 1525 and 1549. The same was true of the location of large rebel camps. Essex rebels converged on the field at Mile End in 1381 and 1450. In 1451, would-be Norfolk rebels gathered at the village of Thorpe, on the edge of Mousehold Heath, which was the location of rebel camps in 1381 and 1549. Blackheath was the location of rebel camps in 1381, 1450 and 1497.[39]

[36] Harvey, 'Was there popular politics', 168; Harvey, *Jack Cade's rebellion*, 161.

[37] Hilton, *Class conflict*, 143.

[38] Harvey, *Jack Cade's rebellion*, 17, 20, 24; Scase, '"Strange and wonderful bills"', 241; Eiden, 'Joint action', 23. For more on popular politics and the textile industry, see J. Walter, *Understanding popular violence in the English revolution: the Colchester plunderers* (Cambridge, 1999), ch. 7; D. Rollison, 'Discourse and class struggle: the politics of industry in early modern England', *Social History*, 26, 2 (2001), 166–89.

[39] Harvey, *Jack Cade's rebellion*, 90, 116, 117, 158; Hilton, *Class conflict*, 62, 144; R. B. Dobson, *The peasants' revolt of 1381* (Basingstoke, 1970), 16; Eiden, 'Joint action', 19; Bush, 'The risings of the commons', 110.

II SOCIAL CONFLICT AND THE ORIGINS OF CAPITALISM
IN MID-TUDOR ENGLAND

In recent years, early modern historians have moved away from polarised descriptions of society and culture, preferring instead to emphasise fluidity and movement in the place of seemingly static distinctions between 'elite' and 'popular'. One result of this trend has been to open up important subjects to new perspectives: the category of popular culture, for instance, now seems more like an open field than an interpretive closure.[40] However, this shift carries with it the risk that inequalities of wealth and power might be obscured. After all, class – either as a structure or as a relationship – was not an invention of the modern period. Rather, early and mid-sixteenth-century England reverberated with a harsh sense of class conflict: as the Henrician pamphleteer Sir Richard Morison observed, 'In time of peace, be not all men almost at war with them that be rich?'[41] Much of this book will be preoccupied with exploring this conflict and with its implications for the ways in which we might understand the formation of early modernity.

Fundamental to understanding the distribution of wealth and power in early modern society was the politicised nature of work. Repeatedly, this book will employ the formulation of 'working people' to describe its key collective agent, the commons, whom it counterposes to the gentry and nobility. Such a formulation might be taken as simplistic. It is not. The interpretive purpose of this dichotomy is not to suggest that all, or even most, early modern workers felt part of a uniform, homogeneous, collective culture; that their interests were always the same; or that internal social distinctions within the commons (of which more below) were unimportant. But this dichotomy, for all that it sits uncomfortably alongside the retreat from class within postmodern social and cultural theory, retains an important historical value.

For contemporary social theorists, physical labour represented the everyday boundary between gentility and commonality.[42] The commonality were those who dirtied their hands; the gentry were those who did not. As Edmund Dudley put it, 'the commynaltie in substance standith in trew labor ... it is behovefull for them to exercise the same both erly and late, and from tyme to tyme, and not to slugg in there beddes, but to be thereat full trewly in the morning'.[43] Moreover, as we shall see in Chapter Three, Tudor workers were

---

[40] See, for instance, T. Harris, 'Problematising popular culture', in T. Harris (ed.), *Popular culture in England, c. 1500–1850* (Basingstoke, 1995), 1–27; B. Reay, *Popular cultures in England, 1550–1750* (London, 1998).

[41] W. G. Zeeveld, *Foundations of Tudor policy* (Cambridge, MA, 1948), 216.

[42] Duby, *The three orders*, 59.

[43] D. M. Brodie (ed.), *The tree of commonwealth: a treatise* (Cambridge, 1948), 67.

expected to labour in silence: 'Theis folke may not grudge not murmure to lyve in labor and pain, and the most parte of there tyme with the swete of ther face.'[44] 'Commonalty', therefore, was a politico-economic term. In late medieval and Tudor social theory it was defined with reference to the relations of production such that, as David Rollison observes, '"Commonalty" [was] used ... to mean the estate or class described ... in 1387 as those to whom "it fallith to travayle bodily and with here sore swet geten out of the erthe bodily".'[45] In contrast, gentility was reserved to those who did not work. As Keith Wrightson has put it, 'the possession of gentility constituted one of the most fundamental dividing lines in society'. This had both political and social implications: 'The gentry of provincial England ... formed an elite of wealth, status and power, internally differentiated and yet united by their shared interests as substantial landowners and agents of government and by their common claim to bear the name of gentlemen.'[46]

The dichotomy employed in this book between working people and their would-be governors therefore highlights one key element of Tudor social discourses, while (unfortunately) obscuring an equally important aspect of social reality. For as Rollison and Wrightson make clear, contemporary descriptions of society invoked work as a political category, drawing a sharp line between those who laboured and those who did not in order to deny political participation to the former. As we shall see, despite their best efforts, such social theorists failed. In fact, working people managed to articulate their own political opinions throughout the period both in large-scale rebellions and (in some respects more powerfully) in everyday, micro-political confrontations with their social superiors.

As I have tried to argue elsewhere, early modern historians remain oddly resistant to the category of class.[47] Given the episodic ferocity of social conflicts in the period, this is strange. It is therefore revealing that one of the leading historians of the Tudor century should feel so unembarrassed about using that term in description of the 1549 rebellions: as John Guy has put it, the 1549 rebellions 'were the closest thing Tudor England saw to a class war'.[48] Certainly, it is hard to look at early and mid-Tudor urban society without reading them (at least in part) in terms of open social conflict. In this period, the enclosure of common land, often seen as the cause of the source of the definitive rural conflict of the period, was probably felt with greatest intensity in urban centres. Thus, for instance, in Coventry in 1509, in

---

[44] *Ibid.*, 45.   [45] Rollison, 'Conceits and capacities', 144.
[46] K. E. Wrightson, *English society, 1580–1680* (London, 1982), 23, 26.
[47] A. Wood, *The politics of social conflict: the Peak Country, 1520–1770* (Cambridge, 1999), 10–26.
[48] J. Guy, *Tudor England* (Oxford, 1988), 208.

Nottingham in 1512, in Gloucester in 1513 and in London in 1514 there were significant crowd disturbances concerning the enclosure of common land.[49] Some of these disputes spilt over into the rebellions of 1549. In Southampton in that year, for instance, the court leet settled a long-running contest over the city's commons in favour of the urban poor. This conflict had been the cause of trouble since 1490, and there had been two earlier enclosure riots concerning such common rights, in 1500 and 1517.[50] Ballads against enclosures in Coventry in 1496 described how 'The cyt[i]e is bond that shuld be fre / The right is holden from the Cominalt[i]e / Our Comens that at Lammas open shuld be cast / They be closed in and he[d]gged full fast.'[51] In early Tudor York, disputes over political participation connected with deeper conflicts which cast the commons against the governing oligarchy. Notably, this had been preceded by conflicts in the fifteenth century, as a result of which the commons had petitioned in 1475 stating their belief that 'forasmuch as we be all one body corporate, we think that we be all in like privileged of the commonalty which has borne none office in the city'.[52]

In Cambridge, matters came to a head in 1549. Despite the humanist pretensions of some of the leading colleges, the dissolution of the monasteries had, according to rebels, resulted in the decay of almshouses, the stopping up of common lanes, the enclosure of common land and the overstocking of those commons that remained by wealthy sheep farmers.[53] Finally, perhaps most importantly, in the city of Norwich, which was to form the epicentre of the eastern rebellions of the commotion time, the later 1520s saw vicious conflict over food prices.[54] At Christmas time in 1527 there were attacks upon corn merchants at the marketplace cross. The following year, the high price of food inspired food riots amongst the women of Norwich and Yarmouth; the 'young people' of Norwich joined in the riots, and were only quelled after public executions.[55] In 1532, the recurrence of high food prices again led the city's women to riot; their leaders were punished with public whippings in the marketplace.[56] Finally, just before the outbreak of Kett's rebellion, the aldermen decided to erect enclosures on the Town Close,

[49] P. Slack, *From reformation to improvement: public welfare in early modern England* (Oxford, 1998), 14.

[50] A. Jones, '"Commotion time": the English risings of 1549', PhD thesis, University of Warwick (2003), 106–7.

[51] R. H. Tawney and E. Power (eds.), *Tudor economic documents: being select documents illustrating the economic and social history of Tudor England* (London, 1924), III, 13.

[52] Hoyle, 'Petitioning as popular politics', 368–73.

[53] C. H. Cooper, *Annals of Cambridge*, 4 vols. (Cambridge, 1843–5), II, 38–40.

[54] Again, conflicts over food prices in the 1520s and 1530s deserve closer scrutiny.

[55] Blomefield, III, 198; NRO, NCR/17B, 'Liber Albus', fol. 18v.

[56] W. Hudson and J. C. Tingay (eds.), *The records of the city of Norwich*, 2 vols. (Norwich, 1906–10), II, 163–5.

a common on the edge of the city. This proved to be one of the causes of insurrection amongst the poor of Norwich in 1549.[57]

For all the intensity of urban social conflicts, it was in rural England that a new socio-economic order was being born. The emergence of agrarian capitalism was regionally specific: East Anglia was especially precocious. In Norfolk in particular, the emergence of capitalism was driven by two motive forces: the entrepreneurial energies of wealthier yeoman farmers and the cash-grabbing fiscal seigneurialism of the gentry. Recently, historians have tended to understate the extent of seigneurial conflict in late medieval and early modern Norfolk. In her very fine study of the agrarian economy of the county in this period, Jane Whittle has claimed that 'on the whole, [Norfolk] landlords of the early and mid-sixteenth century seem to have been content to maintain the status quo rather than "improve" their estates'.[58] This flies in the face of a large body of evidence: of often ferocious riot and litigation between lord and tenant; of the attempted rebellions in the country in 1537, which as we have seen targeted the gentry; and of actual insurrection in 1549. In all of these cases, landlords were faced by unified village resistance. Within early sixteenth-century Norfolk, a seigneurial offensive was underway, as lords increased rents, exploited copyhold customs, emparked land in order to create deer-parks and enclosed commons. This seigneurial offensive receives further attention in Chapter One. In particular, lords were driven to expand their sheep flocks and manipulated customary foldcourse arrangements so as to ensure that they could graze their ever-expanding sheep flocks on tenants' fields. Similarly, lords also overstocked common land. Kett's rebel demands were designed to curtail such lordly exactions. As Bindoff observed, if the Norfolk rebels had succeeded, they would have 'clipped the wings of rural capitalism'.[59] Certainly, this is true of the likely impact of the rebel programme upon fiscal seigneurialism; but, as we shall see below, rebel demands would not have hindered the slower, steadier micro-economic changes within village communities from which the wealthy yeoman class was benefiting.

Inevitably, debates over the origins of capitalism in England have been conducted in the shadow of Karl Marx's theorisation of that subject. But whereas considerable quantities of ink have been consumed in the debate over the relationship between the English Revolution and the origins of capitalism, Marx's more interesting and perceptive discussion of economic developments in the fifteenth and sixteenth centuries have received relatively

---

[57] Neville/Woods, sig. B3v; Holinshed, 964.
[58] J. Whittle, *The development of agrarian capitalism: land and labour in Norfolk, 1440–1580* (Oxford, 2000), 311.
[59] S. T. Bindoff, *Ket's rebellion, 1549* (London, 1949), 9.

little attention. Marx's account of the agrarian origins of capitalism was largely based upon his readership of the mid-sixteenth-century social complaint literature available to him in the Reading Room of the British Museum. Here he encountered the outraged social critique of the 'commonwealth men' whose writings we explore more thoroughly at the start of Chapter One. Combining the mid-Tudor evangelicals' denunciation of avarice with Marx's revolutionary communism resulted in an account of the origins of English capitalism which was both impassioned and in some respects two-dimensional. Nonetheless, that angry denunciation rewards rereading.

Marx saw capitalism as originating from the proletarianisation of small producers during the fifteenth and sixteenth centuries. Overstated though this was – late medieval rural workers often combined wage labour with work on their own land, or as industrial workers – the insight that the period *c*. 1450–1600 saw fundamental transformations in both the ownership of the means of production and in relations of production has been confirmed by later generations of archival research.[60] In Marx's account, the crisis of feudalism resulted in the liberation of serfs from bondage. Although he was vague about the precise periodisation, Marx saw that a substantial period of time separated the end of feudalism from the emergence of agrarian capitalism. As Jane Whittle has observed rather more recently, 'we are left with a lengthy period of time which is neither fully capitalist nor feudal'.[61] Recognising that 'the capitalistic era dates from the sixteenth century', Marx added that 'wherever [capitalism] appears, the abolition of serfdom has been long effected'. He went on: 'In England, serfdom had practically disappeared in the last part of the fourteenth century. The immense majority of the population consisted then, and to a still larger extent, in the fifteenth century, of free peasant proprietors, whatever was the feudal title under which their right of property was hidden.'[62]

If Marx exaggerated when he spoke of rural labourers as having been 'suddenly and forcibly torn from their means of subsistence, and hurled as free and "unattached" proletarians on the labour market', his sense that developments in the rural economy of late medieval England had a long-term, world-historic significance is more apposite: 'The expropriation of the agricultural producer, of the peasant, from the soil, is the basis of the whole process [that is, the origins of capitalism].'[63] His location of the origins of

---

[60] The emergence of capitalism is a key theme in K. E. Wrightson, *Earthly necessities: economic lives in early modern Britain* (New Haven, CT, 2000).

[61] Whittle, *Development of agrarian capitalism*, 11.

[62] K. Marx, *Capital: a critique of political economy*, 3 vols. (Chicago, 1926), I, 787, 788.

[63] *Ibid.*, 787.

this shift in relations of production is equally perceptive: 'The prelude of the revolution that laid the foundation of the capitalistic mode of production, was played in the last third of the fifteenth, and the first decade of the sixteenth century.'[64]

In the light of generations of diligent archival scholarship, it is possible to draw attention to all sorts of difficulties with Marx's analysis. Nonetheless, he makes some important points which will bear heavily upon our study of the relationship between popular rebellion and social change in sixteenth-century England: Marx showed that there was a significant time lag between the end of feudalism and the establishment of agrarian capitalism as a dominant mode; that the late fifteenth and early sixteenth centuries repre-sented the key decades in the emergence of capitalist relations of production in the countryside; and that the free peasantry of the fifteenth century emerged as a result of conflict with the lordly class. This latter point contains important implications for our study of popular politics in Tudor England: Marx illuminates the economic basis of the key conflict in 1549 – a dispute between lord and tenant over relations of production and modes of exploita-tion. In the English case, relations of production and exploitation became the site of a messy, three-way conflict between an aggressive lordly class, an entrepreneurial group of wealthy yeoman farmers and a body of semi-proletarianised labourers. If Marx failed to perceive the significance of the yeomanry, his achievement lay in the recognition that the period witnessed a profound and important social conflict.

The significance of micro-economic change within village communities was contemporaneously overshadowed by the polarised conflict between gentry and commons. In contrast, modern historians have tended to empha-sise the role played by yeoman farmers in the emergence of capitalism. Thus, for Jane Whittle, agrarian change was not the consequence of class struggle between lord and tenant; instead, 'it was the tenants' own choices which exposed them to the market and made them vulnerable to its fluctuations'. Like Keith Wrightson, Whittle notes the 'increased polarisation of wealth in rural society'. In her analysis, this social polarisation resulted from the terminal decline of serfdom; the growing productivity and diversity of the rural economy; the emergence of a cash nexus; and the proletarianisation of much of the labour force.[65]

In the early sixteenth century, the middling social fraction tended to be identified – and to identify itself – as the 'honest men' or the 'honest inhabi-tants'. Alternatively, they might be collectively designated as 'the honesty of

[64] *Ibid.*, 789.   [65] Whittle, *Development of agrarian capitalism*, 97–8, 177.

the p[ar]ishe'.[66] Sometimes, they were known as 'the most substancyall of the comons', or as the 'substanciall yomen'; very occasionally, they might be known as the 'myddel sort of the peple'.[67] The honest men were essential to the functioning of the Tudor state. Thus, in the crisis of October 1536, the Duke of Norfolk placed his trust in the clothiers of Suffolk to maintain order in that county; likewise, he wrote of the importance of maintaining the loyalties of the 'substanciall yomen'.[68] Similarly, the honest men represented an important conduit of popular political opinion: when Sir John Russell and Sir William Parr wanted 'to knowe the certaintie of the state of ... [the] comons herts', they asked 'the moost discrete and substauncall p[er]sons'.[69] In September 1537, the Chancellor wrote to Thomas Cromwell, worrying about unemployment amongst the textile workers; he suggested that the clothiers should be told that they would be responsible if there should 'growe murmor and sedicion amongs[t] the people for lack of worke'.[70] When in 1549 Sir Thomas Smith proposed that the rebels in the Thames Valley should be put down, he recommended that the gentry '& other hed & grave yomen' should be responsible for this suppression.[71] Likewise, the surveillance of popular political speech depended crucially upon the participation of the honest men.[72] This middling social group therefore represented the front line of the state.

Despite the 1549 rebels' identification of a large-scale conflict between the commons and the gentry, the interests of the honest men did not always accord with those of their poorer neighbours.[73] This is especially obvious within the micro-politics of the village, in which competition over scant resources often led to conflict between rich and poor. It was not only the gentry who tried to undermine common rights; Whittle supplies the example of one wealthy farmer in the 1530s who refused to allow his poorer neighbours to put their animals on the common. As his opponents put it, this was

---

[66] Quoting PRO, E36/120, fol. 105r–v. For other examples, see Shagan, *Popular politics*, 194; BL, Cotton MS, Vespasian F XIII, fol. 204r; PRO, SP1/89, fol. 122r; PRO, SP1/114, fols. 251r–253r; PRO, SP1/115, fol. 82r; PRO, SP1/138, fol. 30r.

[67] PRO, E36/118, fol. 116r; PRO, SP1/115, fol. 173r; J. Meadows Cowper (ed.), *Henry Brinklow's complaynt of Roderyck Mors; and, The lamentacyon of a Christen agaynst the cytye of London* (Early English Text Society, extra ser., 22, London, 1874), 51. For another reference to 'the myddell sorte' in 1538: BL, Cotton MS, Nero B VI, fol. 138r. For the emergence of the term 'middle sort', see K. E. Wrightson, 'Sorts of people in Tudor and Stuart England', in J. Barry (ed.), *The middling sort of people: culture, society and politics in England, 1550–1800* (Basingstoke, 1994), 28–51.

[68] PRO, SP1/106, fol. 118r–v; PRO, SP1/115, fol. 173r.   [69] PRO, SP1/107, fol. 115r.

[70] BL, Cotton MS, Titus B V, fols. 195r–197v.   [71] PRO, SP10/8/33.

[72] I hope to write about the surveillance of popular opinion elsewhere.

[73] For frictions between wealthier and poorer villagers in mid-sixteenth-century Norfolk, see A. Greenwood, 'A study of the rebel petitions of 1549', PhD dissertation, Manchester University (1990), 289–97.

to the 'great detriment and pauperisation of the common rights of the said tenants'.[74] Likewise, in 1557, forty-two copyholders of Wighton and Binham complained to the Court of the Duchy of Lancaster against the wealthy yeoman John Smyth whose sheep flocks, by his 'extorte power', were overwhelming the commons.[75] From the other side of the fence, established inhabitants sometimes came into conflict with the village poor, whom they stereotyped as a criminal class. During the reign of Henry VIII, hedge-breakers (that is, the poor in search of firewood) were regularly reported to the court leet of Walden (Essex). In 1545, the court ordered that 'all those cottages in which the paupers of this town dwell' should be searched to see if they had sufficient wood for the winter; those who were 'unprovided' were to be 'regarded, pronounced, and declared breakers of hedges'. By 1554, any inhabitant who broke a hedge for the second time was to be expelled from the village.[76] Marx was surely correct to identify in disputes over firewood one of the most elemental forms of class struggle.[77] Internal village conflicts also pitted rich against poor over the terms of labourers' proletarianisation: in 1558, one Norfolk labourer was indicted at the quarter sessions for attempting to organise a strike, 'counselling many other day labourers' to demand high wages.[78]

Rich and poor, then, despite their periodic self-identification as the 'commons', did not always have the same interests. Importantly, late medieval rebel complaints were biased towards the interests of wealthier villagers. It was this social group that dominated the government of the village and – crucially – of the hundred; it was also from this group that the leaders of rebellion tended to be drawn.[79] In 1549, as rich and poor villagers and townspeople united against the gentry under the increasingly worn label of the 'commons', the honest men placed themselves at the head of popular protest for the last time. One of the defining purposes of this book is to investigate the ideological, linguistic and social basis of this fragile unity; another key aim is to look at why this tradition of late medieval popular protest ended with the commotion time of 1549.

[74] Whittle, *Development of agrarian capitalism*, 61.
[75] PRO, DL3/70/T1.
[76] K. C. Newton and M. K. McIntosh, 'Leet jurisdiction in Essex manor courts during the Elizabethan period', *Essex Archaeology and History*, 3rd ser., 13 (1981), 12.
[77] K. Marx and F. Engels, *Collected works*, 37 vols. (London, 1975–98), I, 224–63.
[78] Whittle, *Development of agrarian capitalism*, 286.
[79] Harvey, *Jack Cade's rebellion*, 111; Goheen, 'Peasant politics?', 47.

Part I
Context

The 1549 rebellions

In every country the process is different, although the content is the same. And the content is the crisis of the ruling class's hegemony, which occurs either because the ruling class has failed in some major political undertaking for which it has requested, or forcibly extracted, the consent of the broad masses ... or because huge masses ... have passed suddenly from a state of political passivity to a certain activity, and put forward demands which taken together ... add up to a revolution. A 'crisis of authority' is spoken of: this is precisely the crisis of hegemony, or general crisis of the State. (Q. Hoare and G. Nowell Smith (eds.), *Selections from the prison notebooks of Antonio Gramsci* (London, 1971), 210.)

Only when members of a society experience structural alterations as critical for continued existence and feel their social identity threatened can we speak of crises ... crisis states assume the form of the disintegration of social institutions. (J. Habermas, *Legitimation crisis* (1973; Eng. trans., London, 1976), 3.)

I 'COMMYNS IS BECOME A KING': LEGITIMATION CRISIS IN MID-TUDOR ENGLAND

On 7 July 1549, as crowds gathered at Wymondham to witness the performance of the *Life of St Thomas Beckett*, an event that would provide the cover for the start of Kett's rebellion, Sir William Paget wrote a sharply critical letter to the Duke of Somerset.[1] In his brutally perceptive critique of the Protectorate's policies, Paget identified a fourfold crisis of the state. This concerned, firstly, a crisis in government policy; secondly, a crisis in social relations; thirdly, a crisis in religious belief; and fourthly, a crisis in popular politics. In particular, Paget was concerned by the growing willingness of labouring people openly to discuss politics and religion. He presented these

---

[1] J. Strype (ed.), *Ecclesiastical memorials relating chiefly to religion and the reformation of it and the emergencies of the Church of England under King Henry VIII, King Edward VI and Queen Mary I*, 4 vols. (Oxford, 1822), 2: II, 429–37; for manuscript versions, see BL, Cotton MS, Titus 3 B, fols. 277r–279v; PRO, SP10/8/4. See also his comments in PRO, SP68/4, fols. 53r–54r (no. 185), fols. 71r–72v (no. 189).

four challenges as together comprising a fundamental legitimation crisis.[2]
Finally, less obvious to Paget, but working their way below the surface of
events, was an economic crisis driven in the short-term by high food prices
and inflation and in the longer-term by the emergence of agrarian capitalism.

Addressing the first of his crises, Paget warned that Somerset's social
reforms, directed against enclosure and seigneurial oppression, had spun
out of control, alienating the traditional ruling class and allowing the rebellious commons into government. 'How say for the law,' asked Paget

where is it used in England at liberty? Almost nowhere. The foot taketh upon him the
part of the head, and commyns is become a king; a king appointing conditions and
laws to the governors, saying, Grant this and that, and we wil go home.[3]

In particular, Paget criticised Somerset's willingness to pardon rebels, recom-
mending instead a policy of repression: the Protector's leniency towards the
rebels meant that 'evell men' had been given the 'boldenes' to think that
Somerset dared not meddle with them, but instead was 'glad to please them'.
Paget warned Somerset that he had alienated himself from the rest of the
Council as a result of this leniency. Paget had already warned Somerset about
the dangerous direction of his policies; in an earlier letter he had noted that
'as the people (which be most inconstant, uncertain, and flexible) vary their
sayings and show themselves to like or mislike; so do the ministers change
their determinations, contrary to all the rules of policies'.[4] Events, Paget now
warned, had reached breaking point.

Paget's second point concerned the breakdown of social hierarchy. In
December 1548, Paget sensed the growing antagonisms which would
explode in the spring of the following year. He saw in these conflicts a
fundamental threat to the social order, in which 'The governor [was] not
feared; the nobleman contempted; the gentleman despised.'[5] In a summary of
key issues which Paget presented to the Council in April 1549, he noted that
'The greater officers [are] not greatlie feared, the people presuminge much of
their goodnes. The inferior officers not regarded but contempned. The
gentleman despised and so nowe contented to endure.'[6] Paget expanded

---

[2] See Giddens' summary of Weber's interpretation of legitimacy, in which it is argued that 'no
stable system of domination is based purely upon either automatic habituation or upon the
appeal to self-interest: the main prop is belief by subordinates in the legitimacy of their
subordination': A. Giddens, *Capitalism and modern social theory: an analysis of the writings
of Marx, Durkheim and Max Weber* (Cambridge, 1971), 156. See also Habermas,
Legitimation crisis, 97.

[3] Strype (ed.), *Ecclesiastical memorials*, 2: II, 431.

[4] B. L. Beer (ed.), 'A critique of the Protectorate: an unpublished letter of Sir William Paget to the
Duke of Somerset', *Huntington Library Quarterly*, 34 (1971), 280.

[5] *Ibid.*

[6] B. L. Beer and S. M. Jack (eds.), 'The letters of William Lord Paget of Beaudesert, 1547–63',
Camden Miscellany, XXV (Camden Society, 4th ser., XIII, London, 1974), 31.

upon this crisis of authority in his third point, a remarkably frank and perceptive account of the impact of the Henrician and Edwardian Reformations:

Consider, I beseech you most humbly with al my heart, that society in a realm doth consist and is maintained by means of religion and laws. And these two or one wanting, farewel al just society, farewel kings, government, justice, al other vertue. And in cometh commonalty, sensuality, iniquity, and al other kinds of vice and mischief. Look wel, whether you have either law or religion at home, and I fear you shal find neither. The use of the old religion is forbidden by a law, and the use of the new is not yet printed: printed in the stomac[h]s of eleven or twelve parts of the realm, what countenance soever men make outwardly to please them in whom they se the power resteth.[7]

An unintended consequence of the Reformation, then, took the form of a crisis of belief in which traditional modes of legitimation – specifically, the role played by the Church in the justification of social inequality – were called into question.

This plebeian critique of the established order was understood by Sir William Paget in terms of assertive speech. As he observed, 'in our old Majesty's time ... all things were too straight and now they are too loose; then it was dangerous to do or speak though the meaning were not evil; and now every man have liberty to do and speak at liberty without danger'.[8] In his note of advice, Paget expanded upon his theme, warning that 'The common people [were] to liberall in speche, to bolde and licentious in their doinges and to wise and well learned in their owne conceytes.'[9] Lastly, in contrast to Somerset's policy of appeasement, Paget argued for the violent repression of the rebellions. Noting 'The disobedience of the people', he advised that military resources be employed against the commotioners rather than against the French, and that the Council should look to the

conservacion of the state of the realme here at home, for what availeth yt to seke to wynne foreyne realmes, and to lose your owne wherein youe dwell ... Bringe the subjectes into the obedience wherin youe founde them and that must be done by force and terrour, and then may youe commaunde them.[10]

Rather than pardoning the rebels, Paget argued that Somerset should have used violence at first, and only then pardoned rank-and-file rebels. He drew upon an analogy with the 1525 German Peasants' War:

In Germany, when the very like tumults to this began first, it might have been appeased with the loss of twenty men; and after, with the loss of an C. or CC. But it was thought nothing, and might easily be appeased; and also some spiced consciences

---

[7] Strype (ed.), *Ecclesiastical memorials*, 2: II, 433–4.
[8] Beer (ed.), 'A critique of the Protectorate', 280.
[9] Beer and Jack (eds.), 'The letters of William Lord Paget of Beaudesert', 31.   [10] *Ibid.*, 78.

taking pity of the poor, who indeed knew not what great pity was, nor who were the poor, thought it a sore matter to lose so many of their even Christian [country folks] saying, they were simple folk, and wist not what the matter meant, and were of a godly knowledg: and after this sort, and by such womanly pity and fond persuasion, suffered the matter to run so far, as it cost ere it was appeased, they say, a thousand or two thousand men's lives.[11]

In his letter of 7 July 1549, Paget advised that Somerset should gather the nobility and gentry. These should then combine with the levies taken from those parts of England that were not in rebellion and with the mercenary forces that were employed to guard against the Scots and French. Following victory, Paget recommended that the leaders of the insurrections should be hanged and the rest should be prosecuted before Star Chamber. Thereafter, Somerset should allow the mercenaries to 'ly in such towns and villages as have been most busiest taking enough for their mony, that rebels may feel the smart of their villany'. This policy, Paget argued, should be applied in every rebellious county. Thereby, he suggested, Somerset would 'deliver the king an obedient realm'.[12]

There was a wider context to Paget's brutal but pragmatic advice. His concerns connected with elite anxieties about popular politics and religious change. There was a close connection between popular perceptions of social conflict and the Reformation, which labouring people understood in more than merely doctrinal terms. The dissolution of the monastic houses and of the chantries, and the seizure of church lands and goods, were felt by many common people to represent an aggressive action by the Crown and the gentry, part of a wider assault upon the traditional social order. Significantly, it was widely recognised in ruling circles that, by the mid-sixteenth century, the Reformation had failed to implant itself within popular culture. Thus, in 1540, Sir Roger Townshend, reporting the spread of a prophecy in north Norfolk concerning Our Lady of Walsingham, worried that 'I cannot perceyve but the seid Image is not yett out of sum of ther heddes.'[13] Edwardian evangelicals were constantly aware that the Henrician Reformation had failed to win over popular religious loyalties. Thus, John Hooper wrote to Henry Bullinger expressing his worry that 'a great portion of the kingdom so adheres to the popish faction, as altogether to set at nought God and the lawful authority of the magistrates'.[14] In his sermon of 19 April 1549, Latimer warned that the Reformation had broken the Church's role in the legitimation of the social order: 'Men will be masters; they will be masters and no disciples. Alas, where is this discipline now in England? The people

---

[11] Strype (ed.), *Ecclesiastical memorials*, 2: II, 435. [12] *Ibid.*, 436.
[13] Moreton, 'Walsingham conspiracy', 39.
[14] H. Robinson (ed.), *Original letters relative to the English Reformation* (Parker Society, XXVI, Cambridge, 1846), 66.

regard no discipline; they be without all order . . . surely in popery they had a reverence; but now we have none at all.'[15] Rulers' recognition of the failure of the Henrician Reformation could sometimes take on a frustrated tone: in a deleted injunction to the Council concerning religion, it was ordered that the new religion should be 'beate in to [the people's] heads by contynuall inculcacon'.[16]

Paget's worries concerning the increasingly assertive nature of popular political speech were to be found elsewhere in the mid-Tudor period. Popular religious belief, and the sites of its articulation, became the key battleground upon which Reformation ideas would be won or lost. Proponents of the Reformation stated an unequivocal desire to silence religious debate. Thus, the preface to the 1549 edition of the English Bible condemned those who 'by theyr inordinate reading, undiscrete speaking, contencious disputing, or otherwise by theyr licentous lyvinge' presented the Scriptures as a subject for debate.[17] A statute of 1543 noted the 'ignoraunce fonde opinions errours and blingnes' into which some of the laity had been thrown by the publication of the vernacular Bible. This had inspired 'greate libertie . . . whereupon diversitie of opinions sayings variauncs arguments tumults and scisms have been sprung'. In answer to this heterogeneous babble, the framers of the statute proposed to nail down scriptural meaning. While accepting that every 'noble man and gentleman' may read the Bible to his household and that every merchant had the right privately to peruse the Scriptures, it ordered that since

a greate multitude of [the King's] . . . subjects, most speciallie of the lower sorte have so abused the same, that they have therebye growen and increased in divers naughtie and erronyous opinions . . . no women nor artificers prentises journeymen serving men of the degrees of yeomen or under, husbandemen nor laborers shall reade . . . the Byble or New Testament in Englishe to himselfe or any other pryvatelie or openlie.[18]

Likewise, in a proclamation of May 1541, Henry VIII ordered that lay subjects who read the Bible should not 'presume to take upon them any common disputation, argument, or exposition of the mysteries therein contained'.[19] Thanks to the state's ambitious desire to regulate popular speech, such injunctions intensified the already politicised terrain of plebeian conversation and religious opinion. Thus, in November 1536, Henry VIII circulated his bishops with a letter that condemned 'dyversitie of opinion'. This, the King saw as stemming from a 'certaine contemptuous man[ner] of speking' against the rituals of the Church. In Henry's analysis, it was the unhindered speech of the commons that was to blame for the frustration of

---

[15] Latimer, *Sermons*, 230.   [16] PRO, SP15/3/47.
[17] *Bible in English* (London, 1549), preface.
[18] *Statutes of the realm*, 11 vols. (London, 1810–24), IV:I, 894–7.   [19] *TRP*, I, 297.

his religious policies, observing that 'oure Labours Travail and desire ... is ... defeated ... by gen[er]all and contemptuous woords spoken by sundry light and sedicious p[er]sons'.[20]

In a series of royal injunctions, the plebeian alehouse was identified as the most important environment for the articulation of popular religious opinion. In 1538, a royal proclamation observed that although the publication of a vernacular Bible had been intended to strengthen obedience, it had led subjects 'arogantly' to voice religious and political opinions 'in churches ale houses Tavernes and other places and congregacions', causing 'slaunder ... by words as wryting oon parte of theym calling the other papist, the other parte calling the other heretyks'. And so it was ordered that no subject should abuse another with the name of papist or heretic, and that only licensed preachers should publicly read from the Bible. Moreover, subjects were told that if any 'dowte shall come to ... you' concerning the Scriptures, they should not give 'to moche to yor owne mynd fantazies and opinions nor having thereof any open reasonyng in yor open Tavernes or Alehowses', but should instead have recourse to 'lerned men'.[21] The alehouse therefore was constituted as a key site within the Reformation battle of ideas: in yet another injunction, Henry VIII noted how 'that most precious jewel, the Word of God, is disputed, rhymed, sung and jangled in every alehouse and tavern, contrary to the true meaning and doctrine of the same'. Similarly, the magistracy of late Henrician Kent expressed anxiety concerning the 'open disputation [that] was in alehouses, and in household reasoning among servants, of which did also arise much debate and strife [would lead to] ... a commotion ... among the people'.[22]

Two points emerge from this. Firstly, it is clear that the Tudor state sought to close down plebeian religious discussion. Secondly, the state attempted to deploy both its hegemonic and its coercive powers in order to fix scriptural meaning, defining biblical ideas in such a fashion as to legitimate its authority. These represented responses to a fundamental crisis of legitimacy in mid-Tudor England. In 1549, long-term processes of structural change and social conflict combined with short-term religious fissure, governmental breakdown and economic catastrophe. All this engendered a massive legitimation crisis on a scale that would not be seen again until the outbreak of the English Revolution. This crisis stemmed from the inability of the mid-Tudor state to inspire sufficient commitment or respect. This was due to the Henrician and Edwardian Reformations.[23] These might be understood as comprising a

[20] PRO, SP1/111, fol. 161r. See also PRO, SP6/7, fols. 155r–157r.
[21] BL, Cotton MS, Cleopatra E V, fols. 344r–345r. See also fols. 313r–326r.
[22] Shagan, *Popular politics*, 198, 232.
[23] D. Beetham, *The legitimation of power* (Basingstoke, 1991), 168.

revolution from above in which the Crown was involved in both a massive intervention into popular culture and a revolutionary attempt to restructure the polity.[24] The best theorisation of the impact of a 'revolution from above' has come from William Hunt. Drawing upon Antonio Gramsci, Hunt has argued that

regimes are legitimate when they are perceived as the vectors of an effective national myth, one which is generally, though never universally, endorsed by the dominant social strata, and at least passively acknowledged by the subordinate. By national myth I understand a complex of shared premises, values and purposes which maintains social solidarity and which justifies or sacralizes social domination. When a regime comes into conflict with a strong national myth by disregarding or contravening its central integrative premises, then it is heading for trouble.[25]

The legitimation crisis that Hunt had in mind was that inspired by the policies of Charles I; but his formulation works equally well for the reigns of Henry VIII and Edward VI. Elite contemporaries were well aware that the religious revolution set in motion by Henry VIII was to be won or lost on the local level. And it had to do so not only through theology and church doctrine but also, because late medieval religion was so intermixed with social practice, Reformation ideas had to penetrate the sphere of everyday life.[26]

Two important aspects of legitimation stand out from this: the significance of symbolism and of the everyday. Firstly, it is clear that successful elites operate through the presentation of an 'entire symbolic universe', in which legitimating ideas are articulated, represented and related to the socioeconomic order.[27] In late medieval England, the dominant form of this symbolic totality took a religious form; as Paget recognised in his letters to Somerset, the Reformation undermined the legitimacy of that belief system. Secondly, effective legitimation strategies occur in ordinary, everyday experience as well as in the world of official ideology. As James C. Scott has observed, the status quo is reaffirmed not only through overt state propaganda but also through daily patterns of social interaction between dominators and dominated.[28] Thus, the everyday emerges as the essential site within which a

---

[24] For the Reformation as 'revolution', see Shagan, *Popular politics*, 1, 176, 236; and from a different historiographical perspective, E. Duffy, *The voices of Morebath: reformation and rebellion in an English village* (New Haven, CT, 2001), 53.

[25] W. Hunt, 'Spectral origins of the English Revolution: legitimation crisis in early Stuart England', in G. Eley and W. Hunt (eds.), *Reviving the English Revolution: reflections and elaborations on the work of Christopher Hill* (London, 1988), 308.

[26] A. Mansueto, 'Religion, solidarity and class struggle: Marx, Durkheim and Gramsci on the religious question', *Social Compass*, 35 (1988), 261–77.

[27] A. Izzo, 'Legitimation and society: a critical review', *Current Sociology*, 35, 2 (1987), 46.

[28] J. C. Scott, *Domination and the arts of resistance: hidden transcripts* (New Haven, CT, 1990).

ruling class must maintain its authority.[29] In this context, Henry VIII's concern with alehouse conversation seems less like paranoia and more like a perceptive awareness of the political significance of the everyday.

The significance of everyday legitimation strategies to the maintenance of established authority has been highlighted in the recent historiography on state formation and social relations.[30] Mike Braddick and John Walter have argued that the early modern English state operated according to a widely shared set of rules and expectations. At those moments at which that normative order was called into question, a crisis of legitimacy occurred. Thus, the early modern state was peculiarly vulnerable to shifts in *ideas*. In the mid-Tudor period, two centrally important territories within which legitimating ideas were supposed to operate – religion and social relations – were simultaneously called into question; in both cases, the source of this crisis of legitimacy was to be found within ruling circles. Firstly, the aggressive fiscal seigneurialism of the gentry and nobility undermined traditional notions of social reciprocity. Secondly, the Reformation undercut fundamental aspects of religious belief, challenged conventional distinctions between Church and state, and alienated that body of (in Gramscian terms) 'traditional intellectuals' upon whom the late medieval state had primarily relied for its legitimation: the clerical estate.

Henry VIII and Thomas Cromwell were well aware of the pivotal role played by parish priests. In the orders that Henry VIII sent to all parishes, he took care to instruct curates to set an example to their parishioners, ensuring that their 'owne lyvinges and conversacon' corresponded to the new religious order.[31] In many parishes, such injunctions were in vain. Rather, as Thomas Cromwell's correspondence makes clear, priests were often to be found voicing strenuous opposition to the Reformation. One priest, for instance, argued in a sermon of 1535 that 'who put Christ to dethe but the peeres of the realm in those dayes tht war . . . and yff Christ war now a lyve agayn, he shuld dye a cruell dethe, as ye see how their hedds goythe off nowe dayly'.[32] The fact that conservative clerics were to be found at the leadership of popular insurrection in 1549 in Devon, Cornwall, Oxfordshire, Buckinghamshire and Norfolk suggests that the Edwardian Reformation met with similar clerical hostility. Other than to encourage local denunciations of dissident priests (an action that was itself potentially corrosive of authority), it was difficult for the central state to do much about clerical criticism of the

---

[29] In early modern history, there is insufficient empirical work within this area.
[30] Braddick, *State formation*; Braddick and Walter (eds.), *Negotiating power*.
[31] BL, Cotton MS, Cleopatra E V, fols. 344r–345r.
[32] PRO, E36/120, fols. 165r–166r; for a similarly problematic sermon, see PRO, E36/120, fols. 5r–6r. For another example of clerical opposition to the Henrician Reformation, see PRO, SP1/115, fol. 122v.

Reformation; the best that Henry VIII could do was to instruct magistrates to look out for priests who mumbled the King's instructions in the pulpit, and who told their parishioners 'to lyve as ther forfathers dyd, that the olde fashion is the best and suche other crafty sedicous parables'.[33]

For mid-Tudor governors, religious division represented a further problem that had been engendered by the Reformation. Thus, one Henrician priest was to be found contending with a fellow cleric over the merits of Latimer's preaching; the evangelical minister warned his conservative counterpart to 'take hede what ye say for it is treason'. Another priest warned the conservative vicar that 'you be my frende and hath been Butt yf ye speke suche words as thes bee I cannot abyde you Therefore use yor Tonge more modestyously for I bore you well And I am lothe to breke w[i]t[h] you for suche wordys'.[34] It was not only priests who were set at odds by the early Reformation; whole parishes could be split down the middle. Thus, the inhabitants of the Kentish parish of Cranmer in 1537 found themselves divided between evangelicals and conservatives. One man, Thomas Sharp, remarked to his neighbour Edward Battarst, 'that he was wery of all togethers for we cannot agree w[i]t[h]in the our selfs well said Edward battarst, I pray God that all may be well that we may be lovers and freends nay said Thomas Sharpe that will never be till v or vi be kylled of thise newe fellowes in our p[ar]ishe'.[35] Such divisions were felt with even greater intensity where some parishioners, perhaps influenced by an earlier tradition of Lollardy, emerged as radical critics of the social order. Thus, one man found himself in trouble in January 1537 for his opinion that 'when so ever ii or iii simple p[er]sons as ii coblers or wevers were in company and elected in the name of God that ther was the trewe church of God'.[36] The same year, an Aylsham man was reported by his neighbours for his opinion that 'he shulde have god aswell w[i]t[h] a forke full of mucke as w[i]t[h] a wax candell'.[37] The previous year, it was alleged that Robert Wymond had observed that there was no purgatory 'for purgatorye ys pissed owte'; one of Wymond's neighbours was of the opinion that 'Yff our Lady were here in erth I wold no more fere to meddyll with her then with a comon hore'.[38]

Such opinions remind us that the mid-Tudor legitimation crisis was engendered not only by negative responses to the Reformation but also by autonomous political and religious opinions amongst the labouring classes. These ideas were contradictory: they endured both in spite of, and *in relationship with*, dominating ideology. Resistance and legitimation were therefore

---

[33] PRO, SP6/7, fols. 155r–157r.   [34] PRO, E36/120, fols. 143r–146r.
[35] PRO, E36/120, fol. 10r–v.   [36] BL, Cotton MS, Cleopatra E V, fol. 415r.
[37] PRO, SP1/120, fol. 247r–v.
[38] PRO, SP1/113, fols. 107r–109r. For a lengthy volume concerning religious dissidence in Kent, see CCCC, MS 128, calendared in *L&P*, XVIII (2), no. 546. For an illuminating discussion of religious radicalism in Norfolk in 1530, see BL, Cotton MS, Cleopatra E V, fol. 389r–v.

intertwined in the late medieval period; what happened in the mid-Tudor period was that this crucial relationship was briefly severed. Between 1532 and 1549, the close integration between religious ideas and state ideology was lost, as the traditional intellectuals upon whom the late medieval polity had relied for its legitimacy – the clerical order – drew away from that role. This occurred at the same time as the gentry and nobility transgressed their stated social roles, thereby provoking growing criticism amongst subaltern classes.

In the mid-Tudor period, therefore, the Crown, the gentry and the nobility faced a profound crisis. This was generated by a combination of short-term Reformation ideology and longer-term social conflict. Both forces undermined popular belief in any organic, interdependent social order. Rebel politics in 1549 were driven not only by ideological ferment, but also by immediate economic crisis. In 1547, prices stood at 46 per cent higher than they had in 1540. Prices fell in 1548, only to rise again in 1549 by 11 per cent on the 1548 average. By the 1550s, agricultural prices were 95 per cent up on those of the 1530s. Devastating as this was for landholding tenants, this surge in prices was catastrophic for the wage labourers who made up a growing proportion of the village economy of agrarian regions. The same was true of urban labourers. As Beer suggests, 'in the 1540s and 1550s the real wages of an urban labourer may have fallen as much as 50 percent, causing his [or her] diet to consist of an increasing proportion of bread in comparison to meat'.[39] Moreover, mid-sixteenth-century changes in the hitherto fluid land market of late medieval agrarian England, in particular the increase in land prices, meant that the landless and near-landless were forced out of the market.[40] For the bottom half of the population of the southern and East Anglian villages, a segment of the rural economy that was increasingly dependent upon fluctuations in food prices, the combination of these economic conditions was catastrophic.[41] The year 1549 was, then, one of crisis: a crisis that encompassed religion, politics, social relations and economic life.[42]

II POLICY AND IDEOLOGY UNDER THE DUKE OF SOMERSET'S PROTECTORATE

For a group of mid-sixteenth-century radical writers whom posterity has labelled the 'commonwealth men', the answer to the crisis that had been

---

[39] Beer, *Rebellion and riot*, 19, 21.
[40] Whittle, *Development of agrarian capitalism*, 102, 107, 110, 152, 167, 175, 190.
[41] *Ibid.*, 277. For an interesting contemporary comment upon the increase in food prices, see NRO, COL/2/1.
[42] For the significance of food prices in the 1549 rebellions, see *CSP, Span*, IX, 397; M. Bryn Davies, 'Boulogne and Calais from 1545 to 1550', *Bulletin of the Faculty of Arts, Fouad I University, Cairo*, 12, 1 (1950), 60.

opened up by the Reformation was obvious: it lay in a combination of preaching, teaching and social reform. Hugh Latimer used his recollections of his father's time to highlight both need for education, and the social virtues of an earlier age. He recalled that 'My father was a yeoman ... he kept me to school, or else I had not been able to have preached before the Kings majesty now ... he kept hospitality for his poor neighbours, and some alms he gave to the poor.'[43] In the reign of Edward VI, such arguments found their way into government policy. The Duke of Somerset likewise regarded education as a hegemonic device, describing learning as that which 'of wild men maketh civil, of blockish and rash persons wise and godly counsellors, of obstinate rebels obedient subjects, and of evil men good and godly Christians'. Without investment in grammar schools and universities, Somerset believed, there would be 'but barbarism and tumult'.[44] The establishment of a preaching ministry was similarly believed to stabilise society. Hence, a printed supplication of 1544 observed that 'Without a doubt, the wante and lacke of preaching of Godes Worde ... hathe bene the very originall grounde and cause of all the insurrection, commotion [and] dyscention which hathe rysen ... within ... [the] realme.'[45] It was argued that ideally, preaching and teaching should be combined in an educative ministry in which godly ministers also acted as schoolteachers. Implicit to the commonwealth writers' case was a critique of the impact of the dissolution of the monastic houses, and of the social changes of the early sixteenth century. Thus, Robert Crowley wrote that social stability would be restored through a combination of preaching, teaching, charity, social responsibility and a wider distribution of wealth. He argued that the wealth of the monasteries, which in his view had been poured away, should instead have been used to establish schools for the education of poor children. Crowley went on to condemn urban authorities, who had failed to provide welfare to the poor in the place of the charity that had been offered by monastic houses. Meanwhile, he observed, rich citizens bought up town houses and let them to the poor at exorbitant rents.[46] One of the earliest of these writers, Henry Brinklow, anticipated Crowley's analysis: to Brinklow, the Reformation was not just a missed opportunity – it also represented an intensification of the oppression of the poor.[47] Brinklow argued that with the

---

[43] Latimer, *Sermons*, 101.

[44] M. L. Bush, *The government policy of Protector Somerset* (London, 1975), 54.

[45] J. Meadows Cowper (ed.), *A supplicacyon for the beggers, with A supplycacion to our moste soveraigne lord Kynge Henry the Eyght, A supplication of the poore commons, The decaye of England by the great multitude of shepe* (Early English Text Society, extra ser., 18, London, 1871), 26; see also Meadows Cowper (ed.), *Henry Brinklow's complaynt*, 52.

[46] Crowley, *Select works*, 7, 10–11, 70–2.

[47] For a revealing new study of Brinklow, see K. Gunther and E. Shagan, 'Protestant radicalism and political thought in the reign of Henry VIII', *P&P*, forthcoming.

dissolution of the monastic houses, substantial properties had passed into the hands of oppressive lords, who raised rents and manorial dues 'so that the pore man that laboryth and toyleth upon it, and is hys slave, is not able to lyve'.[48] For the commonwealth writers, therefore, the Henrician Reformation represented both (in religious terms) an incomplete revolution, and (in social terms) an extension of existent social conflicts. Thus, the anonymous author of the pamphlet *Vox populi, vox Dei* argued that 'We have banished superstition / But we still have ambition / We have shut away all cloisterers / But still keep extortioners / We have taken the lands from the Abbewse / But we have converted them to a worse use.'[49]

The arguments outlined by the commonwealth writers had their immediate origins in the intellectual and political circle around Thomas Cromwell in the 1530s. The commonwealth men's advocacy of education as a means of enabling both social mobility and the communication of ruling ideas into the population was anticipated by Thomas Cranmer, who wrote that 'pore mennys children arr many tymes enduyed with more synguler giftes of nature ... as with eloquence, memorie, apte pronunciacion, sobrietie, with suche like, and also commonly more gyven to applie thair studie, than ys the gentilmannys sonne delicatelie educated'. Cranmer echoed Richard Pace's views of 1517, who wrote that learning was now better 'than ignorance and noble blood'. In the 1530s, seeing that 'penury ever bredyth sedytyon', Thomas Starkey advanced the hope that the profits of the monastic houses would be employed for the maintenance of the commonwealth, rather than being leased to lords and wealthy gentlemen. In the same decade, Sir Richard Morison likewise felt that the roots of sedition lay in the lack of education.[50] But the commonwealth writers need also to be understood in the longer chronological context of late medieval radical Christianity. Thus, Wycliffe's belief that 'the poor, by virtue of their poverty, bore a natural likeness to Christ and the mark of his authority' found its mirror in Ridley's linkage of the plight of the urban poor with 'our good Master Christ's cause', describing how Christ had 'lain too long abroad ... without lodging in the streets of London, both hungry, naked and cold'.[51] The clearest connection between the commonwealth writers and late medieval radical Christian thought was to be found in Robert Crowley's edition of Langland's *Piers Plowman*, in which Christ appears 'in pore man's apparayle'. In the climax of Crowley's

---

[48] Meadows Cowper (ed.), *Henry Brinklow's complaynt*, 9, 33; see also Meadows Cowper (ed.), *A supplicacyon for the beggers*, 79.

[49] Tawney and Power (eds.), *Tudor economic documents*, III, 25–39.

[50] Zeeveld, *Foundations*, 162, 193–4, 218; PRO, SP1/105, fols. 47r–49v; R. Morison, *A remedy for sedition* (London, 1536), sigs. D2r–3r.

[51] Justice, *Writing and rebellion*, 90; Tawney and Power (eds.), *Tudor economic documents*, II, 312.

version of Langland, Piers Plowman himself appears as Christ: 'painted all bloodye and came in with a crosse before the comune people, and right lyke in all lymmes to our lorde Jesus'.[52]

In recent years, historians have grown used to dismissing the radicalism of the commonwealth men. Thus, Michael Bush has written off the radical challenge represented by these writers, arguing that

> Without exception they subscribed to the traditional ideal of the state as a body politic in which every social group had its place, function and desert ... their thinking was paternalistic and conservative ... none questioned the necessary existence of the rich and the poor ... What moved them ... was not the prospect of people starving to death, but the wrath of God and the fear of oppressed peasants failing to provide the state with its military needs or rising to destroy the nobility.[53]

Certainly, it is not difficult to find a conservative strain within common-wealth literature. This took two forms: a tendency to conceive of society in terms of mutually supportive social blocs in which the subordination of the commons was naturalised; and a disavowal of popular politics and of plebeian agency. Gilpin, for instance, advised the poor not to 'murmur' against their rulers, but instead to obey authority. In the place of popular rebellion, Gilpin told the poor that it was God who would punish their 'evill governors'.[54] Robert Crowley wrote in identical terms. His 1550 work, *The voyce of the last trumpet*, is structured around a set of 'lessons' in which beggars, servants, yeomen, lewd priests, scholars, learned men, physicians, lawyers, merchants, gentlemen, magistrates and women all receive instruc-tion as to their duties and obligations. Once again, the poor were enjoined to resist rebellion; to put their faith in ultimate salvation; and to accept the authority even of oppressive governors. Hence, 'The beggars lesson' advises 'do not seke thy lotte to chaunge / If God have layede hys hande on the / And made the lowe in al mens syght / Content thiselfe with that degre'.[55] The rationale underlying Crowley's social vision is clearest in his *Waie to wealth*. Here, class is presented as a product of man's fall. Crowley advises the commons to 'Quiet thy selfe therfore againste the streame. For thi sinnes have deserved this oppression, and God hath sent it the as a just rewarde for thi sinnes.'[56] Crowley disavowed social mobility. Thus, he encouraged yeomen to accept their place, to defer to the gentry, and to give charity to the poor: 'Howe darest thou be bolde, I say / To heape up so much goulde

[52] R. Crowley, *The vision of Pierce Plowman, nowe the seconde time imprinted* (London, 1550), fols. 60v, 103v–104r.
[53] Bush, *Government policy*, 61–2.
[54] B. Gilpin, *A godly sermon preached in the court at Greenwich the firste Sonday after the Epiphanie ... 1552* (London, 1581), 62–3.
[55] Crowley, *Select works*, 57.   [56] *Ibid.*, 138.

in store / Out of the due that thou shouldest paye / To them that be pore, sicke and sore?'[57]

But to categorise the commonwealth writers as 'conservative' is both to simplify and to dismiss their message. What makes the commonwealth writers so difficult to pin down is precisely their contradictory, multifaceted nature. At the same time as Crowley, Latimer and Gilpin denied popular agency, so they denounced the oppressions of the rich in terminology that was strikingly similar to that of the commotioners of 1549. Thus, Latimer argued that it was the rich who were responsible for dearth: 'These rich men ... causeth such dearth, that poor men, which live of their labour, cannot with the sweat of their face have a living, all kind of victuals is so dear.'[58] Henry Brinklow agreed that the gentry were responsible for dearth, arguing that 'the chefe cause of [economic distress] ... be ... the landlordes; for as he encreaseth hys rent, so must the fermer the price of his wolle, catel and all vitels ... And thus I say, the lordes be the only cause of all the dearth in the realme'.[59] To Brinklow, the roots of the mid-sixteenth-century crisis lay in the absence of Christian morality. It was this moral vacuum that, in his analysis, had created a tyrannical class society:

the body of this realme, I meane the comynaltye, is so oppressed ... by wicked lawes, cruel tryann[t]es, which be extorcionars, and oppresors of the common welth. For all men are geven to seke their own pryvate welth only, & the pore are nothing provyded for.

The answer lay in the application of Scripture: 'let all things be reformed, and set forth by the toch stone which is Godds word'.[60] Similarly, the commonwealth writers and the rebels of 1549 both saw the gentry's creation of a sheep economy as an attack upon community; hence, one anonymous writer of 1550 observed that 'where twelf score persons were wont to have meate, drynke, rayment and wages ... now there is nothyng kept there, but onlye shepe'.[61] Like the plebeian dissidents whose words were recorded in prosecutions of seditious speech, Gilpin connected the sumptuary display of elite authority with the destruction of the commons, observing that 'the gentry desire rich clothes and sumptuous buildings and therefore destroy the poor'.[62] Latimer pursued a similar interpretation, arguing that oppressive landlords intended 'plainly to make the yeomanry slavery'.[63]

In the mid-Tudor period, printed critiques of the social order were both more numerous and more bitter than was to be the case at any time before the 1640s. Moreover, while some literature was clearly designed for an elite

---

[57] *Ibid.*, 63–5, 89.   [58] Latimer, *Sermons*, 99.
[59] Meadows Cowper (ed.), *Henry Brinklow's complaynt*, 12.   [60] *Ibid.*, 73, 74.
[61] Meadows Cowper (ed.), *A supplicacyon for the beggers*, 98.
[62] Gilpin, *A godly sermon*, 58–9.   [63] Latimer, *Sermons*, 100.

audience, others were highly populist. One such pamphlet, *A ruful complaynt of the publyke weale to Englande*, echoed the complaints of Kett's rebels in 1549, observing how 'Suche offices as heretofore / apperteyned to the yomans ryght / Be taken awaye . . . / and geven to Lorde or knyght.' Again, echoing rebel criticisms, the pamphlet criticised the blurring of social boundaries: 'Marchauntes they become lordes / and Lordes useth marchaundyse.'[64] There was more than a tinge of radicalism to the commonwealth writers' rhetoric. Thus, in his sermons preached to the court in 1552, Gilpin argued that the 'mightie men, gentlemen and all riche men' intended 'to robbe and spoile the poore'.[65] In his 1550 work, *Waie to wealth*, Robert Crowley engaged in a protracted denunciation of the gentry which verged upon support for the rebels of the previous year and which was, by inference, supportive of Somerset's social reforms. He accused the gentry not only of failing in their duties to the commons, but of disobedience to the law. In particular, Crowley highlighted the gentry's opposition to the enclosure commissions empowered by Somerset: it was this disobedience, according to Crowley, which had caused the rebellions.[66] In his strongest language, Crowley warned the gentry that 'The bloude of . . . the plowemen that laboured sore' whose lands have been lost 'Theyr bloude I wyl of you require'. Elsewhere, Crowley repeated this triangulation of oppression, retribution and bloodshedding, warning the gentry that 'the bloude of [the commons] . . . shalbe required at your handes. If the impotent creatures perish for lacke of necessaries, you are the murderers, for you have theyr enheritaunce and do minister unto them.'[67]

Crowley's belief in divine retribution should not be seen as a conceptual dead end. To him, the anger of a just God against the 'possessioners' seemed real and imminent enough. After all,

Heaven and earth shall not perish, but the wordes of the Spirite shall not perysh, but be fulfylled. Nowe herken you possessioners, and you rich men lyfte up your ears; ye stuards of the Lord, marke what complayntes are layede agaynste you in the hygh court of the lyveynge God.

Crowley assumed that the voice of the poor enjoyed a special force in heaven: thus, he compared divine vengeance upon Egypt with God's judgement upon mid-sixteenth-century English society, promising plagues, dearth and the desertion of great houses: 'Thinke you that you shal dwel upon the earth alone? The Lorde of hostes (sayth the prophete) hath spoken these wordes unto me.'[68] Least wordy and most direct of the commonwealth writers,

---

[64] Anon., *A ruful complaynt of the publyke weale to Englande* (London, 1550).
[65] Gilpin, *A godly sermon*, 45–6.   [66] Crowley, *Select works*, 144–6.
[67] *Ibid.*, 117, 163–4, see also 121.   [68] *Ibid.*, 160, 161.

Latimer warned that 'the greedy pit of hell burning fire' awaited the oppressors of the commons.[69] The anonymous supplication of 1546 followed an equally radical line, citing Scripture to the effect that 'Let none eat that laboureth not.'[70] This was consistent with Crowley's view: he warned the gentry that 'By nature ... you can claime no thynge but that whiche you shall gette with the swet of your faces.'[71] For the commonwealth writers, therefore, work was a moral category: whereas the gentry stood condemned by their idleness, so the values of the commons commended them in the eyes of the Lord: as Latimer observed,

Our Saviour Christ, before he began his preaching, lived of his occupation; he was a carpenter, and gat his living with great labour. Therefore let no man disdain or think scorn to follow him in a mean living, a mean vocation, or a common calling and occupation.[72]

The institution of property itself fell under the critical scrutiny of the commonwealth writers. Expanding the limits of the traditional doctrine that property represented a form of stewardship, Robert Crowley argued that commodity fetishism lay at the roots of social conflict:

If the possessioners woulde consyder themselves to be but stuardes, and not Lordes over theyr possessions, thys oppression woulde soon be redressed. But so longe as thys perswasion stryketh in theyr myndes – 'It is myne owne; whoe shall warne me to do wyth myne owne as me selfe lysteth' – it shall not.[73]

Similarly, Gilpin wrote of how 'covetous cormorantes ... turning poore men out of their holdes ... saie their land is their owne, and forget altogether that the earth is the Lords, and the fulnesse therof'.[74] Latimer was at his bluntest: 'no rich man can say before God, "This is my own." No, he is but an officer over it.'[75]

Far from simply seeking to recall the gentry to their proper social roles, the commonwealth writers engaged in a wider critique of elite values and behaviour. Thomas Some, the author of the preface to Latimer's sermons, called attention to the contrast between the gentry's pretensions and their conduct:

thou that art so gorgeously apparelled, and feedeth thy corruptible carcase so daintily; thou that purchasest so fast, to the utter undoing of the poor, consider whereof thou camest, and whereunto thou shalt return. Where is then all thy pomp? Where is all thy ruff of thy gloriousness become?

A Christian critique of pride could be turned around into criticism of class society: Some advised the gentry to 'Pull down thy sail: say, "Down, proud

---

[69] Latimer, *Sermons*, 102.   [70] Meadows Cowper (ed.), *A supplicacyon for the beggers*, 88.
[71] Crowley, *Select works*, 163.   [72] Latimer, *Sermons*, 214.
[73] Crowley, *Select works*, 157.   [74] Gilpin, *A godly sermon*, 51.
[75] Latimer, *Sermons*, 411. See also 399, 477 and Meadows Cowper (ed.), *Henry Brinklow's complaynt*, 17.

heart."'[76] Anticipating Gerrard Winstanley, Latimer warned the gentry that their enclosures and depopulations would create an alienated, atomised society: 'Woe be to you that join house to house, and field to field! Shall ye alone inhabit the earth?'[77] In Raphe Robynson's 1551 translation of More's *Utopia*, which might be considered as part of this mid-sixteenth-century genre, the disputant Raphael countered the lawyers' objections that sufficient work had been provided for the poor by moving into overt social critique:

there is a great numbre of gentlemen, which can not be content to live idle themselves, like dorres, of that whiche other have laboured for: their tenauntes, I meane, whom they polle and shave to the quicke, by reisyng their rentes ... these gentlemen, I say, do not only live in idlenesse themsleves, but carrye about with them at their tailes a great flocke or traine of idle and loterynge servyngmen, which never learned any craft wherby to gett their livynges.[78]

Again, this criticism of large gentry households would be repeated in the rebel demands of 1549.[79]

Just as, pursuing late medieval radical Christianity, the commonwealth writers argued that the poor were closer to Christ than were the rich, so they claimed that 'the poor be more willing to hear the Gospel, they take more pain in hearing God's word, than the rich do; for the rich commonly least regard the Gospel'. To Henry Brinklow, the complaints of the poor would be heard in heaven, warning the rich that 'the crye of the peple is heard unto the Lord, though ye wyll not heare'. After all, as Latimer put it, 'Christ saith, it is hard for a rich man to come to heaven; speaking of those which set their hearts upon riches.'[80] Equally important in this context was the commonwealth writers' assumption that the commons had a right to petition the Crown: hence, Gilpin warned that 'as Solomon saith, who so stoppeth his eare at the crying of the poore, he shall cry and not be heard'. Citing biblical precedent, he went on to observe that 'We finde that pore me[n] mighte come to complaine of their wronges to the Kinges owne person.'[81] Brinklow claimed that in the German city states, 'the porest man ... may boldly come' and make complaint.[82] The frontispiece of the account of the causes

---

[76] Latimer, *Sermons*, 107, 108. See also Meadows Cowper (ed.), *A supplicacyon for the beggers*, 52.

[77] Latimer, *Sermons*, 109.   [78] More/Robynson, 21–2.

[79] On Robynson's translation of *Utopia*, see D. Weil Baker, *Divulging utopia: radical humanism in sixteenth-century England* (Amherst, MA, 1999), 106–30.

[80] Latimer, *Sermons*, 477, 479; Meadows Cowper (ed.), *Henry Brinklow's complaynt*, 52.

[81] Gilpin, *A godly sermon*, 45–6.

[82] Meadows Cowper (ed.), *Henry Brinklow's complaynt*, 43.

of the decay of England cited Proverbs to the effect that 'A Kyng that sitteth in judgment, and loketh well about him, dryveth away all evell.'[83] It is within this context that Latimer's encouragement to the Duke of Somerset to 'hear poor man's suits yourself' must be understood.[84]

As Elton has demonstrated, there was certainly no coherent 'Commonwealth party'.[85] But it should be obvious that much of the printed literature of the mid-sixteenth century exhibited a deep concern with social conflict, and with the corresponding need for socio-religious reform. In the reign of Edward VI, under both Somerset and (albeit to a lesser extent) Northumberland, such concerns were deepened to produce a genre of social criticism which, while not wholly original, was both pervasive and unusually powerful. Although it is difficult to establish a direct causal link between this literary genre and Edwardian policy, the similarities between the two in both form and language are unmistakable. In this context it seems perverse to deny a link between the commonwealth writers and the Protector Somerset's social policies: the one laid the intellectual ground for the other. It is worth laying out a brief assessment of the policies pursued by the Duke of Somerset in the years preceding the commotion time.

Under the terms of the will of Henry VIII, England was to be governed during Edward VI's minority by a council of leading noblemen headed by the Lord Protector, Edward Seymour, the Earl of Hertford. Within a few days of the death of Henry, Seymour elevated himself to Duke of Somerset. Protector Somerset's exact religious and social beliefs remain vague; but it is at least clear from his policies that he saw himself as both a social and a religious reformer. Between November and December 1547, parliament passed an Act which swept away a huge body of repressive legislation, including both the medieval heresy laws and Henrician additions to those laws, together with all restrictions on printing and the study of the Bible. Importantly, there were no executions for heresy under Somerset's Protectorate. Edward's first parliament also saw the dissolution of the chantries. Echoing commonwealth ideology, the Act justified itself according to the need to fund poor relief and education; in fact the profits were mostly spent on preparations for the confrontation with Scotland and France. Doctrinally, the Act was justified on the grounds that chantries encouraged 'superstition'. The lands and possessions that had supported the chantries were then sold off. The repeal of the Henrician Proclamations Act gave Somerset increased power – he was

---

[83] Meadows Cowper (ed.), *A supplicacyon for the beggers*, 93.   [84] Latimer, *Sermons*, 127.
[85] G. R. Elton, 'Reform and the "Commonwealth-men" of Edward VI's reign', in P. Clark, A. G. R. Smith and N. Tyacke (eds.), *The English Commonwealth: essays in politics presented to Joel Hurstfield* (Leicester, 1979), 23–38.

now able to issue proclamations without consent of the Council.[86] It was Somerset's idiosyncratic combination of autocracy and reformism that drove his attempts to reverse social change. The parliament of 1549 passed an Act of Uniformity which enforced the Prayer Book upon individual parishes, requiring that services be conducted in English. In June 1548 Protector Somerset established an enclosure commission, whose job it was to report upon illegal enclosures. Only one such enclosure commission went into operation, that headed by Somerset's ally John Hales. The target of Hales' commissioners were those who intended to put down not those enclosures which had been made upon private land, which were 'very beneficial to the Commonwealth', but instead were those individuals who had 'taken away and enclosed any other men's commons, or hath pulled down houses of husbandry and converted the lands from tillage to pasture'.[87]

The central problem, however, with Somerset's enclosure commissions lay in the structure of the mid-Tudor state. The commissioners were selected from amongst the country gentry: that is, precisely the class that was per- ceived to be the beneficiaries of agrarian change. Hugh Latimer gave an account of the corrupt handling of one enclosure commission jury. He explained how there was 'a great man, who sat in commission about such matters; and when the townsmen should bring in what had been inclosed, he frowned and chafed . . . and threatened the poor men, that they durst not ask their right'.[88] Conceivably, it was a growing awareness of his inability to operate through the traditional ruling class that drove Somerset's increas- ingly populist approach. Much of the evidence suggests that it was the Protector's criticism of 'private profit, self-love, money and suchlike' as 'the Devils instrument', combined with the force of evangelical preaching, that drove his domestic policies.[89] Certainly, Somerset involved himself in the minute settlement of local disputes, attempting to settle private suits between lord and tenant. It did not take long to communicate this author- itarian populism to the commons: hence, by 1548, the willingness of plebeian dissidents to appeal to Protector Somerset.[90] It was precisely this desire

[86] According to Bush, *Government policy*, Somerset was driven by diplomatic and military imperatives, especially in his policy towards Scotland. More recently, Shagan, *Popular politics*, has partially reinstated the older view presented in W. K. Jordan, *Edward VI, the young king: the Protectorship of the Duke of Somerset* (London, 1968) and A. F. Pollard, *England under Protector Somerset: an essay* (London, 1900).

[87] Bush, *Government policy*, 45.   [88] Latimer, *Sermons*, 248.

[89] Quote from Bush, *Government policy*, 46.

[90] For Somerset's authoritarian populism at work, see, for instance, PRO, SP15/3/47. For Paget's mention of Somerset's interest in 'pore menes cause', see Strype, *Ecclesiastical memorials*, 2: II, 437. For examples of Somerset's intercessions in local conflicts, see PRO, C1/1197/52; PRO, SP15/3/47, 50; PRO, REQ2/18/114; Latimer, *Sermons*, 127; Shagan, *Popular politics*, 293; CLRO, Rep 12 (1), fols. 2r–v, 38v, 39v, 40r, 76r, 96v, 103v. See also

amongst the commons to be included within state structures, at the same time as they found themselves in face-to-face conflict with the gentry and nobility, that characterised the politics of the 1549 rebels.

Nowhere was this more obvious than in the enclosure commissions of 1549 which, at the beginning of the commotion time, stimulated popular opposition to the gentry and which, at its height, invoked the sharpest popular statement of anti-seigneurialism that was to be found in England before the English Revolution. It is this feature of the Protectorate that leads Jim Holstun to characterise Somerset's government as 'an absolutist but also populist regime that would hold off the depredations of agrarian capitalism'. Holstun sees this as a form of 'monarcho-populism' which opposed the 'aristo-capitalism' of the gentry and nobility.[91] Within this 'monarcho-populist alliance', there existed 'a post-feudal but anti-capitalist mode of production that attempted to use the resources of the newly centralised Tudor monarchy to maintain and even extend the relative independence enjoyed by free English small producers during the fifteenth-century golden age'.[92] In this context, Holstun defines 'monarcho-populism' as 'a genuine discursive and practical phenomenon of Tudor England, for monarchists legitimated themselves through paternalist resistance to capitalist encroachments on small producers, while small producers legitimated themselves by invoking loyalty to a reigning monarch or Protector against some menacing middlemen or interloper'.[93] In the short term, it seemed that 'There was a tang of illegality about the [enclosure] commissions of 1549'; yet, the key point was that the enclosure commissioners were conducting their work through the agency of individual village governors, rather than by Act of parliament.[94] This illuminated a wider contradiction: the increasing inclusion of the commons within a polity which was supposed to be closed to popular politics. This contradiction was to be blown open by the rebellions of 1549.

III THE ORIGINS OF THE COMMOTION TIME: THE DISTURBANCES OF 1548 AND THE WESTERN RISING OF 1549

The rebellions of 1549 were preceded by significant trouble in the previous year. The disturbances of 1548 are significant partly as a set of events in their own right and partly for the way in which they anticipated the commotion time of 1549. As with the rebellions of 1549, trouble began in Cornwall. Here, on 5 April 1548, the hated government agent William Body was

---

M. L. Bush, 'Protector Somerset and requests', *Historical Journal*, 18, 3 (1974), 451–64. On Somerset's oppression of his tenants in the Mendips, see PRO, SP10/10/20. For Calvin's letter of support to Somerset, see PRO, SP10/5/8.
[91] Holstun, 'The spider, the fly and the commonwealth', 56–7.   [92] *Ibid.*, 56.
[93] *Ibid.*, 57.   [94] Bush, *Government policy*, 47.

murdered by a crowd at Helston following his attempts to impose one of the earliest elements of the Edwardian Reformation, the removal of 'superstitious' images. By 7 April the crowd at Helston had increased to 3,000. Leaders of the rebels demanded the re-establishment of the Henrician settlement. In response, the local gentry levied an army from Devon and east Cornwall. In the face of this force, the rebel host dissolved. On 17 May, a general pardon was issued by the Crown, which exempted the leaders from its provisions; twenty-eight of the leaders were sentenced to death, of whom ten were subsequently executed.[95]

The next outbreak of serious trouble took place in Hertfordshire, centring on the villages of Northaw and Cheshunt. Here, in early May, rumours of the impending announcement of an enclosure commission led to large-scale enclosure riots and demonstrations. The target of these crowd actions was Sir William Cavendish, a commissioner of the Court of Augmentations who had been responsible for the enclosure of a large part of Northaw common. There had been trouble in Northaw in 1544, leading to riots by large crowds. According to Cavendish's subsequent complaint to the Court of Star Chamber, in 1548 some 700 armed rioters broke down hedges and fences on his land, destroyed his rabbit warrens, besieged his house and threatened him with murder. On 23 May, the rioters assembled with arms and confronted the enclosure commissioners on Northaw common, whom they intimidated. Later depositions given by the commoners of Northaw and Cheshunt accepted that they had destroyed enclosures, but claimed that the purpose of the gathering on the common had been, according to the yeoman John Thompson, 'but ... to speke w[i]t[h] the commission[er]s and to be petition[er]s to them in ther right for the comon'. According to Thompson, it had been 'the interest of his comon and also neighbourhood' that had drawn him into the demonstration before the enclosure commissioners. Significantly, although Thompson denied all charges of riot, he did state that it had been the intention of the demonstrators to 'have made co[mp]laynt to the K[ing]s Counsell for their right [upon the common]'. Another local man, James Butler, admitted that the rioters had destroyed Cavendish's rabbit warrens, drawing attention to the threatening language of his neighbours, some of whom said that 'it shold cost a C mens lyvys or ev[er] they wold lese one fote of the comon'. Importantly, Butler emphasised the wide geographical scale of the protest, describing how protesters came from across Hertfordshire, Middlesex and Essex, including St Albans, Hatfield, Barnett, Enfield, Waltham Cross and South Mimms. The organisers of the protest included both the town constable of Cheshunt and the high constables of the hundred. The protesters justified their protests with reference to the minority

[95] For further detail, see I. Arthurson, 'Fear and loathing in west Cornwall: seven new letters on the 1548 rising', *Royal Institution of Cornwall*, 3, 4 (2000), 68–96.

of Edward VI and to the apparent support of Protector Somerset for the removal of enclosures: in Butler's hearing, one man remarked that 'they would defend their common & kepe it untyll the K[ing]s matie came to hys Full age. Sayeng further that yf my lord p[ro]tectors grace were there p[re]sent he shold gyve none of theyr comon away.'[96]

On 1 June 1548, the enclosure commission that had been anticipated by the Northaw and Cheshunt demonstrators was issued. This covered the counties of Buckinghamshire, Oxfordshire, Berkshire, Bedfordshire, Northamptonshire, Warwickshire and Leicestershire and was led by Somerset's ally John Hales. Evidence that the enclosure commissioners were greeted with popular acclaim came in mid-August, when the Earl of Warwick wrote to oppose the commissions because he objected to their activities 'in this troublesome time'.[97] Following the passage of the enclosure commissioners through the Thames Valley, Somerset was concerned that the commons intended to take matters into their own hands and 'in a marvellous trade of boldness', to introduce 'Reformation' themselves.[98] Trouble came not only in rural areas; urban centres were also affected by the growing assertiveness of the commons. On 2 October 1548, the Colchester scrivener Nicholas Moore was expelled from the town in response to his leading role in articulating popular opposition to the Colchester governors. It was noted that, '[be]yng [n]eyther studyed, lerned, nor ex[per]ienced in the co[mm]en lawes of the Realme', Moore had 'nev[er]theles of late tyme taken uppon hym to be aswell a [comm]en councellor in very many and divrs suts depending … in the Kyngs honorable Coort of his Chauncery, as a co[mm]en councellor and a co[mm]en Atturney before the bayliffs of the said Borough'. When rebellion came to Essex in 1549, Nicholas Moore was to be found at its head: he was one of two men who, in September 1549, were executed for their leading role in the Essex commotion time.[99]

The clearest precursor of the commotion time came in Yarmouth. In this divided town, there was already conflict over the dissolution of religious houses and the corruptions of the civic oligarchy.[100] Popular hostility to the Yarmouth governors boiled over in the winter of 1548.[101] A faction within the town, led by the cooper John Rotheram, claimed to represent the poor

---

[96] For Thompson's deposition, see PRO, STAC10/16, fols. 137r–143v; for Butler's deposition, see PRO, STAC10/16, fols. 168r–172r; for Cavendish's complaint, see PRO, STAC3/1/49. For a detailed account of the Northaw and Cheshunt disturbances, see Jones, '"Commotion time"', 33–83.

[97] E. Lamond (ed.), *A discourse on the commonweal of this realm of England* (Cambridge, 1893), liv.

[98] Bush, *Government policy*, 75.

[99] ERO (Colchester), D/35/R2, fols. 226r–229v; PRO, SP10/8/61.   [100] PRO, STAC3/5/78.

[101] The subsequent discussion is based upon PRO, STAC3/7/32.

of the town. They advanced a series of complaints. These included the imposition of new regulations concerning the sale of herrings, which they argued had resulted in price increases such that the 'pore comons' were left hungry; the enclosure of the town's commons by the bailiffs, 'being insasyable & gredy or covetous'; and the prevention of the commons from articulating their complaints. This resulted from the rejection of a 'supplication' which, as members of one of the town's two courts leet, Rotheram and his supporters had placed before the common council. The result of the bailiffs' denial of Rotheram's faction's right to complain had been that the latter petitioned Protector Somerset for the redress of their grievances.

John Rotheram explained how he and his fellow jurors had prepared a 'supplication ... for the redresse of theyre hayring mony and the inclosur of theyre co[mm]on'. They had been helped in the production of the 'supplication' by an unnamed 'lernyd man'. One of the town oligarchs, William Bishop, remembered the 'supplication' being read before the common council and the bailiffs, and recalled that it contained 'thretts'. It was alleged that, following the rejection of their petition, Rotheram's ally John Long had cried out 'All ye that be sworne to the kyng come to us. All ye that be sworne to the Baylyffs tarye theare stylle.' At some point thereafter, Rotherham's faction had prepared a second supplication, this time addressed to Protector Somerset. This supplication had been conveyed to Somerset by Thomas Trendell, who received payment for the service from the court leet on which Rotheram and his allies sat. In response, the bailiffs and the common council had imprisoned Rotheram and Long. Ominously, it was alleged that while in gaol, Rotheram had warned one of the bailiffs to 'be affraide of an insurrecon ... this is but the begynnyng of an insurrecon'. Rotheram himself recalled that he had told the bailiff 'yow have allwayes saide that the comons went aboute an Insurrection but a man may p[er]ceyve by yor talke that yow go aboute yt yor selfe'. Rotheram and Long were subsequently sent to Norwich castle where they were interrogated by the gentry. As they were taken from the gaol, it was claimed that Long had exclaimed 'that he came of the comonaltie & that he wuld hold w[i]t[h] the comonaltie while he lyved to be torne in peces with wilde horses'. At the same time, Rotheram 'did speke thes words following in the p[re]sens of too hundred p[er]sons of the seid towne ... this have I for holdyng with the poore comunaltie'. Rotheram himself recalled that as he was led from gaol 'he spake to all the people ther being above a C. psons, Farewell masters, for this have I for holding wth the pore com[mon]altye'. Although Rotheram added that 'he ment no hurte by the spekyng of those words', the implication was clear: Rotheram had defined a fundamental antagonism between the town's governors and the 'pore com[mon]altye'. The faultlines within Yarmouth in 1548 broke open in the following year. When Robert Kett sent forces to besiege Great Yarmouth in August 1549, they were led by John Rotheram who, earlier in the insurrection, had apparently been moving freely in and out of the town. Similarly, some of the leading witnesses against Rotheram in 1548 appeared as key figures in the defence of the town against the rebels in 1549.[102]

Aside from such continuities in personnel, the trouble of 1548 displayed a number of other similarities with the commotion time of the following year. Most obviously, the geography of protest in 1548 anticipated that of 1549. In both years, Cornwall was the first county to rise. The commons of Essex, Hertfordshire and Middlesex were all involved in the Northaw and Cheshunt disturbances; St Albans, one of the homes of the demonstrators on Northaw common, was to be the site of a rebel camp in 1549. Both the Cheshunt demonstrators and John Rotheram's faction in Yarmouth attempted to petition Protector Somerset, and at least one of the Cheshunt demonstrators saw Somerset as his ally; many of the rebels of 1549 were similarly drawn into negotiations with Somerset through the process of petitioning. These rebel petitions were sometimes composed by men with legal training such as the Colchester scrivener Nicholas Moore (who was, let us remember, executed in 1549), or the anonymous 'lernyd man' who had drawn up the 'supplication' in Yarmouth. Finally, both in 1548 and in 1549, the Cornish rebels demanded the restoration of the Henrician settlement. It is now time to turn to a narrative of the rising that began in Cornwall in 1549.

The commotion time of 1549 started in Cornwall around Easter.[103] Rebels converged on Bodmin, where they established a camp. The gentleman Humphrey Arundell fell into their hands, and (according to his later testimony), in an attempt to control the rebels' actions, assumed military leadership of the rising.[104] Also prominent in the leadership of the rising were the local clergy, who exercised an important influence upon rebel demands. Those Cornish gentry who remained loyal to the Crown retreated to St Michael's Mount, where they were besieged; upon the fall of the castle,

[102] For Rotheram's association with Kett, see A. W. Ecclestone (ed.), *Henry Manship's Great Yarmouth* (Great Yarmouth, 1971), 89–90. Thomas Clark, who had served on the leet jury with Rotheram in 1548, was also appointed by Robert Kett to raise forces with John Rotheram. William Bishop Junior and John Mylsent, who both gave evidence against Rotheram in 1548, held office respectively as petty captain and captain of the defending forces in Yarmouth in 1549: see Ecclestone, *Henry Manship's Great Yarmouth*, 91. For Rotheram's movement in and out of Yarmouth in 1549, see PRO, C1/1272/64, which also demonstrates that Rotheram survived the post-rebellion repression.

[103] The main sixteenth-century narrative sources for the Western rebellion are those of Hooker and Holinshed; the latter account condenses that of Hooker, who was a member of the editorial team that drew up the second edition of the *Chronicles*, and was an eyewitness to the siege of Exeter: see Hooker, 4, 55; A. Patterson, *Reading Holinshed's Chronicles* (Chicago, 1994), xiv. The best twentieth-century account of the rebellion remains F. Rose-Troup, *The Western rebellion of 1549* (London, 1913), upon whom both Beer, *Rebellion and riot*, and J. Cornwall, *Revolt of the peasantry, 1549* (London, 1977), depend heavily.

[104] PRO, SP10/9/48.

the gentry were looted and imprisoned. Thereafter the rebels, marching under the banner of the Five Wounds of Christ, moved through Cornwall gathering forces. The combination of social antagonism and religious grievance displayed in the early stages of the Cornish rising set the tone for the Western rebellion. The politics of the Western rebellion can be deduced from two sources: the reported actions of the rebels; and the statements of rebel grievances that were sent in early June by the rebel leadership to the Council.[105] Rebel religious demands were relatively limited, centring upon the restitution of the Henrician settlement rather than the wholesale return to Catholicism. As elsewhere during the commotion time, religious demands were mixed up with economic and social critique. Their articles of late June or early July, for instance, contained criticism of the new vernacular Prayer Book; the demand that liturgy be phrased in Cornish; criticism of the Mass; the restitution of the Henrician Act of Six Articles; criticism of the unwillingness of parish priests to explain the King's proceedings and their abuse of baptism and burial and refusal to hold services; criticism of the forcing through of religious change without Edward VI's consent; attacks on taxes on sheep and cloth; criticism of local royal officers and of the Council; and complaints concerning the dearth of food.[106] Hostility to the gentry ran through the stated demands of the Western rebellion.[107] One Devonshire gentleman described the rebels as 'a band of theves' who 'wolde have no State of anye Gentlemen'.[108] Certainly, rebel demands suggested resentment at the gentry's breach of their traditional social responsibilities. Hence, for instance, the insurrectionaries complained that the gentry no longer offered hospitality.[109] Although they did not assume the same prominence as in Norfolk, tenurial disputes were also important to the Western rising.[110]

In early June, the Cornish rebels invaded Devon. On 10 June 1549, an apparently independent rising broke out in Sampford Courtenay (Devon) as a result of the introduction of the newly printed Book of Common Prayer. The Sampford Courtenay rebels were also motivated by rumours of new taxes.[111] Shortly after the Sampford Courtenay rising, the Devon rebels joined with the Cornish forces. On 21 June, representatives of the Devon gentry approached the rebels at the village of Crediton (Devon) where they attempted to negotiate; but following the rebels' rejection of this appeal, the loyalist forces burnt

---

[105] For the date of the first rebel petition, see Greenwood, 'A study of the rebel petitions', 31.
[106] *Ibid.*, 30. [107] *Ibid.*, 185; Beer, *Rebellion and riot*, 62–70.
[108] Rose-Troup, *Western rebellion*, 487–8.
[109] J. E. Cox (ed.), *Miscellaneous writings and letters of Thomas Cranmer*, Parker Society, 18 (Cambridge, 1846), II, 185.
[110] See, for instance, PRO, E321/5/52.
[111] Hooker's account is the most detailed contemporary description of the Sampford Courtenay rising: Hooker, 57–8.

part of Crediton. Word of the burning of Crediton spread across the county; impelled by this news, coupled with hostility to the new Prayer Book, a further rising took place at Clyst St Mary (Devon).[112] As with the Cornish rebels, the Devon commotioners marched under banners depicting the Five Wounds of Christ. On 23 June, the rebels fortified a position in Clyst St Mary alongside the main road to Exeter. Here they were met by a gentry-led force, whose leaders once again attempted to negotiate; but following the break-down of these negotiations, a battle ensued.[113] The weak loyalist forces subsequently retreated from Devon, allowing a rebel force of 2,000 to besiege Exeter on 2 July. A circuit of rebel camps was established around Exeter. Although there were deep-rooted social and religious divisions within the city, the governing elite retained control. As Hooker put it, 'In the citie were two sortes of people, the one & the greater number were of the olde stampe and of the Romyshe religion: The other beinge of the lesser number were of a contrarie mynde & disposicyon for they wholye [gave] them selffes to the reformed religion.'[114] The dearth of foodstuffs induced by the siege led Exeter's poor to clamour for victuals. Sensitive to popular complaints con-cerning prices, the aldermen saw to the equal distribution of food.[115]

Meanwhile, the loyalist forces had been placed under the command of Lord Russell. Initially, as he complained to the Council on 18 July, his forces were too weak to confront the rebels. From their camps, the rebel leadership submitted a sequence of written demands to the Council, which were answered both by printed royal declarations and by denunciations from the pulpit of St Paul's Cathedral by Cranmer.[116] Taking the initiative, on 28 July the rebels advanced to Fenny Bridges, where a battle ensued, resulting in a limited victory for Russell. Hooker claimed that rebel losses amounted to 300 dead. Hearing the sound of parish bells ringing, a sign that further rebel forces were being rallied, and fearing being cut off, Russell retired.[117] Although outnumbered, the loyalist forces launched attacks upon the rebels; these assaults continued until the beginning of August. Martial law was imposed upon the region, allowing Sir Anthony Kingston to carry out a policy of repression: as Holinshed put it, 'Manie ... were executed by order of the marshall law & a great part of the countrie abandoned to the spoile of the soldiers.' Gallows were erected both in Exeter and in the countryside and rebel priests were hanged from their church towers with their 'popish trash' – bells, holy water bucket, beads and robes – about them.[118] On 3–4 August 1549, the

---

[112] Hooker, 60–3.   [113] Hooker, 63–4.   [114] Hooker, 71.
[115] For accounts of the siege see Holinshed, 943–53; Hooker, 68–80.
[116] Greenwood, 'A study of the rebel petitions of 1549', 38; Cox (ed.), *Miscellaneous writings*, 163–87. These declarations are reproduced in Holinshed, 919–24.
[117] Hooker, 83–4.   [118] Holinshed, 924–5, 958–9.

royal army advanced, clashing with rebel forces at Clyst St Mary. Hooker remarked that 'the fighte was verie fierce and cruell & blooddye'. Observing the rebels mustering new forces, and fearing that the prisoners he had taken might turn on his men, Russell ordered his rebel prisoners to be slaughtered.[119]

In early August, Russell was reinforced by cavalry under the command of Lord Grey, fresh from victory over rebels in Oxfordshire and Buckinghamshire (of which more below). Equally important, he was supplied by money from the merchants of Bristol, which enabled him to pay his local levies.[120] On 5 August, Russell's strengthened forces engaged the rebels at Clyst Heath, where, following terrible slaughter, the commotioners were routed. Hooker estimated that the rebels lost 2,000 dead.[121] The following day, Russell lifted the siege of Exeter. Shortly after this, Russell received further new forces, as Sir William Herbert arrived with levies from Wales. Again, repression followed upon royal victory: Hooker reports that the whole area under royal control was put to the spoil. Of Herbert's Welsh forces, Hooker wrote that 'in spoylinge theye were not so cruell as most insaciable'.[122] A further large-scale engagement followed on 16 August 1549 at Sampford Courtenay, where a rebel force was once again defeated. In his description of the battle, Russell made it clear that despite the advantage enjoyed by the royal forces thanks to their strength in artillery, and their Italian arquebusiers, the battle had been a near-run thing. He estimated rebel losses during the engagement at 600, and said that a further 700 had been killed in the ensuing rout; moreover, 'great execucion had followed had not the night come on so faster'.[123] Russell's forces now numbered between 8,000 and 10,000 men.[124] Fragments of the rebel force retreated to Kingsweston in Somerset, where they were joined by local rebels. Here they were run to ground by Russell's army and the remaining rebel force was annihilated. In the course of the whole Western rebellion, Hooker estimated that 4,000 rebels were killed in battle.[125] Of those executed under martial law, there are no figures.

IV THE COMMOTION TIME

While the bloody events of the Western rebellion were unfolding, insurrection spread across much of southern and eastern England.[126] On 11 April

---

[119] For his account of this battle see Hooker, 85–9.
[120] Inner Temple Library, Petyt MS 538/46, fol. 435r.   [121] Hooker, 89.
[122] Hooker, 91; see also Inner Temple Library, Petyt MS 538/46, fol. 451r.
[123] BL, Harl MS 523, fols. 50v–51v.
[124] For accounts of the battle, see Hooker, 94–5; PRO, SP68/4, fols. 90r–94r (no. 195).
[125] Hooker, 96.
[126] Most modern accounts of the 1549 rebellions provide little insight into the insurrections outside the West Country and Norfolk. Beer's account in *Rebellion and riot*, 140–63, has now been superseded by Amanda Jones' magisterial doctoral dissertation.

1549, Somerset issued his second declaration against enclosures, empowering commissioners to rectify recent enclosures of common land. According to the charges brought against Somerset in October, this proclamation 'went forth against the will of the whole Council'.[127] The formation of enclosure commissions, which relied for their work upon popular submissions, stimulated widespread rioting, petitioning and demonstration. The local gentry regarded such action as rebellious, and in many counties they responded with repression. The consequence was that, by summertime, in some parts of England there was an uneasy stand-off between the commons and the gentry, while elsewhere there were armed hostilities.

Although there was an isolated outbreak of enclosure rioting at Ruislip (Middlesex) between 14–23 April, the initial source of significant anti-enclosure protest in 1549 originated in Somerset and Wiltshire.[128] On 5 May 1549, a crowd of 200 weavers, tinkers and artisans broke down enclosures at Frome (Somerset). The following day, they were persuaded to depart by local magistrates, and advised to petition Lord Stourton about their complaints. When Lord Stourton and the Bishop of Bath interrogated some of the rioters, they answered 'that they had done nothing but what was lawful, for they had heard of a proclamation sent into the country whereby they and all others were authorised so to do'. Clearly, Protector Somerset's declaration against enclosures had stimulated assertive popular action. On 8 May, four or five rioters' representatives presented their petition to Lord Stourton and were promptly arrested. Early May saw further enclosure riots in the county; some of the rioters were said to have asked 'why shulde oone manne have all and an other nothinge'; in response, together with the 'best sort', the gentlemen formed a body of armed men. The gentry expressed confidence that they were 'strong enough for the repression of the worst sort'; together with the 'honest yeoman and farmers', they intended to put down any further gatherings.[129]

---

[127] Bush, *Government policy*, 76.

[128] For the Ruislip riots, see Jones, '"Commotion time"', 251–4. Edward VI stated that the commotion time originated in Wiltshire: J. G. Nichols (ed.), *Literary remains of Edward the sixth*, 2 vols. (London, 1857), II, 225–7. Holinshed locates the origin of the rebellions in Somerset: Holinshed, 917. According to Wriothesley's *Chronicle*, the risings began in May in Somerset and Lincolnshire: W. D. Hamilton (ed.), *A chronicle of England during the reigns of the Tudors* (Camden Society, new ser., XX, London, 1877), 13. Wriothesley and Holinshed were probably right to identify Somerset as the earliest example of significant anti-enclosure demonstration. In any event, the Wiltshire and Somerset protests occurred within a few days of one another. Despite what Wriothesley says, there is no evidence of any significant protest in Lincolnshire at this time.

[129] HMC, *Bath*, IV, 109–10. For earlier conflict over enclosures in Somerset, see PRO, STAC3/3/80; PRO, STAC10/16, fols. 247r–249r; PRO, STAC3/7/100.

Meanwhile, similar developments were unfolding in Wiltshire. Trouble centred on Salisbury and the nearby borough of Wilton. This town had once been a substantial settlement, dominated by its abbey. By 1543, Sir William Herbert was destroying the abbey to make way for his mansion house and had enclosed the surrounding land into parkland.[130] This type of empark-ment was exactly the sort of action that Somerset's enclosure commissions were meant to prevent. At some point in May 1549, obviously sensing trouble, Sir William Herbert took the initiative and confiscated the towns-men's weapons. In response, the commons of Salisbury rose against Herbert and destroyed the fences of his park. Taking brutal decisive action, Herbert came with 200 men 'who by his order attacked the commons and slaughtered them like wolves among sheep'. Herbert's precipitous actions stimulated popular action against the gentry elsewhere: 'after this the resentment of the commons fled into a blaze against the gentry who were despoiling them everywhere'.[131] By 25 May, it was reported that

Ther ys a grete number of the commonse uppe abowte Salyssebery in Wylleshere, and they have pluckyd downe Sir Wyllyam Harberde's parke that ys abowte hys newe howse, and dyverse other parkysse and commonse that be inclosyd in that cuntr[y]e, but harme they doo too … [nobody]. Thay saye thay wylle obaye the Kyngs maiste[r] and my lord Protector with alle the counselle, but thay saye thaye wyll nat have ther commonse and ther growendes to be inclosyd and soo taken from them.[132]

As in Somerset, then, the rioting commons of Wiltshire saw a close connec-tion between their actions and the policies being pursued under the Protector.

At the same time as the Wiltshire disturbances, serious trouble developed in Kent. Seditious letters had been circulating in the county in the spring. One leader of popular rebellion was executed at Ashford on 13 May, and another at Canterbury on the following day.[133] On 15 May, the Council noted the insurrections in Somerset and Wiltshire, and warned the magistrates in Hampshire to look out for trouble. Some of the commons of that county were to rise as well, drawing up a 'supplicacon' which they submitted to Lord Wriothesley.[134] On 19 May, a band of young men destroyed enclosures on Bristol's commons; on 23 May the leaders were arrested.[135] By 22 May 1549, enclosure rioting had grown sufficiently serious to warrant a royal

---

[130] VCH, Wiltshire, VI, 2–3, 8.
[131] Bryn Davies, 'Boulogne and Calais', 61–2. R. C. Hoare, *The modern history of Wiltshire*, 6 vols. (London, 1843), VI, 261, cites a 'MS Chronicle of Salisbury', which states that there was an 'uproar' upon Harnham Hill near Salisbury in 1549.
[132] HMC, *Rutland*, I, 36.
[133] Jordan, *Edmund VI*, 446; P. Clark, *English provincial society from the Reformation to the Revolution: religion, politics and society in Kent, 1500–1640* (Hassocks, 1977), 78.
[134] Jones, '"Commotion time"', 86; for the Hampshire disturbances, see PRO, DL3/56/G1d, e, k–g; PRO, STAC3/4/89.
[135] Jones, '"Commotion time"', 99–100.

declaration against such action.[136] Perhaps sensing that, as in Bristol, the young people of London might also represent a potential source of support for rebellion, on 23 May 1549 the Court of Aldermen ordered that house-holders must ensure that all servants and youths be kept indoors during night-time.[137] Although 30 June was to see enclosure riots at Witley (Surrey), where a village had been destroyed in order to make way for a royal park, June 1549 saw a lull in disorder.[138] Hence, Hugh Paulet wrote from Kent on 13 June that 'the lewde uprore of the people in sundrye plac[e]s … resteth nowe in good quiet'.[139] The following day the Council issued a proclamation pardoning the 'rude and ignorant people' who had taken part in the ris-ings.[140] Nonetheless, the London authorities remained jumpy.[141]

By early July, therefore, the only remaining large-scale trouble lay in the West Country. It was at this time, however, that Protector Somerset made two fundamental errors. Firstly, on 1 July, he called the leading gentry of each county to Windsor in order to discuss the raising of an army that could be sent into the West Country.[142] Secondly, on 8 July he issued a third declaration against enclosures which re-established enclosure commissions. The instructions to the new commissioners were notable for their depen-dence upon the commons: the commissioners were instructed to call before them 'sixe persones of every Parishe, that is to saie: twoo freholders, twoo fermers, twoo Copieholders or tenauntes at wil', and ask of them where enclosures or depopulations had occurred.[143] Somerset's declaration there-fore created a new space within which popular complaints could be articu-lated; as with his second enclosure commission, he thereby appeared to legitimate popular protest. The result was a renewed bout of enclosure rioting. This came at the same time as fresh disturbances in Essex, Kent and Hampshire, where, as the Council warned Sir William Paget on 4 July, 'the lyk styrres have byn resumed'.[144] Two days earlier, the Mayor of London ordered the company authorities to assemble the householders of their companies and to instruct them to 'loke to their hole famylyes and men s[er]vants that they suffer none of them to be abrode owte of ther howses' at night-time in 'this tyme of unquyetnes'.[145]

Over 8–10 July, the commons of East Anglia took advantage of the absence of many of the leading gentry of the region to launch a series of co-ordinated insurrections. These are more fully discussed in the next section. The contradictory character of subsequent government reports concerning

---

[136] PRO, SP10/7/18; *TRP*, I, no. 333.   [137] CLRO, Rep 12 (1), fol. 90v.
[138] Jordan, *Edmund VI*, 447; PRO, E178/2244.
[139] Longleat House, Thynne Papers, 2, fol. 70r.   [140] *TRP*, I, no. 334.
[141] CLRO, Journal 16, fol. 15v.   [142] PRO, SP10/8/1A.   [143] PRO, SP10/8/10.
[144] PRO, SP68/4, fols. 30r–36r (no. 180); PRO, SP68/180.   [145] CLRO, Journal 16, fol. 17v.

the East Anglian risings is testimony to the panic that the eastern commotions induced in ruling circles. On 10 July 1549, the Council wrote to Russell, advising him that the rebels in Suffolk, Essex, Kent, Hampshire and Surrey 'have not only confessed theyr faults wth verie lowlye submission, but also for rellygyon declared themselves'. They noted that, save for in Devon and Cornwall, the rebels were 'appeased and . . . quieted in all places saving only in Buckingham shyre ther a fewe Light persons nuely assembled whome we trust to have also appeased wthin twoo or three dayes'.[146] By 12 July, however, the Council was less relaxed about the disturbances in Buckinghamshire, as it wrote to Lord Russell that there had been 'A stirr here in Buck[inghamshire] and Oxfordshire by instigacon of sondrey preists'.[147]

Even by this date, the Council seems not to have registered the significance of the disturbances in East Anglia. In part, this was due to the extent of trouble in the critical area of the Thames Valley. Here, large groups of rebels were breaking down enclosures and plundering deer-parks in Oxfordshire, Buckinghamshire and Berkshire. In particular, Sir John Williams' park at Thame (Oxfordshire) was targeted (Williams was Treasurer of the Court of Augmentations); similarly, all the deer at Rycote Park (Oxfordshire) were killed, and the rebels went on to occupy the house '& dranke theyr fyll of wyne, ale and bere, slew many shepe & ete them'.[148] One later account of these disturbances described how the rebellious commons

seditiously growing together took up arms . . . made spoil and havoc . . . pulling up hedges, breaking down pales, filling up ditches, robbing houses and committing other infinite disorders, so that gentlemen were either forced to leave their houses or with help of their neighbours so to be guarded and strengthened as they might be able to keep their houses and defend themselves against the attempts of this fury.[149]

Lord Grey, who had been sent westwards with a body of 1,500 horse, paused to confront the rebels in the Thames Valley. Here, he assembled the local gentry and engaged the main rebel force at Chipping Norton 'where they [had] encampyd themselves'. Grey defeated the rebels, 'more then hauf of them rann ther wayes, and other that tarried were some slain, some taken, and some hanged'. Lord Grey executed one of their leaders, pardoned another, and before he departed for the West Country he left a series of instructions to

---

[146] Inner Temple Library, Petyt MS 538/46, fols. 435r–436r.   [147] *Ibid.*, fol. 437r.

[148] C. L. Kingsford (ed.), 'Two London chronicles from the collections of John Stow', *Camden Miscellany*, XII (Camden Society, 3rd ser., XVIII, London, 1910), 18.

[149] J. Stevenson (ed.), *The life of Jane Dormer, Duchess of Feria by Henry Clifford. Transcribed from an ancient manuscript in the possession of the Lord Dormer* (London, 1887), 44–6. This account makes much of the paternalism displayed by the Dormers; this rather misleading account has to be compared with evidence of the Dormers as targets of popular fury: see Jordan, *Edward VI*, 448.

the county gentry ordering them to maintain a watch for further seditious activity and to execute any who questioned their authority.[150]

At the same time as the disturbances in the Thames Valley, the government faced what appears to have been co-ordinated action in Kent, Sussex and Surrey.[151] In all three of these counties, the rebels were led by 'a captain they called Common-wealth and made havoc on the wild beasts in many of the parks in these parts'.[152] The rebels themselves were known as common-wealths, and were remembered by this name by later generations. As elsewhere, popular action was directed against enclosures as well as gentry parks.[153] The Kentish rebels established a camp outside Canterbury, inspiring the nervous city authorities to borrow artillery from London.[154] Rebel advance forces reached as far as Greenwich, and threatened to come to London to free their imprisoned leaders. It was perhaps these threats that stimulated the London authorities to order their householders to arm themselves and to establish a watch on each gate; martial law was declared in the capital on 18 July. Three days later, the Spanish Ambassador reported that 'London is very closely guarded; there is artillery at the gates and outlets'.[155]

The authorities responded to the threat from the south-east in three ways, combining repression with negotiation and compromise. Somerset commissioned leading members of the Kentish gentry and royal heralds to negotiate with the camp at Canterbury. The rebels behaved confidently, insulting the royal herald, demanding payment for each day they had been gathered in the camp and sending a list of complaints to the Council. These included the demand that wage rates should be increased.[156] There was a basic mismatch

---

[150] Kingsford (ed.), 'Two London chronicles', 18; Nichols (ed.), *Literary remains*, II, 228; for Grey's instructions, see PRO, SP10/8/9; Inner Temple Library, Petyt MS 538/46, fols. 438v–439r. The best discussion of these disturbances is Jones, '"Commotion time"', 194–233.

[151] These disturbances also overlapped into Hampshire: see PRO, DL3/56/G1k–g. For a good discussion of the rebellion in Kent, see Jones, '"Commotion time"', 167–76. See also B. L. Beer and R. J. Nash, 'Hugh Latimer and the lusty knave of Kent: the commonwealth movement of 1549', *Bulletin of the Institute of Historical Research*, 52 (1979), 175–8; J. D. Alsop, 'Latimer, the "Commonwealth of Kent" and the 1549 rebellions', *Historical Journal*, 28, 2 (1985), 379–83; Clark, *Provincial society*, 78–81.

[152] Bryn Davies, 'Boulogne and Calais', 61.

[153] For the destruction of enclosures, see PRO, E133/6/815; PRO, E134/30&31Eliz/Mich19; for the destruction of the fences of the park at Witley (Surrey), see PRO, E178/2244.

[154] T. Wright, 'On the municipal archives of the City of Canterbury', *Archaeologia*, 31 (1846), 211.

[155] *CSP, Span*, IX, 405, 406; Hamilton (ed.), *A chronicle*, 15–16.

[156] BL, M485/39, Salisbury MS 150, fol. 117r–v. For rebel wage demands, see Clark, *Provincial society*, 423, n. 33. The Canterbury rebels' demand for compensation was mirrored by that of the Norfolk commotioners, who demanded that those officers who had offended them should pay each 4d. to each rebel for every day spent in the Mousehold camp. See A. Fletcher and D. MacCulloch, *Tudor rebellions* (1968; 5th edn, 2004), 158.

in Somerset's responses to the Kentish rebels. On 22 July, rebels from Essex and Kent were executed, one at the Southwark end of London Bridge, the other at Aldgate.[157] Meanwhile, over August and September, Captain Commonwealth, identified as 'Latymer otherwise called comen welthe of kente', was receiving money for conveying messages to and fro.[158] A less confused strategy was followed in Sussex, where the Earl of Arundel sent a message to the rebel camp, 'commanding them to withdraw to their houses, and that as many of them as had just occasion to complain of wrong, should resort unto him to the Castle of Arundel, where with indifferency they should be heard'. Here the rebels were treated to a feast by the Earl, and their complaints against enclosures were given an airing. As a result, Arundel ordered the offending gentlemen to remove their enclosures, and subsequently restored order, ostentatiously punishing the 'mutinying varlets' who had led the rebellion.[159]

Somerset's confused response to the south-east rebels, rewarding Captain Commonwealth at the same time as he hanged other Kentish rebel leaders, formed part of a wider governmental crisis. Mid-July saw Somerset launch 'a major initiative to make official contacts with the various rebel groups from Canterbury to Norwich'.[160] Employing a combination of royal heralds and trusted local gentlemen, Somerset sent letters to rebel camps in Norwich, Thetford, Oxfordshire, Suffolk, St Albans, Hampshire and Essex. These letters highlight the confused nature of Somerset's response to the commotion time, combining standard authoritarian denunciations of plebeian rebellion with sometimes wild offers of compromise.[161] Meanwhile, Somerset placed his faith in the word of God, sending preachers into rebellious areas to condemn the sins of insurrection.[162] Partly, Somerset was constrained by the limited forces at his disposal; by early July, he faced not only significant challenges in Norfolk and the West Country, but he had also to retain troops for the looming confrontations with France and Scotland.[163] Where Somerset had forces on the ground, as in Oxfordshire and Buckinghamshire, he did not hesitate to use force; elsewhere, as in Kent, he was forced to negotiate. Even for some of his supporters, such compromises went too far. Thus, Sir Thomas Smith wrote to William Cecil on 19 July suggesting that the rebellions should be put down with armed force, and proposing that the gentry and leading yeomen should be gathered into cavalry forces, which should be employed in the suppression of what he called the 'camp men'; he

---

[157] Hamilton (ed.), *A chronicle*, 18–19.   [158] Alsop, 'Latimer', 380.

[159] L. Stone, 'Patriarchy and paternalism in Tudor England: the Earl of Arundel and the peasants' revolt of 1549', *Journal of British Studies*, 13 (1974), 19–23.

[160] D. MacCulloch, *Thomas Cranmer: a life* (New Haven, CT, 1996), 434.

[161] Shagan, 'Protector Somerset'.   [162] PRO, E315/258, fols. 78r, 99r, 101v.

[163] Bush, *Government policy*, 89–97.

concluded his letter with the observation that 'if a great no[m]ber of the boysterers were dispached the realme [would] have no losse'.[164]

Meanwhile, the Council had other threats to face. On 13 July, there were large-scale enclosure riots at Enfield (Middlesex). Around the same time, there were disturbances in Hertfordshire.[165] Ominously, two days later, the London authorities ordered a survey to be made of the weapons available in the capital.[166] On 25 July 1549, in the only recorded large-scale trouble in the north of England during the 'commotion time', some 3,000 rebels rose in the East Riding. They were motivated by a prophecy that foretold how 'there shoulde no kynge reigne in England: the noble men and Gentlemen to be destroyed: And the Realme to be governed by 4 governours to be elected and appointed by the Commons, holdyng a Parlament in commotion'. The Yorkshire rebels' plan was to join with their counterparts in Devon and Cornwall. As elsewhere, the Yorkshire rebels captured stray members of the local gentry; unlike elsewhere, they murdered some of their captives.[167]

Government declarations in late July and early August betrayed an increasing anxiety. On 27 July 1549, the Council wrote to Lord Russell concerning the 'evill inclynation of the people' in Somerset, advising that Russell should see that such as 'speak ... traiterous words' should be hanged as traitors, 'and that wilbe the only and the best staye of all those talks'.[168] On 2 August, the London authorities ordered that 'at this p[re]sent danger-ous tyme', the city's defences were to be repaired; householders were instructed to purchase one month's supply of food.[169] Like the Exeter authorities, those in London were highly sensitive to food prices and were careful to ensure the supply of victuals to the capital.[170] In this, they were supported by the Council, who empowered London's butchers to requisition sheep and oxen 'in the tyme of this rebellyon of the people'.[171] Perhaps recollecting the role played by young people in the disturbances of Evil Mayday of 1517, the city authorities were especially anxious to regulate the movement and behaviour of young people, apprentices and servants.[172] Confirmation that such worries were not wholly without foundation came with the arrest of John Wheatley on 5 August 1549, who was committed to Newgate 'for that he entysed mens s[er]vants & app[re]ntices ... to

[164] PRO, SP10/8/33.   [165] Jones, '"Commotion time"', 255–64.
[166] CLRO, Journal 16, fol. 20v.
[167] A. G. Dickens, 'Some popular reactions to the Edwardian Reformation in Yorkshire', *Yorkshire Archaeological Journal*, 34 (1939), 151–69; Jones, '"Commotion time"', 294–301.
[168] Inner Temple Library, Petyt MS 538/46, fol. 444v.   [169] CLRO, Journal 16, fols. 25v, 26r.
[170] CLRO, Rep 12 (1), fols. 99r, 104r, 110r, 111r, 121v–122v, 126r.
[171] CLRO, Rep 12 (1), fol. 114r.
[172] CLRO, Rep 12 (1), fols. 90v, 98r–v, 123r. On the Evil Mayday riots, see Holinshed, 588.

repayre & go w[i]t[h] hym to the rebells at Norwiche'.[173] Certainly, the London authorities were keen to ensure that the watch was made up of older, wealthier men, instructing that it should comprise 'discrete & sad p[er]sons & substancyall householders ... & not ... boyes & nakyd men'.[174] At the same time, censorship was reimposed on the press. Thereafter, the government's fortunes improved. On Saturday 10 August, the news of Russell's relief of Exeter reached London.[175] Two days later, an attempted rising in Hampshire was scotched.[176] On 21 August 1549, the Yorkshire rebels disbanded following the offer of pardon; nonetheless fifteen rebels were executed at Wakefield, and a further eight were put to death at Seamer.[177] A week later, Londoners heard of the defeat of the Norfolk rebels. Throughout this period, repression continued. On 16 August, two rebels were put to death under martial law: one was hanged at Bishopsgate in London, and the other was sent to Waltham to be executed. The same day, there were trials at the London Guildhall of men from Southwark, Wiltshire, Suffolk and Oxfordshire. They were executed on 22 August. The Wiltshire man (a vicar) was executed at Aylesbury; the others were put to death at Tyburn, Tower Hill and Tottenham, and 'their heades and quarters were set at divers gates of London'.[178]

V BONDMEN MADE FREE: THE RISINGS IN EAST ANGLIA

The intense violence that marked Kett's rebellion is difficult to explain without some understanding of the particular sharpness of social conflict in early and mid-sixteenth-century Norfolk.[179] In some ways, the conflicts in

---

[173] CLRO, Rep 12 (1), fol. 122r.   [174] CLRO, Rep 12 (1), fol. 102v.
[175] Hamilton (ed.), *A chronicle*, 20.   [176] PRO, SP10/8/41.
[177] PRO, SP11/6/84; PRO, SP15/14, fols. 46r–48v. The leaders of the rebellion were executed on 21 September 1549.
[178] Hamilton (ed.), *A chronicle*, 20–1.
[179] For the key sixteenth-century narrative accounts of Kett's rebellion, see Sotherton; Neville/ Woods; and Holinshed. Sotherton's manuscript account is probably the earliest of these accounts. Neville's 1575 Latin account, *De furoribus Norfolciensium* (London, 1575), was the first full printed narrative of Kett's rebellion, reprinted with slight changes in C. Ocland, *Anglorum praelia* (London, 1582). Holinshed's 1577 and 1586 accounts add a few extra details, such as an account of the siege of Buckenham Castle, but otherwise largely follow Neville. In 1615, Neville's narrative was translated into English by the Norfolk clergyman Richard Woods, and reprinted in 1622. For an earlier manuscript translation of Neville, see Bodleian Library, Tanner MS 421. The next significant work on Kett's rebellion was that by Blomefield, who made use of the Norwich records, including the Chamberlain's accounts; the quarter sessions and Mayor's Court; and the 'Liber Albus' (NRO, NCR/17B). Importantly, Blomefield also used a document called 'the Norwich Roll', a manuscript eyewitness account of Kett's rebellion. This document was also used in Anon., *The history of Kett's rebellion in Norwich in the reign of Edward the sixth* (Norwich, *c.* 1843), at 25–6, 36–7 and possibly at 66–7, 77, 80–6, 99–118. By the time that F. W. Russell published his remarkable work, *Kett's rebellion in Norfolk* (London, 1859), however, the 'Norwich Roll' had been lost. Much of the twentieth-century work on Kett's rebellion – in particular

Norfolk followed the pattern of many other southern and eastern counties; but what distinguished them was the peculiar rapaciousness of the gentry, coupled with the sometimes violent assertiveness of the commons. One student of the topic has talked of a 'manorial reaction' occurring in Norfolk, in which the lords attempted to squeeze increased rents and dues out of their tenants, at the same time as maximising profits on their own lands, in particular in the form of large-scale sheep farming and commercial beef farming. Greenwood's analysis of the court rolls of Gaywood, which was to be a location of rebellion in 1549, show in detail how in that year the manorial lord raised his animals on the village common in breach of custom; how he likewise abused his foldcourse rights on the common by overstocking it with sheep; and took profitable commodities without licence. Elsewhere within the county, lords aggressively asserted their powers in order to create a large-scale sheep economy. Thus, Sir John Heydon kept 2,600 sheep on two foldcourses in Salthouse and Kelling; at Weating, the lord maintained 4,700 on twelve foldcourses; at Elveden there were eleven foldcourses which maintained 3,200 sheep; in 1521, Sir Henry Fermour maintained 15,500 sheep in Fakenham.[180] Lords also sought to squeeze increased profits out of their lands and tenants by a series of other devices. Seigneurial entitlements to maintain rabbit warrens, for instance, encouraged lords to extend such warrens and increase the number of rabbits upon them; this was a particular source of frustration to tenants, as the rabbits would wander into their fields, destroying their crops.[181] They also attempted to prevent copyholders from taking timber, increased entry fines upon copyhold land and ratcheted up copyhold rents.[182]

J. Clayton, *Robert Kett and the Norfolk rising* (London, 1912); S. K. Land, *Kett's rebellion: the Norfolk rising of 1549* (London, 1977); and Cornwall, *Revolt of the peasantry* – merely repeat Russell's findings. But there was some important work done in the twentieth century. R. J. Hammond's 1933 London University MA dissertation, 'The social and economic circumstances of Ket's rebellion', and Bindoff's 1949 account, *Ket's rebellion*, include some useful material from the records of the Court of Star Chamber and elsewhere. The outstanding work produced in the twentieth century was Diarmaid MacCulloch's brilliant essay, 'Kett's rebellion in context', which transformed the subject. Nonetheless, Beer, *Rebellion and riot*, manages to ignore the implications of MacCulloch's work, largely reiterating Russell and Blomefield's accounts. In contrast, Greenwood, 'A study of the rebel petitions', deserves close attention.

[180] Greenwood, 'A study of the rebel petitions', 17, 263, 268, 277–89.

[181] For a protracted dispute over the warrening rights of Methwold, see PRO, DL4/20/7; PRO, DL4/22/31; PRO, DL4/22/43; PRO, DL4/22/48; PRO, DL4/22/59; PRO, DL4/23/40; PRO, DL4/22/21; PRO, DL4/23/48; PRO, DL4/23/75; PRO, DL4/27/41; PRO, DL4/27/69; PRO, DL4/30/40; PRO, DL4/31/38; PRO, DL4/31/47; PRO, DL4/35/16.

[182] For complaints concerning these issues, see R. Hoyle, 'Communication: agrarian agitation in mid-sixteenth-century Norfolk: a petition of 1553', *Historical Journal*, 44, 1 (2001), 223–38. For a dispute over a copyholder's right to take timber, see PRO, STAC3/6/30.

Most controversially, on some manors – in particular on those of the Duchy of Lancaster and the estates of the Dukes of Norfolk – lords sought to reimpose serfdom.[183] This could entail a certain degree of violence. Thus, in 1528 John Sylk complained to the Star Chamber that his lord, Thomas Boleyn, had identified him as a bondman, and that when Sylk refused to accept this status, Boleyn had assaulted Sylk's wife, seized his cattle and goods and nailed up the doors and windows of his house. Sylk described himself as 'a Freeman and of Free condicyon and no bondeman', emphasising that his ancestors had dwelt in Norfolk beyond memory, 'sometyme dwell-yng in one Towne and sometyme dwellyng in a nother'; Sylk's terminology is revealing – to be a bondman in sixteenth-century Norfolk was not only economically disadvantageous, it was also humiliating and degrading, and the term was used as an insult.[184] On some estates, such as that of the Heydons in north Norfolk, the late fifteenth and early sixteenth centuries saw lords exercising an increasing domination over the local economy. The Heydons held a series of coterminous manors, around which they built a little fiefdom, constructed upon a systematic, integrated monopoly of the local economy. On the commons of their manors, their sheep grazed on foldcourses, protected by shepherds in their direct employment. The wool was moved to the Heydons' castle at Baconsthorpe, which had been con-verted to include weavers' rooms. Here it was made up into cloth, and was then exported to London and the Low Countries through ports which also lay within the Heydons' estate.[185]

When this seigneurial offensive was combined with the assertiveness and independence of the commons of Norfolk, who were used to defending their rights through organised collective litigation, petition, demonstration and riot, the result was explosive.[186] This was all the more the case during the Henrician and Edwardian Reformations, which were perceived of by many labouring people as an element within a wider policy of expropriation. In their complaints to equity courts, the commons presented the seigneurial offensive as part of a project not only to undermine the economic stability of

---

[183] D. MacCulloch, 'Bondmen under the Tudors', in C. Cross, D. Loades and J. J. Scarisbruck (eds.), *Law and government under the Tudors* (Cambridge, 1988), 91–109.

[184] PRO, STAC2/24/270; PRO, STAC2/19/141. For another case illustrative of Norfolk gentry violence, see PRO, STAC2/34/67. For an attempt to reimpose serfdom on a Duchy of Lancaster manor, see C. M. Hoare, *The history of an East Anglian soke: studies in original documents* (Bedford, 1918), 272–313.

[185] S. Evans, 'Gentlemen clothiers in sixteenth century Norfolk', MA dissertation, Centre of East Anglian Studies, University of East Anglia (1999).

[186] For litigation and riot resulting from this seigneurial offensive, see PRO, STAC2/6/13–16; PRO, STAC2/29/117; PRO, STAC2/29/140; PRO, STAC4/3/42; PRO, STAC2/21/93; PRO, STAC2/15/11–13; PRO, STAC2/34/50; PRO, STAC2/24/292; PRO, STAC3/4/35; PRO, STAC3/6/30; PRO, STAC3/4/35.

the tenants' households, but also as an attempt to destroy the polity of the village. Thus, the inhabitants of Stradsett complained against their lords whom they said intended to 'empov[er]isshe and utterly to undo ... the inhabitants of the ... Towne' by squeezing them off their common 'to the distrucon and ruyne of the ... Towne and the utter decay of the husbondry and tyllage of the same of ther owne mere wrong and extorte powre without any rights or title'. In overcharging the common with great flocks of sheep, the lords not only breached ancient customary law; they also undermined the material basis of village life. As the tenants put it, 'the said Towne standeth onely by tillage and husbondry and not by pasturyng of shepe and catell'.[187]

Norfolk labouring people were notoriously litigious and were well used to presenting themselves before lawcourts in the most favourable light. We should not be surprised, therefore, to find that in their legal complaints tenants often stereotyped their lords as vindictive oppressors. Nonetheless, the consistent tendency of lower-class Norfolk complainants to present their lords as part of a network of mutually supportive powerful gentlemen is suggestive of the growing collective antagonisms between commons and gentry that would explode into violence in 1549. Thus, the tenants of Honingham claimed that whereas they were 'poore men, strangers unknowen and w[i]t[h]out Frendes in ... Norff[olk]', their opponents were 'men of greete substaunce & Riches and greetly alyed and Frended in ... Norff[olk]'. Likewise, the tenants of Middleton complained to Protector Somerset that their common land had been stolen from them by their lord, 'p[er]ceiving theym to be vary pore ignorant and symple sp[i]rited people and w[i]t[h]out frends or reputacon in the Cuntrey'. In driving them from their commons, the tenants said that their lord had used 'his grete myght and extorte power wrongfullye ... in most cruell sorte'. It was difficult, the tenants argued, for them to oppose their lord because 'by color of his worship and estymacon and also of the grete favor p[ar]tiality frendship and alliance towarde hym born and shewed in the said County and elsewhere', they were unable to gain an impartial hearing of their case. One of the tenants of Sir Henry Parker used very similar language in description of the authority which his lord wielded over him, presenting it as a product not only of his particular seigneurial position, but as the result of his place within a network that was founded upon the exercise of social power: in his analysis, 'Sr henrye parker [was] ... a man of great worshippe & of a greate powre and auctorytie w[i]t[h]in the said Countie & yor said poore supplyaunte but a verye poore Man.'[188]

---

[187] PRO, STAC2/18/197.   [188] PRO, STAC3/4/53; PRO, REQ2/18/114; PRO, STAC3/6/30.

Warning signs of the growing anger felt by many Norfolk working people towards their rulers were to be found in the conspiracies of 1537 in Oxburgh and Walsingham, in which conspirators planned to kill the gentry.[189] Equally explicit were the alleged words of John Walter of Griston, whose neighbours reported in 1540 that he had proposed that

If iii or iiii good Felowes wold ryde in the nyght w[i]t[h] ev[er]y man a belle and cry in ev[er]y towne that they passe through to Swaffh[a]m to Swaffh[a]m: by the mornyng ther wold be ten thowsand assemblyd At the lest: And then one bold felowe to stande forth and sey: syrs nowe we be her assemblyd you knowe howe all the gentylmen in man[ner] be gon forth and you knowe howe lytyll faver they bere to us Pore men let us therfore nowe go hence to ther howssys and ther shalt we have harnesse and sub-staunce and vytayles and so many as wyll nott turne to us let us kylle them ye evyn ther Chyldern in the Cradells: for that were a good turn if ther were as many gentylmen in Norff[olk] as ther be whyt[e] bulls.

The prominent gentlemen Richard Southwell and Sir Roger Townshend, who had won the praise of Thomas Cromwell for his role in suppressing the Walsingham conspirators, were picked out by John Walter as targets.[190] Of all counties of mid-Tudor England, therefore, social relations in Norfolk were probably the most precariously balanced, and plebeian anger at its most intense.

The first stirrings of trouble in East Anglia appear to have originated in early May at Landbeach (Cambridgeshire), where the tenants were accused of rioting against an unpopular lord.[191] In Essex, there was a disturbance in the county in the late spring.[192] Growing tensions in Norwich may well have been signalled in late June, when the assize judges sat in the city. Instead of the extravagant feast that the justices traditionally received at Norwich they missed their usual banquet, being served only beer. Conceivably, this could have been part of a civic fast; at the least, it points towards a sensitivity concerning conspicuous consumption at a time of high food prices.[193] In May, in a further sign of nervousness concerning the attitudes of the poor, the Norwich authorities ordered a compulsory poor rate.[194] Nonetheless, as late as 14 June, Richard Southwell could write a relaxed letter from Norwich,

---

[189] Moreton, 'Walsingham conspiracy'.

[190] PRO, SP1/160, fol. 157r. For earlier citations of John Walter's reported words, which base their assessments of early modern social relations upon his speech, see C. Hill, *The world turned upside down: radical ideas in the English Revolution* (London, 1972), 23 (where Walter is erroneously identified as one of Kett's rebels); J. A. Sharpe, *Early modern England: a social history, 1550–1760* (1987; 2nd edn, London, 1997), 233. For the dating of Walter's speech, see D. MacCulloch, *Suffolk and the Tudors: politics and religion in an English county, 1500–1600* (Oxford, 1986), 299.

[191] J. R. Ravensdale, 'Landbeach in 1549: Ket's rebellion in miniature', in L. M. Munby (ed.), *East Anglian Studies* (Cambridge, 1968), 109–10.

[192] Jordan, *Edward VI*, 446.   [193] PRO, E368/327.

[194] Hudson and Tingay (eds.), *Records*, II, 126.

which betrayed no hint of trouble.[195] Yet there were ominous signs in the region. On 28 May, Robert Bell of Gazeley committed unspecified treasons in Suffolk which later led to his execution.[196] On 20 June, a crowd destroyed enclosures in Wilby and Attleborough.[197] On 1 July, as we have seen, Somerset made his fatal error of ordering the East Anglian gentlemen to repair to Windsor. The result was to create a power vacuum in the region, which as MacCulloch has shown was filled between 8 and 10 July by a co-ordinated region-wide insurrection. As a further stimulant of trouble, 8 July saw the issue of Somerset's third enclosure commission.

The first signs of this co-ordinated insurrection were in Cambridgeshire, Essex and Norfolk. On Monday 8 July, a rising broke out in Cambridge.[198] Two days later, a crowd broke down enclosures made on the town's commons and then marched to Barnwell Priory where enclosures had been made following the dissolution of that house.[199] Rebel bills circulated in the streets of Cambridge, poking fun at the bailiffs, condemning the corruptions of the town authorities and rejoicing at the riots. One of these bills linked rural and urban grievances against enclosure: 'For Cambridges bayle[ff]s trulye / Gyve yll example to the cowntrye / Ther comones lykewyses for to engrose / And from poor men it to enclose.' The ballad concluded: 'For common to the commons again I restore / wherever it hath been yet common before.'[200] Early July saw renewed disturbances in Essex, which were eventually to be suppressed by Lord Rich. At some time, probably in the early stages of the Essex insurrection, Colchester fell under rebel control. Moreover, as in Cambridge, there were grievances in Colchester against the enclosure by the bailiffs of the town's common lands.[201]

But it was in Norfolk that the most serious of the East Anglian insurrections broke out. On Saturday 6 July, crowds gathered at Wymondham to watch the Wymondham Game, a traditional play which celebrated the life of St Thomas Becket. This was itself tinged with sedition, since the commemoration of the life of St Thomas Becket had been outlawed under Henry VIII.[202] The feast day of Wymondham Game took place on the Sunday; and the festivities ended on Monday 8 July. But, inspired by the news that rebels in Kent had risen, commotioners in Norfolk used the opportunity of the

---

[195] Longleat House, Thynne Papers, 2, fol. 75r.   [196] MacCulloch, 'Kett's rebellion', 38.
[197] Holinshed, 963.   [198] MacCulloch, *Cranmer*, 431.   [199] Jordan, *Edward VI*, 449.
[200] Cooper, *Annals*, II, 40–2.
[201] Jordan, *Edward VI*, 446; PRO, C1/1352/88–90; Walter, *Understanding popular violence*, 78.
[202] TRP, I, 270–6; L. M. Clopper, *Drama, play, and game: English festive culture in the medieval and early modern period* (Chicago, 2001), 132, 135, 301, 302 attests to the popularity of the life of Thomas Becket as a subject for drama in fifteenth-century East Anglia.

Wymondham Game to organise an insurrection of their own. Thomas Becket may have had a special importance for Tudor insurrectionaries: in the Yorkshire rising of 1489, the rebels claimed to stand for 'suche ... poyntes as Seynt Thomas of Cauntyrbery dyed for'. As Fletcher and MacCulloch observe, St Thomas Becket 'was commonly associated with resistance to Henry II's plans for taxes on the poor'; at a time of renewed taxation, this was an important association.[203] Again, as evidence of the links between urban and rural commons that characterised the 1549 rebellions, plans for the Wymondham rising also drew in the poor of Norwich.[204] The Norfolk insurrection began with Robert Kett as one of its targets, rather than its leader. On 9 July, a crowd of rioters broke enclosures in Morley. They then set upon the fences erected in Hethersett by the minor gentleman John Flowerdew. He offered the rioters money to break down the enclosures of his local enemy, Robert Kett of Wymondham. Upon arriving at Kett's estate, they explained their case to Kett, who (according to the later narrative accounts) then offered to lead them in an attempt 'to subdue the power of Great men'.[205]

Robert Kett of Wymondham made an unlikely rebel. He was a yeoman in late middle age with extensive landholdings and a tanning business whose wealth placed him on the edge of the lesser gentry. One of the richest members of his community, he had previously been prosecuted in the manor court for enclosing part of the town's commons, and both he and his brother William (who joined him as a leader of the insurrection) had been members of the town gild of St Thomas Becket.[206] Significantly, Robert Kett had led local opposition to Flowerdew's attempts to strip the assets of Wymondham Abbey following its dissolution.[207] Kett's dispute with Flowerdew was part of a complicated three-way conflict within the Wymondham area between rival yeoman farmers and the local poor over enclosures and common rights.[208] It is difficult to be certain about Kett's motives. Quite possibly, as one of the 'honest men' of his town, he was driven by the desire to assert leadership over an angry crowd of the local poor. Certainly, the 'honest men' often pushed their way into such a leadership

---

[203] Fletcher and MacCulloch, *Tudor rebellions*, 14–15.   [204] Holinshed, 964.
[205] Neville/Woods, sigs. B3r–v.
[206] For the Ketts' involvement in the the pre-Reformation parish gilds of Wymondham, see G. A. Carthew, 'Extracts from papers in the church chest of Wymondham', *Norfolk Archaeology*, 55 (1884), 121–52. Until its abolition, the Kett family also helped to fund the regular performance of the Wymondham Game: see T. Pettit, '"Here comes I, Jack Straw": English folk drama and social revolts', *Folklore*, 95, 1 (1984), 4.
[207] Blomefield, II, 521.
[208] For this context, see PRO, STAC3/3/46, in which in 1548, one farmer from the Wymondham area portrays another as 'an extorcyoner A wretch A suppresser of poore men A Traytoure A Theffe yee and an arant Theffe'.

role. Alternatively, he may have felt a genuine sympathy with the interests of his poor neighbours. We have no direct access to the words of Robert Kett. But for a fleeting moment, the speech of another leader of the East Anglian rebellions is revealed to us: as MacCulloch observes, 'in a scandalized memorandum of 1549 scribbled in the otherwise severely impersonal record of court business at Ipswich; the rebel Richard Wade, it records, "seid to Mr Bayliffes openly in the [borough] halle that there was small favour shewyd to ther pore neybores" '.[209] Perhaps Kett, too, was moved by such considerations.

Whatever his motives, Robert Kett was to prove an energetic leader. As Tuesday 9 July drew to a close, Kett led the rebels to Bowthorpe, on the outskirts of Norwich; as they marched, the rebels broke enclosures, captured gentlemen and plundered their houses, drawing recruits from nearby villages.[210] At Bowthorpe they were met by representatives of the Norwich poor, who had spent the day breaking recent enclosures on Town Close, part of the city's common land, and by a delegation from the Norwich authorities. That same day, perplexed as to how to deal with the rebel force, the Mayor of Norwich, Thomas Codd, had sent news of the arrival of the rebel host to London. The following day, Kett's host encountered Sir Edmund Wyndham, who denounced them as rebels.[211] Less strong-willed than Wyndham, Thomas Codd arrived at the temporary rebel camp at Eaton Wood to negotiate with the commotioners' leadership. Kett demanded free passage through Norwich to Mousehold Heath, a large expanse of common land on the eastern side of the city, upon which he planned to establish the rebel camp; this Codd refused. On 11 July, the rebels skirted north of Norwich, crossing the river Wensum at Hellesdon. Here Sir Roger Woodhouse met them with food and drink, accompanied by his servants. Presumably, it was Woodhouse's intention to negotiate with the rebels, feasting them in the same way as the Earl of Arundel had treated the Sussex rebels. But whereas Arundel's stratagem had drawn the Sussex rebels' sting, the Norfolk commotioners set upon Woodhouse, stripping him of his fine apparel, seizing his horse, throwing him into a ditch and taking him captive.[212] Arriving at the village of Sprowston, on the edge of Mousehold Heath, the rebels damaged a dovehouse that had recently been constructed by the Norwich alderman and lawyer John Corbet; this had been built into the former leper hospital of St Mary Magdalene, and as such represented a symbol of the expropriation

---

[209] MacCulloch, *Suffolk and the Tudors*, 306.
[210] For enclosure riots during the commotion time that were subsequently prosecuted before the quarter sessions, see NRO, NQS C/S3/r8, mm. 15, 16, 19, 21, 35, 39, 40, 54, 63, 64, 65, 76, 104, 108, 125, 146, 153, 154, 159.
[211] For Wyndham's attempts to levy troops in Norfolk, see NRO, NRS 12131/27/B4.
[212] Holinshed, 965.

associated with the Reformation. The rebels established their camp at Mousehold Heath that evening.

Kett occupied the former palace of the Earl of Surrey, Mount Surrey, which offered commanding views over Norwich, where he imprisoned his gentry captives.[213] A rebel council, made up of representatives of Norfolk and Suffolk hundreds, headed by Robert Kett, was established under an oak tree in Thorpe Wood. This tree soon took the name of the Oak of Reformation. From Mousehold Kett issued warrants in the King's name, requisitioning food and organising recruiting. The later narratives say that numbers at the camp soon grew to 20,000; one contemporary source gives their numbers as 8,000; another at six score thousand.[214] Thomas Codd and the leading alderman Thomas Aldrich joined the rebel council. The same ambiguity hangs over Codd and Aldrich's involvement in the early days of the Mousehold camp as over the motives that drove Humphrey Arundel in Cornwall – either they had been coerced into this role, or they took part in the camp out of a desire to moderate the actions of the commotioners.

In contrast to rebel success in Norfolk, the commotioners in Cambridge were easily defeated. By 13 July, Somerset was writing to the Mayor and Vice-Chancellor of Cambridge congratulating them on extinguishing the rising. On 16 July, Somerset pardoned some of the commotioners; entries in the town's accounts demonstrate that others had already been executed. Expenditure was incurred on 'carrying out . . . Gallows, & for a newe Rope'. Nonetheless, a few rebels escaped the harsh justice of the Cambridge authorities: the town clerk also recorded the cost of 'mendinge . . . the prison after the prisoners brake out'.[215] Meanwhile rebel camps were multiplying across East Anglia. By 14 July, there were rebel gatherings at Ipswich and Bury St Edmunds. A day later, a camp was established at Downham Market.[216] The rebels in Suffolk criticised the high price of food, unemployment in the textile industry and the oppression of copyholders, and called for the return of rents to the level at which they had stood in 'the old tyme'.[217] King's Lynn, whence those Norfolk gentlemen who had not fallen into rebel hands had fled, was besieged by rebel forces camped at Castle Rising; the rebels had come from Watton, Thetford, Dereham and Brandon, as well as from the

[213] On Mount Surrey, see W. T. Bensly, 'St Leonard's Priory, Norwich', *Norfolk Archaeology*, 12 (1895), 195.

[214] *CSP, Span*, IX, 405; BL, Lansdowne MS 2, fol. 60r (no. 25).

[215] Russell, *Kett's rebellion*, 197–8; Cooper, *Annals*, II, 36–7. But note that repression was combined with compromise: the Cambridge rebel complaints were almost immediately addressed. See Cambridgeshire Record Office, CCA Shelf C/57, fols. 33r, 34v.

[216] MacCulloch 'Kett's rebellion', 40. The Ipswich camp subsequently moved to Melton.

[217] Hatfield House, Cecil Papers, 201, fols. 58r–61v. The microfilmed version in the British Library of this badly faded and damaged document is illegible, and the document needs to be read in the original at Hatfield House. For the microfilm, see BL, M485/53.

area around King's Lynn. The siege was characterised by intermittent fighting between the gentry and the rebels.[218]

Somerset responded to the East Anglian rebellions with a combination of coercion and compromise. On 16 July, he issued a declaration offering a pardon to those rebels who were prepared to disband which also invoked martial law against those who held together. He was also heavily involved in correspondence with rebels across southern and eastern England. At around this time, the only surviving set of rebel grievances from Norfolk were drawn up.[219] These Mousehold articles contained criticisms of corrupt office-holders and of seigneurial oppressions; proposals for educational reform that implied support for Somerset's evangelical programme; a resonant demand that serfdom be abolished ('We pray thatt all bonde men may be made fre for god made all fre with his precious blode sheddyng'); and demands that the commons should select Somerset's enclosure commissioners. Somewhat overlooked by historians, but nonetheless significant, was the demand that the commons should be allowed to select commissioners to uncover corruption amongst the local magistracy. Even more striking, and indicative of the creative interplay between Somerset and the rebels, the Protector wrote to the Thetford rebels, acknowledging that they were not 'satisfyed' with some of the enclosure commissioners, and asking that the rebels should instead nominate 'suche names has been required by them eyther to be added to thoth[e]rs or put in steade of their places'.[220]

The discussion between Somerset and the rebels was conducted through royal heralds. One such herald arrived at Mousehold Heath on 21 July. He offered a pardon to the rebels, some of whom accepted it, including Codd and Aldrich, who departed for Norwich. Kett, however, refused to accept that he was in arms against the Crown and so denied that he needed any pardon; the herald therefore denounced Kett and his followers as traitors. The legal status of Kett's host having been clarified, that evening Thomas

---

[218] BL, Lansdowne MS 2, fol. 60r (no. 25); BL, Add MS 8937, fol. 3r; Blomefield, III, 221–2. Blomefield misdates these clashes as occurring in 1548. A rather eccentric account of the siege of King's Lynn, which includes some (unreferenced) useful information, plus some blind alleys, is to be found in H. J. Hillen, *History of the Borough of King's Lynn*, 2 vols. (Norwich, 1907), I, 261.

[219] The original is at BL, Harl MS 304, fols. 75–7. On the dating of the Mousehold articles, see Greenwood, 'A study of the rebel petitions', 213. By 19 July, the Mousehold articles had arrived at the court: see *CSP, Span*, IX, 405. The original framers of the document did not give it any title. In a scrawled hand, different from that which drew up the document (fol. 79v), is the note '[torn] artacles of the [torn] Requests and demands'. Alongside this, in another hand, probably of the seventeenth century, is the title 'keates demaundes beinge in Rebellyon'. It is by this name that the document has been known to twentieth-century historians, who in their editions have numbered the articles. See Fletcher and MacCulloch, *Tudor rebellions*, 156–9; Beer, *Rebellion and riot*, 105–7.

[220] Shagan, 'Protector Somerset', 58.

Codd convened a meeting of the common council, who agreed to close the city to the rebels. The same day, Somerset's Council was forced to admit the scale of the East Anglian risings, explaining to Russell that the commons of Essex, Suffolk, Norfolk and Kent 'were not been so good ordre and quiet ... though theyr articles be not suche as yor matters [i.e. the West Country's demands for a halt to the extension of Protestantism] ... They [the East Anglian and Kentish rebels] stand for p[res]ent reformation and yet must they tary a p[arl]yament tyme.'[221]

On the following day, the first organised violence of Kett's rebellion occurred. Facing a closed and barred city, the rebels began an artillery duel with the guns of Norwich. They then launched an attack across the eastern curve of the river Wensum; this assault proved highly successful as the rebels drove the armed citizens out of the Hospital meadows and seized the city's artillery. Norwich's resistance to the rebels rapidly evaporated, and as the commotioners reasserted control over the city they seized Codd, Aldrich and the evangelical preacher Robert Watson.[222] On 23 July, the Council wrote to Russell explaining that the Marquis of Northampton had been sent to bring back to obedience 'some of the Light sorte ... but no greate nomber at and abowte Norwhiche'. Somerset continued to believe, however, that the Norfolk rebellion would not last long, because the rebels had already opened negotiations: 'for p[re]sentlye ther: hither half a dosen chosen of theyr compayny who seke the kyngs ma[jest]ie mercie and redresse of things and be returned to receyve p[ar]don by dyrrecions of the M[ar]ques'.[223] It is possible that, like Norwich, the town authorities of Yarmouth had originally yielded to the rebels in their locality; certainly, at one stage of the commotion time, the town was open to the rebels. Moreover, the bailiffs of Yarmouth fell into rebel hands; according to the bailiffs, they subsequently escaped. However, by 26 July, the town was closed to the rebels and had declared its loyalty to the Crown.[224]

On 26 or 27 July, Northampton's force departed for Norwich.[225] It comprised about 1,500 men, including foreign mercenaries and those Norfolk and Suffolk gentlemen who had originally been called to Windsor. The small force was probably intended to persuade the rebels to submit. On 31 July, Northampton arrived at Norwich, where he was met by the leading alderman Augustine Steward who handed over the city's sword, thereby symbolically submitting Norwich to royal power. Steward did his best to

---

[221] Inner Temple Library, Petyt MS 538/46, fol. 440v.
[222] On Watson's evangelical beliefs, see BL, Cotton MS, Cleopatra E V, fol. 409r.
[223] Inner Temple Library, Petyt MS 538/46, fol. 438r.
[224] Ecclestone (ed.), *Henry Manship's Great Yarmouth*, 89; PRO, C1/1376/34.
[225] MacCulloch, 'Kett's rebellion', 43.

conceal the support of many of the poor of the city for Kett, explaining to Northampton that 'although a great rowt of the lewd citisens were partakers with the rebelles, yet a number of the substantiall & honest citizens would never consent to their wicked doings'.[226]

Northampton's force marched to the main marketplace, where they spent the night. During that time, there were clashes on Magdalen Hill to the north of the city between Northampton's Italian mercenaries and Kett's rebels, followed by more serious attacks on the royal lines. The following day, Northampton was distracted by the false offer of negotiations at Pockthorpe Gate with the rebel leader John Flotman. While Northampton was absent, rebels again attacked across the Wensum, moving through the meadows of the Great Hospital and clashing with royal forces near the parish church of St Martin-at-Palace-Plain. In the course of this encounter, Lord Sheffield, Northampton's second-in-command, was killed by a butcher called Fulke. Sheffield's death took the heart out of the royal forces, who fled the city in disorder. A number of leading Norfolk gentry fell into rebel hands, along with eleven artillery pieces.[227]

Again, the rebels established control over Norwich. They reduced the city's defences, breaking down the gates; some of their more disorderly elements plundered the mansions of the county gentry and the homes of those notables who had supported Northampton.[228] The richer citizens were systematically intimidated by the rebels: as the anonymous author of the Norwich Roll explained

the city at this time was in the most disordered state, and such was the fear of the rebels, that the wives and daughters of the citizens resorted twice a day to the churches to prayer ... When Kett's messengers were sent to any private house, the inhabitants were compelled to bake, brew, and do any work for the camp, otherwise they were taken prisoners, and carried to the 'Oak of Reformation'.

The author added that

I, the writer, who was then above 22 years of age, and an eye witness of these things, was present after prayer, during this dolorous state, when people met both of the miserable estate they were in, and like to be in, holding up their hands to heaven, praying with tears, that God would deal so mercifully with them, that they

[226] Holinshed, 972.
[227] Edward VI gives Northampton's losses in Norwich at 100 men, as does the Council's letter of 23 August: see Nichols (ed.), *Literary remains*, II, 231 and Inner Temple Library, Petyt MS 538/46, fol. 454r–v. For another account of the defeat of Northampton, see *CSP, Span*, IX, 423. For a fuller discussion of Northampton's failure, see A. Wood, 'Kett's rebellion', in C. Rawcliffe and R. Wilson (eds.), *Medieval Norwich* (London, 2004), 287–9.
[228] For one detailed example of rebel plunder, see C. E. Moreton, 'Mid-Tudor trespass: a break-in at Norwich, 1549', *English Historical Review*, 108 (1993), 387–98.

might live to talk of it, thinking it impossible at that time, they were so devoid of hope.[229]

In contrast to rebel successes in Norwich, the rebellions elsewhere in East Anglia were steadily extinguished. This left Kett's force isolated. Attempts to broaden the Norfolk insurrection also failed. Early August saw an abortive rebel attempt to seize Yarmouth. A second attempt to take the town on 20 August also failed. In their frustration, and in a further sign of their hostility to the process of expropriation represented by the Reformation, the rebels destroyed the new harbour that the town authorities had constructed, which had been funded from the sale of church goods. By 3 August the Suffolk gentry, carrying offers of pardon from Somerset, had persuaded the leaders of the camps within the county to disband.[230] Twelve days later, apparently in breach of these pardons, the authorities arrested the Suffolk rebel leaders.[231] By 11 August, Lord Willoughby lifted the siege of King's Lynn before moving north towards Walsingham with the 1,500 men he had recruited from Lincolnshire, Cambridgeshire and Norfolk; the remnants of the rebel camp at Castle Rising retreated to Mousehold Heath.[232] Most significantly, the Council raised a large army, numbering at least 6,000 foot and 1,500 cavalry. This was dispatched to confront Kett's host. The force comprised men levied from Wales, the Midlands and East Anglia, together with a substantial force of mounted gentry and several thousand foreign mercenaries.[233] Initially, this force was to be led by Somerset himself; by 11 August, however, the Earl of Warwick had been appointed as its commander.

Passing through Cambridge, where he received the submission of those Norwich citizens who had escaped rebel hands, Warwick was reinforced by Willoughby's troops. On 23 August, Warwick's army arrived on the western side of city. The next day, an attempt was made to negotiate with the rebel leadership; following its rejection Warwick forced an entry to the city at the Brazen Gate. During vicious fighting, he captured forty-nine rebels whom he promptly hanged at the market cross. Warwick then imposed a night-time curfew. In a further display of his willingness to use violence, that night Warwick executed 'the son of one Wasey, a cobler, who with two or three

---

[229] Anon., *History of Kett's rebellion*, 25–6. See also Blomefield, III, 231–2.

[230] MacCulloch 'Kett's rebellion', 43; Ecclestone (ed.), *Henry Manship's Great Yarmouth*, 90–1; NRO, Y/C18/1, fols. 55v–57v.

[231] *APC*, II, 311. See also 313, 315–16, 317 for further arrests.

[232] BL, Lansdowne MS 2, fol. 60r (no. 25); PRO, SP15/3/52. For Willoughby's expenses, see PRO, E351/217. For King's Lynn's contributions to his forces, see NRO, KL/C7/6, fols. 112r, 118v, 125r.

[233] Bush, *Government policy*, 87; *CSP, Span*, IX, 432; Nichols (ed.), *Literary remains*, II, 231; Inner Temple Library, Petyt MS 538/46, fol. 453r; BL, Cotton MS, Titus B II, fol. 5r.

more, were found in the marketplace'.[234] Vicious fighting followed for the
next three days and nights in the narrow lanes and alleyways of Norwich. In
these encounters, the rebels often had the advantage; with many of the poor
of Norwich within their ranks, they were better able to negotiate the complicated urban topography of the city; equally important, Warwick was
unable to deploy his cavalry and artillery.[235] Certain incidents stand out.
At one point, the rebels ambushed Warwick's artillery train, seizing many of
the guns from their Welsh guards. At another point, Warwick's forces drove
the commotioners out of Blackfriars Place, hanging those stragglers who fell
into their hands on the spot. On 25 August 1549, in a sign of his increasing
desperation, Warwick attempted to reimpose control over the city, fortifying
the gates, trying to place guards at every corner and passage and breaking
down White Friars Bridge in order to deny the rebels entry to the centre of
Norwich. That same day, in another sign of his possession of the initiative,
Kett launched an attack into the south of the city, burning down the staithe
and a number of large warehouses. But the decisive moment came on
Monday 26 August, when Warwick received reinforcements in the shape
of 1,000 fresh mercenaries. He used these troops to cut the rebels' supply
lines into the countryside.[236] As a result the rebel camp at Mousehold was
rendered untenable and Kett was forced to move his base. At this point, a
prophecy circulated amongst rebel ranks that if they fought a battle in the
low valley of Dussindale, just south of Mousehold Heath, they would be
victorious.[237]

On Tuesday 27 August, Kett's force moved to Dussindale. Here, the rebels
readied themselves for attack, digging entrenchments, positioning their guns
and chaining their gentry captives at the front of their ranks. Leaving his
levies behind, Warwick moved with his mercenaries, artillery and mounted
gentry to confront the rebels. Eyewitness accounts confirm that the subsequent battle mirrored the violence of earlier encounters. As a boy, Ambrose
Dudley was present in his father's army at the battle of Dussindale, and in his
later years well remembered the rebels' furious hail of arrows. He recalled
that 'the battaile was so manfullie fought on both sides, that it could be
hardlie judged by the best soldiers that were there, which side was like to
prevaile'. Royal bombardments were met with the rebel artillery; hails of
arrows decimated Warwick's forces; the mercenaries had the worst of it;
nonetheless, in a cavalry charge that followed another bombardment, the

---

[234] Anon., *History of Kett's rebellion*, 77.
[235] On support for the rebels amongst the urban poor, see *ibid.*, 36–7; Blomefield, III, 235.
[236] BL, Harl MS 523, fols. 53v–54v (also in BL, Cotton MS, Galba B12, fols. 115v–116v);
Nichols (ed.), *Literary remains*, II, 231.
[237] On the location of the valley, see A. Carter, 'The site of Dussindale', *Norfolk Archaeology*,
39 (1987), 54–62.

rebel ranks were broken. Some of the commotioners craved pardon. Others gathered in a last stand. Warwick again offered pardon; some accepted; others refused, and so met their death. Kett fled the catastrophe, only to be captured the following day.[238]

Estimates of the losses vary. Edward VI noted that rebel losses numbered 2,000.[239] In a circular letter of 31 August 1549, reproduced the following day, English ambassadors were told that 1,000 rebels had died at Dussindale.[240] A less-informed witness gives the rebel casualties as 10,000, adding the grisly detail that the country people buried the corpses in mass graves.[241] Some indication of the intensity of the fighting can be gleaned from Captain Thomas Drury, who led a troop of professional English soldiers. Pressing his case for the payment of his soldiers' wages, he stated that between the defeat of the Marquis of Northampton and the battle of Dussindale, he had lost 60 out of his 180 men.[242] On both sides, the casualties had been appalling. Kett's defeat left the rebellious commons traumatised and broken.

---

[238] M. Champion, 'Kett's rebellion 1549: a Dussindale eyewitness?', *Norfolk Archaeology*, 43 (2001), 643; Longleat House, Thynne Papers, 2, fol. 148r–v.

[239] Nichols (ed.), *Literary remains*, II, 231.

[240] PRO, SP68/4, fol. 91v; see also BL, Harl MS 523, fols. 53v–54v and BL, Cotton MS, Galba B12, fols. 115v–116v.

[241] Bryn Davies, 'Boulogne and Calais', 63.   [242] PRO, SP10/8/59.

2

'Precious bloody shedding': repression and resistance, 1549–1553

I CLEANSING THE BODY POLITIC

In September 1549, large parts of Norwich lay in ruins. Immediately following the defeat of the rebellion, the city authorities set about its reconstruction. At the same time as they saw to the cleansing of the streets, lanes and open spaces of bodies, dirt and detritus, so the authorities sought to wash the taint of rebellion from the urban body politic. The Chamberlain's accounts provide a detailed picture of their desire to repair, cleanse and purify the city.[1] There was much to be done: the common staithes and the warehouses were burnt. The gates were broken. The city's bridges, so vital to its role as a marketing centre, were damaged. Fighting had been particularly intense in a number of key sites: around the Great Hospital; in Tombland, Elm Hill, Pockthorpe and Bishopsgate; outside Blackfriars Hall and in the marketplace. A substantial number of dwellings had been destroyed, either in the fighting or burnt by the rebels. Amongst the corpses, ashes and ruined buildings, there was work to be had. A number of labourers appear repeatedly in the Chamberlain's accounts, 'makyng clene the m[ar]ket place', carrying loads of earth and 'mucke', rebuilding the walls, cleaning the guildhall and washing the streets. The enclosing fences around the Town Close fields which the city's poor had destroyed at the beginning of the insurrection were rebuilt. New locks, rivets, planks and hinges were set on the city's gates. The 'dorestalle & dore loope of the tresyr house' that had been 'sore hewyn and mankyld by that kette and his kytlyngs' were repaired. The clerk paid particular attention to the 'newe mendyng & makyng' of locks on the treasury, the assembly house and the chests within which the city's funds were stored: 'iiii locks & hespys' were fitted onto the 'iron chest' in the treasury; 'iii oy[ther] locks in the same howse, ii locks on the [Ex]chekyr in the [As]sembly chambyr, and iii gret locks & keys on the dore to the Tower ov[er] the treasyr howse all whiche locks keyes & hespys war broken by the ... Traytor Kette and hys rebels'.

[1] NRO, NCR/18A/7, fols. 304v–312r.

Before anything else, bodies needed to be carted away to burial pits: 3 shillings 9 pence was spent on the removal of the bodies of the forty-nine rebels 'that war hangyd at the [market] Crosse' by Warwick. The instruments of mass execution had also to be repaired: 3 pence was spent on mending the ladder from which the condemned had been tossed. At the same time as the physical damage to the city was repaired, so its governors looked to the re-establishment of its rights and liberties. The autonomy of Norwich, which had been revoked when the city's sword had been surrendered to the Marquis of Northampton, was re-established by the grant of a new charter. From the costs of aldermanic journeys from Norwich to London down to the price of vellum, wax and paper the Chamberlain's clerk duly recorded the costs incurred in gaining the new charter.

As the Chamberlain's clerk laboured over his accounts, enumerating (for instance) the cost of the 'nayles Ryvetts, stapylls, plat[e]s, brads, nayles made of dyv[er]s leng[t]his with square heds spekyngs and sondry ay[ther] iron work' used in the repair of the city's gates, so new boundaries were redrawn within the political order of the city. At the command of the authorities, the Earl of Warwick's family arms, the bear and the ragged staff, were erected alongside the royal arms on all of the city's gates. Members of the civic elite also put up Warwick's arms over the entrances to their houses.[2] The message was clear: politically, symbolically and militarily, the forces of order had returned. Yet there remained a certain nervousness. As Stallybrass and White have observed, 'Differentiation . . . is dependent on disgust.'[3] The Chamberlain's accounts situated the civic authorities on the side of cleanliness and order, and placed the rebels on the side of dirt, disgust and disorder.

But at the same time as labourers worked to clean the streets and repair the gates, so those same gateways became the site of mass execution and the location for the display of dismembered bodies. Since records do not exist for the period during which the city lay under martial law, and the records of the assizes and the Court of Oyer and Terminer which sat in the city following the re-establishment of the city's liberties have not survived, the extent of repression within Norwich is difficult to retrieve with any accuracy.[4] Nonetheless, the surviving sources suggest that the repression was severe.[5]

---

[2] For the erection of the bear and the ragged staff on aldermen's houses, see NRO, NCR/16A/6, fols. 32v, 33r.

[3] P. Stallybrass and A. White, *The politics and poetics of transgression* (London, 1986), 191.

[4] Moreover, the poor survival of the State Papers for the reign of Edward VI, compared with those of Henry VIII, means that it is not possible to describe the repression of the 1549 rebellions with the detail possible for those of 1536–7. The records of the Norfolk quarter sessions shed some light upon the pursuit of rebels. See NRO, NQS C/S3/8, fols. 132r, 133r.

[5] The evidence presented here demonstrates the inaccuracy of McClendon's claim that 'the [Norwich] magistrates quickly re-established civic rule without wreaking vengeance on residents who had co-operated with or supported Kett': M. C. McClendon, *The quiet*

Although Warwick stood by his promise of pardon, there remained a large number who had refused to yield to the royal forces in the final stages of the battle of Dussindale and so who could legitimately be executed.[6] On the day following the battle of Dussindale, the Earl of Warwick celebrated his victory in the parish church most favoured by the civic elite of Norwich: St Peter Mancroft.[7] That evening, he witnessed a masque performed in his honour.[8] Warwick remained in the city, conducting executions under martial law until around 7 September.[9] The leaders of the rebellion were the first to feel the hard hand of Warwick's justice. On 29 August, 'nine of the chiefest procurers of all the mischiefe', including Fulke the butcher (the killer of Lord Sheffield), Miles the gunner (who had commanded the rebel artillery) '& two of their prophets', were hanged on the Oak of Reformation. Meanwhile, 'divers' others were hanged within the city.[10] At Magdalen gates, on the northern perimeters of the city, thirty rebels were hanged, drawn and quartered in a single day; the author of the Norwich Roll estimated the total number of executions in Norwich at about 300.[11] A measure of the loss of life in rebellion and repression can be gleaned from the rentals levied upon stall-holders in the Norwich market. Six months after the battle of Dussindale, the rental recorded a number of stalls that remained empty either as a consequence of their holder's death, or, like the trader John Kyng, who 'was a rebell in Mushold kenell', because the holder had fled the city 'and was nevyr hard of syns'.[12]

It is a revealing reflection upon the character of social relations in mid-Tudor Norfolk that the county gentry, furious at the humiliation they had suffered, felt that the Earl of Warwick was insufficiently severe in his treatment of the rebels. Early on in the repression, the Norfolk gentlemen came to Warwick and demanded that a larger number of rebels suffer execution. Warwick answered, in black humour, that

---

Reformation: magistrates and the emergence of Protestantism in Tudor Norwich (Stanford, CA, 1999), 114. McClendon claims that 'no action' was taken in the cases of seditious speech heard in the aftermath of Kett's rebellion: *ibid.*, 146. She appears to have overlooked the punishments handed down in such cases by the Norwich magistrates: these are at NRO, NCR/16A/6, p. 82.

[6] Norfolk gentry whose houses and goods had been plundered by pardoned rebels were forced to sue for the return of their goods at central courts: see, for instance, PRO, C1/1206/15; PRO, C1/1277/39; PRO, STAC3/1/74.

[7] Holinshed, 984.   [8] Anon., *History of Kett's rebellion*, 104–6.

[9] S. Brigden (ed.), 'The letters of Richard Scudamore to Sir Philip Hoby, September 1549–March 1555', *Camden Miscellany*, XXX (Camden Society, 4th ser., XXXIX, London, 1990), 87.

[10] Holinshed, 983; Sotherton, 91.

[11] Blomefield, 255; Anon., *History of Kett's rebellion*, 100.

[12] NRO, NCR/18A/7, fols. 283r–285v.

He knew ... [the commons'] wickednesse to be such, as deserved to be grievously punished; and with the severest judgement that might be. But how farre would they goe? ... Would they bee Ploughmen themselves, and harrow their owne Lands?[13]

Certainly, a letter from Sir Thomas Woodhouse highlights the initial severity of the repression within Norfolk. Complaining that he had been left off the Commission of Oyer and Terminer that had been established for the purpose of punishing rebels, he observed that within Yarmouth alone there were between 140 and 160 prisoners, all of whom would be dealt with by the Commission. He added 'that my lorde of Warwicke dothe execution of meany men at Norwiche. And the gentlemen crave at his hande the gyft of the rychees of them, and do dayly bring in men by accusatyon.'[14] Ellis Griffith recorded that, following the battle of Dussindale, 'many honest men were hanged, many of them without deserving it for any harm they had done, and some who had not even raised a stick to go to the field'.[15]

As to Robert Kett, immediately following his capture on 29 August he was taken to Norwich Castle where he was interrogated. Soon afterwards, he and his brother William were conducted to London; by the evening of 6 September 1549 they were brought before the royal court 'and after long examynacyon they were both caryed on horseback ... with people suffycyent wondryng at them, to Nuegate this present day [7 September], and Keyte rode not lyke no stoute captain, for his sadell was but a shyp skynne'.[16] Another witness described how the Ketts arrived at court 'pynned by th[e] armes in penny halters according to ther degrees'.[17] By 22 October, the brothers were incarcerated in the Tower of London, along with Robert Bell of Gazeley, one of the leaders of the Suffolk insurrection, and Humphrey Arundel.[18] Royal retribution was swift. On 23 November, charges of high treason were drawn up. On 26 November, alongside the leaders of the Western rebellion, the brothers stood trial. Scudamore described how, 'confessing theyr fawltes [they] weare all condemned to be hanged, drawn and qwarteryd'. On 29 November, following their conviction for high treason, the Kett brothers began their journey back to Norfolk.[19] At some point, the form of the brothers' execution was changed, and it was decided to hang them in chains.[20] On 7 December, Robert and William Kett were executed.

---

[13] Neville/Woods, sigs. K3v–4r.   [14] PRO, SP10/8/55(1).
[15] Bryn Davies, 'Boulogne and Calais', 63.
[16] Brigden (ed.), 'The letters of Richard Scudamore', 88.
[17] Longleat House, Thynne Papers, 2, fol. 140r. This gives the date for the arrival of the Ketts as 8 September. On the same day, Thomas Audley received £50 from the Council 'for bringing Ket': *APC*, II, 323.
[18] PRO, SP10/9/48. For a similar list of prisoners from around the same time, see BL, Cotton MS, Titus B II, fol. 67r–v.
[19] Holinshed, 984; Hamilton (ed.), *A chronicle*, 30.
[20] For hanging of rebels in chains, see, for instance, PRO, SP1/116, fols. 22r–v, 108r–v.

William was hanged from the tower of Wymondham Abbey, and Robert was hanged in chains from Norwich Castle. Their bodies remained suspended in chains, as Neville/Woods put it, 'for a continuall memory of ... [their] great villanie'.[21]

Elsewhere, the defeat of rebellion was also followed by repression. In Oxfordshire, Buckinghamshire and Berkshire, Lord Grey pursued an identical policy as that followed by Warwick in Norfolk. Before moving on to join Russell's forces in the West Country, Grey left a letter for the magistrates of those counties ordering that rebels should be executed in market towns and 'the heddes of every of them in the said Townes severally to be sett upp in the highest place ... for the more terror of the said evell people'. He also ordered that constables should 'Lye in wayt for tale berers Rysers of rumours and newes and spekers of sedicious words'.[22] Grey's orders were followed: it was reported in late August that 'the Oxfordshire papists are at last reduced to order, many of them having been apprehended, and some gibbeted, and their heads fastened to the walls [of Oxford]'.[23] Likewise, Yorkshire saw executions following the rising in the East Riding.[24] When Sir William Herbert arrived in the West Country, he set up gallows 'in sundrie places ... and did command and cause manie to be executed and put to death'.[25] By 21 August the Council was ordering Lord Russell to execute the leaders of rebellion and other 'obstinate rebelles' in order to make examples 'of the[m] by ther punishment to the teror of all others'.[26] Following the defeat of the Western rebels, many 'were executed by order of the marshall law, & a great part of the countrie abandoned to the spoile of the souldiers'.[27]

In July 1549, the accounts of Exeter yield references to the purchase of timber with which to make new gallows.[28] In Colchester, the Earl of Oxford and Sir Thomas Darcy, who oversaw the trials 'by law marshall', had six men hanged on 31 August: 'wherof two was hanged by the pillory & one at ev[er]y of the foure gates'. For his services in quieting the 'uprours' within Colchester, the town authorities later provided Darcy with the gift of two oxen.[29] The Suffolk, Essex and Sussex rebel leaders were still being rounded up in the winter of 1549; their executions continued into the following year.[30]

By collating a variety of sources, some of them taken from the repression of the rebellions of 1549, others concerned with the suppression of the 1536–7

---

[21] Neville/Woods, sig. K4v.

[22] PRO, SP10/8/9. For some dark stories of the application of martial law in the West Country, see Holinshed, 925.

[23] Rose-Troup, *Western Rebellion*, 393.   [24] PRO, SP15/14, fols. 46r–48v.

[25] Holinshed, 958.   [26] PRO, SP10/8/47.   [27] Holinshed, 926.

[28] M. Stoyle, *Circled with stone: Exeter's city walls, 1485–1660* (Exeter, 2003), 190.

[29] BL, Stowe MS 829, fols. 24r, 32r.

[30] PRO, E315/258, fols. 82v, 83v, 85r; Kingsford (ed.), 'Two London chronicles', 21.

insurrections and subsequent prosecutions of seditious or treasonable speech, it is possible to sketch a picture of the form of public execution in mid-Tudor England. In particular, detailed receipts submitted to the Exchequer by Sir John Thynne, sheriff of Somerset and Dorset, for costs incurred 'concernyng dyvers execucons by hym don uppon dyvers rebells' allow some insight into the organisation of judicial retribution at that time.[31] His bill specified the expense of conveying rebel captains to the trials and subsequently of their executions. Fifty-four prisoners taken at Kingsweston were conveyed to trial, incurring the costs of 'cords to make fast the said pryson[er]s'. Two prisoners were taken from Bruton to Wells, 'where they sufferd as was appointed'. On that occasion, 2 shillings were paid 'to a poore man to do execucon'. Further disbursements, of 4 shillings and 4 pence on 'Irons to hang them with', suggest that these West Country rebels, like Robert and William Kett, were hanged in chains. At Frome the accounts provide a closer picture of the grim process of execution. Eight pence was spent on 'irons to hang one of'. 'Wood for fier to burne the intrailes' cost a further 8 pence. Very similar expenses were incurred during executions carried out at Wells, Shepton Mallett, Glastonbury, Bridgwater and Taunton. Specific items ranged from the macabre to the quotidian – money was spent on irons for cages of gibbeted men; feed for horses; food for Thynne and his men; watchmen; shoeing a horse; fuel for fire used in burning the entrails of men being hanged, drawn and quartered; and for a ladder from which the condemned men were thrown. In one town, for instance, Thynne and his men spent 4 shillings at supper, 6 shillings for chains, 12 pence for 'a carte to cary the dedd man to the jebbet', 2 shillings for horse feed and 3 shillings for dinner.

As to the executions themselves, these took repetitive forms. Executions were preceded by sermons and often drew great numbers.[32] The condemned were drawn upon a hurdle to the place of execution – generally, a market-place, or, in the case of walled towns, perhaps the city gates – where they were meant to ask 'forgyvenes' for their treason.[33] Sometimes, this might go wrong – the spirited Raphe Rogerson, one of the Walsingham plotters of 1537, when offered the opportunity to recant, responded by speaking 'according to his cankrede stomake'.[34] What Robert Kett had to say we do not know. In July 1538, however, eight men and two women who were executed in Worcestershire were more willing to accept their place. It was

---

[31] PRO, E368/327.
[32] BL, Cotton MS, Cleopatra E IV, fols. 122r–123r.   [33] PRO, SP1/124, fol. 124r.
[34] PRO, SP1/120, fol. 224r–v. For a condemned man who used his opportunity of public speech to cast doubt upon the validity of the verdict, see PRO, SP15/3/78. For a study of execution speeches, see J. A. Sharpe, '"Last dying speeches": religion, ideology and public execution in seventeenth-century England', *P&P*, 107 (1985), 144–67.

reported that after the bishop's chaplain 'sett forrthe the kings auctorytie of supremacye & p[er]suadyd the prisoners to take ther deathe charitablye and to take the same deathe for the satysfacion of the worlde onely and Crist for the satisffacon of their synes', the condemned 'by reason of ... [the] sermon ... gave thanks to the kyng and his officers for ther just execucion and deathe and so dyed repentantlye'.[35] The execution would then be carried out: women found guilty of treason were burnt; men were hanged, drawn and quartered unless, as in the case of Robert and William Kett, a special fate had been reserved for them.

Public executions were intended to imprint repression upon popular memory. Hence, in 1536, Henry VIII wrote to the Earls of Shrewsbury, Rutland and Huntingdon ordering them to carry out executions 'to theexeample and ter[ro]r of all others herafter in what state and t[e]rmes soever'.[36] With this in mind, the heads and quartered bodies of the executed were dispatched to market towns within the locality wherein the treason had been committed.[37] Quartered heads and bodies would be displayed upon spikes and were intended to provide emblems of the awful consequences of rebellion. They made grisly sights: one Londoner recalled how 'Upon London bridge I sawe iii or iiii mennes heedes stande upon poles ... Upon Ludgate the fore quarter of a man is set upon a pole ... upon the other side hangeth the hawnce of a man wth the legge ... It is a straunge sight to se the here of the heedes fase or moose away & the grystell of the nose consumed awaye.'[38] The priest William Forrest remembered how, passing through Thame (Oxfordshire) in 1537, a town which saw public executions both in that year and in 1549, he had seen 'Goddys servauntes used with muche crudelytee / Dysmembred (like beastes) in thopen highe waye / Their inwardys pluckte oute and harties wheare they laye / In suche (most grievous) tyrannycall sorte / That to shamefull weare here to reporte'.[39] William Baldwin had an equally disgusted reaction at the sight of 'quarters of men' on the gates of London: 'I call it abhominable because it is not only against nature but against Scripture; for God commanded ... Moses that, after the sun went down, all such as were hanged or otherwise put to death should be buried ... and I marvel where men have learned it or for what cause they do it, except it be to feed and please the devil.'[40] By the autumn of 1549, the market crosses and gates of

[35] PRO, SP1/134, fol. 298r. [36] PRO, SP1/108, fols. 139r–143r.

[37] For an example, see PRO, SP1/129, fol. 161r.

[38] B. White (ed.), *The vulgaria of John Stanbridge and the vulgaria of Robert Whittinton* (Early English Text Society, 187, London, 1932), 69.

[39] W. D. Macray (ed.), *The history of Grisild the Second: a narrative, in verse, of the divorce of Queen Katherine of Arragon. Written by William Forrest* (London, 1875), 81.

[40] W. A. Ringler and M. Flachmann (eds.), *Beware the cat, by William Baldwin: the first English novel* (San Marino, CA, 1988), 10.

towns across much of England were decked out with such grotesque reminders of the commotion time. It is all the more surprising, therefore, that despite these reminders of retribution, popular conspiracies continued to be hatched.

II RESISTANCE AND POPULAR CONSPIRACY, 1549–1553

The rebel defeat at Dussindale did not bring popular resistance to an end in Edwardian Norfolk. Rather, persistent grumbling was mixed with enclosure rioting and protest. This suggests an identifiable continuity within popular political culture, linking plebeian complaint in Henrician and early Edwardian Norfolk with that of the later part of the reign of Edward VI. In February 1550 the Star Chamber ordered that William Whitered of Whissonsett should lose an ear for seditious words. At East Dereham there was an accusation of rebellion. Occasional pardons were handed out to Norfolk husbandmen and yeomen for treasonable activities committed after the defeat of Kett's rebellion.[41] The quarter sessions and the Star Chamber heard a number of complaints brought by the gentry concerning enclosure rioting within the county. In some cases, a clear continuity with the events of the commotion time can be observed: at Hellesdon and Cringleford, on the northern and western edges of Norwich, enclosures were destroyed and grain seized in October 1549. The same villages had seen trouble earlier in the summer. Like later complaints of 1551, the indictments brought against the alleged enclosure rioters of October 1549 stated that they had carried out their actions 'in the manner of a new insurrection'. Elsewhere, sheep were stolen from gentry estates.[42] At Lakenham, another village on the edge of Norwich, an esquire complained of the theft of corn, fattened cows and large numbers of sheep by a group of men including one John Oldman; a man of the same name was prosecuted by the Norwich magistrates for seditious words in 1550 when, perhaps significantly, he wished that he was still in the rebel camp on Mousehold Heath, eating stolen mutton.[43]

The Norwich magistrates were kept busy in the aftermath of Kett's rebellion by the seditious speech of former rebels. The display of Warwick's arms alongside those of Edward VI provided an opportunity for the articulation of dangerous speech, as also did the sight of Kett's body, hanging in chains from Norwich Castle. John Redhead, a weaver, was accused by George Redman,

---

[41] *APC*, II, 385; *APC*, III, 131; *CPR, Edward VI*, III, 295, 328–9.
[42] NRO, NQS C/S3/8/146, 150, 154, 155; NRO, NQS C/S3/3A/16, 47, 113, 148, 161, 235; PRO, STAC10/16, fol. 24r–v; PRO, STAC3/6/44. For continuing trouble over enclosures in Suffolk, see PRO, STAC3/6/3.
[43] PRO, STAC3/4/83; NRO, NCR/12A/1(a), fols. 9v–10r, see Chapter Six.

servant to a gentleman called Barton, of having said in February 1550 that the bear and the ragged staff should be taken down from Mr Barton's house, where it was displayed as a sign of Barton's loyalty to the Earl. Redman also accused Redhead of having said

That afore it were Lammas day next comyng That Kette shuld be plukked downe from the toppe of the Castell sayeing also It was not mete to have any more kings Armes then one.

John Redhead answered by saying that he was only repeating a conversation he had overheard in the market a month earlier. On that occasion, he heard

ii or iii . . . men of the Countrithe standing to gethers having co[n]versation betwixte them selfs [and] . . . th[e] one of them speke to thother loking uppon Norwiche Castell towards Kette thus words viz. Oh Kette god have mercye uppon thy sowle and I trust in god that the kings Majestye and his Connsaill shalbe enformed ones betwixte this and Mydsomer even. That of their owne gentylnes thowe shalbe taken downe and by the grace of god and buryed and not hanged uppe for wynter stoore and sett a quyetnes in the Realme. And that the ragged staff shalbe taken downe also of their owne gentylnes from the gentylmens gates in this Cittie, and to have no more kings arms but one within this Cittie under Christ but king Edwarde the Syxe god save his grace; whiche persons he saithe he never knewe them nor cannot name them.[44]

Redhead's careful attempt to sidestep the accusation of seditious speech reveals some repetitive themes within popular politics in post-rebellion Norwich: the continuing hostility to the Earl of Warwick; the significance of the marketplace as a site for the articulation of political speech; the continuing trust in Edward VI; and the bitterness felt by many labouring people at the symbols of their recent defeat – in this case, the display of the bear and the ragged staff on the houses of the city's mercantile elite and the sight of Kett's body. Redhead's evidence also highlights the significance of one particular date: 'Mydsomer'. In a number of cases of seditious speech in Norwich, we find references to midsummer 1550 cited as the occasion at which scores would be settled, or at which there would be a new rebellion.

In 1551, the Norwich magistrates heard a case which indicates that despite the rebel defeat, some labouring people retained the confidence to offer open complaint. In the June of that year, the gentry of the county met in Norwich. This gathering presented one particularly assertive individual, Joysse of Trowse, with the opportunity to articulate popular complaints.[45] Thomas Nykson, a Suffolk gentleman's servant, gave evidence to the Norwich Mayor's Court on 27 June 1551 concerning his conversation in Bere Street with a man called Bretten. Nykson claimed that Bretten extolled Joysse of Trowse's qualifications as a tribune of the people, explaining how

[44] NRO, NCR/16A/6, pp. 32, 33.   [45] Trowse is a village on the southern edge of Norwich.

ther were many gentylmen come to town, to a good purpose, And sayed that if one Joyce had ben there he wold have tolde suche a tayle that it shulde have ben a shame to the[m] all.

Nykson replied, criticising Bretten's speech, to which Bretten answered that

thowe art a gentylmans s[er]vante, And that you woll not leave tyll ye famysshe all the poore peopull and further sayed ... that those that be nerest to the counsaill ... were very traytors.

The following week, Joysse himself articulated similar views to a Norfolk gentleman, who alleged that

Joyse of Trowce sayed thies words That there was a gentylman called Mr Woodhouse of Kymberley had v.l. combe of Maulte uppon his Chambr, And that Joyse shulde have boughte thereof a C combe; and that Mr Woodhouse wolde not gyf it under viii s a combe; And that he that had so muche by him was a traytor to the kyng.[46]

In the face of such popular complaint, the Norwich oligarchy were keen to display their paternalism. In May 1550, anticipating possible trouble in midsummer and painfully aware of the dearth of food, the governors of Norwich bought in stocks of corn.[47] At the same time, both the aldermen and the common councillors donated money and grain to a common fund for the relief of the poor.[48] In January 1551, they repeated the measure, noting that 'there is like to ensewe a scarcytie of grayne for that the market is unserved and many pore folks want it', and they ordered that the aldermen of each ward should instruct each 'substancyall Citizen' to prevent their servants from buying corn in the market, instead seeing that their households were provided for 'pri[vat]ely'. The magistracy thereby sought to avoid the repetitive accusation that the rich of the city bought all the corn, leaving the poor to starve. The Mayor and two of the leading aldermen were also deputed to persuade prominent members of the county gentry to bring food into the city. Finally, the council conferred with the fishmongers, ensuring that cheap fish was provided for the poor.[49] In the following winter, similar measures were put in place, as the magistracy attempted to control the price of grain during yet another dearth year. At the same time, a note of anxiety was sounded as the aldermen were ordered to return to their wards in order to 'make a perfect Serche of all suche poore peopull as ben residente within their lymyts, according to the statute; and to Certyfie Mr Mayor of all the names of them, and also the names of every p[er]son in wryting which shalbe chargeable to the Releif of the poore within their parissh'.[50] Not for the first time, in their desire to monitor the settlement of the poor at the same time as

---

[46] NRO, NCR/16A/6, pp. 124, 418–19. [47] NRO, NCR/16D/1, fol. 236r.
[48] NRO, NCR/16A/6, pp. 62–3. [49] NRO, NCR/16A/6, pp. 92, 93, 94.
[50] NRO, NCR/16A/6, pp. 162, 173.

they regulated the market, the oligarchs of Norwich placed themselves at the cutting edge of urban social policy.[51]

Many of the Norwich authorities' actions were carried out at their own initiative. Similarly, in post-rebellion Yarmouth, the bailiffs and the 'Twenty-four' who governed the town were careful to regulate food supplies and to monitor the movements of the town's poor. According to a series of injunctions, 'the people' were prevented from 'ther contynuall & daly hawntyng the taverns & alehouses'; the price of food was lowered; two members of the 'Twenty-four' were sent to negotiate with the 'honest men of the Contrith' concerning the supply of food; and the constables were ordered to make a survey of the poor in their wards.[52]

The London authorities were perhaps the most successful of all urban oligarchies in containing popular complaint. Throughout the reign of Edward VI, the London authorities regulated food prices and saw that the city was supplied with food during periods of dearth.[53] In periods of particular tension, the 'good and substancyall ... householders' of the city were ordered to muster with armour and weapons to keep a night watch. 'Weake and insufficient p[er]sones and nakyd men' were specifically exempted from such service on the council for unreliability. Significantly, in midsummer 1550, the Mayor ordered a double watch.[54] There were rumours of a rising on Mayday, another traditional day for disorder.[55] As during the commotion time, in November 1549, the city supervised plays.[56] The city authorities also encouraged the livery companies to monitor any seditious words amongst their members.[57] Especially sharp anxiety was demonstrated concerning disbanded soldiers. The mayor heard reports that the soldiers said 'that thei cannot worke ne will not worke', and that they intended to

appoynte them selfes in severall companyes in London and come owte of severall lanes & stretts in London & mete all together in some one place ... and thereupon sett uppon the Cytezens and their howses and take there suche botyes and spoylle as thei can leye hande upon.

It was also alleged that the soldiers said that if they did not receive some aid from the authorities, 'that then thei will turne all England upsidowne at their pleasures'.[58]

Following Warwick's seizure of power the Privy Council combined paternalism and coercion. The terminology employed in the Council's declarations

[51] P. Slack, *Poverty and policy in Tudor and Stuart England* (Harlow, 1988), 123.
[52] NRO, Y/C19/1, fols. 11r, 12r, 32r, 78r.   [53] See, for instance, CLRO, Journal 16, fol. 32r.
[54] CLRO, Journal 16, fols. 65r, 91v; CLRO, Rep 12 (1), fol. 271v; CLRO, Rep 12 (2), fols. 315r–326v.
[55] Beer, *Rebellion and riot*, 205.   [56] CLRO, Rep 11, fol. 162v.
[57] CLRO, Rep 12 (2), fol. 335r.   [58] CLRO, Journal 16, fols. 64v, 66v, 91v.

highlights the slipperiness of political language in the mid-sixteenth century: like Somerset's declarations, those issued under the new regime often mimicked the language of popular politics. Hence, a declaration of August 1551 against forestalling and regrating within Essex, Suffolk, Norfolk and Lincolnshire was intended to amend 'the gredie malice of covetouse men'.[59] Without fanfare, the Council met many of the rebel demands of 1549: the negative consequences of the Henrician Reformation were addressed, as the Court of Augmentations was instructed to establish schools and manumit bondmen.[60] In Thame and Rycote (Oxfordshire), which had seen trouble in 1549, new chaplains were appointed and a poor house established.[61] But the defining concern of the new regime lay with the preservation of order. Hence, the military successes of the summer of 1549 were consolidated by parliamentary legislation which tightened statutory provision against rioters and rebels; strengthened the Edwardian Reformation; made the spread of 'Phantasticall' prophecies an offence; and sought to regulate the urban labour market.[62]

The Council's concern with disorder had some basis in reality. Following the commotion time, the authorities received a steady stream of information concerning conspiracies, riot and seditious speech.[63] Significantly, many of the counties that had been involved in the commotion time were also heavily represented in post-rebellion evidence of popular complaint and attempted risings. In November and December 1549, unnamed 'prisoners and sedicous persons' were still arriving in London gaols from Suffolk and Sussex. Early in 1550, 'certene lewde personnes' were conducted from Essex and Sussex into the hands of the Crown.[64] Seditious speech and 'matter of rebellion' in Suffolk worried the Council in 1550.[65] In Essex, there were seditious bills in Colchester and Chelmsford.[66] Likewise, the Council was keen to track down the authors of similar bills in Bristol.[67]

Security in the London area remained a constant source of anxiety. In Middlesex in 1550, 'Captain Redde Cappe, one of the rebelles of the last yere' was being feasted by the commons; the Council wanted to know who had released the man. The Mayor of London was ordered to prevent criticism of his office by the 'idle, seditious persones whereof that place is full'.[68] Similarly, the Council was worried by the 'seditious behaviour' shown towards

[59] *CPR, Edward VI*, IV, 140. [60] *CPR, Edward VI*, III, 214–16.
[61] *CPR, Edward VI*, IV, 11.
[62] See Beer, *Rebellion and riot*, 194 for a fuller discussion of this legislation, and Wood, *Riot, rebellion and popular politics*, 32–42 for the development of legal definitions of riot, rebellion, sedition and treason in the early modern period.
[63] See also PRO, SP10/15/34. In the months after the commotion time, the Council granted occasional pardons for attempted rebellion. See *CPR, Edward VI*, III, 403, 418, 419; IV, 343.
[64] PRO, E315/258, fols. 82v, 83v, 85r. [65] *APC*, III, 18, 31.
[66] *APC*, II, 407; III, 138, 161, 390, 410. [67] *APC*, II, 421. [68] *APC*, III, 6, 390.

the Mayor and aldermen of Chichester.[69] Along the Thames Valley, another centre of trouble in 1549, there were continuing reports of popular conspiracies. In Oxfordshire, there were riots in the demesne lands of Banbury Castle; two individuals from Thame were examined by the Council 'tooching insurreccion'.[70] The Council was notably delicate in its dealings in a local dispute over common rights in Oxfordshire and Buckinghamshire.[71] In Berkshire, there was the spread of 'lewde prophecies' and a conspiracy intended to achieve 'the destruction of the gentlemen'.[72] May 1552 saw the grant of a Commission of Oyer and Terminer to the magistracy of Hampshire, empowering them to inquire into 'a conspiracie lately attempted by dyvers lewde persones there', which had resulted in a 'commotion'.[73] In another echo of 1549, reports from Nottinghamshire in May 1550 spoke of how 'certein conestables, by twoo and twoo, rode from parish to parish to rayse the commons in the Kinges name'.[74]

Most worrying of all were those reports that linked the commons of one formerly rebellious county with another. Thus, the Council heard how debates concerning religious practice drew crowds of sixty people from Kent and Essex.[75] A report of 23 May 1550 described how there was 'a conspiracie ... wrought amonge the commons as well of [Kent] ... as of Sussex, to assemble at Hethfelde upon Whitson Mondaye next'.[76] Two years later, a Buckinghamshire tanner attempted to organise rebellion in Berkshire, calling upon the commons to rise in order to lower the price of rents and food to the level at which they had stood in the time of Richard III.[77] An attempted rising in August 1551 in Uppingham (Rutland) was intended to draw together the rebellious commons of Rutland, Leicestershire, Northamptonshire, Lincolnshire and Norfolk. The magistracy of Rutland and Leicestershire, together with other 'Jentilmen' stamped on the conspiracy, arresting and executing the leading conspirators. The plan had been to rally 400 men 'upon a Playne nere Uppyngham, called the Broad, and so to have vysyted certen Jentilmen, and so to have proseded to ther further Purpose'. The Council was assured by Lord Clinton that 'the Contry ys very redy to serve with us, except thes certen lyght Knaves, Horsecorsers, and Craftsmen', and that 'good watche' was to be kept 'in every Towne and that every Jentilman have Horses in there Houses for themselves and there Servants nightly, that uppon the soden thei may without tract of Tyme repayre where thei shalbe commanded'.[78] These preparations showed that the gentry had learnt the harsh lessons of 1549: as in Wiltshire in that year, where an

---

[69] *APC*, IV, 225.   [70] *APC*, III, 34, 181.   [71] *APC*, IV, 116; III, 247, 252.
[72] *APC*, III, 35; Beer, *Rebellion and riot*, 205.   [73] *APC*, IV, 45.   [74] *APC*, III, 31.
[75] *APC*, III, 198–200.   [76] *APC*, III, 35.   [77] *CPR, Edward VI*, IV, 343.
[78] BL, M485/39, Salisbury MS 151, fols. 26r–27r. For the execution of one of the accused plotters, and doubts over the validity of the testimony against him, see PRO, SP15/3/78.

immediate recourse to force had prevented rebel success, the magistracy of post-rebellion Edwardian England displayed a consistent willingness to use the sword wherever they deemed necessary.[79]

III THE INTERMINGLING OF ELITE AND POPULAR POLITICS: OCTOBER 1549 AND JULY 1553

Due to historians' arbitrary separation of elite and popular politics, studies of the two major coups d'état of the mid-Tudor period – that led by the Earl of Warwick in October 1549 against the Duke of Somerset, and the seizure of power by Queen Mary in July 1553 – have tended to neglect the significant role played by the commons in these events.[80] While Somerset's half-hearted attempt to drum up popular support in October 1549 ultimately led nowhere, as MacCulloch has argued, popular participation on the side of Queen Mary proved decisive. Criticism of Somerset's populist reformism, and of his lack of harshness towards the 'camp men', had been growing within ruling circles since July 1549. In particular, in September 1549, members of the Kentish gentry articulated their resentment of Somerset's failure to deal with the rebels in their county.[81]

In early October, as tensions mounted between Warwick and Somerset, Warwick drew his affinity about him; sensing danger, the London authorities commanded aldermen to patrol the streets with weapons. On 5 October, Somerset issued a proclamation for a general array to gather at Hampton Court, where the King was lodged with the Protector. On 6 October, in a sign of Somerset's popular support 'over 4,000 peasants' assembled at the court. Following Somerset's production of Edward VI, who gave a speech in support of the Protector, he had the 'peasants divided into squadrons, and assigned them quarters as if he expected to fight'. But by the late afternoon, the 'peasants' had been sent home, and in the early evening the King and Somerset headed off to Windsor Castle, 'where a great number of peasants [were] daily assembling'. Back in London, almost the whole nobility had assembled and charged Somerset with having 'called in the peasants to oppress the nobility and make himself master and tyrant of all'.[82] The

---

[79] For examples, see Clark, *Provincial society*, 80.

[80] B. L. Beer, *Northumberland: the political career of John Dudley, Earl of Warwick and Duke of Northumberland* (Kent, OH, 1973), 88–91, 155–6, wholly ignores popular politics; D. Loades, *John Dudley: Duke of Northumberland, 1504–1553* (Oxford, 1996), 257–64, 131–40, notes popular involvement, but fails to analyse it. In contrast, MacCulloch, *Suffolk and the Tudors*, 309–10, provides an incisive account of the role of the commons in the 1553 coup; and Shagan, 'Protector Somerset', makes some perceptive remarks about the October 1549 coup.

[81] PRO, SP10/8/56; Longleat House, Thynne Papers, 2, fol. 145r.

[82] *CSP Span*, IX, 456–8. For the mustering of support for Somerset in Kent, see PRO, SP10/10/18.

following day, Lord Russell and Sir William Herbert, key members of Warwick's affinity, wrote to the Duke of Somerset condemning him for encouraging popular rebellion: 'Your graces proclamacons and billets put a brode for the raysing of the Com[m]ons we myslike very moche,' they said.[83] Further proof of Somerset's willingness to draw the commons into state affairs took the form of bills, which were scattered in London's streets, calling on the people to rise and defend the Crown against 'certen Lords and gentil-men' who intended to depose the Protector.[84] Immediately the Council, backed by the London authorities, issued declarations against the bills.[85]

As Somerset appealed for support from amongst the commons, so Warwick and the Council looked to the gentry and nobility. Both sides issued warrants to raise troops.[86] Warwick's affinity made much of Somerset's actions, por-traying him as a threat to the social order: the Council accused Somerset of having attempted 'an alteracon of the maner and order of governement of the kings maties affayres', stating that he was 'the very orygynall' of the commo-tion time, describing how he had sown 'sedicion betwene the nobillytie and the comons whereof have ensued suche tumults and hurlye Burlyes' and accusing him of having supported 'the chiefest Captaynes and ringleaders of the said comotyons', rewarding them 'wth rewardes and gyftes and some of them wth Annual lyvinges'.[87] This was a clear reference to Somerset's appea-sement of the Kentish rebels. In the aftermath of the commotion time, such remarks touched raw nerves within the gentry and nobility. The support demonstrated by the Mayor and aldermen of London for the Council was central to Somerset's defeat. The London authorities put into effect the same precautions against popular disorder as they had deployed during the spring and summer, ordering aldermen to maintain watches at night-time, doubling daytime watches, raising armed forces from amongst the livery companies, locking the gates and issuing declarations of support for the Council during 'the tyme of this dissencon & unquyetnes'.[88] Seeing that the leading members of his own class had deserted him and that his supporters primarily comprised 'peasants', Somerset gave up the game and on 11 October was arrested and conveyed to the Tower.[89]

---

[83] Inner Temple Library, Petyt MS 538/46, fol. 92r.   [84] PRO, SP10/9/12.
[85] PRO, SP10/9/40; CLRO, Journal 16, fol. 37r–v.
[86] PRO, SP10/9/1–4, 23. For Russell and Herbert's proceedings against troops raised for Somerset, see PRO, SP10/9/31.
[87] BL, Add MS 48018, fols. 404r–405v, 407v–408r.
[88] CLRO, Rep 12 (1), fols. 149r, 149v–150v; 153r–v; CLRO, Journal 16, fols. 33r, 34r–35v, 36r, 36v–37r. S. Brigden, *London and the Reformation* (Oxford, 1989), 497–501, offers an excellent account of events in London.
[89] For the Council's version of events, see PRO, SP68/4, fols. 128r–130v (no. 201), 132r–140r (no. 202).

Two key themes stand out from these events. Firstly, Somerset's capacity to draw upon the support of the 'peasants' demonstrates his popularity with the commons; as Ethan Shagan has suggested, this drew from his deliberate and ostentatious populism.[90] Secondly, Somerset had consciously drawn the commons into state affairs; rather like the Duke of York in 1452, the Protector was pursuing a strategy characteristic of a late medieval populist nobleman. In this respect, as in others, the events of 1549 have more in common with the Wars of the Roses than they do with early modern political crises. Four years later, Mary I was to pursue a similar strategy, albeit with greater success.

On 6 July 1553, Edward VI died. John Dudley, now Duke of Northumberland, backed by his powerful affinity, supported the Protestant Lady Jane Grey for the throne. But despite such support, Queen Jane's accession commanded little popular backing: on her entry into London on 10 July, the citizens stood silent with 'sorrowful and averted countenances'.[91] By then, Queen Mary was ensconced in her residence at Kenninghall. The loyalty of East Anglia's common people was to be critical in deciding the outcome of the contest between Mary and Northumberland. MacCulloch has suggested that 'the memory of Northumberland's commanding role in the destruction of the Mousehold camp four years earlier' must have been a powerful influence upon popular allegiances.[92] Certainly, the Spanish Ambassador observed that on Mary's arrival in Kenninghall 'the people were very glad to see her'. His report went on to emphasise the speed with which key members of the local gentry and the commoners of East Anglia resorted to Mary's banner:

As soon as the news of the King's death arrived, [Mary] had herself proclaimed Queen, to the great delight of the people and of many gentlemen who went to offer her their services. The great concourse of people were moved by their love for her to come and promised to support her to the end and maintain her right to the Crown, bringing money and cattle as their means enabled them.[93]

MacCulloch has shown how key sources described how the 'common people' of Norfolk and Suffolk backed Mary against the local gentry's candidate, Queen Jane. Notably, as in his coup against Somerset, Northumberland attempted to blacken Mary's name by her popularity, describing her supporters as 'the concurrance of a fewe lewd base people' and describing his backers as 'all other the nobilies and gentilmen remaining in their dueties to or soveraiigne lady queene Jane'. In particular, Northumberland noted that 'bicause the co[n]dicions of the baser sorte of people is understoud to be

[90] Shagan, 'Protector Somerset'.   [91] Brigden, *London*, 520.
[92] MacCulloch, *Suffolk and the Tudors*, 310.   [93] *CSP, Span*, XI, 106–7.

unruly if thei be not governed and kepte in order', he had sent forces to control the region.[94] Certainly, the detailed borough records of Yarmouth demonstrate that it was the wealthy mercantile elite, supported by the local gentry, who backed Queen Jane. In contrast, the commons of the town supported Mary. Shortly before Mary's putsch, one Norfolk yeoman debated with Sir Thomas Woodhouse as to the meaning of treachery: Woodhouse was told by the yeoman that he was a traitor to the Crown: 'What a traytor ... said the said Sir Thoms well well I dought nott but w[i]t[h]in the monyth to se xxtie such traitor knaves as thou arte hanged.' Woodhouse, who had led the defence of Yarmouth against Kett's rebels, obviously sensed the increased tension between commons and gentry.[95] On 9 July, the borough assembly sent representatives to talk to Mary at Kenninghall, 'to knowe hyr graces pleasure co[n]cernyng hyr l[ett]re to us sent this p[re]sent nyght sygned w[i]t[h] hyr hande'. The following day, the assembly met in order to 'make A playne & determyt Agreament: whether the Lady Mary his [sic] grace shalbe p[ro]claymed quene of yngland'. So sensitive were these discussions that the clerk of the council scored out the minutes of the meeting. Again, the assembly prevaricated, sending three representatives to 'Ryde imedyately to Norwyche to knowe the advce & councell of the worshypfull there & of there councell: & that the p[ro]clamacon shalbe delayed & defferred untyll there Retorne'; meanwhile, four other assemblymen were given 'Full powre and Auctorytie' to see to the town's defences and artillery. Finally, by 14 July the assembly appears to have decided to support Mary.[96] Meanwhile, the sailors aboard the naval force sent by Northumberland to stand off Yarmouth had mutinied in support of Mary. The decisive role played by the commons in the Marian coup was made clear as Northumberland's recruits drained away. Finally, Northumberland surrendered and was watched by rejoicing crowds as he arrived at the Tower of London.[97] The Spanish Ambassador gave a vivid account of the popular rejoicing in London at Queen Mary's accession: there were 'expressions of popular rejoicing ... a clamour and din and press of people in the streets ... it was all the more marvellous for coming so unexpectedly ... the people were mad for joy, feasting and singing, and the streets crowded all night long'.[98]

In East Anglia, popular expectations of the new regime were high. Shortly after her accession, camps were established in the Marshland area of Norfolk

---

[94] BL, Harl MS 523, fol. 43r–v.   [95] NRO, Y/C4/252, m. 29r.

[96] NRO, Y/C19/1, fols. 82r–84r. For a fuller discussion of events in Yarmouth and other East Anglian towns, see R. Tittler and S. L. Battley, 'The local community and the Crown in 1553: the accession of Mary Tudor revisited', *Bulletin of the Institute of Historical Research*, 57 (1984), 131–9.

[97] CLRO, Rep 13, fol. 68r.   [98] *CSP, Span*, XI, 108.

and in the Isle of Ely, and it was reported that 'all the people in M[ar]shland are holly & ernestly by the Quenes highnes true subjects so that this day & tomorow ij c or iij c wold come from thens to s[er]ve her where her highnes doth abyde'. Popular support for Mary within Marshland was strong: 'the comenyst people in m[e]rshlond ar fully reconsyled to spend ther lyves w[i]t[h] her highness & at her comand'.[99] Meanwhile, an 'insurreccon' was underway in the Isle of Ely. The numbers involved were clearly large: the Council heard that 'ther was of the same confederacye the nombre of Fyve thousand p[er]sons or mor'. Moreover, it was reported that the commons were moved by the spirit of the commotion time: 'they seye p[ro]fyselye that they wylle not trust to the informacon or reporte of any Jentyleman butt have them in the same dyspyte & reproche as the late Rebells hadd in Norff[olk]'.[100] In Norfolk, meanwhile, a new petitioning movement briefly flourished. The evangelicals of Norfolk, noting the support that they had given to the Catholic Queen in opposition to the Protestant Duke, petitioned for the toleration of their religion.[101] The commons of Norfolk likewise petitioned for the relief of their grievances, observing that they were 'sore obpressed borne & grudged att by dyv[er]s & sundry gentylmen' who were 'inflamed & embraced w[i]t[h] suche covetousnes unlawfull desyres of such thyngs as be not ther owen'.[102]

Early hopes of a new reformist leadership proved unfounded. Nonetheless, as late as December 1553, some Norfolk commoners retained a belief in the Marian regime. One Norwich man found himself 'at a poore mans house nere Magdalen gates' in that month, where he met 'One Bonor a taylor', who said that

This yere woll be as towblous a yere as ever was and that he wold Jeopard his lyef uppon it and one of the company asked … whye, and Bonnor sayd … if there be not a way founden to compleyn to the quens grace & the Duke of Norff[olk] … The gentylm[en] shalbe taken sleapers in their bedds & kylled all in a nighte.[103]

In reality, Mary's regime proved just as hostile to popular politics as had that headed by Northumberland. Hence, Queen Mary's instructions to magistrates dwelt upon the 'libert[i]e and insolencye' of the 'commun sort of people', and warned them of the risk of rebellion.[104] The Council continued to badger magistrates to seek out seditious speech; one Londoner's diary

---

[99] Oxburgh Hall, Muniments, Letter of Leonard Smythe of Shouldham to Sir Henry Bedingfield. For trouble in Marshland later in Mary's reign, see PRO, STAC4/3/6.
[100] Oxburgh Hall, Muniments, Edward Beawpre to the Council.
[101] J. Foxe, *Acts and monuments*, 8 vols. (London, 1837–41), VIII, 127.
[102] PRO, E163/16/14. For a full discussion of this document, see Hoyle, 'Communication'.
[103] NRO, NCR/12A/1(a), fol. 80v. For a later apology for offering a petition on behalf 'of the poor people' to Queen Mary, see PRO, SP11/14/26.
[104] BL, Cotton MS, Titus B II, fol. 99r–v.

noted a stream of unfortunate individuals who were pilloried for their dangerous words.[105]

Both in October 1549, and again in July 1553, the lower orders had entered confidently into the political world of their social superiors. In October 1549, this provided the Earl of Warwick with the opportunity to condemn the Duke of Somerset as a dangerous stirrer of revolt. In contrast, in July 1553, popular support for her coup guaranteed Mary the throne. Despite their very different outcomes, however, both cases highlight the significance of popular politics in the mid-Tudor crisis and the capacity of elite political culture to generate populist appeals to the people. This stands at odds, of course, to the repeated statements of conventional authoritarianism both by Mary and by Somerset in which the people were enjoined to live in quietness and obedience to their social superiors. And here lay the conceptual gap between political theory and political practice in mid-sixteenth-century England. We turn now to the politics of speech and silence in Tudor England, and to the characteristics of popular political language.

[105] J. G. Nichols (ed.), *The diary of Henry Machyn, citizen and merchant-taylor of London, from AD 1550 to AD 1563* (Camden Society, 1st ser., XLII, London, 1848), 24, 34, 35, 36, 37, 42, 49, 60, 63, 64, 69, 71, 75, 96, 102, 150, 154, 164, 178. See also, for example, CLRO, Rep 13 (1), fol. 73r.

Part II

Political language

3

Speech, silence and the recovery of rebel voices

In the voices we hear, isn't there an echo of now silent ones? Nothing that has ever happened should be regarded as lost to history. (H. Eiland and M. W. Jennings (eds.), *Walter Benjamin: selected writings*, 4 vols. (Cambridge, MA, 2003), IV, 390.)

It is high time for a social history of language, a social history of speech, a social history of communication. (P. Burke, 'Introduction', in P. Burke and R. Porter (eds.), *The social history of language* (Cambridge, 1987), 1.)

I SPEAKING FOR THE COMMONS IN TUDOR ENGLAND

The voice of Robert Kett seems both angrily eloquent and irretrievably silent within the documentary traces left by the Norfolk insurrection. In the main narratives of the rebellion, Kett speaks almost constantly; yet rarely for, or on behalf of, himself. Instead, his speech provides a conduit for other voices in two important respects: at the same time as he articulated the rebel politics of 1549, he was ventriloquised by the hostile authors of the narratives. Throughout their accounts of the rising, Holinshed, Sotherton, Neville and Woods placed long, impassioned speeches into Robert's mouth. Confronted, for example, by the Wymondham rebels at the beginning of the insurrection, Neville and Woods have Kett say

That hee was ready ... to subdue the power of Great men, and that he hoped to bring to passe, that ... those of their pride should repent ere long ... And promise[d] moreover, to revenge the hurts don unto the Weale publike, and common Pasture by the importunate Lords therof.[1]

The Kett of Holinshed's *Chronicles* spoke in a similar, albeit more abbreviated, fashion: he

willed them to be of good comfort, and to follow him in defense of their common libertie, being readie in the common-welths cause to hazard both life and goods.[2]

---

[1] Neville/Woods, sigs. B3r–v.　[2] Holinshed, 964.

Sotherton's manuscript account placed the following words into Kett's mouth:

Robert ... pretending to doe good thereby to the commonwealth sayd hee would assist [the rebels] with body and goods.[3]

Here as elsewhere, the three narratives offered consistent accounts of the thrust of Kett's speech, but differed as to its precise content. Whereas Robert Kett's speeches in the printed accounts of Holinshed, Neville and Woods tended to be lengthy, articulate and highly rhetorical, those presented in Sotherton's manuscript were laconic and to the point. Holinshed, Neville and Woods' accounts of Kett's speeches were to be repetitively plagiarised and embellished by later writers. Of course, the precise accuracy of any of these accounts of Kett's words remains dubious; rather than any claim to factual reportage, their value lies in how they represent rebel politics in 1549.[4]

In this section we therefore look at the ways in which the rebel voice was represented in literary and archival sources. Towards the end of the section, we go on to consider the repressive mechanisms that produced many of the archival sources upon which we depend for information concerning popular political language. By the end of this section, it will be clear that plebeian political speech represented an especially sensitive field of social relations. In the next section, we develop this insight further, looking at how speech and silence constituted power relations. In the succeeding section, we study how far plebeian speech represented a form of agency. The closing section looks at the ways in which the spread of political rumour helped to constitute plebeian politics within distinct speech communities. In order to illuminate the reasons for the peculiar sensitivity of early modern people towards speech, at various points in the chapter we draw upon the insights of social anthropology and sociolinguistics. Throughout, the chapter seeks to explore the politics and representation of speech and silence in sixteenth-century England. Necessarily, this leads us to reflect upon the political interests that underwrote the production of the archival and literary sources upon which standard histories of the 1549 rebellions have depended.

Rather than deploying the standard Tudor accounts of Kett's rebellion as though they formed unproblematic, 'objective' accounts of the insurrection, we ought to employ them as a way into the complex interplay between memory, fact and literary narrative in the representation of rebel politics. Most obviously, Robert Kett's speeches fulfil a *function* within Holinshed

---

[3] Sotherton, 80.

[4] Although it is worth noting that twentieth-century historians have tended, rather naively, to deploy this evidence as though it represented an accurate report of Kett's speech: see, for instance, Beer, *Rebellion and riot*, 83.

and Neville/Woods' accounts, developing their predetermined plot, enabling interaction between opposing characters and articulating rebel politics. Yet in contrast to the deceptive richness of the standard narratives, the archival record reveals nothing about Kett's speeches. Like the leaders of the 1536 rebellions, following the defeat of their insurrection, Robert and William Kett were subject to close examination. On the day following the battle of Dussindale, the Earl of Warwick sat in Norwich Castle, conducting 'examinations to find who were the principal beginners and promoters of this unhappy rebellion'. Upon their removal to London, the Kett brothers remained the focus of such attention. Sir Richard Southwell took a leading role in the London interrogations, conducting the legal examinations which led to their indictment, and questioning them as to the whereabouts of Crown money which he had disbursed rather mysteriously in Norfolk during the commotion time.[5] Yet the record of these examinations has not survived. The loquacity of Robert Kett within the Tudor narrative accounts therefore provides a stark contrast to his silence in the archival record.

Just as the pre-trial examinations of Robert and William Kett have been lost, so the surviving judicial records do not provide any insight into their speech. Similarly, the established narratives of the rebellion provide little insight into the trial, focusing instead upon its inevitable outcome. The only direct evidence that survives of the Ketts' trial comes from Richard Scudamore's letter of 27 November 1549, in which he states that Robert and William were brought before the King's Bench where they confessed their 'ffawltes' and were condemned to be executed.[6] In contrast to this contemporary letter, one rather less direct source suggests that the Kett brothers refused to follow the established conventions of Tudor show trials, but instead used the opportunity of the trial to condemn their opponents. *The history of Kett's rebellion in Norwich in the reign of Edward the sixth*, a work that apparently enjoyed access to the now lost Norwich Roll, an eyewitness account of Kett's rebellion, provides a detailed account of heated exchanges between Robert Kett and the presiding judge, the Lord Chief Justice, at his trial at King's Bench in November 1549.[7] Kett was accused

[5] PRO, E351/221; Russell, *Kett's rebellion*, 215–17; Blomefield, III, 255. The leaders of the Western rising were also subject to examination shortly after their capture: see N. Pocock (ed.), *Troubles connected with the Prayer Book of 1549* (Camden Society, 2nd ser., XXXVII, London, 1884), 65–6. For the examination of Robert Aske, see M. Bateson, 'Aske's examination', *English Historical Review*, 5 (1890), 550–73; for further evidences, see M. Bateson, 'The Pilgrimage of Grace', *English Historical Review*, 5 (1890), 331–43. Such material has enabled the careful examination of the motives and actions of the leadership of the 1536 rebellions. See, for instance, R. Hoyle, *The Pilgrimage of Grace and the politics of the 1530s* (Oxford, 2001), 190–9, 412–14.

[6] Brigden (ed.), 'The letters of Richard Scudamore', 94.

[7] Anon., *History of Kett's rebellion*, 110–15.

of having subverted the normal procedures of the court: 'On the question being asked, "How will you be tried?" instead of making the usual reply, "By God and my Country" . . . Kett answered "By unjust judges, and by tyrants."' The Attorney General denounced the Kett brothers as traitors, offered an account of the rebellion which centred upon the leadership role of Robert and William, and concluded by highlighting the relative affluence of the Ketts: 'The prisoners had not the excuse of the poor – they did not rebel from want, or from poverty; but . . . were traitors at heart.' The account mentioned the examination of

a great number of witnesses . . . among which, were many of the principal citizens of Norwich . . . Kett and his brother, however, endeavoured to shew in cross examination, that they had always endeavoured to restrain the people – that had not the rebels been commanded by men like themselves, their outrages would have been greater – and that, but for them, the city of Norwich must have perished.

Robert was then invited by the Lord Chief Justice to offer his defence. Kett denounced the magistrates and jury as prejudiced, stating that 'he had no hope of being acquitted' before offering his own account of what had led him to rebellion:

Although he did not originate the rising of the people, he rejoiced at being able to serve them when in arms. The people of England had been cruelly used by the gentry, their oppressors – and when he looked around that court and saw many present who he knew were tyrants, he bade them beware – for he was sure the time must come when the English people would level the pride of their oppressors.

Kett was interrupted by the Lord Chief Justice who told him 'that he could not allow such observations to be made'. Robert proceeded to an account of the rebels' grievances:

The people had been oppressed – they had been trampled on – their rights had been denied them – their commons were enclosed – and tens of thousands were now literally starving, the poor having since the dissolution of the monasteries, no means of obtaining casual relief. To remedy these grievances, he had assisted the poor. He had not taken arms against his lawful sovereign King Edward – whom he prayed God to bless. But he had opposed his evil councillors, and the tyrant gentry.

Kett concluded his defiant peroration by expressing his hope that 'the remembrance of his name might live in the minds of his fellow countrymen, and incite them in after ages to resist oppression and tyranny in any shape'. William Kett spoke in similar terms,

urging on the rich men present, the necessity of shewing more kindness to their poorer countrymen, and telling them that a time would assuredly come, when the people of England would most fearfully avenge themselves on those oppressors, who had for centuries trampled on their own, and their forefathers' liberties.

Robert Kett's voice seems therefore to speak to us, offering a fulsome account both of his own motives, and of the collective grievances of those whom he led; but there may well be yet another form of ventriloquism at work here. Instead of providing direct access to the words of a mid-sixteenth-century rebel leader, the speech may have emerged from the mid-nineteenth-century radical imagination. Robert Kett's forceful speech may well have been a product of early Victorian artifice. The confrontation between Kett and the Lord Chief Justice is reminiscent of courtroom struggles between nineteenth-century radicals and a repressive judiciary.[8] Quite conceivably, the Victorian author's transparent identification with the rebel cause of 1549 might have tempted him or her to speak for Robert Kett, inventing rebel speech which both elucidates mid-sixteenth-century social conflicts, and yet at the same time hinting at their similarities to early Victorian class struggles. There are, therefore, good reasons to be suspicious about the factual accuracy of this account. Nonetheless, I am reluctant to wholly dispense with this trace. Partly, because there remains at least a possibility that it retains some slight tinge of historical authenticity; but more importantly because it directs our attention towards the retrieval of the rebel voice from the unyielding grip of the historical record.

Whereas the accounts of Robert Kett's speech proffered in Holinshed, Neville and Woods portray him confronting authority on equal terms, the description of his trial speech presents Kett as the defiant advocate of the commons. The power of Kett's trial speech therefore contrasts with the impotency of his own situation. Whether fictional or not, this account of his speech highlights one circumstance within which plebeian rebellious speech might imprint itself upon the historical record: in deliberate, conscious moments of bloody-minded defiance. As such, Kett's trial speech illuminates the politics of speech and silence within early modern England, and the tension between the content of reported rebel speech and the nature of that reportage. Although the archival record is loaded with such evidence, the rebellious commons' furious anger is articulated most systematically and with the greatest clarity in an opening passage in the Neville/Woods narrative. But this time, instead of channelling popular complaint through the mouth of Robert Kett, the passage describes the collective speech of the commons as a whole.

The standard narrative accounts of Kett's rebellion might be read as products of an interchange between elite and popular cultures. In particular, the opening pages of the Neville/Woods narrative illuminate the capacity of

---

[8] J. Epstein, '"Our real constitution": trial defence and radical memory in the age of revolution', in J. Vernon (ed.), *Rereading the constitution: new narratives in the political history of England's long nineteenth century* (Cambridge, 1996), 22–51.

elite writers to comprehend the rebel voice. Like medieval monastic chronicle accounts of the 1381 rising, early modern historical accounts of popular insurrection hovered uneasily between ideologically driven condemnation and the need to represent the real content of rebel politics. In an opening passage, the Neville/Woods narrative highlights this contradiction, presenting rebellion not as a senseless insurgency, but as a rational response to meaningful grievances. Prior to commencing its blow-by-blow description of the Wymondham insurrection, the Neville/Woods narrative offers the following account of rebel complaints, couched as a collective speech act:

many base and vile persons ... bitterly inveighed against the authoritie of Gentlemen, and of the Nobilitie. For, said they, the pride of great men is now intollerable ... [the gentlemen are] consumed with vain pleasures, thirst only after gaine and are inflamed with the burning delights of their desires: but themselves [that is, the commons] almost killed with labor and watching, doe nothing all their life long but sweate, mourne, hunger, and thirst ... they and their miserable condition, is a laughing stock to most proud and insolent men ... that condition of possessing land seemeth miserable & slavish, they hold all at the pleasure of great men: not freely, but by prescription, and ... at the will, and pleasure of the Lord. For as soone as any man offend any of these gorgious Gentlemen, he is put out, deprived, and thrust from all his goods ... so farre are they now gone in cruelty and covetousnesse, as they are not only content to take by violence all away, and by force & villainy to get ... except they may also suck ... our blood & marrow out of our veines and bones. The common pastures left by our predecessours for the reliefe of us, and our children, are taken away. The lands which in the memory of our fathers were common, those are ditched and hedged in, and made severall; the Pastures are inclosed, and we shut out: whatsoever fowles of the ayre, or fishes of the water, and increase of the earth, all these do they devoure, consume and swallow up ... while we in the meane time, eat herbs and roots, and languish with continuall labour ... Shall they, as they have brought hedges about common Pastures, inclose with their intollerable lusts also, all the commodities and pleasure of this life, which Nature the parent of us all, would have common ... We can no longer bear so much, so great, and so cruell injury, neither can we with quiet minds behold so great covetousness, excess and pride of the Nobilitie: we will rather take Armes ... then indure so great cruelty ... While we have the same forme, and the same condition of birth together with them, why should they have a life so unlike unto ours, and differ so far from us in calling? We see that now it is come to extremitie, we will also prove extremity, rend down hedges, fill up ditches, make way for every man into the common pasture: Finally, lay all even with the ground, which they no less wickedly, then cruelly & covetously have inclosed. Neither wil we suffer our selves any more to be pressed with such burden against our willes, nor indure so great shame as living out our dayes under such inconveniences, we should leave the Commonwealth unto our posteritie, mourning, and miserable, and much worse then we received it of our fathers.[9]

This passage has attracted the attention of Annabel Patterson, who sees it as part of a 'trope of reported speech'. Apparently uninterested in the accuracy,

[9] Neville/Woods, sigs. B1v–2v.

provenance or literary function of the reported speech, Patterson takes the passage at face value. For her, it represents an 'extraordinary document' which 'offers an ethical model of how socioeconomic inequality is perceived as by no means inevitable by the losers'. Most importantly, she sees in the passage the validation of James Scott's proposal that 'subordinate classes – especially the peasantry – are likely to be more radical at the level of ideology than at the level of behaviour, where they are more effectively constrained by the daily exercise of power'. This leads her to conclude that the passage represents a 'utopian [ideology] of classlessness'.[10] For all its methodological naiveté, Patterson's remark is nonetheless perceptive. She is not the first to discern within this passage a broader statement of rebel ideology. Earlier discussions of the rebellion also deployed the passage as evidence of rebel intentions. Writing in the 1730s, Blomefield saw the passage as proof that the rebels intended to level 'all men to an equality of fortunes'. From a very different ideological standpoint, the socialist writer Reg Groves also saw the passage as a fundamental statement of rebel politics, presenting it in full transcription alongside the Mousehold articles as exemplars of the rebel ideology in his 1947 work *Rebels' oak*.[11] In contrast, later twentieth-century academic historiography has avoided the passage (possibly seeing it as nothing more than a hostile exaggeration of rebel complaints), preferring instead to assess insurgent ideology on the basis of the Mousehold articles alone. Certainly, the passage is fictitious in the sense that it does not constitute an accurate report of any specific incident, but rather represents an imagined condensation of rebel complaint. Like Robert Kett's speeches, the passage fulfils a function within the Neville/Woods narrative, its location in the opening pages of their works enabling the reader to contextualise the subsequent story of violent social conflict. But the literary qualities of the passage do not deprive it of historical value; for in consciously mimicking the style of popular political speech, the passage provides important insights into both the representation of the rebel voice and of plebeian political language.

There is an important parallel to be drawn between the contemporary depictions of the 1549 and 1381 rebellions. Both Paul Strohm and Steven Justice have argued that, despite their evident bias, the monastic chroniclers' accounts of the 1381 rebellion reflect genuine aspects of the rebel politics of that year. Strohm suggests that although the monastic chronicles were 'designed to deny the rebels either coherent ideology or rational intent', because 'an action must be at least partially evoked before it is condemned', the chroniclers nonetheless provide 'an implied or shadowed representation

---

[10] A. Patterson, *Shakespeare and the popular voice* (Oxford, 1989), 42–4.
[11] Blomefield, III, 223; R. Groves, *Rebels' oak: the great rebellion of 1549* (London, 1947), 101–2.

of a rebel rationale'. Thus, when the chroniclers represent rebel speech, Strohm argues that they provide 'a key to the rebels' understanding of their own actions'. Yet he finds only 'a few … scraps' of such speech, leading him to the pessimistic conclusion that 'we have not heard the rebel voice and we are not going to hear it'. In its place, Strohm bases his analysis of 'rebel ideology' upon the actions attributed to the rebels in the chronicle accounts. Thus, on the basis that 'a narrator who wishes to discredit an actor or group of actors must first, in however grudging or distorted a fashion, *represent* their actions or words', Strohm believes that it is possible to retrieve 'rebel ideology' from otherwise profoundly hostile sources. Like Strohm, Steven Justice argues that a rational ideology can be construed from reports of rebel actions in the chronicles, but is more optimistic about their potential as a source for the rebel voice. His re-examination of rebel politics in 1381 turns upon a distinctive reading of six rebel letters included in the chronicles of Henry Knighton and Thomas Walsingham. Working from the methodological assumption that 'taciturn records can be squeezed until they talk', Justice deploys these letters in order to explode the myth that the 1381 rebels were illiterate and hostile to writing; to probe the content of their ideology; to scrutinise the stylistic similarities between rebel language and that of Langland and Chaucer; and to investigate rebel organisation. In transcribing the rebels' letters, Justice argues, 'Knighton slipped: and a whole world opens up', that of 'a rural political culture'. Whereas, like the rest of their class, the monastic chroniclers found the rebel letters to be 'full of riddles', Justice's readership of the letters enables him to defeat the 'ideological work' of the chronicle accounts, to retrieve a whole submerged ideology and so 'to make the rebels live'.[12]

Strohm and Justice's insights help us to make sense of the long passage of collective rebel speech presented at the beginning of the Neville/Woods narrative. Most obviously, Strohm's proposal that 'an action must be at least partially evoked before it is condemned' casts the collective plebeian speech act in a very different light. Rather than seeing the passage as nothing more than the hostile textual projection of ideological domination, designed to stereotype the 1549 rebels as mindless insurrectionaries, it becomes possible to read it more positively. Most importantly, in order to present its reader with a credible reconstruction of popular complaint, the passage knowingly mimics plebeian political idiom.

When the collective voice of the 1549 rebels compares the greed and pride of the 'great men' with the oppression of the commons, and concludes that 'their miserable condition, is a laughing stock to most proud and insolent

---

[12] P. Strohm, *Hochon's arrow: the social imagination of fourteenth-century texts* (Princeton, 1992), 33–5, 49, 51; Justice, *Writing and rebellion*, 7, 8, 14, 206.

men', it alludes to the everyday mockery of the poor by the rich within early modern society. Similarly, the suggestion that the economic and cultural power of the rich was displayed by their conspicuous consumption of food, leaving the poor to 'hunger and thirst', was a repetitive cliché within early modern popular speech. During the hungry February of 1550, for example, John Cobbe was reported to the Norwich magistracy for having said 'in the open corn markette att the [market] crosse ... The poore can bye no corne here for the ryche chorles take it from them.' A month before Kett's rebels rose in Norfolk, the Ipswich mason William Poynet was jailed for his opinion that the 'Gents & Richemen have all catell & wolles & suche like things in ther hands nowe a dayes & the pore peple are now Famysshed but C of us wyll rise one daye agenst them.' The Neville/Woods narrative seems also to reflect the conclusion which many of the 'poor commons' drew from their belief that the rich denied sustenance to the poor: that the rich men intended to 'suck ... our blood & marrow out of our veines and bones'. In June 1550, it seemed self-evident to one former Norwich rebel, Robert Burnam (whom we shall meet again), that 'If the gentylmen might have the higher hande styll the poore commons shulde be trodden under Foote ... if the Gentylmen do go furwarde as they have begonne they wolde destroy the Realme.' The commoners of Landbeach (Cambridgeshire) understood their social world in similar terms. In June 1549, they complained that their lord 'intentyth the dystruccon of the rest of the towne for he wysshyth tht ther were no more houses in the towne but his owne and no more'. The rebellious commons' collective speech reported by Neville/Woods presented enclosure as a meta-phor, whereby the commons were 'shut out' not only from common land, but also from 'all the commodities and pleasure of this life', while the gentry 'seeke from all places, all things for their desire'. Over and again, the com-mons' collective speech reiterated the 'covetousness ... of the Nobilitie'. In their petition to Queen Mary, the Norfolk commons developed a similar interpretation. Claiming that 'we ar soo sore obpressed borne & grudged att by dyv[er]s ... gentylmen beyng soo sore inflamed & enbraced w[i]t[h] suche covetousnes unlawfull desyres of such thyngs as be not ther owen', the petitioners accused the 'insacyable & covetous' gentry of attempting to destroy the commons through the enclosure, emparkment and the increase of rents and dues. Just as the rebel voice in the Neville/Woods narrative complained of how 'cruelty and covetousnesse' led the gentry 'to take by violence all away', so at some time around 1548 some Norfolk bondmen complained of how their prosperity and freedom had been 'by plain force and violence ... taken' by the Duke of Norfolk 'in suche sorte as neyther theimselfe should peaceably enjoye any parte thereof nor yet any relief or coumforte should redounde to their wives and children by their peinfull labours and travaillis'. The collective rebel speech in the Neville/Woods narrative developed a similar critique of bondage, which was presented as an attempt to undermine tenurial rights, such that the commons were unable to hold land 'freely, but [only] by prescription ... at the will, and pleasure of the Lord'. Both the Norfolk commons' petition to Queen Mary and the rebel speech offered by Neville and Woods presented this as an attack not only upon plebeian economic rights, but also upon local memory and the commons' duty to 'posterity'. According to Neville and Woods' report of popular speech, land which 'in the memory of our fathers were common' had been stolen by the gentry; the Norfolk commons' petition defined present rights with reference to the past, complaining of how tenants had lost lands which 'ther Auncestors have ben in possessyon w[i]t[h]oute tyme of mynde of man'. All of this meant that, according to Neville and Woods, the commons would leave 'the Commonwealth unto our posteritie ... much worse than we received it of our fathers'. We find the same echo in the condemnation offered by the Southampton court leet of the enclosure of the town's common in 1579. They denounced the enclosure on the grounds that it represented an attack both upon their material well-being and upon their duty to the past and to the future: because 'our ancestors of their great care and travail have provided [the common] ... so we thinke it our dutie in conscience to keepe, uphold and maintaine the same as we found yt for our posteritie to come'. In similar vein, the copyholders of Walsham regarded Sir Nicholas Bacon's increase of seigneurial dues as an assault upon 'themselves and their posterity'.[13]

Two implications emerge from this melange of popular complaint. Firstly, comparison of Neville/Woods' lengthy passage of collective plebeian speech with archival records suggests that, despite their avowed hostility to their subject, they offer genuine insights into rebel political vocabulary. This finding is important for the investigation of rebel ideology, as it both broadens the range of historical documentation available to our study and raises the wider issue of the power relations embedded within that documentation. Secondly, our discussion raises the nature of such representation, and the motives which underlay educated writers' attempts to articulate the popular voice.

Annabel Patterson was right to suggest that Neville/Woods' lengthy passage was formed within a contemporary 'trope of reported speech'. As she shows, Shakespearean drama also mimicked plebeian political speech, most notably in *Henry VI Part Two* and *Coriolanus*.[14] This was also true of other

---

[13] K. Thomas, 'The place of laughter in Tudor and Stuart England', *Times Literary Supplement*, 21 (January, 1977), 76–83; NRO, NCR/16A/6, pp. 98, 418–19; NRO, NCR/16A/4, fol. 61v; NRO, NCR/12A/1(a), fol. 8r; CCCC, XXV/194, 'Articles agaynst Richard Kyrby of land-ebeche – 1549, 8 Juni'; PRO, E163/16/14; PRO, C1/1187/9; R. H. Tawney, *The agrarian problem in the sixteenth century* (London, 1912), 245–6; PRO, C2/2Eliz/P12/48.

[14] Patterson, *Shakespeare and the popular voice*, ch. 2.

contemporary dramatic work, which sometimes presented plebeian complaint as personified in allegorical figures. The 1592 play *A knack to know a knave*, for instance, presented a character called Honesty, 'a plain man of the country', who spoke for the rural lower orders. The play's targets were the familiar enemies of sixteenth-century popular politics: corrupt priests, royal favourites, the gentry, usurers and middlemen. Like much of the plebeian seditious speech of the period, the play is built around a revenge fantasy. Honesty condemns the middleman to punishment at the market cross, with his 'cursed tongue pinned to [his] breast'; the priest and the corrupt courtier are executed; the landowner is taken to a cornfield 'there [to] have your legs and hands cut off, because you loved corn so well, and there rest till the crows pick out of thine eyes'.[15] The resonances of this play, performed during the hungry 1590s, are obvious enough. But printed depictions of the plebeian language of class are most clearly stated in the writings that formed the mid-Tudor commonwealth tradition.

The commonwealth tradition, with its strong social critique and powerful mixture of economics, religion and morality, provides the outstanding mid-Tudor example of the overlap of elite and popular political culture. In particular, this is true of Robert Crowley's writings. He not only articulated a similar world-view to that of the rebellious commons of 1549 but also appropriated their voice. In many passages of his work, Crowley deployed common phrases which are more typically to be found in accusations of seditious speech. In a discussion of the corruption of urban government, for example, he concluded that 'The pore men are pold / and pyled to the bare / By such as shoulde serve them.' To 'poll and pill' was a popular euphemism for financial extortion, such as unfair parliamentary taxation, or the imposition of financial penalties by lords or town authorities. Thus, John Este of Great Yarmouth was fined in June 1553 for having said openly in the town's court that the bailiffs 'have taken my goods from me & now you rewarde me with indyting me & yf yowe were as redy to gyff as you are to pill & powle me you showlde do better wth me than you do'. Like so much of the language of mid-sixteenth-century popular politics, this terminology had enjoyed a long life, dating back to the fourteenth century. A poem of 1300, for instance, denounced the oppressions of village bailiffs who 'pilethe the pore and pyketh ful clene'.[16]

[15] D. Bevington, *Tudor drama and politics: a critical approach to topical meaning* (Cambridge, MA, 1968), 227–9.
[16] Crowley, *Select works*, 13; NRO, Y/C4/252, m. 28r; R. Hope Robbins (ed.), *Historical poems of the fourteenth and fifteenth centuries* (New York, 1959), 8. For other references to 'pilling and polling', see PRO, E36/120, fols. 96r–97r; PRO, DL5/4, fol. 138r; More/Robynson, 21–2; Cockburn (ed.), *Essex indictments*, no. 1783; NRO, NCR/16A/2, fols. 36r–v, 37r (pp. 16–18); PRO, SP1/89, fol. 122r; PRO, SP1/126, fols. 136r–139r.

Robert Crowley dreamt of lynching the oppressors of the commons: 'because he shewed no mercie / no mercie shall he have / The sentence is geven / go hange up the slave'. Again, Crowley echoed popular sentiment. In October 1551, during conversation in the bakery of William Mordewe 'touching the hard world' and the recent devaluation of the currency, the baker remarked that 'if it pleased the king to make him hangman to a greate meany of Gentylmen he could fynde in his harte to hange a greate meany of Gentylmen'. A number of Norwich women confirmed how 'One Suttons wief' replied 'That her husband was in the same mynde'. Mordewe the baker added his opinion that the gentry were 'extreyomers and brybours of the countrith'. Twelve years later, in the course of a discussion of the evils of urban life, Thomas Eton remarked that one of the city's magistrates, Mr Mychells, was 'allweys A mortall foe to all pore men & hath the good wyll of no pore man within norwyche'; since 'mychells ... was never pore mans frynd', Eton held such hatred for the magistrate that 'yf ther wer no men alyve but mr mychells I coulde fynde in my hart to be his hangman'. Such fantasies carried with them an obvious threat: in 1553, one enclosing Norfolk gentleman was faced by a pair of gallows that had been mysteriously erected at the threshold of his house.[17]

Most notably, in a remarkable passage in his 1550 work, *The way to wealth*, Robert Crowley strove to articulate the angry speech of the opposed classes of mid-sixteenth-century England.[18] First of all, Crowley identified the collective speech of the gentry (whom he named 'the gredie cormerauntes') as full of hostility to the commons. His articulation of the common voice was much more sympathetic:

If I shuld demaunde of the pore man of the contrey what thinge he thinketh to be the cause of Sedition, I know his answere. He woulde tel me that the great fermares, the grasiers, the rich buchares, the men of lawe, the marchauntes, the gentlemen, the knightes, the lordes ... they are doares in al thinges that ani gaine hangeth upon. Men without conscience. Men utterly voide of Goddes feare. Yea, men that live as thoughe there were no God at all! Men that would have all in their owne hande; men that would leave nothyng for others; men that woulde be alone on the earth; men that bee never satisfied ... yea, men that would eate up menne, women & chyldren, are the causes of Sedition! They take our houses over our headdes, they buye our growndes out of our handes, they reyse our rentes, they leavie great ... fines, they enclose our commens! No custome, no lawe or statute can kepe them from oppressyng us ... Very nede therefore constrayneth us to stand up ageynst them! ... we must nedes fight it

[17] Crowley, *Select works*, 40; NRO, NCR/12A/1(a), fols. 37r, 123r; NRO, NCR/12A/1(c), fol. 55r. For another reference to a labourer's fantasy of executing the gentry, see *CPR, Elizabeth I*, V, *1569–72*, no. 1818. For another example of the erection of mock gallows, see PRO, SP12/252/94 (II). For the depiction of gallows on a manuscript libel attached to the gate of a gentleman's house, see NRO, NCR/16A/4, fol. 65r.
[18] Crowley, *Select works*, 132–3, 142–3.

out, or else be brought to the lyke slavery that the Frenchmen are in! These idle bealies wil devour al that we shal get by our sore labour in our youth, and when we shal be old and impotent, then shal we be driven to begg ... Better it were therfore, for us to dye lyke men, then after so great misery in youth to dye more miserably in age!

The structure of Crowley's writing is both dialogic – constructing an imagined argument between two opponents – and multivocal – enabling the expression of many voices within a single text. This structure allowed Crowley to evade accusations of sedition, while freeing him to develop a markedly hostile assessment of the attitudes of the dominant class of mid-sixteenth-century England. The conscious mimicry of popular speech lent authenticity to Crowley's prose while also encrypting elements of plebeian political dialect within his text. Some of the fundamental assumptions of rebel ideology of 1549 are stitched into this extract: the broad specification of the oppressing class ('the great fermares, the grasiers, the rich buchares, the men of lawe, the marchauntes, the gentlemen, the knightes, the lordes'); the sense that England's ruling elite was devoid of morality ('Men without conscience'); the belief that the gentry, moved by an avaricious individualism, had become the enemies of plebeian community ('men that woulde be alone on the earth'); the lack of faith in the ability of the legal system to constrain that covetousness ('No custome, no lawe or statute can kepe them from oppressyng us'); the fear of being driven into poverty by the gentry ('when we shal be old and impotent, then shal we be driven to begg'); and, finally, the motivating impulse to insurrection, couched in the contemporary cliché of rebellious plebeian masculinity: 'Better it were therfore, for us to dye lyke men'.

Historians used to despair of finding meaningful evidence concerning the political views of early modern labouring people. Lawrence Stone, for instance, justified his concentration upon 'the acts, behaviour and thoughts of the ruling elite, rather than of the masses' on the grounds that 'this is the only group whose lives and thoughts and passions are recorded in sufficient detail to make possible investigation in full social and psychological depth'.[19] In recent years, historians have grown wary of the feasibility of aiming at any 'full social and psychological' study of any particular group. This greater willingness to accept the partial, fragmentary nature of historical traces has developed alongside the emergence of a new tradition of early modern social history. Stone's gloomy assumption that the history of the lives of the commons lay beyond the limits of the historical enterprise now seems as dated as his heavy-duty positivism. This is especially true of research

---

[19] L. Stone, 'Lawrence Stone – as seen by himself', in A. L. Beier, D. Cannadine and J. M. Rosenheim (eds.), *The first modern society: essays in English history in honour of Lawrence Stone* (Cambridge, 1989), 585–6.

into power relations and popular politics in early modern England.[20] As we have seen, it was difficult to escape from the popular political voice in Tudor England, which impinged upon formal political discourse and drama just as it seethed within the alehouse environment. The main problem for the historian of popular political speech arises not from an absence of material, but from its excess: an excess of contexts (so much reported speech, presenting the voices of so many individuals; so many possible motives that might underwrite that documentation); an excess of archives (so many documents, so difficult to collate and assess); and an excess of meaning (so many possible interpretations of reported words).

Those historians who have exploited the legal and administrative records of seditious speech in early modern England have not tended to dwell upon the difficulties involved in their interpretation. Yet, for all their richness, such material is loaded with interpretive and ethical problems. Self-evidently, these records were the product of an unequal power relationship between the interrogator and interrogated; equally self-evidently, the records had many authors: the interrogator, the interrogated and the clerk responsible for the transcription of the records all had their role in the production of the text. As Garthine Walker puts it, 'Legal narratives may be conceptualized . . . as containing a series of dialogues.'[21] In this respect as in others, the early modern English evidence bears close similarities to the inquisitorial records deployed by, amongst others, Emmanuel Le Roy Ladurie in his study of the villagers of Montaillou and Carlo Ginzburg's reconstruction of the mental world of the sixteenth-century Friulian miller, Menocchio.[22]

The historical analysis of inquisitorial records has been a source of vigorous historical debate. Importantly for our purposes, Jacques Rancière charges Le Roy Ladurie with having suppressed the individuality of the heretical voices in the inquisitorial record, instead deploying them as a source for social history. In situating the heretic villagers of Montaillou 'in the flesh of the social, in the heart of a village', Rancière complains that Le Roy Ladurie has suppressed the originality of the heretic voice:

The inquisitor suppresses heresy by eradicating it: he marks it, he locks it up, he kills it. The historian, on the contrary, suppresses it by giving it roots. He removes it . . .

---

[20] Three recent collections illustrate social historians' current interest in power relations: Braddick and Walter (eds.), *Negotiating power*; Harris (ed.), *Politics of the excluded*; and H. French and J. Barry (eds.), *Identity and agency in England, 1500–1800* (Basingstoke, 2004).

[21] G. Walker, 'Just stories: telling tales of infant death in early modern England', in M. Mikesell and A. Seeff (eds.), *Culture and change: attending to early modern women* (Newark, DE, 2003), 100.

[22] C. Ginzburg, *The cheese and the worms: the cosmos of a sixteenth-century miller* (1976; Eng. trans., London, 1980); E. Le Roy Ladurie, *Montaillou: Cathars and Catholics in a French village, 1294–1324* (1978; Eng. trans., London, 1978).

from the inquisitorial condemnation by giving it the colour of the earth and the stones, by rendering it indiscernible from its place.

In attempting to situate the dissenting rebel voices of mid-Tudor England within a wider political culture, a similar critique might be mounted against the argument developed in this chapter. It is therefore important to note that individual plebeian dissidents in sixteenth-century England often claimed to speak on the behalf of, and in the language of, the collectivity. In the hand-written confession which he submitted to his interrogators following the betrayal of the Walsingham conspiracy, the yeoman George Guisborough, for instance, claimed to speak for both 'the pore pe[o]pyll & comyns [who] . . . say the[y] be sore oppressyd [by the] gentyll men'.[23] The conscious desire of plebeian rebels to speak within a collective rebel voice suggests that Rancière's critique of Le Roy Ladurie is not wholly transferable to the records of the prosecution of seditious speech in Tudor England. Nonetheless, Rancière's critique is illuminating. Most importantly, it should act as a warning against mounting a search for a single, homogeneous 'rebel voice'; instead, in seeking out common themes and formulations within popular political language, we must also identify frictions and contradictions and illuminate individual rebels' verbal originality. We need also to keep constantly in mind the ways in which popular and elite political languages were intertwined, the one threading in and out of the other. Finally, Rancière's critique requires us to attend to the power relations which produced this documentation, and which scripted its form. It is therefore worth pausing to consider the ethical issues involved in the use of such documentation.

A number of historians have addressed the ethical dilemmas faced in the analysis of inquisitorial records. As Ginzburg notes, 'The "archives of repression" certainly provide us with rich evidence' about lower-class people. But, as he recognises, the 'inequality in terms of power' that produced the document also structured its content. As Lara Apps and Andrew Gow acknowledge, present-day historians 'remain in the uncomfortable position of benfiting – intellectually and professionally – from the ordeals of others'. Therefore, as Ginzburg puts it, 'In order to decipher [the documents], we must learn to catch, behind the smooth surface of the text, a subtle interplay of threats and fears, of attacks and withdrawals.'[24] This is certainly true of the record of early modern English popular political speech. Only occasionally,

---

[23] PRO, SP1/119, fol. 33r. J. Rancière, *The names of history: on the poetics of knowledge* (1992; Eng. trans., Minnesota, 1994), 73.

[24] C. Ginzburg, 'The inquisitor as anthropologist', in C. Ginzburg, *Myths, emblems, clues* (1986; Eng. trans., London, 1990), 157, 158, 160–1; L. Apps and A. Gow, *Male witches in early modern Europe* (Manchester, 2003), 67.

however, does the pressure exerted upon the examinant become apparent. The examination of the would-be rebel Richard Vassinger, who became involved in a plot to raise the commons of Hampshire in 1586, provides some hints of the pressures exerted upon him. Repeatedly, the record of his examination indicates how, despite his initial attempts to conceal the names of those involved in the plot, he was forced to release increasing amounts of information. Thus, the record described how Richard called 'to himself better to remembraunce' details of the plot; how 'beinge better examyned', he recalled the names of those involved in the plot; how he repeatedly hesitated in his testimony, claiming that 'he doeth not nowe remember' certain details, only subsequently to acknowledge that he 'remembrethe' them well enough after all.[25] Ginzburg acknowledges in himself his 'emotional identification with the defendant'; I must acknowledge a similar loyalty. But, as John Arnold points out, there is 'an uneasiness here': only through the deployment of inquisitorial records produced out of a repressive state mechanism – in the case of early modern England, the lawcourts or the Privy Council – has the 'subordinate' voice been allowed to speak.[26] After all, some examinations were conducted following the use of state-sanctioned torture; and it is clear that many others were extracted in an environment of fear and intimidation.[27]

It is therefore important that the historian recognise her or his subjective position in relationship to such documentation. Moreover, it is also necessary to keep in mind that the texts with which we are dealing were not produced for the benefit of the historian, but were rather created as part of a process of examination and that the content and form of the resulting depositions and examinations were structured by the application of legal rules. As Peter Rushton reminds us, 'The meaning of archival texts, far more than that of the printed word, is bound up with the context of their production and use.'[28] The legal basis for the prosecution of seditious speech drew from two sources: statute and common law precedent. After 1534, the reign of every Tudor monarch saw at least one statute passed concerning seditious or treasonable speech. Moreover, prosecutions could be legitimised by the sanction of precedent flowing from earlier judgements. Seditious and treasonable speech could be prosecuted by quarter sessions, the assizes, the Court

[25] BL, Cotton MS, Vespasian F IX, fols.147v–148v.

[26] J.H. Arnold, *Inquisition and power: Catharism and the confessing subject in medieval Languedoc* (Philadelphia, 2001), 2–3.

[27] For examples of the use of torture, see BL, Cotton MS, Caligula B I, fols. 130r–131r; BL, Cotton MS, Cleopatra E IV, fols. 122r–123r; PRO, SP1/108, fol. 42r; PRO, SP1/106, fols. 138r, 213r.

[28] P. Rushton, 'Texts of authority: witchcraft accusations and the demonstration of truth in early modern England', in S. Clark (ed.), *Languages of witchcraft: narrative, ideology and meaning in early modern culture* (Basingstoke, 2001), 22.

of King's Bench and in some cases by lesser institutions such as the Norwich Mayor's Court.[29] Moreover, the Privy Council and the Council of the North also held authority over treason and sedition.[30] Finally, the Crown could declare a state of martial law, in which all sorts of speech and behaviour might be deemed dangerous and result in severe punishment.

In normal circumstances, a variety of punishments might be applied by courts, including requiring the guilty party to enter into a recognisance; being placed in stocks or the pillory; being ridden around a marketplace with a label attached describing the crime in question; ears being nailed to, or cut off at, the pillory; whipping; hanging; and finally, in the case of treasonable speech, hanging, drawing and quartering for men, or burning for women.[31] The subject defies any quantitative analysis, but it is clear that a fair proportion of felons deemed guilty of seditious or treasonable speech might receive a royal pardon.[32] Despite the severity of some punishments, it is important to bear in mind that, apart from in the unusual circumstances of martial law (which applied across much of England during the commotion time of 1549), the repression of seditious speech was constrained by the operation of the law. Hence, for instance, even in the extreme conditions of September 1536, the Duke of Norfolk sought the advice of the lawyer Sir Roger Townshend following his examination of would-be rebels in Norwich, asking Townshend to 'loke on [his] boks and ... advertise me how [the rebels] wold wey in the law'.[33] Nonetheless, the treason and sedition legislation provided the state with a sufficiently flexible code to allow for the prosecution of all sorts of political speech. Even Latimer was accused of being a 'seditious fellow' following his highly radical first sermon to Edward VI.

---

[29] For the earlier punishment of seditious speech, see S. Walker, 'Rumour, sedition and popular protest in the reign of Henry IV', *P&P*, 166 (2000), 31–65. For the development of sedition and treason legislation in the early modern period, see J. Bellamy, *The Tudor law of treason: an introduction* (London, 1979); R. B. Manning, 'The origins of the doctrine of sedition', *Journal of British Studies*, 12, 2 (1980), 99–121. For a rare example of a court leet hearing a case of seditious speech, see NRO, NRS 12131/27/B4.

[30] For the Council of the North, see PRO, SP15/3/47. For the Council of the West, see BL, Cotton MS, Titus B I, fols. 172r–175v.

[31] For punishments of seditious or treasonable speech, see PRO, SP1/127, fols. 123r–135r; PRO, SP15/3/78 (whipping); NRO, NCR/16A/5, p. 511; NRO, NCR/16A/6, pp. 98, 123, 128 (pillory); Cockburn (ed.), *Essex indictments*, no. 1094; NRO, NCR/20A, 1553–6, fol. 24v; CLRO, Rep 13 (1), fol. 73r: (nailing of ears); *CPR, Edward VI*, IV, 139–40 (severing of ears); Cockburn (ed.), *Essex indictments*, no. 1243 (hanging, drawing and quartering); NRO, NCR/16A/6, pp. 39, 104–5, 254 (recognisances); NRO, NCR/16A/6, p. 82 (various punishments).

[32] For pardons in sixteenth-century England, see K. J. Kesselring, *Mercy, authority and the Tudor state* (Cambridge, 2003).

[33] PRO, SP1/106, fol. 183r. For other examples of the legalism of Tudor repression, see BL, Harl MS 6989, fol. 97r; PRO, SP1/124, fol. 34r; BL, Cotton MS, Cleopatra E IV, fols. 122r–123r; PRO, SP1/116, fols. 132r–133r; PRO, SP15/3/78; NRO, NCR/16A/6, p. 107.

In answer, he pointed out 'that Christ himself was noted to be a stirrer up of the people against the emperor; and was contented to be called seditious'.[34]

II SPEECH, SILENCE AND SOCIAL RELATIONS
IN EARLY MODERN ENGLAND

Elite anxieties concerning popular political conversation need to be under-stood as a peculiarly fraught aspect of the politics of speech and silence. In this section, we address the relationship between speech and social power and assess the logic that underlay contemporary connections between silence and social order. Attention is drawn to the ways in which the frustration of elite expectations of plebeian silence generated anxieties concerning popular political speech. In particular, the section explores the insight that speech represents a sharp indicator of power relations. Here, we draw upon anthro-pological work which points towards the intimate connections between speech and power. Hence, as Maurice Bloch puts it, within any social order, 'a central issue is who gets to be heard ... who is worth hearing'. Bloch was especially interested in the formal presentation of political speech. In his pioneering study of the speechmaking in Merina councils in mid-twentieth-century Madagascar, Bloch observed that 'the right to speak – who speaks rather than what is said – is important in reproducing the ranking system by displaying it'. In Bloch's analysis, 'the rules for regulating speech-making' formed a means by which 'social control was exercised' within Merina society.[35] Bloch's perspective forms a useful starting point for the historical investigation of speech and silence. While Bloch saw Merina speech events as echoing pre-existent inequalities of wealth and power, it will be argued here that speech had a greater autonomy and force: that it helped to *define* social relations. Moreover, just as Bloch described Merina speech councils as a central arena within which power relations could be represented and enacted, so, within early modern England, those in authority utilised a variety of formal institutional contexts for the verbal display of hierarchy.

Anthropologists often deploy the terms 'oratory' and 'speech events' in order to make sense of those formal occasions at which public speech occurs. Within such formulations, public modes of speaking possess a peculiar performative authority. As a form of structured discourse, public oratory is

---

[34] Latimer, *Sermons*, 134. See also *ibid.*, 240, and Meadows Cowper (ed.), *Henry Brinklow's complaynt*, 49.

[35] F.R. Myers and D.L. Brenneis, 'Introduction: language and politics in the Pacific', in F.R. Myers and D.L. Brenneis (eds.), *Dangerous words: language and politics in the Pacific* (New York, 1984), 4; M. Bloch, 'Introduction', in M. Bloch (ed.), *Political language and oratory in traditional society* (London, 1975), 6, 12.

understood to follow tight rules which are intended to reproduce dominant power relations.[36] Certainly, anxieties concerning the relationship between speech and social authority coloured the rules by which the governing villagers of Swallowfield (Wiltshire) decided to run their village council in 1596. Whereas the villagers agreed that during their deliberations, 'no man shall skorne an others speech, but tht al tht shalbe spoken may be quyetly taken & hard of all', rather more prescriptive injunctions governed the speech of the village poor. It was ordered that 'suche as be poore & will malepertlye compare wth their betters & sett them at nought' were to be 'warned'; if such individuals continued to speak out of place, they were to be prosecuted as 'comon disturbers of the peace'.[37]

Such verbal restrictions often become accessible to historical scrutiny only at the moment of their transgression. Thus, in 1551, the manorial jurors of Cawston were evidently disturbed to hear Alice Lambe, the wife of Simon Lambe, a tenant of the manor, speak openly in their court. In so doing, Alice trespassed upon one of the prohibitions of village society: married women were not meant to speak at manorial courts. Alice explained that she had done so because her husband Simon had lost his mind; on one occasion Simon had told his neighbours that 'I am as wyse as a cuckowe.' Yet, as Alice explained, despite his condition, Simon had gone on to make a will and to sell some of their estate. The jurors nonetheless presented Alice for 'sayeinge openlye before the companye then p[rese]nte That her husbonde had not wyte to take money owte of his owne pourse'.[38] In speaking in the formal setting of the manorial court, Alice Lambe challenged not only the injunctions that governed the practice of the court, but, as Bloch would have it, the oratorical rules that expressed power relations. Symbolically, Alice Lambe thereby called into question the patriarchal order of Cawston during a centrally important speech event: the meeting of the manor court. As Bloch reminds us, 'this sort of political event is a kind of self-presentation of the social system'; hence, to challenge such a 'political event' was to challenge the 'social system' that it reflected.[39]

Bloch's formulation raises a fundamental issue in the social history of language: does linguistic practice merely *reflect* pre-existent power relations, or does it *constitute* those relations? For Bloch, the answer was obvious. He proposed that 'Speech events ... do not exercise power so much as they reproduce already existing relations of dominance.' Hence, 'ultimately the

---

[36] For a survey, see R. Grillo, 'Anthropology, language, politics', in R. Grillo (ed.), *Social anthropology and the politics of language* (London, 1989), 1–24.

[37] S. Hindle, 'Communication: hierarchy and community in the Elizabethan parish: the Swallowfield articles of 1596', *Historical Journal*, 42, 3 (1999), 849–50.

[38] NRO, DN/DEP/6/5A, fols. 32v–33v, 37v–39v.   [39] Bloch, 'Introduction', 26.

power of formalised oratory does not simply spring from its form, it springs from the forces of social power ... it implies the acceptance of who is top, it does not produce it'.[40] This aspect of Bloch's theorisation of the relationship between language and power is not helpful to an understanding of early modern patterns of speech and silence. As we shall see in this section, the rulers of sixteenth-century England often represented both authority and its subversion in auditory terms: the former as 'quietude'; the latter as a threatening 'murmuring'. Such contemporary formulations were more than merely accidental. Rather, governors' attempts to impose silence upon their subordinates, like subordinates' attempts to resist that imposition, helped to constitute early modern power relations.

The relationship between language and power suggests that Raymond Williams was correct to criticise the view that language is 'a simple "reflection" or "expression" of "material reality"'. Instead, he argued that language represents 'practical consciousness [which] is saturated by and saturates all social activity, including productive activity'. For Williams, 'language is ... a dynamic and articulated social *presence* in the world'.[41] This implies something very different from Bloch's formulation. Instead of presenting linguistic practice as a passive echo of social practice or economic relations, we might perceive of language as a key element in the everyday constitution of power relations.[42] As Norman Fairclough characterises the issue, 'language is a part of society, and not somehow external to it ... language is a social process'.[43] Of all historians of early modern society, Jane Kamensky has been the most alive to the conceptual implications of the contemporary obsession with speech and silence, observing how in early New England, 'speech codes', or 'ways of speaking had "social meaning"'.[44] Hence, the conspicuous disregard that the Tudor governing elite were meant to exhibit towards popular speech did more than simply express their economic and political power; rather, that contempt both re-enacted and confirmed the social order. After all, as one widely read conduct book put it, 'when the rich speaketh, every one keepeth silence, but when the poore speaketh, it is saide, what fellow is that?'[45]

There was, therefore, a powerful politics to speech and silence in Tudor England. But this politics was open to contestation. The verbal expression of authority required daily sustenance by its proponents and regular acceptance

---

[40] *Ibid.*, 24.   [41] R. Williams, *Marxism and literature* (Oxford, 1977), 39–40.
[42] For which see, *ibid.*, 21–44; V. N. Voloshinov, *Marxism and the philosophy of language* (Cambridge, MA, 1986).
[43] N. Fairclough, *Language and power* (Harlow, 1989), 22.
[44] J. Kamensky, *Governing the tongue: the politics of speech in early New England* (Oxford, 1997), 10.
[45] S. Guazzo, *The civile conversation*, 2 vols. (1581–6; London, 1925), I, 190; on language as constitutive of power relations, see Burke, 'Introduction', 15.

by inferiors. For all that early modern rulers affected to despise popular political speech, their ears remained ever attuned to the sound of that plebeian 'murmuring' which they understood might lead to 'commotion'. It is therefore revealing that early modern rulers tended to characterise popular politics in auditory terms. Thus, for instance, the Duke of Norfolk warned Thomas Cromwell in February 1537 that 'the people were never in the i[n]surrection tyme more full of ill wordes then they be nowe'. Plebeian opposition to new taxes was defined as 'a grett clamor among the pepull'; 'insurrection' became a 'rage of horley borley'.[46] The nervousness of rulers concerning popular 'clamor' led some labouring people to understate their demands, thereby tactically manipulating their rulers' fears while also advancing their own interests. Others, keen to infuriate their betters, flagrantly and deliberately broke the established conventions according to which speech was governed. Language was therefore not only a site of domination, but could also become a field of contestation, and even of creativity by the dominated.

Picking up Bloch's concept of the 'speech event', and applying it to sixteenth-century England, we can observe the sometimes violent contempt which individual labouring people displayed towards the assumption that they should remain silent and subservient. Indeed, such formal speech events sometimes provided the opportunity for the deliberate, conscious rejection of authority. Hence, a year before Kett's rebellion, the clerk of a manorial court of Aylsham recorded how Robert Backhouse, after being fined as a barrator by the court, 'publicly asserted' to the manorial court 'that the hedburghs whych have Annoyed hym before thys tyme were all knaves and by the masse he wold breake ther heades'. Still worse, he went on to warn two of the jurors that 'by godds blode I and a hundred more wylbe upon the noses of the mowest of you', following which he drew his dagger and attacked the jurors.[47]

Within the urban environment, the guildhall occupied a still more obvious site for the enactment of hierarchical speech events; sitting as magistrates, the Mayor and aldermen gathered in their best robes in finely decorated, panelled courtrooms in order to administer justice. As Douglas Hay has noted, there was a deliberately theatrical element to the dispensation of justice, in which magisterial power was supposed to be ritually re-enacted, and popular subordination reinforced.[48] Such occasions were ripe for

[46] PRO, SP1/178, fol. 178v; BL, Cotton MS, Cleopatra E IV, fol. 319r; E. Hall, *Hall's chronicle; containing the history of England during the reign of Henry the Fourth and the succeeding monarchs, to the end of the reign of Henry the Eighth* (London, 1809), 823.

[47] NRO, NRS 12131/27/B4.

[48] D. Hay, 'Property, authority and the criminal law', in D. Hay, P. Linebaugh and E. P. Thompson (eds.), *Albion's fatal tree: crime and society in eighteenth-century England* (London, 1975), 17–64.

subversion. Thus, the denunciation of the Mayor of Canterbury as a 'Chorle' was given greater efficacy by its location, in a council meeting in the guild-hall.[49] Similarly, in the aftermath of Kett's rebellion, Johanne Bray defended her husband from the dangerous charge of having been a rebel, saying in the Norwich guildhall that 'she defyed Mr Mayor and all them that shud saye' that her husband was a rebel; rebuked for such speech, the clerk recorded how, nonetheless, 'she repeated thus words twycs or thrycs I defy Mr Mayor'.[50] Parish churches also provided an important space for verbal dissidence. Thus, the parishioners gathered in Orford (Suffolk) church on Michaelmas day were singing the psalm 'Magnificat' when their service was disturbed by the constable of the town who, in a loud voice, denounced the authority of the unpopular lord's bailiff, warning him that he should remove the lord's sheep from the common fields of Orford 'or ells I & my Fellowes will dryve them awaye'.[51] The leader of the 1549 rebellion in Watford (Hertfordshire) likewise chose his parish church as the location for his denunciation of a local magistrate as 'a false Justice'. The rebel was said to have 'revyled hym w[i]t[h] moste sklanderouse wordes that could be spoken & sayd he was a Theife & had robbyd hym of his goods'.[52] In 1597, one parishioner denounced the priest of Horsforth 'uppon a Sabaoth daye in the chauncell . . . callinge him foole, dowlte, & asse, & at an other tyme in open courte holden for the mannor said he was as bad a man as could goe uppon the earthe'. Likewise, in New Buckenham that year, Jane Hayward came into the church during service '& further used many Rayling & obbrobrius speeches' callinge the minister 'blacke sutty mowthed knave'.[53]

All of this stood in overt opposition to the proper ordering of speech. According to contemporary patriarchal logic, people were expected to be discrete in their speech. William Perkins advised that 'Men shoulde be slow to speake, and swift to heare.' He saw talkativeness as sinful: 'A foole poureth out al his mind, but a wise man keepeth in til afterward . . . the foole . . . is the ungodlie person, that maketh no conscience of any sinne'; 'The lippes of the righteous know what is acceptable; but the mouth of the wicked speaketh froward thinges.'[54] A century earlier, Robert Whittinton had articulated a similar formulation: 'A foole is so ful of wordes that he dassheth out all that lyeth on his herte.'[55] Authoritarian social theorists assumed that such discretion was socially specific: since the gentry possessed greater rationality than the plebeians, the vulgar multitude was both noisy and

---

[49] PRO, STAC2/8/100.   [50] NRO, NCR/16A/6, p. 254.
[51] PRO, STAC2/21/93.   [52] PRO, STAC3/7/53.
[53] J. F. Williams (ed.), *Bishop Redman's visitation, 1597: presentments in the archdeaconries of Norwich, Norfolk, and Suffolk* (Norfolk Record Society, Norwich, 1946), 47, 95.
[54] W. Perkins, *A direction for the governmente of the tongue* (Edinburgh, 1593), fols. 5r, 6v, 7v.
[55] White (ed.), *Vulgaria*, 76.

garrulous. Such formulations were ubiquitous within elite descriptions of popular politics. The courtier Ellis Griffith, witness to the rising at Lavenham (Suffolk) against Wolsey's Amicable Grant in 1525, described the crowd of weavers and labourers gathered in the town as a tumultuous, chaotic multitude, speaking 'all at the same time like a flock of geese in corn', devoid of order, each member of the crowd 'began to babble and shout, every man with his plan', all of them representative of 'the characteristic indiscretion of the ignorant'.[56] Similarly, Sir Philip Sidney characterised the rebellious lower orders of Arcadia as noisy, credulous and irrational: 'hearkening on every rumour, suspecting everything, condemning them whom before they had honoured, making strange and impossible tales of the King's death ... infinitely disagreeing'.[57] In some formulations, popular political speech was presented as not only inappropriate, but as grotesque. Hence, in Thomas Wilson's *Arte of rhetorique*, in 1549 the actions of 'The rebelles of Northfolke' proved clearly that 'Thou lives wickedly, thou speakes naughtely.' As Cathy Shrank has pointed out, such depictions of the 'recurrent link between disorderly, disobedient or "deviant" behaviour and incomprehensible or redundant speech' contrasted with the linkage between 'language, reason and civil living'.[58]

The Privy Council's periodic declarations against rumour and sedition provided an opportunity for the restatement of the need for plebeian silence. The 1551 declaration against 'Rumour mongers', for instance, developed a stark assessment of the threat posed by loose popular speech: 'false lies, tales, rumours, and seditious devices against his Majesty' abused 'that most precious jewel, the word of God'. Within this overarching belief system, political rumour was an offence against both secular law and divine order. Plebeian obedience was synonymous with silence: the proclamation was meant to ensure that 'every man [should live] within the compass of his degree, contented with his vocation, every man to apply himself to live obediently, quietly, without murmur, grudging, sowing of sedition, spreading of tales and rumours'.[59] Just as rebellion was presented as the greatest human sin, so its perceived precursor, rumour, was represented as diabolic. In 1599, the Star Chamber was told that the authors of seditious libels were 'instruments of the divell', who intended 'to fill the Ruder sorte wth lies and stirre upp careles men unto contempt of state and move the comon sorte unto

---

[56] HMC, *Welsh*, I, iii.
[57] R. Kegl, *The rhetoric of concealment: figuring class and gender in Renaissance literature* (Ithaca, NY, 1994), 49.
[58] T. Wilson, *The arte of rhetorique, for the use of all suche as are studious of eloquence* (London, 1553), fol. 108r; C. Shrank, 'Civil tongues: language, law and reformation', in J. Richards (ed.), *Early modern civil discourses* (Basingstoke, 2003), 19.
[59] *TRP*, II, 514–18.

sedicon'.[60] Nicholas Breton pursued a similar analysis in 1607, claiming that it was 'a worke of the Devill to sow sedition'. Such verbal transgression was equivalent to 'the sin of witchcraft, and what greater transgression, then Rebellion? Which chiefly have her breeding in murmuring.'[61]

The combination of anxiety and contempt which defined elite attitudes to plebeian political opinion underwrote governors' perceptions of popular politics as a whole. The gentry and nobility tended to conceive of popular politics either as bestial – as a 'many headed monster' which required the bridle of elite authority, in bodily terms, as a rebellion of the limbs or lower organs against the brain – or in auditory terms, as an intimidating collective roar, a rumour, a murmur.[62] One frightened gentleman summed up this conceptualisation of popular politics with greatest clarity: for Arthur Wilson, an appalled eyewitness to the Stour Valley riots which preceded the outbreak of the English Civil War, he described the crowds he saw as alternatively 'the Beast', the 'Guidie Multitude' or simply as 'The Mouth'.[63] This latter image is especially revealing. The idea that popular politics took the form of dangerous sound possessed a long history. Medieval monastic chroniclers recalled the Peasants' Revolt of 1381 as 'The Noise: *rumor, rumor magna, rumor pessima*'.[64] In the 1450 rebellion, the origins of the popular insurrection were said to have lain in what 'Comun voyses' had 'noysed'.[65] There was a direct continuity between medieval and early modern formulations of popular politics. Mid-sixteenth-century readers of Hall's *Chronicles* read of how in 1450 'the furye of the mutable comons' led them to 'openly denouncyng' established authority; 'of these wordes sprang dedes, and of this talkyng, rose displeasure'; 'rumor ope[n]ly spoken, & como[n]ly published' eventually culminated in Jack Cade's rebellion. The Cornish rebellion of 1497 was presented as a consequence of unbridled popular 'angre': 'lamentying, yellyng, & criying maliciously', the Cornish 'compleyned and grudged ... forgettynge their due obaysaunce, beganne temerariously to speake of the kyng him selfe'.[66] Perhaps the clearest expression of the connection between clamour and disorder was to be found in Holinshed's account of the spread of the Western rising. Holinshed described how news of the outbreak of the Devon rebellion spread

[60] PRO, SP12/273/37.
[61] A. B. Grosart (ed.), *Nicholas Breton: the works in verse and prose* (1879; repr. Darmstadt, 1969), 5, 9, 10, 11.
[62] On bestial images of the lower orders, see C. Hill, 'The many-headed monster', in C. Hill, *Change and continuity in seventeenth-century England* (1974; 2nd edn, New Haven, CT, 1991), 181–204.   [63] Walter, *Understanding popular violence*, 42–3.
[64] Justice, *Writing and rebellion*, 208.
[65] M. L. Kekewich, C. Richmond, A. F. Sutton, L. Visser-Fuchs and J. L. Watts (eds.), *The politics of fifteenth-century England: John Vale's book* (Stroud, 1995), 204–5.
[66] Hall, *Chronicle*, 218, 477.

as a cloud caried with a violent wind, and as a thunder clap sounding at one instant through the whole countrie, are carried and noised even in a moment throughout the whole countrie; and the common people so well allowed and liked thereof, that they clapped their hands for joy, and agreed in one mind, to have ... [rebellion] in everie of their severall parishes.[67]

The governing elite of Tudor England therefore continued to conceive of popular politics in auditory terms: as a 'commotion', a 'murmur', as 'complaining and murmuring', as a 'great hurlie burlie among the multitude', or as Sidney described Arcadia's 'mutinous multitudes', a 'confused rumour'. In *Coriolanus*, Shakespeare likewise depicts popular politics as a dangerous, clamorous noise: meeting the plebeian Tribunes, Coriolanus describes them as 'The tongues o'th'Commonwealth'.[68]

For the rulers of Tudor and early Stuart England, popular politics was therefore about noise; and in particular about threatening, anonymous collective speech. This formulation betrays important aspects of elite perceptions of popular politics: characterised by constant anxiety, periodic incomprehension and occasional terror. Most intimidating were those moments at which popular politics seemed to close itself to the elite. Hence, the London disturbances that culminated in the Evil Mayday of 1517 were said to have been preceded by 'a common secret rumour, [that] ... no man could tell how it began'.[69] Similarly, the origins of a rumour in Norfolk and Suffolk concerning new taxes proved impossible for the Duke of Norfolk's agents to track down because 'the words were so universallie spoken that they coulde not [find] the furst authours notwthstanding they had examined many p[er]sones'.[70] Over the course of the seventeenth century, elite formulations of crowd actions, popular organisation and plebeian speech came gradually to emphasise the collective mobility of the 'vulgar' – the *mobile vulgus*, later shortened to the enduring label of 'mob'.[71] But before the Civil Wars, the gentry and nobility tended to favour auditory descriptions of popular politics.

The ubiquity and force of such formulations remain most apparent within the archives of the Court of Star Chamber, which enjoyed a special jurisdiction over riotous offences. Gentry complainants to the court routinely represented plebeian crowds in auditory terms, as 'a great shuffling'; 'a great

---

[67] Holinshed, 940. See also Hooker, 57.
[68] Hall, *Chronicle*, 218, 220, 477; Holinshed, 969–70; Bryn Davies, 'Boulogne and Calais', 60; Kegl, *Rhetoric of concealment*, 49; *Coriolanus*, III.1.22.
[69] Hall, *Chronicle*, 588.   [70] PRO, SP1/135, fol. 49r.
[71] T. Harris, 'Perceptions of the crowd in later Stuart London', in J. F. Merritt (ed.), *Imagining early modern London: perceptions and portrayals of the City from Stow to Strype, 1598–1720* (Cambridge, 2001), 250–72.

uprore of people'; an 'uprore and Tumulte of a multitude of people'.[72] In Star Chamber complaints, riots were described in terms of noisy, transgressive speech: to Henrician and Elizabethan gentlemen alike, rioters seemed full of 'grete showtts and cryes'.[73] The speech of demonstrating or rioting crowds was represented as 'garboilinge and shuffelinge together'.[74] Popular political attitudes were likewise identified as 'tumultes and uprore'.[75] Individual verbal complaint was rendered in collective terms as 'a greate murmuringe and discontentm[en]t'. Such speech was defined by its seditious homogeneity; crowds were seen as a faceless collectivity that 'murmored' together.[76] Reconstructing their experiences of hearing such 'murmuring', gentry complainants emphasised the terror that the sound of popular politics held for them. The description proffered to the Star Chamber of the negotiations between the gentry commissioners and the anti-enclosure demonstrators at Northaw in 1548 emphasised how the 'Ryotous p[er]sons' spoke 'obstynatly and Rebellyously' to the gentry, giving forth 'cruell Terryble menassyng and sedycyous wordes'. Full of 'fury and rage', the crowd 'made sundry greate showts exclamacons and cryes'. When they subsequently descended upon Sir William Cavendish's house, he recalled the terror of hearing their angry collective speech: 'spekyng further in theyr said Rage and Rebellyous fury aswell dyv[er]s other most dysobedyent and Rebellyous words', Cavendish reconstructed for the court how hearing these 'many fearefull menassyng and spytefull wordes' against himself and the Crown, he was put 'in great danger feare and joperdy' for 'the losse of his lyff'.[77] The noise of popular politics was contrasted to the silence of social order. Hence, one Lincolnshire gentleman established a contrast between the 'sedicious factions and turbulente spiritts' who were 'apt to raise tumults and rebellion' and the proper auditory order which they threatened: 'the quiett and settled state and peace of [the] ... whole kingdome'.[78]

We should not dismiss such descriptions as mere legalistic rhetoric. Instead, Star Chamber complainants both reflected and fashioned the authoritarian instincts that dominated the elite's social paradigm. Gentry complainants dwelt upon the terrifying sound of popular politics both because they knew that the propertied and powerful privy councillors who sat in Star Chamber were socialised into thinking of popular politics in terms of intimidating noise and because they too were brought up to such ideas. Such formulations were ubiquitous within elite culture, characterising both

---

[72] PRO, STAC8/4/3.18; PRO, STAC8/4/3.3; PRO, STAC8/5/21.17.
[73] Compare PRO, STAC5/S76/16 and PRO, STAC2/34/50.
[74] PRO, STAC5/A57/5.   [75] PRO, STAC5/P14/21.
[76] PRO, STAC8/227/4.38; PRO, STAC5/P14/21.
[77] PRO, STAC3/1/49.   [78] PRO, STAC8/125/3.4.

Star Chamber complaints, and literary and historical descriptions of popular politics. In both types of material, the leaders of popular rebellion were represented as especially voluble. Thus the Norfolk rebel leader John Flotman was described in the Neville/Woods narrative as 'a man alwaies of a voluble tongue, and ready by nature to speake reprochfully', who spoke 'arrogantly and threatningly' in his encounter with the Marquis of Northampton at Pockthorpe Gate on 1 August 1549. For Holinshed, 'the wicked speech of ... the rascall sort' was backed by the 'lowd voice' of Robert Kett himself.[79] Similarly, individuals singled out as providing the leadership for popular politics in Star Chamber complaints were identified as having spoken 'wth a high & a lowd voice'.[80] Significantly, the speech of women rioters was seen as especially disturbing: one group of women enclosure rioters was said to have been 'clamorous, loude', possessed of 'highe voices', giving out 'outcries shout[s] hallowe[s]'.[81] The political speech of individual women was equally disturbing. Thus, the wife of a Hertfordshire rebel leader in 1549 was described as having denounced a local gentleman in 'the moste dispitefull words that she could ymagen'.[82]

Socialised into an authoritarian world-view, it was sometimes difficult for the early modern elite to comprehend popular complaint as anything other than seditious. In Shakespeare's play, individual plebeian representation is comprehended by Coriolanus and his patrician supporters as but 'The horn and noise o'th'monster's'; Cranmer spoke in similar terms in 1549, describing rebel demands as intimidating, collective speech acts in which 'unlawful assemblers mutter ... They make exclamations ... They charge ... They say.'[83] In some accounts, popular politics was personified as a 'murmurer': Edmund Dudley warned the 'commyners' against a messenger he called 'discontentacion or murmurr', explaining how 'This messenger will induce you to grudge or to make some inward displeasure in doing your Dewtie, as in paing your farme rentes ... or to do some other particuler service ... or to murmur at paymentes of taxes.'[84] Within such descriptions, seditious speech was rendered equivalent to rebellion. Instructions sent by the Council in September 1549 to the magistrates of those counties that had been affected by risings ordered the arrest of 'tail tellars vagabonds and others going about to rayse or people', and placed the 'spreding of sedycyous tales and rumors' on the same level as organising rebellion, instructing that such murmurers should be 'executed openly to the terror of others'.[85] A discussion document prepared for Queen Mary concerning the military and fiscal weaknesses of

[79] Neville/Woods, sig. G2r; Holinshed, 969.   [80] PRO, STAC8/290/22.
[81] PRO, STAC8/184/24.   [82] PRO, STAC3/7/53.
[83] *Coriolanus*, III.1.97; Cox (ed.), *Miscellaneous writings*, 193, 195.
[84] Brodie (ed.), *The tree of commonwealth*, 87.   [85] PRO, SP10/8/66.

the state warned how, amongst other perils, the people had 'growne stub-burne and liberall of talk'.[86] Such constructions went beyond a hard-headed awareness of the power of speech within popular political culture, instead reifying assertive plebeian speech, presenting it as equivalent to rebellion.

The gentry and nobility represented popular politics in auditory terms because speech formed such a sensitive point within the everyday practice of power relations. In particular, social theorists criticised excessive speech before superiors: Thomas Wright observed in 1604 that he 'who talks much before his betters, cannot but be condemned of arrogancie, contempt, and lacke of prudence'. Since speech was understood as reproducing power, so 'familiaritie aspireth to equalitie'.[87] Nicolas Faret likewise drew attention to the appropriately respectful tone with which inferiors should address super-iors, suggesting that inferiors or equals might be addressed with greater ease.[88] Indeed, labouring people were expected to be grateful that the gentry might bestow words upon them: as Shakespeare observed, 'We grace the yeoman by conversing with him.'[89] Such formulations also fed into social criticism: one ballad of 1550 that depicted popular grievances introduced a character called 'Little John Nobody, that durst not speak' who, despite his name, gave voice to anti-evangelical opinions; asked to expand, however, he retreated to his original position: that he is 'Little John Nobody, that durst not speak'.[90] Speech, demeanour and body language therefore formed powerful emblems of power relations. The judges in Star Chamber, brought up to expect a proper absence of eye contact from their social inferiors, discussed in appalled terms how those who spoke seditious words were now 'daringe to speake in the face they care not of whom'; this was taken as proof that they were equivalent to 'Jacke Cade or Jacke Strawe'.[91]

Within the elite mindset, quietude was synonymous with order, and plebeian silence equivalent to proper deference. In sermons, homilies and prescriptive tracts, the lower orders were repeatedly told to remain silent in the face of authority: thus, Edmund Dudley stated bluntly that the 'com-mynaltie ... may not grudge nor murmure to lyve in labor and pain'.[92] The Homily against Rebellion of 1570 invoked 'the wyl of God' as justifica-tion for the need to 'stoppe the mouthes of ignoraunt and foolishe men'.[93] Mid-Tudor editions of the Bible made an explicit connection between

---

[86] BL, Cotton MS, Titus B II, fol. 74r–v.
[87] T. Wright, *The passions of the mind* (1604; London, 1630 edn), 139–40.
[88] N. Faret, *The honest man* (London, 1632), 197–9.   [89] *1 Henry VI*, II.4.81.
[90] T. Percy (ed.), *Reliques of ancient English poetry: consisting of old heroic ballads, songs, and other pieces of our earlier poets*, 3 vols. (London, 1889), II, 133.
[91] PRO, SP12/273/37.   [92] Brodie (ed.), *The tree of Commonwealth*, 45.
[93] R. B. Bond (ed.), *Certain sermons or homilies (1547) and A homily against disobedience and wilful rebellion (1570): a critical edition* (Toronto, 1987), 211.

'murmuring' against magistrates and 'murmuring' against God. The 1570 Homily went further, seeking to reach into subjects' souls: it suggested that even when silent, autonomous plebeian opinion was harmful to the social hierarchy and warned the ruled to expect to incur 'the heavie wrath and dreadfull indignation of almightie God' against those 'as do only but inwardly grudge, mutter and murmure against their governours'. In a similar vein, the Marian statute against sedition warned that 'we ar forbidden to thinck evill and muche more to speake evell' against the sovereign. Such 'inward treason', although it might avoid earthly retribution, remained known to an omniscient God.[94]

These idealised notions structured everyday power relations, producing unattainable expectations amongst the elite and so helping to frustrate communication between social groups. Assertive speech was understood as the province of the educated, rational gentleman; women, servants, the young and the poor were expected to remain silent. Subordinates' speech could therefore be understood by their rulers either as threatening or as absurdly inappropriate. Some labouring people may have internalised such expectations.[95] The fragmentary evidence of seditious speech suggests also that some plebeians might have placed more weight upon the opinions of wealthier men and women than they did upon their peers. In 1537, in order to lend credibility to his report of the death of Henry VIII, the Kentish fisherman Thomas Graunt emphasised how he had heard the story from 'honest men in this countraye', including 'a man like a m[er]chaunte man'.[96] We should not, therefore, overdraw the distinction between the idealised expectations expressed in the conduct book literature, and the hurly-burly messiness of everyday life. Conduct manuals stressed how speech denoted rank and hierarchy, simultaneously embedding and naturalising social distinctions: 'the rude speeche of the countrie Clowne, is as naturall to him, as the fine and polished, is to the Citizen and Gentleman'. For Guazzo, 'It behooveth a Gentleman to speake better then a Plebeian.'[97]

Contemporary elite representations of popular resistance frequently stressed the dangerously inappropriate nature of plebeian speech. The Norfolk gentleman Sir Henry Parker, for instance, explained to the Star Chamber how he had set one of his tenants in the village stocks for using 'yll & lewde language' against him, deploying such 'unsemely & unfittyng words not to be named but also fell in such ragyng and raylyng . . . as were not

---

[94] *Ibid.*, 230; *Statutes of the realm*, IV, 1, 240–1.
[95] For more on this, see A. Wood, 'Fear, hatred and the hidden injuries of class in early modern England', *Journal of Social History*, 39, 3 (2006), 803–26.
[96] BL, Cotton MS, Appendix, L, fols. 73r–74r.   [97] Guazzo, *Civile conversation*, I, 124, 145.

decent for any ten[a]nt to use nor any honest p[er]son to have spoken'.[98] To the governing elite of early modern England, such conduct was dreadful. It seemed self-evident to Guazzo that poverty bred humility. Thus, 'a poore man proud' seemed as damaging to proper order as 'a yong man without obedience, a rich man without charity'.[99] These expectations structured elite attitudes to charity, poverty and poor relief. Paupers were advised to repress their speech before their superiors: 'Keep a good tongue though men deale not very well with you ... carry yourselves dutifully and humbly towards the rich and all your superiors,' be 'not saucy, surly, ill-tongued: [be] patient and meek when you receive a reproofe and [do] not swell or give ill words'.[100] Such expectations made it difficult for the poor to negotiate claims to poor relief or charity. Mary Stracke of Hempnall found herself in trouble in 1597 as 'a comon drunckard & sower of discord betweene neighboures, & a breaker of the Christian Charity'. In answer, she emphasised her material needs, contesting her characterisation as a trouble-causer and claiming 'that she had three children and is verie poore, and when she spoke for her releef ... they saye she skoldeth'. The parish priest trod a middle path, denying that she was a drunkard, but confirming that she was 'busie with her tongue'.[101]

The dangerous position within which Mary Stracke found herself in 1597 reminds us that it was not only the gentry and nobility who felt anxiety concerning the inappropriate speech of their inferiors. Part of the appeal of patriarchalism lay in its postulation of a link between the narrow interests of the gentry and nobility and the wider interests of adult, settled, propertied men. Within authoritarian social theory, both were set in authority over subordinates. Just as lords ruled over tenants, so patriarchal writings advised adults to expect deference from children; masters to expect deference from servants; employers to expect deference from workers; village officers to expect deference from paupers; and husbands to expect deference from wives. The effect of this linkage between public and private authority was to invoke a wider set of interests in the maintenance of the social order. And since speech and silence represented such sensitive indices of authority, so superiors were encouraged to expect their authority to be expressed within speech. The connection established within authoritarian social theory between domestic, magisterial and divine authority defined any subordinate's improper speech as an assault upon the whole social order. In 1543, the *King's book* recommended 'a reverence and lowliness in words and outward gesture, which children and inferiors ought to exhibit unto their

---

[98] PRO, STAC3/6/30.   [99] Guazzo, *Civile conversation*, II, 17, 71.
[100] S. Hindle, 'Exhortation and entitlement: negotiating inequality in English rural communities, 1550–1650', in Braddick and Walter (eds.), *Negotiating power*, 114.
[101] Williams (ed.), *Bishop Redman's visitation*, 105.

parents and superiors', manifest in 'a regard to their words'. Such verbal and bodily deference was owed 'not only [by] ... children ... unto their parents, but also all subjects and inferiors to their heads and rulers'.[102]

Verbal criticism of any authority figure within this divinely constituted patriarchy was understood as the work of Satan. As Breton wrote: 'If thou be a man, and murmurest against God, thou art a Devill, if thou bee a Subject, and murmure against thy King, thou art a Rebell; if thou bee a Sonne and murmure against thy father, thou shewest a bastard's nature.'[103] The politics of speech and silence not only structured relations between Crown and subject and between gentry and commons, but also underwrote the political structure of households and communities. Like some of the small-scale societies studied by twentieth-century anthropologists, speech was mixed up with the micro-politics of sixteenth- and seventeenth-century communities, producing what must sometimes have seemed like an 'oppressively hierarchical ... society which manifested itself in Elders continually telling younger men what to do, in fathers similarly telling their sons, older brothers telling their younger brothers, and men telling women'.[104] Like the people of the later twentieth-century Trobriand Islands, early modern English women and men regarded 'language as dangerous and powerful'. For them, 'speech [contained] the possibility and ... the inherent power to provoke disruptive and destructive events'.[105] Hence, the aldermanic opponents of the populist Mayor of Cambridge spiced the allegations of sedition that they offered against him to the Council in November 1551 with the observation that he 'hathe used abrode straunge and dawngerous talke, wch brideth mytche variance and troble in the town', alleging that the Mayor had stirred sedition by claiming that the 'welthest' would take the town's common land from the poor 'wch is entred into light heads, and dawngerous talke hathe alredye folowed'.[106] Truly, in early modern England, 'Words were serious business.'[107]

In recent years, the records of the criminal, church, equity and manorial courts of early modern England have been extensively explored by social historians interested in studying the communal, social and gender relations in the period. One of the key findings of such studies concerns the power accorded to both individual and collective speech. In particular, recent research into gender relations has addressed the identification of scolds and barrators – respectively, women and men who were considered by

---

[102] C. Lloyd (ed.), *Formularies of faith put forth by authority during the reign of Henry VIII* (Oxford, 1856), 311–12.

[103] Grosart (ed.), *Nicholas Breton*, 9.   [104] Bloch, 'Introduction', 3.

[105] Myers and Brenneis, 'Introduction', 17.   [106] PRO, SP10/13/68.

[107] G. Walker, *Crime, gender and social order in early modern England* (Cambridge, 2003), 100.

their neighbours to have disrupted the proper flow of power relations through their inappropriate speech. Just as deviant speech acts were central to the construction of the identity of the 'scold' or 'barrator', so, too, socially dangerous speech identified individuals who were deemed to be unneighbourly, unreliable, seditious or even, in the case of witchcraft accusations, diabolic.[108] Words therefore constituted the 'credit' upon which reputation depended; styles of speech identified collectivities, whether based upon religion, class, gender, age or localities; who spoke, when and with what force, both formed and articulated everyday power relations in the household, street, alehouse, field and village. Collective opinion, often identified as the 'common fame', 'common voice', 'report' or 'rumour' of a place, defined both relationships between individuals and the customary rights which obtained within a locality. Within some contexts, such as an individual's long-standing reputation or the customs of a village, collective speech could be defined in terms of stasis, a commonplace 'daily speeche & reporte of the neighbors', or the 'comon report in the contrey'.[109] In other cases, such as the speedy transmission of alarming political news, collective speech seemed much more fluid and immediate, comprising a 'flyinge reporte'.[110]

III SPEECH ACTS, POPULAR AGENCY AND SOCIAL POWER

The social chauvinism embedded within early modern elite culture sometimes limited the capacity of the gentry and nobility to construe meaning from their conversations with what they called the plebs. This tendency was heightened by their willingness to conceive of popular politics as a senseless, collective voice. The Elizabethan narratives of Kett's rebellion reproduced such prejudices. In its account of the confrontations under the Oak of Reformation, for instance, the Neville/Woods account developed a powerful contrast between the 'eloquent words and sentences' of Matthew Parker's sermon and the reactions of the 'common people [who] began to murmur, and openly to rage'.[111] Such blind-spots presented rebels with an opportunity, allowing individual leadership and organisation to be concealed behind the roar of the common voice. On other occasions, however, labouring people displayed an evident irritation at their rulers' deafness. The

---

[108] See, for instance, D. E. Underdown, 'The taming of the scold: the enforcement of patriarchal authority in early modern England', in A. Fletcher and J. Stevenson (eds.), *Order and disorder in early modern England* (Cambridge, 1985), 92–115; M. Ingram, '"Scolding women cucked or washed": a crisis in gender relations in early modern England?', in J. Kermode and G. M. Walker (eds.), *Women, crime and the courts in early modern England* (London, 1994), 48–80.
[109] PRO, STAC3/1/76.4; PRO, STAC10/6/182.   [110] PRO, STAC8/19/10.16.
[111] Neville/Woods, sig. C4v.

description offered by Sir William Cavendish to Star Chamber concerning the demonstrations at Cheshunt in 1548 replicated the tendency to conceive of popular politics as collective, uniform and clamorous. He reported to the court how 'Ryotous p[er]sons' spoke 'obstynatly and Rebellyously' to the enclosure commissioners, offering them 'cruell Terryble menassyng and sedycyous wordes'. In answer, the demonstrators emphasised how 'the cause of theyr comyng [to speak to the commissioners] was ev[er]y ma[n] to speke for his owne right of comen'. The Cheshunt man John Thompson explained how he and his neighbours had told the intimidated members of the commission that the crowd comprised 'poore men that ment no harme but came to speke w[i]t[h] the commission[er]s and to be petition[er]s to them in ther right for the comon'.[112] The Cheshunt inhabitants' clear intention was to individualise their speech, presenting it as grounded in reason and common right, and thereby to undermine Cavendish's representation of their politics as a senseless, collective clamour.

Fundamental to both the practice of social relations and the organisation of popular political culture, therefore, were the meanings given to plebeian speech. At no times was this more obvious than during the insurrections of 1549. It was characteristic of both the constrictions placed upon popular speech and the frustrated desire of labouring people to find a voice, that some individual working people claimed to speak for the collective interests of the commons. Robert Kett was not the only rebel leader of 1549 whose speech was used by the later narrative authors to articulate collective plebeian complaint. In the account offered by Neville/Woods of John Flotman's confrontation with the Marquis of Northampton at Pockthorpe Gate on 1 August 1549 we find a similar articulation by an individual of a collective political agenda. Flotman, characterised as 'a man alwaies of a voluble tongue, and ready by nature to speake reprochfully', was said to have addressed the Marquis with 'a loud voice'. Following a denunciation of Northampton, he went on to discuss the rebel cause:

For we are to restore to her former dignitie the Common wealth, now almost utterly over throwne, and daily declining (and inforced through the insolency of the Gentlemen) out of her miserable ruines, wherein she hath long continued, either by these courses, or else (as become valiant men, and such as are indued with courage) fighting boldly (with the perill of our lives) to die in battell, and never to betray our libertie, though it may bee oppressed.[113]

In other cases, those claiming to speak for the commons positioned themselves beyond the plebs. One petitioner to Queen Mary consciously appropriated the common voice, justifying that claim on the grounds that the poor

---

[112] PRO, STAC3/1/49; PRO, STAC10/16, fols. 137r–143v.
[113] Neville/Woods, sigs. G2r–3r. See also Sotherton, 90–1.

had been denied a voice: 'I have heard many pore men say they durst not complain for fear of displeasure.' In complaints to central equity courts, richer individuals often claimed to speak 'in the name of all the pore Inhabitants and p[ar]isioners' of their communities. On some occasions, the apparent willingness of poorer people to allow their wealthier neighbours to ventriloquise their interests could prove disastrous. The poor inhabitants of Cottenham (Cambridgeshire) learnt this lesson in the 1550s. Here, following an 'Intreaty ... of the welthiest and ... the best sorte ... in ther ow[n]e behalfe and on behalfe of the rest of the seyd tennantes and Inhabyt[a]ntes of ... Cotenhame', the lord and wealthier villagers came to a settlement concerning access to the village commons which excluded the poorest inhabitants.[114] But on many other occasions, individual leadership emerged from amongst the poor, manifesting itself through assertive speech. In the course of crowd disturbances in Elizabethan Blythburgh (Suffolk) concerning the right of the poorer inhabitants to the town's commons which had been enclosed by a local farmer, Luke Fennell presented himself as the key defender of the popular case. On the third day of rioting on the commons, magistrates commanded the rioters to depart. In answer, Fennell said 'they would not [depart] for it was ... there comon'. A local gentleman implored the crowd to disperse, asking them 'if this were the lyffe they mente to leade', whereupon Luke Fennell *'in the name of them all'* (my emphasis) confirmed defiantly 'that this was the lyffe they mente to leade'. The gentleman warned them that 'it would breede there trouble more than they were awarr', to which Luke repeated his assertion that 'it was there comon'. The consistency of Fennell's verbal assertiveness landed him in gaol.[115]

Compared to the fate of George Guisborough, who was hanged, drawn and quartered for his role in the popular conspiracy in Walsingham in 1537, Luke Fennell was fortunate. Yet there remain similarities in how Guisborough and Fennell specified their relationship to the collective interest. Notably, both defined themselves as the representatives of a larger movement. In his handwritten confession, Guisborough manipulated his obligatory admission of guilt in order to identify himself as the representative of a wider set of plebeian 'co[m]play[n]ts', stating that he had intended to stand for 's[er]ten causys the whych co[n]cer[n]s the lyvy[n]gs of the pore pepyll and comyns *the which say* [my emphasis] the[y] be sore oppressyd be gentyll men be cause ther lyvy[n]gs is taken away'.[116] Such leadership sometimes came with its peculiar satisfactions. When in 1496, Lawrence Saunders was imprisoned for his opposition to the enclosure of the common fields of Coventry, the town's elite was troubled by the appearance of 'seducious billes' criticising

---

[114] PRO, SP11/14/26; PRO, STAC4/3/8; PRO, STAC4/3/17.
[115] PRO, STAC5/B96/39.   [116] PRO, SP1/119, fol. 33r.

his imprisonment. One bill observed how the town's governors had 'hunted the hare / You holde him in a snare'; another lamented how 'he that speketh for our right is in the hall / And that is shame for yewe and for us all / You cannot denygh hit but he is your brother'.[117]

The willingness of some labouring people to assume such leading roles, coupled with the record of their punishment, presents the historian of popular politics with both an opportunity and a dilemma. The opportunity lies in the clarity with which the deliberately transgressive speech of such popular leaders was recorded by the scripting hand of repression. Nowhere does the archival record of the suppression of popular political speech represent the plebeian voice with greater clarity or with less methodological complexity than in those cases where labouring people stood forth before the authorities and without apparent regard to the consequences, spoke their minds. But such moments also present us with a dilemma: that of accounting for the motives for that dangerously public speech. Were such individuals reckless? Or foolish? Or brave? Or were they so frustrated by the imprisoning structures of contemporary power relations that their anger simply burst out? How, therefore, should we explain the meaning, context and significance of such deliberately transgressive speeches? Such problems are best illuminated through example.

Robert Burnam of Norwich had been one of Kett's rebels in the summer of 1549. He felt little respect for his rulers and was prepared to voice such contempt at the most dangerous of times. Less than a month after the defeat of the insurrection, Burnam stood before the Norwich Mayor's Court and uttered a defiant statement of contempt for the city's magistracy. The clerk of the Mayor's Court recorded the ensuing exchange between Robert Burnam and the Mayor as follows:

Mr Mayor ye do me wrong to kepe me here w[i]t[h]out any cause where unto Mr Mayor answered and sayed noo Burnam I kepe the not here, and he sayed yes, ye scribes and pharisees ye seke innocent bloude, But if I cannot have Justice here, I shall have it of bettermen and I ask no favour at your hands.

Following this encounter, Burnam was offered the opportunity to retract his opinions. The churchwardens of his parish came to him 'and did advyse him to turne his harte and become a newe man'. Upon Burnam's reply that he had given no offence, he was reminded of his reputation: that one gentleman who had been captured by the rebels had said that 'he was not affrayd of his lief of no man but of the saide Burnam'. Upon Burnam's angry response that 'There are to many gentylmen in Englande by five hundred,' the churchwardens warned him that he faced prison. The following midsummer, Burnam was

---

[117] Tawney and Power (eds.), *Tudor economic documents*, III, 12–13.

appointed to the watch. While touring the streets, he treated his fellow watchman to a protracted diatribe concerning the ills of the nation.[118] He began by denouncing the Norfolk gentry as traitors and 'theves', saying that the watch should be maintained against them. Recollecting the camping time, he wished that the rebels had treated the gentry with greater severity and concluded that 'If the gentylmen mighte have the higher hande styll the poore comons shulde be trodden under Foote; and [the gentry would] destroye the Realme.' Like other speakers of dangerous words, 'he was requyred to leave such talke But he wolde not'. As the watch passed Burnam's parish church, St Gregory's, he burst into criticism of the Crown's recent confiscation of parish goods, regretting that the money he had donated to the church had been seized by the gentlemen. These were dangerous words, linking social and religious critique at a time of renewed anxiety about popular disorder: across southern England, the authorities braced themselves for a repetition of the events of the midsummer of 1549.[119] Like his fellow watchman, who promptly revealed his speech to the magistrates, some of Burnam's neighbours also felt that he had become a liability: John Petyver remarked that 'a goode worde were as sone spoken as an evell and that Burnam were a foole'. This opinion seemed confirmed by the judicial punishment inflicted upon Burnam: in 1550, as a consequence of his errant speech, his ears were cut off at the pillory.[120]

Burnam's verbal dissidence therefore highlights three significant issues: firstly, the truculent refusal of some individuals to be silenced, whatever the threat; secondly, the active co-operation of others in maintaining surveillance of popular opinion; thirdly, the contempt shown by some labouring people towards dissident members of their community. The social historian of popular politics, distant from the terrifying exercise of power in post-rebellion Norwich, may choose to see Burnam as articulating some wider plebeian ideology; but at the time, at least for some of his neighbours, we should remember that it seemed self-evident that 'Burnam were a foole'.

Whether foolish or not, Robert Burnam's words were recognised as dangerous. In part, this recognition flowed from the content of his speech; but it also concerned their context. Robert Burnam was not the only plebeian dissident to use the Norwich guildhall as a stage. In Easter 1550, the fishmonger Jerome Quasshe was recorded as having 'sayd openly' to the Norwich magistracy

---

[118] NRO, NCR/16A/6, pp. 1–2; NRO, NCR/12A/1(a), fols. 8r–9v. Burnam's use of the term 'pharisee' may identify him as an evangelical: see Shagan, *Popular politics*, 21, 232.

[119] A midsummer watch was ordered by the London authorities in 1550: CLRO, Journal 16, fol. 65r. For other trouble in Norwich during the midsummer of 1550, see Chapter 2.

[120] NRO, NCR/16A/6, pp. 52, 82.

That their satte on the benche That w[i]t[h]in theis xxxtie yeares had no shepe; and nowe have a thousande and more then they oughte to have; and ii or iii fermes; and yet nothing is spoken of them.

Quasshe's hostile analysis of the increased wealth of the Norwich magistrates was apparently inspired by their decision to lower the price of fish at a time of dearth of other foodstuffs. But clearly, his dismissive critique of elite social mobility both touched a sore spot amongst the occupants of the Bench and hinted at the rebel politics of 1549. It is therefore unsurprising to find that Jerome was imprisoned and condemned to the pillory for his words.[121] As he underwent his humiliating punishment, some of his neighbours came to talk with him. In their subsequent testimony, these men and women explained how Quasshe had continued to revile the Bench as 'knaves', remarking that

the clog he had uppon his heele was for no matter neyther felony nor treason And he might as well speke the words that he spake of Shepe as they mighte speke the words that they spake of hering [that is, the recent reduction in the price of fish].

Johane Greene responded that the magistracy had lowered the price of herrings 'for a comon wealthe', but Quasshe replied 'Thenne lette the knaves do thereafter.' Another of his neighbours called him 'a folisshe knave', remarking that 'Ye talke ye cannot tell whereof.' Finally, Robert Collerd told Quasshe that he was 'a folysshe brabling fellowe for ye shuld talke in place as ye shulde talke for there was no place for to utter any suche matter'.[122]

   Like Robert Burnam, Jerome Quasshe had therefore to face popular scorn for his lack of discretion. But also like Burnam, Quasshe had made use of the public space afforded by the guildhall to speak his dangerous words. Just as the poverty of 'poor men' sometimes compelled them to speak, so the religious transformations of the mid-Tudor period forced angry words into men and women's mouths. On 8 December 1550, the King's Lynn carpenter Thomas Derling found himself in trouble for having opined 'That ther is nothing set forth this daye in the Church of this Realme of Inglande That is justely agreable to Goddes worde'. Those present at his speech included the Mayor, Sheriff and other leading aldermen. The following April, Derling once again gave vent to his religious opinions before the Norwich magistracy, exclaiming in the guildhall that

if prayor and supplication be not made the realme of Englande woll come to destruction; and that my lord riche and his company woll make the kyng . . . a poore king and dysceyve him if the king do not take hede.[123]

---

[121] NRO, NCR/20A/2, fol. 40r. For Quasshe's trade, see NRO, NCR/16A/6, p. 93.
[122] NRO, NCR/16A/6, pp. 54–5.   [123] NRO, NCR/16A/6, pp. 90, 103.

Shortly after Derling's rash words in the guildhall, Lord Rich wrote to the Norwich magistracy, instructing them to send Derling to London in order to be interrogated by the Council.[124]

In order to explain the significance of this key site for the statement of rebellious speeches, we must return to the concept of the 'speech event' outlined in the preceding section. Edifices such as the Norwich guildhall were designed to both spell out magisterial authority within the urban landscape and provide a location for structured speech events, such as formal speeches and presentations, the impanelment of lawcourts and the convocation of aldermanic councils. In using the guildhall as the stage for their dramatic rebel speeches, Burnam and Quasshe deliberately broke the established rules for such speech events and thereby inverted the civic hierarchy in its most sensitive site; for early modern urban rulers were especially conscious of the importance of guildhalls to the display of their social and political authority. Robert Tittler has identified a close connection between the increasing assertiveness of sixteenth-century urban oligarchs and the construction or extension of guildhalls. In Tittler's analysis, the development of a distinct mayoral role inspired the 'corresponding emergence of "mayoral space" as a specialised development within civic halls and structures ... No office better exemplifies the growth of oligarchy than this, none better illustrates the adaptation of the built environment for political ends.'[125] The location of the guildhall, with its attendant pillory and whipping post standing alongside the plebeian swirl of the marketplace, spelt out the presence of oligarchic authority, backed by legal and physical force, within the heart of the city. Thus, the Norwich guildhall represented more than simply the site of magisterial domination; it also formed the physical and symbolic projection of that domination into the urban landscape.

Guildhalls were intended to provide the site for the retraction of seditious speech, not its elaboration. Within early modern culture, the retraction of dangerous speech represented a moment of ritual purgation.[126] In 1517, for instance, one vocal critic of the magistracy of Leicester was given the opportunity to rescind his words; he did so 'apon his kne[e]s' and 'askyt the meyr and his bredir oponly forgyfnes in the face of the cort and so was pardonyd'.[127] After the Norwich magistracy judged that Thomas Butte had committed sedition in criticising the distribution of food within the city in 1551, he responded by 'being sory and p[ro]mysing ammendeme[n]te hereafter',

---

[124] NRO, NCR/16A/6, p. 110.
[125] R. Tittler, 'Political culture and the built environment of the English country town, c. 1540–1620', in Hoak (ed.), *Tudor political culture*, 150.
[126] Kamensky, *Governing the tongue*, 127–49.
[127] M. Bateson (ed.), *Records of the Borough of Leicester, 1509–1603*, 3 vols. (Cambridge, 1905), III, 4.

agreeing that he would 'accomplisshe and p[er]forme' whatever act of contrition the court demanded of him by way of penalty.[128] Similarly, after exhibiting a seditious bill against the government of London at St Paul's Cross, the grocer John Wilson was required to submit to the Mayor and aldermen 'moost humblye upon his knees', confessing his offence and asking their mercy.[129]

James C. Scott's theorisation of authority is alive to the significance of such rituals of humiliation and repentance. He observes how power reasserts itself through dissidents' public retraction of their actions:

the subordinate, who has publicly violated norms of domination, announces by way of a public apology that he disassociates himself from the offence and reaffirms the rule in question. He publicly accepts, in other words, the judgment of his superior that this is an offence and thus, implicitly, the censure or punishment that follows from it.

Scott concludes that such moments 'offer ... *a show of discursive affirmation from below*, which is all the more valuable since it contributes to the impression that the symbolic order is willingly accepted by its least advantaged members'.[130] In breaking such rituals, and in transgressing 'mayoral space', Burnam, Quasshe and the others therefore gave a special power to their insulting words.

How should we make sense of such speech? Peter Clark describes 'levelling' outbursts such as those spoken by Burnam and Quasshe as 'naive and often hysterical'.[131] This seems unfair. Although Burnam's words carried considerable risk, his hostility to elite social mobility made sense to many members of the commons in the mid-sixteenth century. Regarding Burnam and his peers as simply irrational seems both to reproduce contemporary elite stereotypes and to underestimate popular politics. Nonetheless, Burnam's willingness to articulate such dangerous opinions in the face of implacable authority demands explanation.

We may find some help in the task of explaining Robert Burnam's brazen speech in Michel Foucault's borrowing of the concept of parrhesia, or 'truth-telling', from ancient Greek political philosophy. Foucault identified parrhesia as 'the practice of speaking one's mind, often in situations in which it is dangerous to do so because of the power of one's interlocutor'.[132] Deploying this formulation, we might understand Robert Burnam as a parrhesiast. Indeed, there are hints that in certain circumstances, lower-class speakers might expect contemporary governors to grant them unusual liberties of free

---

[128] NRO, NCR/16A/6, p. 107.
[129] CLRO, Journal 16, fol. 95r. For other examples, see CLRO, Rep 12 (1), fols. 83v, 86r; NRO, NCR/16A/6, p. 294; NRO, NCR/16A/5, pp. 314, 549; NRO, NCR/16A/4, fol. 59v.
[130] Scott, *Domination*, 57.   [131] Clark, *Provincial society*, 250.
[132] J. Simons, *Foucault and the political* (London, 1995), 93–4.

speech. Such expectations flew in the face of the proper silence expected from subordinates within contemporary elite political theory and so remained dangerous; yet parrhesia represented a small and hitherto unobserved fissure within that otherwise unyielding system of thought.

The conventional notion that poor men spoke plainly and with honesty ran through Protector Somerset's social policy, and underpinned his communications with the 1549 rebels. It is most clearly apparent in an exchange between Somerset and the London butchers who were called to account for the high price of meat. In answer, the butchers explained the high prices as a consequence of the domination of the beef trade by covetous gentlemen. Notably, Somerset's Council was warned by one butcher how their oppression of the commons would bring them down:

> Look ye my lords, although I am only a poor man, I will tell you plainly, for I would rather that you knew, even though I may be punished for my boldness, than that the poor people should suffer as they do.

Upon being told by the Protector that he 'might speak what he had in his mind without fear', the butcher proceeded to denounce Sir William Paget for his 'notorious' oppression of the poor commons of Northamptonshire.[133] In the end, Somerset's willingness to accept the rebellious commons' rhetorical strategies led to his fall from power. Yet in allowing a voice to the commotioners, Somerset extended an established social practice. We find similar examples of gentlemen, noblemen and monarchs displaying a tolerance for and attention towards honest plebeian social critique. In 1525, when the Dukes of Norfolk and Suffolk encountered armed rebels at Lavenham (Suffolk) demonstrating against Cardinal Wolsey's Amicable Grant, they asked the rebels to send out delegates to present their case. The weavers' representatives were led by 'a little man, wizened and ill-formed' called John Grene. The old weaver impressed the Dukes' retinue: Ellis Griffith recalled how he 'heard Sir Humphrey Wingfield, who was esteemed one of the ablest lawyers at Gray's Inn, say that no four of the ablest lawyers in the kingdom, even after a week's consultation, could make an answer so meet as did the weaver within less than two hours' space'.[134] Grene's eloquent advocacy of the weavers' case persuaded the Dukes to represent the rebels' complaints to Henry VIII.

Parrhesia, therefore, may have had a function within early modern society, enabling communication up and down the social hierarchy within a polity that was otherwise supposed to be closed to the popular voice. Ironically, it seems that plebeian status could in some circumstances *guarantee* the right to

---

[133] M. A. Sharp Hume, *Chronicle of King Henry VIII of England* (London, 1889), 170–1.
[134] HMC, *Welsh*, I, iv.

speak. Just as labouring people might manipulate their social status in order to avoid entrapment in dangerous political situations by protesting that they were but poor men and women with weak memories, so popular claims to powerlessness, 'poverty' and 'simplicity' opened many complaints to equity courts.[135] Contemporary dramatic works echoed such assumptions. The character 'People', who articulated popular complaint in Nicholas Udall's 1553 play *Respublica*, spoke in 'a stylised literary dialect intended to represent the language of humble provincial folk'.[136] A generation later, dramatists of Shakespeare's era worked within similar assumptions. The character Honesty introduces himself to the monarch as a man who goes 'plaine, and my name is Honesty / a friend to your Grace, but a foe to flatterers'. Later in the play, Honesty introduces the King to Piers Plowman, who personifies the commons and who asks the King to put down the oppressors of the commons. The King responds positively, remarking that 'I perceive, though Honesty be simple / yet manie tymes he speakes trueth . . . For manie tymes such simple manners he / Bewray much matter in simplicitie.'[137] It seems, therefore, that on certain occasions the plebeian voice was allowed to speak truth to power. The special significance accorded to such moments both highlights the typicality of elite expectations of plebeian silence and points towards the power that words enjoyed within early modern culture.

Whereas modern western culture conventionally distinguishes between words and action, early modern people did not. Instead, as Garthine Walker has observed, 'in early modern culture . . . verbal utterance was understood to be a form of action, not merely its weak, binary other'.[138] Since speech was about power, it was also about agency: as Catherine Belsey puts it, 'to speak is to possess meaning, to have access to the language which defines, delimits and locates power. To speak is to become a subject.'[139] The power of speech was ubiquitous within early modern culture. The practice of oath-taking, for instance, was understood as a forceful speech act in which intent, veracity and divinity were intermingled. Instead of perceiving of oaths as a mere formulaic precursor to the presentation of the real business – the evidence itself – contemporaries understood that oaths bound their takers in the eyes of God: one errant oath-taker was warned by a magistrate that 'in swearing the truthe you shall but doe yor duety & yf you forsweare yor self God will

---

[135] For an example of 'poor men' protesting that they could not remember certain seditious words, see PRO, SP1/123, fols. 47v–49r.

[136] A. Fox, *Oral and literate culture in England, 1500–1700* (Oxford, 2000), 70.

[137] Anon., *A most pleasant and merie new comedie, intutled, a knacke to knowe a knave* (London, 1594), sigs. A3r–v, E3r.

[138] Walker, *Crime*, 99.

[139] C. Belsey, *The subject of tragedy: identity and difference in Renaissance drama* (London, 1985), 191.

punishe you'. Witnesses were expected to have 'the feare of God before [their] eyes'. Such assumptions were borne out by the experience of one false witness who, while giving untruthful evidence, 'did sudaynly fall downe as dead wth a fearfull and pittifull cry'; he was carried from the courtroom and after taking two hours to recover, cried out 'O lord have mercy upon me I have sworne I knowe not what.'[140]

Just as some words had the power to *do*, so other words had the power to *undo*: in her study of the power of speech in early American society, Kamensky emphasises 'the ways in which speech was tangible' within that world, including the multiplicity of means by which words could be 'eaten, recanted – in the period vernacular, *unsaid*'.[141] This was equally true of Tudor England. Here, too, public recantation could form an especially powerful speech act, in which dangerous words could be withdrawn through bodily and verbal rituals of repentance and regret. In 1533, the Suffolk shoemaker Guye Glason employed such a strategy in order to escape further punishment for having stated that

I wolde not wurship the crosse ner the crucyfyxe and if that I hade the Rode that standeth in the monasterye of Eye in my yerde I wolde brenne it. And shyte upon its hed to make it a foote hyegher then it is. And that I wolde wurship noon ymages of Sayntes.

In his 'Admission' to the Bishop, Guye swore never again to 'kepe or affyrme or speyke the same', and 'humbly' offered himself 'with contricon of herte'. The Norfolk labourer Richard Clarke took a similar path in April 1606 when he had admitted to the county magistracy that he had proposed a popular insurrection to his workmates, 'but he did speake yt unadvisedlye, and is sorrye for it'.[142]

This awareness of the power of words was most clearly evident in the practical exercise of popular politics. Underlying the repression of popular political speech was more than a pragmatic desire to shut down the public sphere; governors' actions were informed by the perception that words acted and that, in particular, political words constituted political worlds. This sensitivity to language coloured Sir Anthony Aucher's denunciation of Somerset's negotiations with the Kentish rebels known as 'Commonwealths'. In his influential letter of September 1549, Aucher warned 'that yf wordes maye doe harme or maybe be treason or any ylle come of them, ther was never none that ever spake so vyllye as these called Common Welthes doe'.[143]

[140] PRO, STAC8/18/1.34; PRO, STAC5/D23/29.
[141] Kamensky, *Governing the tongue*, 120–1.
[142] NRO, DN/ACT/4b, fol. 36r; NRO, NQS C/S3/15, information of Richard Braye. For other examples of verbal recantations, see, NRO, NCR/16A/5, p. 549; NRO, NCR/16A/6, p. 99.
[143] PRO, SP10/8/56.

The early modern sense that words could act anticipates twentieth-century theories of the relationship between speech and power. Especially important in such theorisations has been the work of J. L. Austin, who proposed that certain types of speech – 'speech acts' – rather than simply offering a descriptive label for reality, actually *operate* within the material world. Hence, Austin observed that 'language can ... make things happen, bringing a previously non-existent state of affairs into being'. In this formulation, such 'performative utterances' 'do not "describe" or "report" ... anything at all; they are, instead, "the performing of an action"'; hence, 'to *say* something is to *do* something'. For Austin, such speech acts can only be successful if they are recognised and accepted as transformative of a situation or relationship.[144]

When combined with sensitivity to class relations, this interest in the material effects of speech brings us close to early modern appreciations of the power of words. This allows us to understand the historical relationship between language, popular politics and social conflict in new ways. Most importantly for our purposes, it allows us to sidestep sterile confrontations between materialist and postmodernist historians concerning the now hoary question of whether class is an 'economic' or 'linguistic' category.[145] Instead, this conjoining of linguistic and social interpretation liberates us to see language as both operative within and potentially transformative of material contexts. Thus, successfully rebellious speech acts can *call* social identities into existence, providing a unifying political language that renders on-going social conflicts comprehensible within a larger framework and thereby *makes* class identities. In the case of the 1549 rebellions, the capacity of rebel organisers to identify a unifying set of interests that defined the 'commons' as a political entity, coupled with a strategy to effect a lasting 'reformation' of English society, grew from a political language which provided a unifying set of concepts. As Donald Sassoon puts it, the 'act of [social] identification was also one of creation'; thus, the invention of class-based political categories – in 1549, the opposition between the interests of the 'poor commons' and the 'rich men' – is proof that 'Those who define, create.'[146] In Edward Thompson's enduring formulation, 'class' therefore

---

[144] J. L. Austin, *How to do things with words* (Cambridge, MA, 1975), 5–6, 12.

[145] For representative texts in this debate, see N. Kirk, 'History, language, ideas and postmodernism: a materialist view', *Social History*, 19, 2 (1994), 221–40; P. Joyce, *Democratic subjects: the self and the social in nineteenth-century England* (Cambridge, 1994), 1–20. For ways out of this now sterile debate, see P. Curry, 'Towards a post-Marxist social history: Thompson, Clark and beyond', in A. Wilson (ed.), *Rethinking social history: English society, 1570–1920 and its interpretation* (Manchester, 1993), 158–200; Epstein, *In practice*, 1–56, 106–25.

[146] D. Sassoon, *One hundred years of socialism: the West European left in the twentieth century* (London, 1996), 7–8.

happens when some men [and women], as a result of common experiences . . . feel and
articulate the identity of their interests as between themselves, and as against other
men [and women] whose interests are different from (and usually opposed to) theirs

but with the added twist that this moment of class 'feeling' is rendered
politically meaningful through the creative power of language.[147]

IV SOCIAL SOLIDARITIES AND SPEECH COMMUNITIES

It was an awareness of how words acted within the social world, just as much
as a principled stubbornness, which caused plebeian dissidents to refuse to
retract dangerous words despite even the greatest of threats. The Norwich
Protestant Cicely Ormes found herself moved to dangerous speech at the
execution of two of her faith on 13 July 1557. The wife of a poor weaver, she
exclaimed that 'she would pledge them of the same cup that they drank on'.
Her words were heard by John Corbet, a prosperous lawyer and a prominent
member of the civic elite, who presented her to the diocesan authorities.
During protracted examinations, she continued to uphold her beliefs.
Notably, she was asked by her interrogator 'if she would go to the Church
and keep her tongue'. Such verbal censorship was beyond her: Ormes
answered that if she closed her mouth, 'God would surely plague her'. She
was burnt on 23 September 1558.[148]

The deliberate force given by labouring people to their criticism of the
world in which they lived could be heightened by their willingness to spice
their speech with oaths and profanities. Exclamations such as 'By the mass'
or 'By God' represented more than simple punctuations but instead were
intended to give an added weight to an outburst. Witnesses to seditious
speech often mentioned how such oaths preceded especially dangerous
phrases. In December 1540, for instance, a Norwich constable's demand
for payments towards city tolls met with the response from one citizen that
'by godds sowle he wold had rather [the aldermen] were sleyne than he wold
paye itt'. In June 1550, Robert Ederych betrayed the speech of the weaver
John Whyte, who had exclaimed to him 'That by the masse we shall have as
hoote a somere as ever was; and . . . sayed that this somere shulde be as evell
and busy as the last somer was'. A few days later, the Norwich magistrates
heard testimony from another weaver concerning the words of William
White, who had claimed that the Duke of Northumberland had been over-
thrown. Warned 'to take heede what he spake', White defiantly responded
'by the masse he durst be bolde to speke it'.[149]

---

[147] E. P. Thompson, *The making of the English working class* (London, 1963), 10–11.
[148] McClendon, *The quiet Reformation*, 175.
[149] NRO, NCR/16A/5, p. 37; NRO, NCR/12A/1(a), fol. 5r–v.

William White's words were intended to elicit a positive response from his audience, drawing them into a favourable but potentially dangerous response to his inaccurate account of Northumberland's troubles. White's speech, then, was intended to act *socially* – to invoke a collective response within which individual opinions would be validated by the wider group. Sociolinguistics supplies us with another useful concept that enables us to come to a fuller understanding of such words: that of the speech community. The originator of the concept of the speech community has explained how

> tentatively, a speech community is defined as a community sharing rules for the conduct and interpretation of speech, and rules for the interpretation of at least one linguistic variety ... self-conceptions, values, role structures, contiguity, purposes of interaction, political history, all may be factors ... the essential thing is that the object of description be an integral social unit. Probably it will prove most useful to reserve the notion of speech community for the local units most specifically characterised for a person by common localities and primary interaction.[150]

This emphasis upon the interrelationship of language, social relations and place – that is, in Hymes' terms, common localities and primary interaction – has a special resonance for the early modern period. Contemporaries were well aware of how accents and dialects defined 'countries' and neighbourhoods and hence how speech patterns represented the conjunction between social identity and local belonging.

Local knowledge, then, was intermixed with local speech. In 1519, John Jovy substantiated his claim that Agnes Drake was a heretic on the grounds that it was commonly reported by trustworthy persons in the streets of Wymondham.[151] Similarly, William Thurston knew that the gentleman Roger Woodhouse was a violent and disorderly man because 'beinge a neighbor he hearde it comonly talked in the towne' of New Buckenham; Richard Watts cited the 'daily speeche & reporte of the neighbors' to the same effect.[152] This was full of political potential. Most obviously, the everyday life of the village revolved around rumour and gossip – that a neighbour was a witch; that a man was a bad husband; that customary laws had once been challenged by a tyrannical lord.[153] The inhabitants of a locality were thereby brought together as members of a speech community that was united as the 'common voice'.

---

[150] D. Hymes, 'Models of the interaction of language and social life', in J. J. Gumperz and D. Hymes (eds.), *Directions in sociolinguistics: the ethnography of communication* (New York, 1972), 54.

[151] NRO, DN/ACT/3a, 1518–19, fols. 67r, 69v.   [152] PRO, STAC10/6/182.

[153] For an example of the everyday politics of rumour, see S. Hindle, 'The shaming of Margaret Knowsley: gossip, gender and the experience of authority in early modern England', *Continuity and Change*, 9 (1994), 391–419.

But plebeian politics could generate a wider, macro-political community. Here the 'common locality' might span a neighbourhood, a county, a region or the realm; and the 'primary interaction' in question concerned state politics. The best examples of moments at which such larger speech communities emerged within popular politics are the crises of 1536–7 and 1549. In both cases, we see the rapid dissemination of specific rumours occurring over a wide geography. The precise content of such rumours varied – in 1536 in Yorkshire and Lincolnshire it was said that the King intended the destruction of half the parish churches of the realm; in the south in 1537 it was reported that the King was dead; in Devon and Cornwall in 1549 that new taxes would soon be levied; in Norfolk in the same year that the treacherous gentry prevented Protector Somerset from communicating with the commons – but their political significance was nonetheless identical. In all cases, the spread of such rumours proved a unifying force, binding together the inhabitants of disparate regions, towns and villages to form a single speech community. Thus, when two Northamptonshire men visited Leicester in 1538, they were told that 'it is comonyd in thys countrey that the kyng and the prynce be bothe deade'.[154] Similarly, 'the comon voyce' spoke in Orford against the local lord.[155] In both cases, a unified common voice spoke.

The tendency of Tudor governors to perceive of popular politics as a 'common voice' presented dissidents with certain advantages. Most obviously, it cloaked political organisation behind a screen of anonymity. Thus, the rioters who gathered together to drive off an intruding flock of sheep from one Norfolk common in 1553 hid the leadership of the protest by claiming that they came together because 'there was a voice ymongest theym' that they should do so.[156] Following the defeat of the Lincolnshire rising of 1536, the vicar of Louth obscured the identity of those of his parishioners who had first argued for a rebellion. Firstly, he denied any personal involvement in the organisation of the rising: 'towchyng the Insurrection yt was yet unknowne to hyme'. Secondly, although he knew that 'certaine words ... was spoken' in which it was alleged that the King intended the dissolution of every second parish church in the realm, he declined to identify who spoke such words, instead observing simply that it caused 'the peple [to] grudge very sore'. He made no pretence as to the gravity of the rumour, observing that this rumour was 'The immediat cawse' of the insurrection, which 'the pore men herd tell' on 1 October 1536; but who did the telling, the vicar replied that 'I can not tell who shuld be the deviser of yt,' instead claiming that he could only describe the collective speech as 'yt was reported'. Finally, he experienced a further lapse of memory: 'But who yt were that grudge against the supremacy of the kynge &

---

[154] PRO, E36/120, fol. 57r.   [155] PRO, STAC2/21/93.   [156] PRO, STAC10/16, fol. 24r–v.

puttyng downe of the Popes auctoritie he can not tell the naymes severally bycause yt ys not in hys remembraunce.' This lack of precision was compared to the clarity of his memory concerning the collective 'brutys & voys' within the locality.[157]

A few months later, John Halom experienced similar difficulties in identifying those responsible for the spread of rumours that the commons of Beverley (Yorkshire) should take their weapons and rise: asked who had given forth such speech, he 'answered that he coulde specifie no mans names more than other ... but that it was a hole co[mm]en voyce'.[158] Similarly, the protesters at Cheshunt in 1548, asked to identify the individuals who had passed on news concerning the arrival of the enclosure commissioners on the common, responded in an equally enigmatic fashion. The Cheshunt yeoman John Thompson remembered hearing of the arrival of the commissioners but explained that 'that he cannot now tell who told it him. But hard it reported in the towne.' Likewise, Simon Pon heard 'a voice' to this effect; and Thomas Chayer, remembered a 'comon voyce and brute'. None of them, however, could remember the names of any who had articulated this 'comon voyce'. John Thompson denied the existence of any organisation behind the appearance of the crowd that met the enclosure commission on Cheshunt common. Still more unlikely, Thompson went on to deny any unity of popular interest in the defence of the common: 'he knowith of no man[ner] of frendshipp shewed in this matt[er] ... but that ev[ery] man is glad to do the best he can to save his right in the comon'.[159]

The notion of the 'common voice' therefore proved useful to those attempting to occlude popular political organisation or to avoid accusations of seditious speech. There were other strategies for evading prosecution for sedition. Perhaps the most common was to accuse others of involvement in a dangerous conversation, an action which tended to initiate a chain of prosecutions. Only in a few cases did an individual admit their seditious speech without attempting to further implicate others.[160] Another strategy was simply to deny the alleged speech. A third was to prevaricate, claiming that there were subtle but important differences in the actual speech from that which was alleged.[161] Alternatively, the accused might offer an apology, claiming that they misunderstood the words spoken, or that they failed to understand its significance altogether: Richard Branborowe, accused of spreading a seditious prophecy, responded that 'yor pore orator neve[r] thoughte nor spake nor nev[er] dyd knowe whatt the p[ro]phese[y] dyd

---

[157] PRO, SP1/110, fols. 157r–158v.   [158] PRO, E36/119, fol. 25r.
[159] PRO, STAC10/16, fols. 137r–152r.   [160] For example, see PRO, SP1/119, fol. 37r.
[161] For an example of the latter strategy, see PRO, SP1/106, fol. 134r–v.

meane'.[162] Another common strategy was to blame an outburst of seditious speech upon alcohol: Margaret Chaunseler explained away her description of Anne Boleyn as 'a goggyll-eyed hoore' on the grounds 'that she was drunken when she did speke them & that the evill sperite did cause hir to speke them'.[163]

There were other ways of evading implication in seditious speech. One frequent tactic was to claim to have forgotten certain events. Thus, following an accusation made against him by a neighbour that, during an argument, he had uttered seditious words, Thomas Poole claimed that 'because they were bothe in fury he dothe not fully rememb[e]r ... [his] very words'.[164] Another tactic was to plead ignorance. When the neighbours of a Nottinghamshire man who had criticised the Council as 'pollyng harlotts' found themselves in trouble for failing to denounce him, they answered that 'they nev[er] knewe howe daungerous nor heynous the wordes were agaynst the kyngs grace for if they had knowne the p[er]ill of them they wolde have opened them as sone as they were spoken'.[165] Similarly, John Cook of Orford remembered 'well' how, during the 1549 rebellion, the widely disliked bailiff of the town 'was set in the stoks in the Rebellyon time for the space of iii daies and iii nyghts but by whom he knowethe not'.[166] The rebellious people of Cheshunt suffered similar lapses of memory in 1548, when they were asked to name the organisers of their protests: Henry Dellow, for instance, told the Star Chamber that he 'doth not now rememb[e]r' who spread the rumour of the arrival of the enclosure commissioners on the town's common. His neighbour William Carle was similarly vague. He remembered that 'the people' had gone to 'entret' the commissioners 'to be good unto them for ther comon', but he could not remember the names of any person who was present amongst that crowd: 'ther names he cannot tell, nor yet ... who p[ro]cured them to be ther'. He denied that 'the people' carried weapons to the mass lobby of the commissioners, but admitted that he had carried a bow and arrow; but this was, he claimed, only 'to pas the tyme'; further pressed, he answered that 'he cannot now declare the names of them all that had wepons ther bicaus of the nombre that was ther'.[167]

Alternatively, the accused could simply deny that dangerous words had been spoken: Anne Folfar of Diss denied widow Miles' allegation that she

[162] PRO, SP1/108, fol. 250r. For another example, see PRO, SP1/108, fol. 250r.
[163] PRO, SP1/89, fol. 158r. For other examples of the link between alcohol and dangerous speech, see NRO, NCR/16A/3, pp. 15–16; NRO, NCR/16A/4, fol. 61v; NRO, NCR/16A/5, pp. 268–9; NRO, NCR/12A/1(a), fol. 136. For a later but nonetheless revealing example of how alcohol could be used as a cover for seditious speech, see PRO, SP16/185/55(II).
[164] PRO, SP1/116, fol. 356r.   [165] PRO, E36/120, fols. 96r–97r.   [166] PRO, STAC4/10/76.
[167] PRO, STAC10/16, fols. 133r–137r, 143v–145r.

had spread the rumour that the unmarried Queen Mary was pregnant, 'taking god to recorde that she never thought nor spake any such words as the said widow miles dowghter hath declared towching the Quenes heighnes nor any other p[er]son or p[er]sons hard spoken'.[168] Wider rebel networks could be concealed behind a smokescreen of forgetfulness. Zachary Mannsell, interrogated in 1586 for his role in an attempted insurrection, explained that the proposed rising stemmed from his seditious conversation with 'a mann travelinge to London, whose name this Exam[inant] knoweth not' who complained about the price of food, and opined 'that poore men could not contynue longe in this sort'.[169] Likewise, four shoemakers from Eye and Harleston (Suffolk) were accused of heresy in 1533. An important element in the accusation involved the claim that one of their number, Thomas Fenne, had acquired his erroneous opinions from a 'man p[re]tending hymself to be lernid'. The authorities were keen to identify this heretical preacher, but Fenne did not prove tractable. At first, the clerk of the court noted simply that 'Thomas Fenne . . . wold make noo direct aunswer.' Fenne proved more talkative after a spell in prison; but even then he remained insistent that the heretical preacher was unknown to him, claiming that he had conversed with a man 'p[re]tending hymself to be lernid whose name he saith he knoweth not, and he shewid him that he not to worship noon ymages nor the crucifix'.[170]

In contrast to those situations in which neighbourly and popular solidarities collapsed, resulting in a bustle of denunciations, subordinates' capacity to maintain that they had learnt political gossip from the anonymous 'common voice' presented their governors with the hard, unbreakable face of a united commonality. Just as political gossip constituted speech communities, so it also constituted communities of silence. This perhaps explains the (sometimes misplaced) confidence with which labouring people gave voice to their political opinions in public. Quite correctly, the plebeian alehouse has been identified as a primary location at which seditious speech was uttered. James Scott even goes so far as to suggest that alehouses represented 'a privileged site for the transmission of popular culture . . . that was usually at odds with official culture'.[171] Yet, even so, a surprising variety of both public and secret locations were selected for the articulation of dissenting speech: not only in alehouses, but also 'in the strete'; at the church; in the churchyard; at the church-ale; in the marketplace; at the market cross; at

[168] BL., Cotton MS, Titus B II, fols. 182r–184v.
[169] H. T. White, 'A Hampshire plot', *Papers and Proceedings of the Hampshire Field Club and Archaeological Society*, 12 (1934), 55.
[170] NRO, DN/ACT/4b, 1532–3, fols. 34–7.   [171] Scott, *Domination*, 121.

fairs; in private houses, or outside in the courtyard; on the village green; at a
wedding; while out ferreting; even upon the deathbed.[172]

The willingness of some labouring people to spread political gossip may
have stemmed from the hostility exhibited towards those who betrayed plebeian political speech to the authorities. The evangelical Edward Underhill,
for instance, remembered how, during the reign of Edward VI, he was libelled
in a ballad as a 'spye ffor the duke off Northumberlande', and how this earned
him universal hostility: 'Thus became I odious unto most men, and many
tymes in daunger off my lyffe'.[173] Similarly, in their petition to Queen Mary,
the godly of Norfolk complained how

> now a man can go to no place, but malicious busybodies curiously search out his
> deeds, mark his words, and if he agree not with them in despising God's word, then
> will they spitefully and hatefully rail against him . . . calling [the godly] 'traitors' . . . we
> poor subjects, for speaking of that which is truth, and our bounden allegiance, are
> daily punished, railed upon, and noted for seditious, and not the Queen's friends.[174]

Popular gossip concerning the betrayal of the Walsingham rising emphasised
the contemptible nature of such treachery: one Bungay man told his neighbour that the 'Companye' had been betrayed by 'on[e] falsse knave that
discovered them'.[175] Likewise, in 1543, a Kentish clergyman told his parishioners that 'As Christ was accused by ii or iii false knaves, so a man may be
accused by ii or iii false knaves & the iu[d]ge as false a knave as the rest & so
be co[n]de[m]ned.'[176]

Of course, such hostility towards accusers indicated that the state could
sometimes rely upon accusations of seditious speech in order to repress
popular political gossip; but it is also indicative of the converse: that labouring people hid their political views behind a mask of compliance. In this way,
distinctions between a secretly articulated 'hidden transcript' of plebeian
dissidents and a 'public transcript' of apparent acquiescence begin to break
down. In its place, we find labouring people constantly monitoring one

---

[172] Alehouses: BL, Cotton MS, Caligula B I, fol. 156r–v; NRO, NCR/16A/4, fol. 61v; NRO,
NCR/12A/1(a), fol. 123r; streets: PRO, STAC10/16, fols. 133r–137r; PRO, SP1/106; PRO,
SP1/119, fol. 38r; churches: PRO, E36/120, fol. 69r; BL, Cotton MS, Titus B II, fols.
182r–184v; markets: NRO, NCR/16A/6, pp. 33, 68; NRO, NQS C/S3/12A, Presentment
of Gallow Hundred; BL, Cotton MS, Titus B II, fols. 182r–184v; market cross: NRO, NCR/
12A/1(a), fol. 33r; churchyard: PRO, SP1/119, fols. 35r, 36r; church-ale: PRO, SP1/123, fol.
122r; village green: NRO, NQS C/S3/15, information of Richard Braye; deathbed: NRO,
NCR/12A/1(a), fol. 1v; private houses: NRO, NCR/12A/1(a), fols. 9v–10r, 80v; at a wedding: NRO, NCR/12A/1(a), fols. 11v–12r; while out ferreting: BL, Cotton MS, Titus B I,
fols. 78r–79v; fairs: NRO, NCR/12A/1(a), fol. 44r.
[173] J. G. Nichols (ed.), *Narratives of the days of the Reformation* (Camden Society, 1st ser.,
LXXVII, London, 1859), 158–9; for other examples, see P. Collinson, *Godly people: essays
on English Protestantism and puritanism* (London, 1982), 406.
[174] Foxe, *Acts and monuments*, VIII, 127.   [175] PRO, SP1/120, fol. 104v.
[176] CCCC, MS 128, p. 10.

another's reactions to political gossip and hiding behind pretences of inno-
cence. Thus, in 1554, John Smith passed on a story concerning the alleged
pregnancy of Queen Mary to his neighbour John Wilby, adding the warning
'I pray you tell yt no further if you do I will denye yt.'[177] Similarly, in 1596,
the husbandman Edward Ewer was hanged for saying that 'yt would never be
a merrye worlde till her majestie was dead or killed; and that her majestie was
ruled by her lordes at ther pleasure, *but we must not saye soe*' (my emphasis).[178] This produced a kind of cognitive dissonance between appearance
and action, speech and silence. Quoting Shakespeare's Duke of York ('You
lose a thousand well-disposed hearts / And prick my tender patience to those
thoughts / Which honour and allegiance cannot think'), David Norbrook has
observed that 'absolutism depends for its maintenance on self-censorship, on
keeping subversive thoughts away from the threshold of consciousness'.
There is an agency at work here, but only of the most limited and self-
protective kind. Where the Tudor state could rely upon popular denunciations, plebeian dissidents perhaps felt that popular political culture had been
'poisoned ... with mistrust'.[179] An account of a political conversation conducted in the shadow of the difficult negotiations between the Crown and the
leaders of the Pilgrimage of Grace gives a striking impression of the difficulties involved in political talk: one loyalist gentleman remembered how he had
been at dinner with his peers when one of them asked what the rebel demands
were 'and evri man lokyd upon other & no man made answer'.[180] Certainly,
the evidence suggests that would-be rebels learnt to be careful in their
conversations. The very terminology employed in description of political
gossip suggests something of the hushed nature of such conversation: labouring people referred to the betrayal of their neighbours as having 'oppened &
disclosed' their neighbours' sayings.[181] One of the Walsingham rebels, having recruited a neighbour to the rebel cause, 'instantly desired [him] ... that
he wuld kepe his councell secretly'.[182]

Popular conspiracies, then, could be betrayed, sometimes even by those
involved in their organisation; hence popular politics faced the sometimes
insuperable obstacle of disclosure. Notably, Latimer remembered the 1530s
as 'a dangerous world, for it might soon cost a man his life for a word

---

[177] BL, Cotton MS, Titus B II, fols. 182r–184v.
[178] J. S. Cockburn (ed.), *Calendar of assize records: Kent indictments, Elizabeth I* (London,
1979), no. 2442.
[179] D. Norbrook, '"A liberal tongue": language and rebellion in *Richard II*', in John M.
Mucciolo (ed.), *Shakespeare's universe: Renaissance ideas and conventions: essays in honour of W. R. Elton* (Aldershot, 1996), 43; and quoting one former East German dissident:
B. Miller, *Narratives of guilt and compliance in unified Germany: Stasi informers and their
impact on society* (London, 1999), 101.
[180] PRO, SP1/113, fol. 70r–v.   [181] PRO, SP1/128, fol. 110v.   [182] PRO, SP1/119, fol. 36r.

speaking'.[183] But as a counterweight to the evidence of betrayal, it is worth recalling the obvious surprise of the Council to the outbreak of the East Anglian rebellions in July 1549.[184] Popular politics, it has been argued in this chapter, depended crucially upon the flow of political information and opinion. Similarly, in criminalising plebeian political speech, the treason and sedition legislation intended to break up popular politics, atomising and localising it. Yet the evidence of the wide geography and co-ordinated outbreak of the 1549 rebellions, like that of the 1536, provides stark evidence that at certain moments popular politics could remained closed and opaque to rulers. The evidence presented here therefore demonstrates how the organisation of the 1549 rebellions represented an *achievement*. Having assessed the politics of speech and silence, in the next chapter we consider the ideological content of that language.

[183] Latimer, *Sermons*, 149.   [184] MacCulloch, 'Kett's rebellion'.

4

Rebel political language

Class does not coincide with the sign community . . . Thus different classes will use one and the same language. As a result, differently oriented accents intersect in every ideological sign. Sign becomes an arena of the class struggle . . . The very same thing that makes the ideological sign vital and mutable is also, however, that which makes it a refracting and distorting medium. The ruling class strives to impart a supraclass, eternal character to the ideological sign, to extinguish or drive inward the struggle between social value judgments which occurs in it, to make the sign uniaccentual. (Voloshinov, *Marxism and the philosophy of language*, 23.)

Questions of language are basically questions of power. (Noam Chomsky, *Language and responsibility* (Hassocks, 1979), 191.)

I OF COMMONWEALTHS AND COMMOTIONERS

In September 1549, Sir Anthony Aucher wrote to William Cecil, warning him about the intentions of the rebels in Kent. Describing them as 'these men called comon welthes', he informed Cecil that the 'comon welthes' were declaring that 'yf they have not reformacyon befor the Feast of Saynt Clement' they intended to rise again.[1] Aucher's letter is important for what it reveals of the gathering criticism of Somerset's policies. But it also highlights another important aspect of the 1549 rebellions: the way in which the rebellion entailed conflict over words and meaning. Perhaps the two words that were most freighted with significance in mid-sixteenth-century England were those mentioned by Aucher: 'reformation' and 'commonwealth'. In attempting to stabilise the meaning of these terms, the governing class sought also to restore the social order. Likewise, in giving different meaning to 'reformation' and 'commonwealth', the rebels asserted themselves as an autonomous political force.

---

[1] PRO, SP10/8/56.

For the rulers of Tudor England, the term 'commonwealth' referred to a fixed polity in which the gentry were born to command and the commons to obey. Thus, for Edmund Dudley, his 'Tree of commonwealth' was rooted in an unchanging social hierarchy bonded by authority, duty and reciprocity:

The common wealth of this realme ... may be resembled to a faier and might[i]e tree growing in a faier field or pasture, under the ... shade wherof all beastes, both fatt and leane, are protectyd and comfortyd from heate and cold as the tyme requireth. In all the subjectes of that realme wher this tree of common welth doth sewerly growe are ther by holpen and relyved from the highest degree to the lowest.[2]

'Commonwealth' was ubiquitous in ideal definitions of the social order. When the Mayor of Canterbury faced criticism during Henry VIII's reign, he called a meeting of the aldermen to organise the defence of 'the comon welthe and good rule of the same Cyty'.[3] Likewise, 'reformation' was taken to refer to a top-down process of religious and social reconstruction. When the Mayor of London, Richard Gresham, wrote to Henry VIII to request that the city be allowed to take over a number of hospitals for the punishment of sturdy beggars, he asked that this be done in the name of the 'reformacion' of the 'comon welthe'.[4] In neither case, according to their conventional meanings, did these keywords of governance allow any political space to the commons.

It is therefore significant that the rebellious commons of Kent, Surrey and Sussex rallied under 'a captain they called Common-wealth'.[5] The rebels themselves were known as 'commonwealths', or as 'councillors of the Commonwealth'.[6] The rebellious meaning given to the term became embedded in local memory: aged witnesses in a Sussex legal case in 1609 retained clear memories of how, sixty years earlier, 'commonwealths' had destroyed enclosures in their village; a Kentish man in 1588 similarly recalled the 'rebellion of comon welth'.[7] Within popular language, 'commonwealth' meant not an ordered hierarchy, but rather denoted the collective interests of the commons: critics of the governing oligarchy in Edwardian Boston (Lincolnshire) complained that, in enclosing the town's commons, the corporation operated without 'any comen welth towardes the pore inhabitaunts'.[8] In 1549, the leaders of rebellion in the Norfolk village of Tunstead persuaded their neighbours to sign a declaration against a local encloser, telling them that 'it was for a Commonwealth'.[9] According to Holinshed, at

---

[2] Brodie (ed.), *The tree of commonwealth*, 31–2.   [3] PRO, STAC2/8/100.
[4] BL, Cotton MS, Cleopatra E IV, fol. 263r. For similar usage see NRO, Y/C19/1, fol. 31v; Slack, *From reformation to improvement*, 30–1; Tawney and Power (eds.), *Tudor economic documents*, II, 317.
[5] Bryn Davies, 'Boulogne and Calais', 61; Longleat House, Thynne Papers, 2, fol. 145r.
[6] Clark, *Provincial society*, 79.   [7] Jones, '"Commotion time"', 130–5; PRO, E133/6/815.
[8] PRO, STAC3/5/11.   [9] PRO, DL1/27/T8.

his assumption of the leadership of the Norfolk rising, Robert Kett told his followers that he was engaged in the defence 'of their common libertie, being readie in the common-welths cause to hazard both life and goods'.[10] The leaders of the popular cause in Yarmouth in 1548 likewise mobilized the language of 'reformation' and 'commonwealth' in justification of their political project: they denounced the bailiffs and common council as 'insasyable & gredy or covetous', and as oppressors of the 'comynaltie'. As the Yarmouth men put it, the town's oligarchs risked the 'undoyng of the comen welth of the seid town'; what was needed was the 'reformation' of Yarmouth's government.[11] Like the commotioners of 1549, the Northern rebels of 1536 and the would-be Norfolk rebels of 1537 also deployed commonwealth terminology in justification of their cause. Thus, one rebel captain in 1536 said that the Pilgrimage of Grace assembled 'for the weale of us all'. A 1536 rebel warrant justified the restoration of the Church, purgation of the Council of 'vylan blode' and the suppression of all heresies as necessary for the maintenance of the 'comon welth'; the warrant was signed 'in this or pilgrimage for grace to the comon welth'.[12] The Walsingham plotter George Guisborough promised his supporters that 'we will put do[w]n the gentilmen ... for a comon wele'. After their execution, the Walsingham plotters were remembered as those that 'dyd for a comyn welthe'. Likewise, one of the Fincham conspirators, who also planned to massacre the gentry of their locality, intended that 'the comynaltie ... wuld ryse ... for the comon welthe'; significantly, the Fincham plotters defined the 'comon welthe' as 'the wele of the comynaltie'.[13] It was because of such popular connotations that Sir Thomas Elyot preferred to define the Tudor polity as a 'public weal' (*res publica*) rather than the dangerous-sounding 'common weal' (*res plebeia*).[14]

The contested meanings given to 'commonwealth' were nothing new: it was not the case, as Ethan Shagan suggests, that the rebellious commons of 1549 simply 'co-opted' government language; rather, the terminology of commonweal was deeply lodged in late medieval popular political language.[15] In a duo of remarkable essays, David Rollison has shown how 'the provenance of "commonweal" as a term of political and constitutional discourse is linked to a tradition of popular resistance and rebellion that emerged between 1381 and 1450'. Rollison quotes one contemporary account of the attack on London by Cade's rebels: 'in that furynys they went, as they said, for the comyn wele of the realme of Ingelonde'. This highlights the

---

[10] Holinshed, 964.   [11] PRO, STAC3/7/32.
[12] PRO, SP1/115, fol. 252v; PRO, SP1/109, fol. 222r.
[13] PRO, SP1/119, fols. 35r; PRO, SP1/121, fols. 22r, 174v.
[14] T. Elyot, *The book named the governor* (1531; London, 1962), 2.
[15] Shagan, *Popular politics*, 280.

relationship between socio-political conflict and linguistic uncertainty. Language, suggests Rollison, is not neutral; instead, the use of the term 'comyn wele' by the 1450 rebels highlights 'causal links between actual social struggles and the development of languages of politics'. Most ambitiously, Rollison argues that 'Running through the generations from 1381 to 1649 ... is a distinctive populist politics, centred on the words common weal.'[16] In the same way, 'reformation' was given a different meaning by mid-sixteenth-century rebels: referring not to government attempts to restructure religion and government, but rather to the commons' attempt to alter the distribution of wealth and power.

Both the words and the actions of the rebels were opposed by their rulers. Sir John Cheke condemned the rebels for twisting around one of the key-words of governance: addressing the Norfolk rebels, he argued that though 'Ye pretend a commonwealth', the rebels brought only chaos.[17] Archbishop Cranmer agreed, asking 'is it the office of subjects, to take upon them the reformation of commonwealth?'[18] In this formulation, Cranmer was unwittingly groping towards one of the defining concerns of modern sociolinguistics. As Fairclough puts it, 'Politics partly consists in the disputes and struggles which occur in language and over language.'[19] In mid-Tudor England, the ruling ideology sought to fix the meaning of certain keywords of political discourse, rendering them static and unchanging. But as Fairclough suggests, words resist such domination, easily slipping away to acquire different meanings. Thus, 'commonwealth' and 'reformation' are best understood as floating signifiers over whom opposing groups struggled. In 1549, like in 1381, 1450 and 1536–7, an important element of the conflict between ruler and ruled involved not only a physical contest, but also a linguistic and ideological struggle. Over and again, terms like 'commonwealth', 'reformation', 'traitor' and 'thief' were twisted around by rebels, transforming them from the keywords of governance into weapons to be used against the gentry and nobility. As J. G. A. Pocock has noted, it is possible for the ruled to 'use ... the language of the rulers in such a way as to empty it of its meanings and reverse its effects'.[20] Like the nineteenth-century French workers whom William Sewell has studied, even when

---

[16] Rollison, 'Specter'; Rollison, 'Conceits and capacities'. For a revealing assessment of the meaning of commonwealth in 1536, see M. L. Bush, 'The Pilgrimage of Grace and the pilgrim tradition of holy war', in C. Morris and P. Roberts (eds.), *Pilgrimage: the English experience from Becket to Bunyan* (Cambridge, 2002), 189–90.

[17] Holinshed, 989.   [18] Cox (ed.), *Miscellaneous writings*, 193.

[19] Fairclough, *Language and power*, 22.

[20] J. G. A. Pocock, 'The concept of a language and the *métier d'historien*: some considerations on practice', in A. Pagden (ed.), *The languages of political theory in early-modern Europe* (Cambridge, 1987), 24.

sixteenth-century labouring people opposed their rulers 'or the state, their opposition was necessarily expressed in terms that their opponents could understand; the bitterest of battles bear witness to the workers' engagement in a common, if contested, frame of discourse'.[21] Language, then, was slippery: both rulers and plebeians plucked keywords from one another's political cultures, twisting them around in order to give them different effects. In studying political language, then, we study an ever-shifting world of nuance, complexity and flux.

Nowhere is this process of linguistic interchange more obvious than in the commonwealth writings of the 1530s–1550s. Within this body of literature, many of the organising concepts of governance were questioned. In the commonwealth writings, as also in Somerset's reformist agenda, the gentry were found particularly guilty of avarice, covetousness and corruption. The language of the commonwealth writers overlapped in important respects with that of rebels in 1536–7 and again in 1549. Thus, Robert Crowley described the gentry as 'men that would eate up menne, women & chyldren'.[22] 'Beholde', Crowley warned the gentry,

you engrossers of fermes and teynementes, beholde, I saye, the terrible threatnynges of God, whose wrath you can not escape. The voyce of the pore (whom you have ... thruste out of house and home) is well accepted in the eares of the Lorde, and hath steared up hys wrathe ageynst you.[23]

Perhaps most striking were the similarities between Raphe Robynson's translation of *Utopia* and the rebel political language of 1549. In Robynson's translation, Sir Thomas More's social criticism was given a new and urgent force:

there is a great numbre of gentlemen, which can not be content to live idle themselves, like dorres, of that whiche other have laboured for: their tenauntes, I meane, whom they polle and shave to the quicke, by reisyng their rentes ... these gentlemen ... do not only live in idlenesse themselves, but carrye about with them at their tailes a great flocke or traine of idle and loterynge servyngmen, which never learned any craft wherby to gett their livynges.[24]

More's character Raphael Hythloday argued that there were two reasons for the economic hardships of the period: the large households maintained by the gentry, and agrarian change, in particular enclosure, rack-renting and

---

[21] W. H. Sewell, *Work and revolution in France: the language of labor from the Old Regime to 1848* (Cambridge, 1980), 12. For other revealing studies of political language, see O. Figes and B. Kolonitskii, *Interpreting the Russian Revolution: the language and symbols of 1917* (New Haven, CT, 1999); J. Epstein, *Radical expression: political language, ritual and symbolism in England, 1790–1850* (Oxford, 1994); P. A. Pickering, 'Class without words: symbolic communication in the Chartist movement', *P&P*, 112 (1986), 144–62.
[22] Crowley, *Select works*, 132. [23] Crowley, *Select works*, 161–2.
[24] More/Robynson, 21–2.

the depopulation entailed in the creation of a sheep economy. Finally, Hythloday charged that the whole social order was predicated upon a giant act of theft:

besides this the riche men not only by private fraud but also by commen lawes do every day pluck and snatch awaye from the poore some parte of their daily living ... Therefore when I consider and way in my mind all these commen wealthes, which now a dayes any where do florish, so god help me, I can perceave nothing but a certein conspiracy of riche men procuringe theire own commodities under the name and title of the commen wealth.[25]

Again, then, we see a struggle waged over the meaning of commonwealth. Less important here is the question of More's authorial intention at the time at which he published these words in 1516; rather, for our purposes, what is significant is the way in which Robynson's translation echoed popular political speech in the mid-sixteenth century. Edwardian social policies were justified in similar language. Thus, John Hooper criticised vicars who maintained multiple benefices, and described the increase of lords' sheep flocks and the decay of cottages as leading to the impoverishment of the commons.[26] A proclamation of 1551 against forestalling grain sought to amend 'the gredie malice of covetouse men'. Likewise, inflation was blamed upon avarice and greed.[27] Under Somerset, it was difficult to find a dividing line between John Hales' criticism of landlords and that articulated by the commotioners.[28]

Political language, then, was difficult to pin down: in many respects, gentleman and labourer shared a lexicon of political keywords; sometimes (but not always) this carried with it joint political assumptions. One of these assumptions concerned gender. Like depictions of the 1525 German rebels, both the representation of the 1549 rebels by their opponents, and their dominant self-definition were 'relentlessly male'.[29] In the narrative accounts of Kett's rebellion, it is not until an adder bites Mrs Kett's bosom (from which was drawn the disastrous prophetic portent that led to the rebel departure for Dussindale) that we learn that Kett's camp included any women at all.[30] The definition of rebellion as a male activity is explicit in one of the characteristic clichés of rebellion: male rebels' frequent statement that insurrection was a brave, bold, masculine activity, in which they intended either to triumph or to die. Thus, the rebels at Lavenham in 1525

---

[25] *Ibid.*, 112.   [26] PRO, SP10/13/13.
[27] *CPR, Edward VI*, IV, 140; PRO, SP10/13/33. For similar examples, see PRO, SP10/11/5; PRO, SP10/10/40–3.
[28] PRO, SP10/4/33; PRO, SP10/2/21; PRO, SP10/5/22; PRO, SP10/5/21.
[29] L. Roper, '"The common man", "the common good", "common women": gender and meaning in the German Reformation commune', *Social History*, 12, 1 (1987), 3.
[30] Neville/Woods, fol. Kr.

were said to have 'protested to die like men in their quarrel with such as were daily despoiling them of whatever God sent them for the labour of their hands'.[31] Likewise, the Neville/Woods narrative explained how, at the last stand of the rebels in the closing stages of the battle of Dussindale, the commotioners exclaimed 'that they had rather dye manfully in fight, then ... to be slaine like sheepe'.[32] Holinshed puts similar words into the rebels' mouths: in one passage, John Flotman responded to a herald's denunciation by exclaiming that the rebels intended either to 'restore the common-wealth from decaie, into the which it was fallen, being oppressed thorough the covetousnesse and tyrannie of the gentlemen; either else would they like men die in the quarrell'. Elsewhere, Holinshed's account of rebel speech deploys a similar formulation, in which, at their last stand, the Mousehold rebels denounce the royal offer of a pardon as nothing but 'a barrell of ropes and halters, with which [the gentry] ... purposed to trusse them up: and therefore they would rather die like men than to be strangled at the wils and pleasures of their mortall enimies'.[33]

In some of its formulations, therefore, rebel political language was distinctly gendered. This reflected a wider tendency within early modern popular politics, in which the recourse to petitioning, demonstration, litigation or riot by plebeian men was justified in terms of their responsibility to defend weaker members of their households.[34] Thus, when the bondmen of Norfolk petitioned the Duke of Somerset for their release from servitude, they returned constantly to the manner in which their patriarchal duties were undermined by bondage. Within the village community, they argued, their private authority as fathers was undercut by their humiliating public subordination to their lord. In particular, they dwelt upon the manner in which their lord, the Duke of Norfolk, 'would not in any wyse permitte any of your oratours to marrye acordyng to the lawes of god ne yet to sette any of their children to schoole'.[35] In this respect, as in others, the Mousehold articles, with their stated desire that 'bondmen' be made free, 'reflect[ed] a male set of political priorities'; as such, it also illuminates the shared linguistic and ideological terrain that could exist between elite and popular politics.[36]

Women were therefore constituted 'as non-political'. This represents a methodological challenge: as Roper observes, 'we ... need to discover where [women] are absent, and [to] uncover the processes by which they are excluded. This is particularly true for the realm of political history, where we need to ask new questions in order to see how the public realm came to be constituted as male territory.'[37] Running alongside this silencing of female

---

[31] HMC, *Welsh*, I, iii–v.   [32] Neville/Woods, sigs. K2v–3r.   [33] Holinshed, 974, 983.
[34] For a good example, see PRO, E134/29&30Eliz/Mich8.
[35] PRO, C1/1187/9.   [36] Roper, '"The common man"', 5.   [37] *Ibid.*, 20.

speech was a male anxiety about women's speech: following the Evil Mayday riots in London in 1517, the authorities sought to control the dangerous spread of rumour by commanding that 'no women should come togither to babble and talke, but all men should keepe their wives in their houses'.[38] In fact, at various points in this book, we have already encountered women's political speech. Throughout this book, they can be found arguing with one another, and with men, about the implications of Kett's rebellion; denouncing the oppressions of rich men; communicating seditious speech; and passing on treasonable prophecies. These scattered examples suggest that, in contrast to the lack of male interest in recording female political speech, men and women did not inhabit 'separate spheres', but rather were willing to argue and debate with one another over political matters. Popular political speech therefore crossed gender lines, spreading amongst 'diverse and many p[er]sons both men and women neighbours'.[39] Messy social reality, in which men and women argued together about politics, therefore was not reflected in dominant political discourses which, both in elite and popular circles, represented both politics and rebellion as a masculine activity.

This chapter will probe the linguistic similarities that link the commotion time with the 1381 rising, Jack Cade's rebellion of 1450, the Pilgrimage of Grace, and the attempted risings of 1537. It will suggest that these rebellions are best understood as manifestations of a deeper popular political culture which, after the defeats of 1549, was broken. The chapter will describe both the form and the content of popular political speech, and will argue that rebel political language was reflective of a wider, strikingly ambitious, popular politics. In this respect, it will challenge conventional interpretations of sixteenth-century popular protest, which tend to write off popular politics as 'overwhelmingly defensive and inward-looking'.[40] In particular, the chapter will criticise Perez Zagorin's dismissal of the 1549 rebellions as 'lacking in a political horizon'. In his study of protest and revolution in early modern Europe, Zagorin has cited the example of Kett's rebellion as evidence that rural protest possessed 'no political goals'. Claiming that 'the movement lacks an ideology' or 'a social or political perspective', Zagorin has argued that Kett's rebellion

failed to articulate principles and possessed no ideology. The time had apparently not yet come in England when a revolt of the lower orders could develop broad ideas or

---

[38] Holinshed, 622.

[39] Quoting PRO, SP1/106, fol. 138r. For other examples of mixed-gender political conversations, see NRO, NCR/16A/6, p. 40; NRO, NCR/12A/1(a), fol. 37r; PRO, E36/120, fol. 176; BL, Cotton MS, Titus B I, fols. 78r–79v; PRO, STAC10/16, fols. 133r–200v; BL, Cotton MS, Titus B II, fols. 182r–184v.

[40] H. Buszello, 'The common man's view of the state in the German Peasant War', in Scribner and Benecke (eds.), *German Peasant War*, 112.

programs to counter the hegemonic, all-pervasive principles of hierarchy and subordination that maintained the Tudor state and society.[41]

In place of this formulation, it will be argued here that in many parts of England, and in Norfolk in particular, the commotioners voiced an ambitious set of proposals aimed at the radical reform of the social and political order.

II ORDERING DISORDER: POPULAR MONARCHISM, AND REBEL ATTITUDES TO STATE FORMATION

This section, like that which follows it, focuses on conflict within rebel politics. It proceeds from the assumption that, although there existed a coherent language of popular politics in 1549, there was no unified, homogeneous ideology. Most obviously, Kett's rebellion projected an entirely different set of religious affiliations from that of the Western rebels. Perhaps as importantly, it will be argued that rebel politics hovered uneasily between order and disorder. In his path-breaking essay of 1979, Diarmaid MacCulloch highlighted the orderly and disciplined conduct of the rebels, arguing that 'The insurgent leaders were seeking good government, not rejecting all government ... It is a moot point, indeed, whether one should consider the affair a rebellion at all.' More recently, MacCulloch has suggested that 'it is only a convenient and rather misleading shorthand device to label those involved [in the commotions in the Midlands, Home Counties and East Anglia as] "rebels"'. Elsewhere, he has referred to the commotioners as merely 'well-meaning demonstrators'.[42] MacCulloch's analysis represents an early example of the more nuanced approach to early modern popular politics that has characterised work on the subject in the past generation. But in assuming that the political intentions of the village rulers were the same as those who followed them, he attributes an inappropriate ideological homogeneity to rebellion. In particular, MacCulloch's emphasis upon the orderliness of the rebellion understates the significance of anger, vengeance and violence apparent in rebel behaviour. Instead, in assessing the politics of 1549, these two sections will balance order against disorder, arguing that the disciplined leadership exercised by men such as Robert Kett contrasted with

---

[41] Zagorin, *Rebels and rulers*, I, 208–9, 212, 214. See also Beer's observation that 'The counties of Tudor England were a world to themselves ... The husbandman or townsman ... knew only what he was told or managed to overhear. Uninformed gossip and wild rumours, blended with generous doses of wishful thinking, often comprised the commons' understanding of government policy, unless they were informed otherwise by the parish priest.' Beer, *Rebellion and riot*, 24.

[42] MacCulloch, 'Kett's rebellion', 50; D. MacCulloch, *Tudor church militant: Edward VI and the Protestant Reformation* (London, 1999), 44; MacCulloch, *Cranmer*, 437.

a spirit of violent class antagonism amongst many of his followers. That
contrast within rebel politics manifested itself in the heart of Kett's camp, at
the Oak of Reformation.

On 24 August 1549, the Herald of Arms offered a pardon to the Norfolk
rebels. Since rebellion represented a means by which the commons could
open a dialogue with government, representatives of the Crown expected
rebels to display proper deference: at Lavenham and Bury St Edmunds in
1525, for instance, rebel representatives had come before the Dukes of
Norfolk and Suffolk wearing their nightshirts, with nooses around their
necks, presenting themselves both as penitents, and as suitable objects of
royal punishment.[43] On 24 August, it initially seemed that Kett's rebels were
going to play their part within the structured rituals of late medieval rebellion: on being conveyed to Mousehold Heath, the Herald was

> received on every side with great shouts & out cries. For every [rebel] . . . uncovering
> their heads, as it were with one mouth and consent all at once (for the most part) cried,
> God save King Edward, God save King Edward . . . The Herald . . . at the length came
> unto the top of the hill, having on his rich Coat of Armes, as solemne ensignes of his
> Office.[44]

The Herald then delivered a lengthy denunciation of the insurrection. This
stratagem was unwise. The Herald's peroration only enraged the rebels:
according to Neville

> they reviled the Herald . . . some calling him Traytor, not sent from the King: but had
> received his lesson from the Gentlemen, and suborned by them, to bring them a sleepe
> with flattering words & faire promises to deceive them in the end . . . Others said, that
> pardon in appearance seemed good & liberall, but in truth would prove in the ende
> lamentable & deadly, as that which would be nothing else; but Barrels filled with
> Ropes and Halters. And that painted coate distinct, and beautified with gold; not to
> be ensignes of an Herald: but some peeces of Popish Coapes sewed together.[45]

In Kent, the Herald of Arms, who had been sent to negotiate with the
'commonwealths', was also mocked by the rebels: it was reported that 'a
greet meyny of [the rebels] . . . rudely behaved themselves toward the seid
officer'.[46] Royal heralds were not used to being treated like this. The trappings of royal authority were meant to intimidate rebels, not infuriate them:
discussing the suppression of the Lincolnshire rising of 1536, Henry VIII
assumed that 'the presence of o[u]r coat was a greate means to abashe' the

---

[43] This incident is more fully discussed in A. Wood, '"Poore men woll speke one daye": plebeian
languages of deference and defiance in England, *c.* 1520–1640', in Harris (ed.), *Politics of the
excluded*, 67–98.

[44] Neville/Woods, sig. H3v.   [45] *Ibid.*, sig. I1r.

[46] BL, M485/39, Salisbury MS 150, fol. 117r–v.

rebels.[47] Undismayed by this angry reception on Mousehold Heath, the Herald of Arms proceeded to the Oak of Reformation, where

an ungracious boy, putting down his breeches, shewed his bare buttockes, & did a filthy act: adding therunto more filthy words. At the indignity whereof, a [royal soldier] ... with a bullet from a Pistoll, gave the boy such a blow upon the loines, that sodainely strooke him dead. Which when the traytors perceived, there came [twelve rebels] ... crying: O my companions, we are betrayed. Doe you not see our fellow Souldiers cruelly slaine before our eyes ... surely this Herald intendeth nothing else, but [that we] ... may most cruelly be slaine [by] ... the Gentlemen.[48]

Following the murder of the rebel 'boy', the negotiations collapsed, and Warwick began his assault upon Norwich.

The events of 24 August 1549 point not only towards a lack of trust amongst the rebels in the negotiations, but also to a fundamental tension in rebel politics. Within the drama enacted under the Oak of Reformation, we can perceive two conflicts: firstly, that between the rebellious commons and the gentry, who were castigated as traitors and oppressors; and secondly, that *within* rebel politics between the rebel leadership, comprised of older, office-holding, wealthier men, and the angry clamour of the insurrectionary 'boys'.[49] Importantly, the narrative accounts emphasised how Kett's council had its origins as an attempt to impose discipline upon these unruly elements within the rebel camp:

the governours ... appoynted a place of ascemblye emonge them in an oken tre ... uppon which tre at the first did none come but Kett and rest of the governours where the people ... wer admonishid to be ware of their robbinge, spoylinge, and other theyr evill demeanors.[50]

The Neville/Woods narrative likewise emphasised how Thomas Codd was joined by other members of the rebel council in seeking 'by all means possible ... to restraine the needy, and hungry common people, from ... [their] importune liberty of rifling, and robbing'.[51] Holinshed stated that the rebel council issued edicts against plunder from the Oak, and that they imprisoned commotioners who broke this order:

it was decreed, that a place should be appointed, where [j]udgements might bee exercised, as in a [j]udiciall hall ... Afore whom ... would assemble a great number of the rebels, and exhibit complaints of such disorders, as now and then were practised amoung them; and there they would take order for the redressing of such wrongs and iniuries as were appointed, so that such greedie vagabounds as were

[47] PRO, SP1/108, fol. 67r.   [48] Neville/Woods, sig. I1v.
[49] For the relatively wealthy backgrounds and record of office-holding amongst members of Kett's council, see Greenwood 'A study of the rebel petitions', 289–97.
[50] Sotherton, 83.   [51] Neville/Woods, sig. C3v.

readie to spoile more than seemed to stand with the pleasure of the said governors, and further than there commissions would beare, were committed to prison.[52]

The Oak of Reformation therefore emerges as a site of ordered authority, from which Kett's council maintained their hold over the rebel rank and file. The Neville/Woods narrative, however, drew attention to the Oak as a site of conflict:

a day was appointed, when [the rebels' gentry prisoners] ... should be brought forth openly as malefactors, that (after a preposterous manner of Judgement) a quest might passe on them. Then Kett ... went upon the ... Oake of Reformation ... his manner was to inquire of his ... companions in that villany, what they thought of [the captives]. The furious varlets being made inquisitors, and Judges of the lives of innocent men; if they found nothing of the man in question, cryed out, A good man, hee is a good man; and therefore ought to bee set at liberty. But if by the least suspicion of any small crime, his same that was named, was but once touched; or if any thing ... were found wherein perhaps hee had offended any one of them: some one (of the people) answered ... Let him bee hanged, let him bee hanged.

The Oak of Reformation represented a key nodal point in rebel politics: it was more than simply the location of the commotioners' council; it was also the site for conflict between order and disorder. The narratives stressed that Kett's authority was precarious; Neville/Woods, for example, described how the rebels

were come to such great rage and madnesse, as the fury and force of so great tumults, could not be restrained neither by the governours, nor yet by Kett himselfe.[53]

Holinshed concurred:

the rebels grew to such unmeasurable disorder, that they would not in manie things obeie neither their generall capteine, nor anie of their governors, but ran headlong into all kind of mischiefe.[54]

The manuscript evidence concerning the rebellions both in Norfolk and Suffolk confirms the narrative accounts' claims that rebel councils assumed the trappings of lawcourts. In a minute of the municipal proceedings of Norwich from July 1549, the Mousehold council was described as 'the hundred', meaning a hundred court.[55] This was the legal body that maintained criminal justice over the administrative unit of the hundred (that is, a cluster of parishes) and which in earlier rebellions had also provided the key organisational unit for insurrection. Typically, hundred jurors were selected from wealthier, established villagers: exactly the same social group as that represented on the rebel council.[56] That Kett's council styled itself as a legal

---

[52] Holinshed, 967.   [53] Neville/Woods, sig. D2v.
[54] Holinshed, 968.   [55] NRO, NCR/16A/4, fol. 67r–v.
[56] On hundred juries, see Goheen, 'Peasant politics?'

body and followed the form of a hundred court are apparent from another scrap of evidence: the only surviving list of demands from the Norfolk rebels – the Mousehold articles – are preceded by a list of the rebel council, each named for the hundred he represented. Certainly, the Norfolk gentry recognised that Kett's council had assumed legalistic powers: the lord of Great Elmingham explained how he had been imprisoned by the rebels after 'a bill' had been exhibited to the rebel council against him, following which he was forced to seal an 'obligacon' to his tenants for £20 in compensation for having denied them their common rights. A complaint to the Court of Chancery suggests that, during the brief period when Yarmouth appears to have lain under rebel control, the commotioners followed the same legalistic practices as their comrades on Mousehold Heath: Johanne Perse explained how she had been expelled from her house in the town after a Yarmouth man 'dyd make a tytle & clayme' upon her home. The Melton camp in Suffolk was also influenced by legal forms: the rebels imprisoned another manorial lord following a 'complaynte' made against him by a merchant. Likewise, local people came to the rebel camp at Ipswich to 'compleyne' about the oppressions of their landlords.[57] These examples provide clear confirmation of the significance of the law within early modern plebeian political culture.[58]

Like Jack Cade's rebels, whose leaders instructed them to let 'alle men know that we wulle neyther robbe nor stele', so the 'commonwealths' in Kent, Surrey and Sussex 'paid for their food in every place'.[59] The narrative accounts of Kett's rebellion provide a revealing anecdote of how some rebels restrained their comrades from plundering the citizens of Norwich. Holinshed described how, on this occasion, those rebels who had committed acts of theft were 'reprooved for the wrongfull robberies by some that were in credit among them', and were persuaded to return the stolen goods.[60] A similar sense of legitimacy informed the Somerset rebels' actions in May 1549, who, when they broke down enclosures, said 'that they had done nothing but what was lawful, for they had heard of a proclamation sent into the country' whereby they were authorised to remove enclosing walls.[61] Likewise, John Paston reported that the rebels of Wiltshire said that 'thay wylle obaye the Kynges maj[e]st[y]e and my lord Protector with alle the counselle, but thay saye thaye wyll nat have ther commonse and ther gro-wendes to be inclosyd and soo taken from them'.[62] In early July 1549, the Spanish Ambassador noted that the rebels 'commit no violence on anybody

---

[57] PRO, C1/1206/15–16; PRO, C1/1376/34; PRO, STAC2/24/78; PRO, C1/ 279/78.
[58] For this, see J. A. Sharpe, 'The people and the law', in B. Reay (ed.), *Popular culture in seventeenth-century England* (London, 1985), 244–70.
[59] Harvey, *Jack Cade's rebellion*, 190; Bryn Davies, 'Boulogne and Calais', 61.
[60] Neville/Woods, sigs. G4v, H1r; Holinshed, 975; Sotherton, 92.
[61] HMC, *Bath*, IV, 109–10.   [62] HMC, *Rutland*, I, 36.

and profess themselves willing to obey the King and his laws'.[63] A year earlier, during the first Cornish rising, the leaders of the crowd that had murdered William Body made speeches calling for the restoration of the Henrician religious settlement until Edward VI reached maturity. Other rebels exclaimed that their actions were sanctioned under the Testament of Henry VIII, which forbade any religious change until Edward came of age.[64] The same legalism influenced the Norfolk rebels who, when Matthew Parker preached at the Oak of Reformation against the sin of rebellion, 'began to question with him about his licence, whereby he was authorised to preach'.[65] The 1536 rebels in Beverley even set the common seal of their borough upon a letter instructing the neighbouring commons to rise.[66] Commotioners, like other protesters, presented themselves not as rebels, but as legitimate petitioners to the Crown or to the lawcourts. Robert Bell, the leader of the Suffolk rebels, paid a man with legal training to write a formal supplication concerning popular grievances. Likewise, the Essex rebels were led by Nicholas Moore, a man with legal training who in 1548 had led the popular cause in Colchester.[67] Popular political action was often conceived in terms of petitioning: in 1553, Thomas Wood of Norwich promised to 'make a supplicacon to the kyng that wold make th[e] aldermen to sweate'; in 1548, the labourer William Busshio explained that the crowd had gathered in the near-insurrection at Cheshunt in order to 'be all sutors and petitioners' to the commissioners for their common.[68]

This willingness to deploy the symbolism and injunctions of authority in justification of crowd actions has been identified as one of the defining characteristics of early modern popular politics.[69] Rebel belief in the legality of their actions influenced the organisation of popular protest. Town and village funds were used to finance rebel activities; the records of such disbursements were carefully entered into account books. The parishioners of North Elmham, for instance, noted the expenditure upon wages for 'suche as sholde tarye at the ... Campe'. It was observed that the parish had sent 'Eyght of them w[i]t[h] the Constable' to the camp at Mousehold. Further expenditures were sanctioned upon food and drink. Likewise, the parishioners of Morebath (Devon) recorded disbursements in support of the Western rebels. Earlier protesters were similarly keen to account for expenditure, and to mobilise local government networks in support of rebellion. In Yarmouth in 1548, for instance, one of the protesters against the borough

---

[63] *CSP, Span*, IX, 396.　　[64] Beer, *Rebellion and riot*, 52.
[65] Holinshed, 968.　　[66] PRO, SP1/107, fol. 137r.
[67] ERO (Colchester), D/35/R2, fols. 226r–229v; PRO, SP10/8/61.
[68] NRO, NCR/12A/1(a), fol. 76r; PRO, STAC10/16, fols. 150v–152r.
[69] J. Walter and K. Wrightson, 'Dearth and the social order in early modern England', *P&P*, 71 (1976), 22–42.

oligarchs explained that he was owed money from the Inquest for drawing up a legal statement of popular grievances. The participation of the 'pore men' of Horncastle (Lincolnshire) in the rising of 1536 was financed out of parochial funds.[70] In their organisational forms, as well as in their rhetoric, therefore, mid-Tudor rebels presented themselves as legalistic, disciplined and ordered.

An appreciation of this legalistic and orderly aspect of late medieval and early modern popular politics is essential to any understanding of one of the defining aspects of the 1549 rebellions: the claim to be acting in the name of, and in support of, Edward VI. Late medieval rebels' attachment to the Crown is characteristically dismissed as 'naive monarchism', a reactionary desire to reverse social change in the name of a distant, beneficent Crown.[71] Hence, rather than analysing popular monarchism, students of the subject have preferred to dismiss it.[72] This plebeian monarchism was one of a number of ideological threads that linked the 1549 rebellions with those of 1381, 1450 and 1536–7. The main chronicle accounts of the 1381 rising described how the rebels would ask 'With whom haldes yow?' anticipating the correct response 'Wyth Kyng Richarde and wyth the trew comunes'.[73] Likewise, the 1536 rebels demanded that those they encountered swear 'to be true to God and to the king and to the commons'. Rebels found it difficult to accept that the Crown might act against their interests: in 1536, one member of a crowd of rebels told a servant of the King that 'thy master is a thief, for he pulleth down all our churches in the country'. In response, others in the crowd argued that 'It is not the King's deed but the d[eed] of Crumwell, and if we had been here we would crum him . . . that he was never so crummed, and if thy master were [here] we would new crown him.'[74] George Guisborough, the Walsingham plotter, remarked to one of his fellow insurrectionaries that

ther was moche penery and scarcenes among the Comons and poor folks for remedy therof he thought it were very well don that ther might be an insurrection . . . he said he thought after the kyng and his councell had knowledge of it he wuld take suche an order that a redress shuld be hadde in theis things that were not wele.[75]

---

[70] NRO, PD209/153, fols. 23r–25r; Duffy, *Voices of Morebath*, 134–9; PRO, STAC3/7/32; PRO, SP1/110, fols. 138v, 143r.

[71] For a revealing assessment, see Scott, *Domination*, 96–103.

[72] For an exception, see M. J. Braddick and J. Walter, 'Introduction. Grids of power: order, hierarchy and subordination in early modern society', in Braddick and Walter (eds.), *Negotiating power*, 37.

[73] Justice, *Writing and rebellion*, 59.

[74] M. L. Bush, *The Pilgrimage of Grace: a study of the rebel armies of October 1536* (Manchester, 1996), 129, 249–50; Shagan, *Popular politics*, 111.

[75] PRO, SP1/119, fol. 36r.

John Rotheram, the leader of the popular cause in Great Yarmouth in 1548, was accused of having identified the bailiffs as opposed to the King's interests, and his comrades as loyalists to the Crown, demanding before the court leet: 'All ye that be sworne to the kyng come to us. All ye that be sworne to the Baylyffs tarye theare style.'[76] We should not be surprised, therefore, to discover that the warrants that issued from the Mousehold camp identified the commotioners as 'the King's friends and deputies', who sought to defend 'the King's honour and Royal Majesty, and the relief of the Commonwealth'.[77] After the defeat of Kett's rebellion, Norfolk people continued to speak of Edward VI as a good ruler. Thus, in February 1550, Margaret Adams told William Mason 'That the kings ma[j]estie had p[ar]doned all [the rebels] . . . so that they come in by a day'. Three years later, a rumour was spread in Norwich alehouses 'that the kings grace' had ordered the destruction of recent enclosures, including those made by the Norwich governors on the Town Close. Interestingly, the Duke of Somerset seems to have inspired similar loyalty amongst some Norwich people: in November 1549, John Rooke stood accused of having proposed establishment of the new rebel camp upon Mousehold Heath, claiming that allies would come out of 'the lorde protectors Countrathe to strenkith' any new Norwich rebels.[78]

Given the depth of rebel identification with the monarchy, it is perhaps unsurprising to find that both mid-sixteenth-century rebels and their late medieval counterparts often branded their opponents as 'traitors'. The main narrative accounts of Kett's rebellion described the commotioners' repeated use of that term: at the Oak of Reformation, it was reported how 'boyes & Country clownes' mocked their gentry captives 'calling them Traitors'; in his tirade against the Marquis of Northampton on 1 August, John Flotman denounced Northampton as 'one stained with all disloyalty, and filthinesse of treason'; the Herald sent to negotiate terms with Robert Kett on 24 August found himself surrounded by a crowd of angry rebels, 'some calling him Traytor'.[79] The anonymous author of the Norwich Roll confirmed this usage, providing an account of how, following the initial fall of the city of Norwich on 22 July, the commotioners ran into the city 'crying about the streets, Traitors! Traitors! and great nombre enter'd houses, robbed shops, and did much violence'.[80] The archival evidence also provides repeated examples of the use of the term. At the start of Kett's rebellion, the constable of Aylsham found his authority challenged by Edmund Chosell, who exclaimed 'Com[e] out thou traytor & goo to the campe meanyng ketts

[76] PRO, STAC3/7/32.
[77] Eccelestone (ed.), *Henry Manship's Great Yarmouth*, 89–90; Holinshed, 966.
[78] NRO, NCR/16A/6, pp. 3, 33, 40; NRO, NCR/12A/1(a), fol. 123r.
[79] Neville/Woods, sigs. E4v, G2v, I1r.   [80] Russell, *Kett's rebellion*, 206.

campe or I shall draw the[e] fourth w[i]t[h] an halter.' On 27 June 1552, one Norwich man reportedly exclaimed that 'those that be nerest to the counsell of all were very traytors'; ten days later, it was said that Joysse of Trowse (who as we saw in Chapter Two had been identified as the potential leader of a future insurrection) had named the gentleman Roger Woodhouse as 'a traytor to the kyng'. A year earlier, Woodhouse had faced denunciation by Robert Burnam, who 'marveyled that Mr Woodhouse of kymberley had so many men. It wolde be knowen what he meant by it, he take him not for the kings frende.' In October 1551, in the course of a dangerous conversation in a baker's shop, 'Suttons wief' remarked of the Norfolk gentry that 'by the masse theye were veary traytors'. The consistent allegations of treachery that were levelled against the Norfolk gentry by their inferiors were given added fuel by the allegation that the gentry intercepted messages sent to Protector Somerset, intending thereby to prevent the negotiations between Crown and commotioners.[81]

The rebels of 1381 had similarly identified their opponents as traitors: when they stormed London, the rebels were said to have cried out 'Where is the traitor to the realm? Where is the despoiler of the common people?' Jack Cade's rebels protested against gentry corruption in similar terms. One rebel bill of 1450 claimed that the King's advisers had committed 'the higheste poynt of tresone', and that they now stood 'enpechid by all the comynealte of Ynglond'; another bill made a similar assumption that only popular agency could restore royal power, arguing that the 'commyns of Englonde [should] Helpe the kynge'. Like in 1549, in the 1450s the meaning of treachery was contested: one man was executed in 1450 for threshing the ground before Henry VI, 'saying that this was how the Duke of York should deal with traitors'. In November 1449, a group of would-be rebels gathered at Thorpe near Mousehold Heath with the intention of doing away with the 'traitors'; a rebel bill of the following year described the King's councillors as 'ffalse traytours that callen hem selfe his ffrendes'.[82]

Rebel monarchism is difficult to square with modern understandings of the state: it was the state, after all, that provided funding, organisation and legal sanction for the suppression of the 1549 risings. For Marxists in

---

[81] NRO, NRS 12131/27/B4; NRO, NCR/16A/6, pp. 124, 418–19; NRO, NCR/12A/1(a), fols. 8r, 37r; BL, Lansdowne MS 2, fol. 60r (no. 25). For an interesting exchange between Sir Thomas Woodhouse and a Norfolk yeoman over the meaning of treachery, see NRO, Y/C4/252, m. 29r. Instead of denouncing the gentry as 'traitors', labouring people might instead describe them as 'thieves', or as 'churles'. For the former, see NRO, NCR/12A/1(a), fol. 9v; PRO, STAC3/7/53; for the latter, see NRO, NCR/16A/6, p. 98; NRO, NCR/12A/1(a), fol. 29r; PRO, STAC8/7/3; ERO (Chelmsford), Q/SR 136/111.

[82] Justice, *Writing and rebellion*, 93; Harvey, *Jack Cade's rebellion*, 70, 158, 187, 189, 190; T. Wright (ed.), *Political poems and songs relating to English history: composed during the period from the accession of Edw. III to that of Ric. II*, 2 vols. (London, 1859–61), I, 230.

particular, who have tended to see the state as the executive arm of the ruling class, it has been hard to comprehend why plebeian rebels, in arms against their rulers, should seek to ally themselves with the Crown.[83] Closer scrutiny of the process of state formation, however, can cast sharper light on the topic: it was not so unusual to find populist monarchies strengthening their power by opposing the sectional interests of the nobility and so winning popular support.[84] Central to this populist process of state formation was the role played by royal courts as neutral, adjudicating forces in disputes between lord and tenant. This connected with popular legalism. Hence, Stephen Justice has argued that 'In 1381, the rebels' "trust" in the King derived less from the mysterious and mythicizing distance of the King's person than from the extraordinary accessibility of his name at law.'[85] In England, increasing popular litigation, combined with the growing authority of the principles of equity practised by central courts, produced both a powerful plebeian legalism and the strengthening of state structures at the expense of the power of local magnates. It is therefore significant that in John Heywood's poem *The spider and the fly*, in which the Spider represents the gentry and the Fly the commons, the Fly threatens legal action over manorial custom against the Spider in 'westminster halle', which the Spider describes as a place where 'I nor no spider maie cum'.[86] Popular monarchism, in other words, was not as naive as it might seem. In particular, on occasions such as that in 1549, where state power was held by a reformist aristocrat, it made sense for labouring people to ally themselves with central government against their local rulers.

Demands for the reorganisation of local government and for access to equal justice at royal courts lay at the heart of the tradition of late medieval popular protest. Hence, the 1450 rebels protested against gentry corruption:

thees false traytours wulle suffer no mane to coome to the Kynges presense for noe cause withoutune brybe whereas ther owte no brybe to bee but that every mane myghte have his dewe comynge in dewe tyme to hyme to aske justyse or grace as the cause requireth.[87]

A poem of around the same time demanded 'good governaunce'.[88] All this was also true of the 1525 German Peasants' War. Here, 'Peasants' and

---

[83] For a rather blunt Marxist account of the relationship between the state and ruling-class power, see G. Therborn, *What does the ruling class do when it rules? State apparatuses and state power under feudalism, capitalism and socialism* (London, 1978).

[84] The subject deserves much fuller study, but see for now T. Ertman, *Birth of the leviathan: building states and regimes in medieval and early modern Europe* (Cambridge, 1997); P. Blickle (ed.), *Resistance, representation and community* (Oxford, 1997).

[85] Justice, *Writing and rebellion*, 61.

[86] Holstun, 'The spider, the fly and the Commonwealth', 62.

[87] Harvey, *Jack Cade's rebellion*, 189.   [88] Wright (ed.), *Political poems*, 238.

burgers' demands for local autonomy within village and town ran like a red thread through all the petitions and proposals of the Peasant War'; the rebels sought to 'put the village community in as autonomous a position as possible'.[89] As Wunder observes, the peasants of the Samland region 'stood in a tradition of corporative self-organisation of their communes and attempted to organise the rebellion too on this model'.[90] Likewise, the 1381 rebels sought to replace seigneurial authority with that of village governors:

> the 1381 rising's notion of the new political order, if utopian, was at least not vaguely so: it was that local communities should continue to exercise their acknowledged and conventional authority *in place of* – not, as was already the case, in addition to – the authority of the lords.[91]

Goheen makes a critical distinction between the institution of the manor and the social world of the village: in Goheen's view, the late medieval village 'expresses [the commons'] communitarian norms', whereas the manor is the 'symbol of their subordination within a larger hierarchy'.[92]

These perspectives form the key to understanding the place of monarchism in popular political culture. Whereas labouring people seem to have perceived of the manor as a relatively abstract institution of seigneurial power, the village represented a genuine unit of everyday life. Hence, whereas plebeian witnesses in mid-sixteenth-century Norfolk church court cases spoke of manorial institutions as administrative entities controlled by lords ('A Courte of Sr James Bulleyne knight holden at Cawston'), the village was represented as a much more immediate, communal entity: 'the . . . towne of Cawston'.[93] By way of contrast, deponents slipped with far greater ease between the village and the parish: within many parts of Norfolk, whereas manors cut across genuine units of communal life, such that landholdings within a given community might fall into three or four manors, the parish and the village were linked together in everyday life, providing the bases for both communal feeling and local administration. Hence witnesses in a 1552 case concerning the parochial customs of Thorndon conflated 'the custom of that p[ar]ishe' with 'the custome of that towne'.[94]

The clearest example of the linkage between the authority of the Crown and popular demands for local autonomy is to be found in Orford (Suffolk). Here, a long-standing conflict pitched the local lords, the Willoughby family, against the local inhabitants. The latter claimed that the town of Orford was held by the Crown, who had granted the inhabitants a charter which allowed

---

[89] Buszello, 'The common man's view of the state', 110, 111.

[90] H. Wunder, 'The mentality of rebellious peasants: the Samland peasant rebellion of 1525', in Scribner and Benecke (eds.) *German Peasant War*, 158–9.

[91] Justice, *Writing and rebellion*, 173.   [92] Goheen, 'Peasant politics?', 44.

[93] NRO, DN/DEP/6/5A, fols. 37v, 38v.   [94] NRO, DN/DEP/6/5A, fols. 104r, 105r.

them substantial self-government. The authority of the Crown was invoked by town officers to challenge the power of the Willoughbys' bailiff, Thomas Spicer. He described in one Star Chamber complaint how the parson of Orford and his parish priest, together with four members of the town's elite, drove the Willoughbys' sheep flocks off the common. Spicer also gave an account of how he had been in the parish church during divine service when Matthew Farrier, the constable of the town, shouted out

Spicer, I comande yowe in the kings behalff & in the name of all the [w]hole Towne here and by vertue of or Charter that yowe medle no further here in yor office of yor bayllywke under the name & tytle of Mr Willoughby Esquier And that ye . . . put away yower Masters sheepe nowe beynge in Newton Felde Between this & Saterday next comyng or ells I & my Fellowes will dryve them awaye.

Witnesses on behalf of the town of Orford emphasised how they 'knoweth no other lorde ther then the Kings highnes'. In 1549, matters came to a head when, during the commotion time, Spicer was arrested by the town constable and placed in the stocks. Spicer's humiliation was given a charivaric touch: he was escorted to the stocks by a man 'with a drome and xxx horsemen'.[95] Plebeian litigants and witnesses to central courts routinely emphasised the power wielded by local lords, their contempt for customary law and their desire to drive the commons out of their villages. Hence, one Suffolk copyholder described how the lord of the manor sought the 'subverson of the whole state of the towne'.[96] The gentry of mid-Tudor England, and of Norfolk in particular, were represented not only as the enemies of the common people, but also as impediments to the administration of royal justice.[97]

The answer to such manorial depredations was outlined in the petition submitted by the commons of Norfolk to Queen Mary.[98] The petitioners noted the chaotic manorial arrangements in Norfolk, observing that in some towns and villages there were three or more manors. According to the petitioners, lords exploited the complexity of the manorial structure of the county to impoverish the poor commons. In this, lords breached both ancient custom and statute law. Authority, therefore, ought to be vested within the 'Townes & vyllages', rather than in manors. Where lords offended against the new arrangements, they should be subject to financial penalties, and the resultant fine shared between the Crown and the individual who had brought the case to one 'of yor gr[ac]es Courts of record'. As Richard Hoyle has

---

[95] PRO, STAC2/21/93; PRO, STAC2/21/100; PRO, STAC4/10/76. See also MacCulloch, *Suffolk and the Tudors*, 306–7.
[96] PRO, C3/154/6.   [97] See, for instance, PRO, STAC2/18/197; PRO, STAC3/4/53.
[98] PRO, E163/16/14.

recognised, a close similarity existed between the Norfolk commons' Marian petition and the Mousehold articles of 1549.[99]

It is worth pausing for a moment to consider the significance of the Mousehold articles as a source for information about rebel politics. In this document, we find the final, and in many respects the clearest, expression of late medieval popular politics. Amongst the list of rebel complaints was placed a partial statement of support for evangelical reform. The document has often been compared with the Swabian articles produced in the course of the German Peasants' War. Both documents had more than a single author: the Swabian articles were a condensation of 300 separate petitions into a single statement of rebel grievances; likewise, the Mousehold articles are multivocal in character.[100] Although they are written in a single hand, they clearly result from the intersection of a series of interest groups in the rebel camp. Surprisingly absent, given the depth of popular support for Kett within the city of Norwich, are any specifically urban demands. Instead, the almost random nature of the demands suggests that representatives of individual villages added their own particular grievances to the document – some concerning servitude, for instance, while others were more exercised by lords' overstocking of commons, or clerical involvement in the land market – so that the resultant document has a rather jumbled appearance. Moreover, as Shagan has demonstrated, the Mousehold articles were drawn up in the course of a protracted process of negotiation with Protector Somerset: as such, they are best understood as comprising a few phrases in a wider conversation.[101]

In both the later petition to Queen Mary and the Mousehold articles a vision was articulated of a process of state formation from the bottom up. The programme outlined in the Mousehold articles and the Marian petition represented an attempt by local inhabitants to create some governmental unity within their communities, taking power from the lords and placing it instead within the village. In this programme, the commotioners sought to link the extension of state authority with local attempts to wrest power from lords. Most notably, the authors of the Mousehold articles envisaged the freezing of the long-term processes of social and economic change that were fissuring village communities.[102] The gentry were to be excluded from the village economy: 'no lord of no mannor shall comon upon the Comons'. It is important that the Mousehold articles echo evangelical proposals for

---

[99] Hoyle, 'Communication'.   [100] Buszello, 'The common man's view of the state', 114.
[101] Shagan, 'Protector Somerset'.
[102] For examples of rebel hostility to social mobility, see NRO, NCR/12A/1(a), fols. 11v–12r; NRO, NCR/16A/6, p. 1; NRO, NCR/20A/2, fol. 40r. For a good example of social mobility in an early sixteenth-century village, see NRO, DN/DEP/6/5b, fols. 100(ii)v–101v.

reshaping the clergy's role in parochial life: priests were to be chosen by the parish; they were to cease dabbling in the land market and should instead dedicate themselves to preaching and to the education of parishioners' children.[103] It is equally important that there was no statement made on doctrinal matters. Overall, the Mousehold articles spelled out a corporatist vision of an alternative social order 'in which society consisted of watertight compartments, each with its own functions and each interfering as little as possible with the others'.[104] This new order was to be fostered within a dispersed polity comprised of autonomous village communities, bound together by the force of the monarch's law. It was in this reform programme that we see the logic of popular monarchism, in which the forces of legalism and orderliness within late medieval popular politics were linked to early modern processes of state formation.

III THE SPIRIT OF THE CAMPING TIME: DISORDER, REBEL DIVISIONS AND CLASS CONFLICT

Preserved in the archives of the city of Norwich is a curious survival from Kett's rebellion. It is an unsigned letter from the wife of a sheep farmer, apparently addressed to the leadership of the rebel camp, complaining about the theft of her sheep.[105] In it, she explained how she had 'geven to the camppe a certen number of wethers [that is, sheep] in myn husbands absences wher w[i]t[h]', but that some of the rebels had stolen a further 180 sheep, 'saying that they wer of the best ende of wethers that myn husbande hadde'. The woman therefore asked that 'myn husbands she[e]p may be From hensforth spared'; furthermore, she explained that she expected 'to be payed For the same [180 sheep] this daye'. The letter illuminates the tension within the rebel camp between order and disorder: firstly, it points to some rebels' willingness to use the rebellion as an opportunity to plunder the local elite; secondly, the orderly aspect of the rebellion is highlighted by the anonymous woman's expectation of payment for the stolen sheep.

Rebel plunder of the gentry's sheep flocks, deer-parks and rabbit warrens comprised one of the most notable features of the 1549 rebellions. In Hampshire, rebels from Sussex stole deer from the gentry estates. In Oxfordshire, the rebels 'drank their fill of wine, ale and beer, slew many sheep and ate them'. In Suffolk, the rebels dined upon rabbits stolen from the

---

[103] For Robert Crowley's advocacy of a preaching and teaching ministry: Crowley, *Select works*, 70–2. For an example of popular hostility to clerical involvement in the village economy, see Oxburgh Hall, Muniments, Letter of William Hulyer to Henry Bedingfield, 16 December 1553; for parochial customs that allowed parishioners to appoint their own minister, see PRO, E134/28Eliz/East29.
[104] MacCulloch, 'Kett's rebellion', 47.   [105] NRO, NCR/26B/59.

warrens which, throughout the sixteenth century, were so hated by local farmers. Across southern and eastern England, the rebels stole 'cows and flocks of fat wethers from the farms of the wealthy which they consumed unsparingly with great show and bragging'. In Norfolk, where the gentry's maintenance of large sheep flocks had been such a cause of conflict between lord and tenant, it was unsurprising to find that, after the rebellion, gentlemen returned to their estates to find them denuded of sheep.[106] The narrative accounts agree that the Norfolk rebels delighted in their plunder: Neville/ Woods wrote of how, on Mousehold Heath, 'the miserable common people [were] drowned in drink, and excesse ... over-charged with meate and drinke'. It was estimated that 'besides Swannes, Geese, Hennes, Ducks, and all kind of fowles without number, about three thousand Bullocks, and twenty thousand Sheepe, were ryotously spent in the Campe within few dayes'.[107] The Spanish Ambassador gave a vivid account of the rebels' riotous assault upon seigneurialism, describing in early July 1549 how 'the peasants are still tearing down the enclosures of parks, and draining fishponds and preserves appropriated by the nobleman'.[108] This represented more than mindless plunder; there was a treble significance to the ostentatious consumption of meat and drink. Firstly, the theft of deer was accompanied by the destruction of enclosing walls around deer-parks: in eating the deer, as in destroying the pales of the deer-parks, the rebels were both symbolically and physically destroying the landscape and economy of lordship. Secondly, we must remember that the 1540s had seen significant inflation and dearth of foodstuffs: how often did labouring people eat meat in this hard decade?[109] The consumption of lords' cattle, rabbits, deer and sheep needs to be seen as a collective act of revenge. Lastly, there was a deliberately burlesque, humorous quality to rebel plunder, epitomised by a letter left by Norfolk rebels who had stolen one gentleman's sheep flock: 'Mr Pratt, your sheep are very fat / And we thank you for that / We have left you the skins to pay for your wife's pins / And you must thank us for that.'[110]

Rebellion, therefore, was about more than grim social conflict: it was also about play, festivity, plunder, excess and fun. MacCulloch has noted that the term 'camping time' had a double meaning: camping referred not only to the formation of rebel camps, but also to the season of disorder characterised by football, again played by riotous young men, the East Anglian name for which was 'camping'. The camping time, in other words, was about both the

---

[106] PRO, DL3/56/G1k–g; Beer, *Rebellion and riot*, 149; MacCulloch, 'Kett's rebellion', 41; Bryn Davies, 'Boulogne and Calais', 63; PRO, STAC3/1/74; PRO, SP10/8/55(1).
[107] Neville/Woods, sigs. C4r, D3r; Sotherton, 84; Holinshed, 968. [108] *CSP, Span*, IX, 397.
[109] On food fantasies in early modern Europe, see P. Camporesi, *Bread of dreams: food and fantasy in early modern Europe* (1980; Eng. trans., Oxford, 1989).
[110] Tawney, *Agrarian problem*, 331.

orderly formation of rebel camps under the disciplined leadership of grave elders, *and* the violent playtime of young men. The association between festivity and rebellion was further evident in the fact that, as in the example of the Wymondham Game, which coincided with the outbreak of Kett's rebellion, commotioners used sporting competitions and traditional festivals as covers for the organisation of rebellion. The rebellions also had their charivaric elements, in which the local forces of authority were humiliated. In Orford, the lord's hated bailiff was marched to the village stocks to the sound of a drum; in 1596, elderly men recalled how during the 'rebellion time' the commotioners had 'sette div[er]se of the better sorte of Buckenham in the stocks & greatly threat[e]ned them'; the village constable of Tunstead led the inhabitants of the nearby settlements to Mousehold Heath with a banner displayed before him, 100 horsemen, and drums beating; Robert Kett met him at Mousehold Heath 'with drums and drumilettes' and gave them thanks.[111]

There may have been a politics of age at work in the East Anglian rebellions. Paul Griffiths has shown how age represented a key determinant of authority: within the patriarchal ideal, power was based not only upon gender, but also longevity. Furthermore, Alex Shepard has argued that age was interwoven with class: just as older men tended to be wealthier, so younger men, some of whom had yet to inherit estates, and others of whom would never do so, tended to be poor. Jane Whittle has demonstrated that within mid-sixteenth-century East Anglia there existed a marginal, wage-dependent population of young men who moved from village to village in search of work, and whose existence, while necessary to the functioning of the agrarian economy, was a source of anxiety to village governors. Notably, these landless wage labourers were, in Jane Whittle's analysis 'criminalised' by their wealthier employers and characterised as vagabonds. Moreover, although already a substantial proportion of the population, the pressures of the mid-sixteenth century meant that seasonal, casual wage labour increased. Finally, Alex Shepard points out that unmarried men were designated 'boys', and were deemed to be shiftless and dangerous; the term 'boy', therefore, did not denote a male child, but instead referred to poor young men in their teens and twenties.[112] This is important to the interpretation of some key moments in the history of Kett's rebellion.

---

[111] MacCulloch, 'Kett's rebellion', 38, 40, 41, 46; Dymond, 'A lost social institution'; PRO, E134/38Eliz/Hil24; PRO, DL1/27/T8. For examples of fatalities during football games, see Cockburn (ed.), *Essex indictments*, nos. 308, 1323, 1361.

[112] P. Griffiths, *Youth and authority: formative experiences in England, 1560–1640* (Oxford, 1996); A. Shepard, *Meanings of manhood in early modern England* (Oxford, 2003); Whittle, *Development of agrarian capitalism*, 222, 223, 225, 256, 281, 283, 287, 298–9, 304.

It will be recalled that, in the incident with which we began the previous section, the rebel who defecated in front of the Herald of Arms on 24 August 1549 was described as a 'boy'. This was not the only occasion upon which rebel 'boys' took the initiative. In the initial rebel attack on Norwich, on 22 July 1549, according to Neville/Woods, the rebel attack was led by 'beardlesse boyes of the countrey (whereof there were a great number) and others of the dregs of the people, men most filthy'. Sotherton described these individuals as 'vagabond boyes brychles and bear arssyde'.[113] Neville/Woods agreed that the young rebels were 'very naked', and described how, during the rebel attack, they combined nakedness with obscenity:

the boyes ... (as though a certaine frenzie had bereaved them of the sense of understanding) running about, provoked our men with all reprochfull speeches. There was added also to their importune cursed words, an odious, & inhumane villany: for ... one of these cursed boyes, putting downe his hose, and in derision turning his bare buttockes to our men, with an horrible noise and out-cry, filling the aire (all men beholding him) did that which a chast[e] tongue shameth to speake, much more a sober man to write: but being shot thorow the buttocks, one gave him, as was meet, the punishment he deserved.[114]

The Cambridge rebels also revelled in their lack of proper clothing: 'How sayst thou Harry Clowte?', asked one rebel bill, 'Thy bryches botom is torn owte.'[115] Finally, when gentry captives were presented to the rebel band under the Oak of Reformation, it was the 'boyes & Country clownes, which stood round about, mocked them, calling them Traitors'.[116] Both physically and politically, therefore, these bare-arsed boys formed the angry, violent and dangerous vanguard of Kett's rebellion; in contrast, it was the proper-tied, office-holding men of the rebel council who tried (often in vain) to restrain them.

If the orderliness of the 1549 rebellions has therefore been overstated in the recent historiography, so also has the relative lack of rebel violence. Certainly, it is true that, rather than killing them, Kett's rebels mostly imprisoned those gentry who fell into their hands.[117] But it is also true that, during the last battle at Dussindale, the rebels chained their gentry captives in front of their lines, intending that the prisoners would be killed by Warwick's barrages. Likewise, on two occasions, the Western rebels executed evangelicals who fell into their hands.[118] The Yorkshire rebels also murdered four gentlemen, possibly because some of them had acted as Chantry Commissioners in the previous year, and 'stripped them of their

---

[113] Neville/Woods, sig. E4r; Sotherton, 87.
[114] Neville/Woods, sig. E4r. For similar imagery elsewhere, see P. Freedman, *Images of the medieval peasant* (Stanford, CA, 1999), 150–6.
[115] Cooper, *Annals*, II, 41.   [116] Neville/Woods, sig. E4v.
[117] For an exception, see PRO, C1/1277/39.   [118] Holinshed, 958–9.

clothes & purses, [leaving] them naked ... in the plaine fields for crowes to feed on'.[119] In their willingness to use targeted violence, the 1549 commotioners behaved more like medieval rebels than early modern rioters. Whereas the latter tended to prefer to displace their anger against their opponents onto physical emblems of popular fury – enclosing fences, Laudian altar rails, gentry heraldry in stained-glass windows and so on – the former were much more willing to murder their leading opponents. In 1381 and in 1450, leading courtiers, noblemen and clerics were executed by rebels in a quasi-judicial fashion. In 1489, Yorkshire rebels killed the Earl of Northumberland.[120] In 1536, the Chancellor of the Diocese of Lincoln was murdered by rebels.[121] The 1537 Walsingham rebels told their supporters that they intended to 'reyse the Coutr[i]e and to take such Gentilmen which wille resyst them and Cutte off ther heads and take ther goods and substance'. In the same year, a plot was hatched in Old Buckenham to take the gentry who had come to dissolve the local monastic house and 'kyll theym in ther bedds'.[122] In 1548, William Body was killed by Cornish rebels. Furthermore, the 1549 rebels used the threat of violence to recruit supporters. Holinshed recorded how 'these rebels ... ranging about the countrie from towne to towne, to inlarge their ungratious and rebellious band, [took] those with force which were not willing to go, & leaving in no towne where they came anie man above the age of sixteene yeare'.[123] Again, this behaviour was similar to that of earlier rebels. In 1540, John Walter of Griston's neighbours accused him of proposing a rising against the gentry, threatening that those 'as wyll nott turne to us let us kylle them ye evyn the[i]r Chylder[e]n in the[ir] Cradells'. The Lavenham rebels of 1525 threatened those who were willing to pay the Amicable Grant that 'they shuld be hewen yn peces'.[124] In 1536, rebels recruited supporters under threat of having their houses burnt. One vicar was intimidated into joining the Lincolnshire rebellion by the threat that, if he did not join the rebels, 'thowe shalt loose thy head'.[125]

If the intended or actual violence of mid-Tudor popular politics seemed closer to the pattern of medieval rebellion than that of early modern popular protest, the angry words spoken concerning their rulers by mid-sixteenth-century labouring people enjoyed close similarities both with late medieval

---

[119] Holinshed, 986; *VCH, Yorkshire: North Riding*, 485; W. Page (ed.), *The certificates of the commissioners appointed to survey the chantries, guilds, hospitals, etc., in the County of York*, 2 vols. (Surtees Society, 91, Durham, 1894), I, xvi.

[120] M. A. Hicks, 'The Yorkshire rebellion of 1489 reconsidered', *Northern History*, 22 (1986), 39–62.

[121] Hoyle, *Pilgrimage of Grace*, 132–3.

[122] PRO, SP1/119, fol. 30r; PRO, SP1/120, fol. 179r–v.   [123] Holinshed, 986.

[124] PRO, SP1/160, fol. 157r; G. W. Bernard, *War, taxation and rebellion in early Tudor England: Henry VIII, Wolsey and the Amicable Grant of 1525* (Hassocks, 1986), 137.

[125] PRO, SP1/107, fols. 147r–148r; PRO, SP1/110, fol. 191v.

popular political language and with that of the early modern epoch. As with rebel disorder and violence, this angry language of class suggests that the orderly dimension of the 'camping time' has been overstated. It seemed commonsensical both to rebels of the fifteenth century and to those of the sixteenth century that their rulers intended their destruction. Thus, the rebel statement of complaints issued from Blackheath in 1450 observed that 'hit is opynly noysyd that Kent shuld be dystroyd with a r[o]yall power & made a wylde fforest'. Similarly, in 1470, rebellion was inspired by a rumour that the King intended to come into Lincolnshire and have 'a great number of the common people hanged and drawn'.[126]

The records of the Norwich magistracy demonstrate that little had changed by the mid-sixteenth century. It was a common belief that the gentry intended to starve the commons to death. In 1552, John Cobbe was set in the cage for observing at the market cross that 'The poore can bye no corne here for the rych chorles take it from them.' Just before the outbreak of Kett's rebellion, the Ipswich mason William Poynet stood accused of having said, while drunk, that 'Gentes and richemen have all catell and wolles and such like thinges in ther handes nowe a dayes and the pore peple are more Famysshed.' The Walsingham rebels of 1537 were motivated by similar concerns. Raphe Rogerson initiated the planned insurrection by remarking to William Guisborough that 'the gentle men buye upp all the grayn, kepe all the catal in their handes and hold all the farmes that poor men cann have no living'. Likewise, George Guisborough remarked to John Semble that 'ther was moche penery and scarcenes among the Comons and poor folks'.[127]

Lords' abuse of their seigneurial powers was seen through the same lens. Bondmen of the Duke of Norfolk complained how their state of servitude meant that the Duke took everything that 'thei truly gotte with the sweate of theire broughes ... by plain force and violence'. The inhabitants of mid-sixteenth-century Salthouse and Kelling believed that, in establishing great sheep flocks upon the commons and in impounding the commoners' cattle, their lords intended 'the utter undoing and distrucon of yor poore subjects their wiffes and children'. The inhabitants of Stradsett spoke in very similar terms about two gentlemen who had enclosed part of their commons and overstocked the rest with sheep and cattle. The lessee of the manor of Landbeach (Cambridgeshire), Richard Kyrby, was suspected by his tenants of intending the destruction of their community, alleging in their complaints of June 1549 that 'he beinge so small a frend to the Comon Weale ... he intentyth the dystruccon of the rest of the towne for he wysshyth tht ther

---

[126] Harvey, *Jack Cade's rebellion*, 186; Harvey, 'Was there popular politics', 164.
[127] NRO, NCR/16A/6, pp. 98, 418–19; NRO, NCR/16A/4, fol. 61r; PRO, SP1/119, fols. 36r, 38r; NRO, NCR/12A/1(c), fols. 18r–19v.

were no more houses in the towne but his owne and no more'. The people of Stradsett told the Star Chamber that it was the intention of these gentlemen to 'empov[er]isshe and utterly to undo ... the inhabitants of the ... Towne' by squeezing them off their common 'to the distruc[ti]on and ruyne of the ... Towne and the utter decay of the husbondry and tyllage of the same of ther owne mere wrong and extorte powre without any rights or title'.[128]

Such complaints, of course, were highly rhetorical. But the overstated nature of plebeian complaints to central courts illuminates the willingness of mid-sixteenth-century labouring people to describe their world in terms of overt social conflict. Both the contemporary evidence and that of the later narrative accounts highlight the fear and hatred which the gentry inspired amongst the commotioners. Neville/Woods gave an account of the speech of the 'ignorant and rude multitude' under the Oak of Reformation who, when presented with gentry captives,

with one mouth cryed out: Let them be hanged, Let them be hanged. And when the Gentlemen inquired ... why they should use such cruell speeches, [the rebels replied] ... that they were Gentlemen, and therefore to be taken out of the way: for they knew well, if once they might get the victorie, they should indure at their hands all kinde of torment, and crueltie.[129]

The Cambridge rebels understood clearly that the local conflicts which pitched the town governors against the poor were based upon attempts to expropriate land and resources from the commons. In the rebel ballad addressed 'To all false flattering Freemen of Cambridge, open and secrete enemies of the poore', Harry Clowte warned that the town elite should not 'take into ther handes / That be other mennes landes'. In the ballad, Jake of the Style responded 'That thus doth all encroche / To ther gret shame and reproche / Ever beyng to ther pore / Heavy grevous and sore'.[130] The priest Sir John Chaundeler, who fled from the Castle Rising camp following its dissolution, was accused of having wished that King's Lynn and all the gentlemen there were on fire and of spreading the rumour that the besieged gentry at Lynn 'went abrode & killed poore men in their harvest work And also kylled women there wyth Chyld'.[131] The gentry and nobility recognised the significance of such popular anxieties: when the gentlemen of Leicestershire were advised by the Council on 11 June 1549 to arm themselves, they were told to keep their distance from the commons 'Lest the peple shuld by brutes conceyve you wolde overrune them'.[132]

---

[128] PRO, C1/1187/9; PRO, STAC3/3/42; CCCC, XXV/194, 'Articles agaynst Richard Kyrby'; PRO, STAC2/18/197.
[129] Neville/Woods, sigs. D4r–v; see also Holinshed, 963, 969.   [130] Cooper, *Annals*, II, 40–2.
[131] BL, Lansdowne MS 2, fol. 60r (no. 25).   [132] PRO, SP10/7/31.

Popular fear of their rulers engendered powerful feelings of hatred towards the gentry. In the immediate aftermath of Kett's rebellion, Sir Thomas Clere was warned by an anonymous letter that if he kept the company of Sir Thomas Woodhouse, who had been a leading figure in the defence of Yarmouth, that 'he shuld be in danger of his lyffe for they were determyned to kyll [Woodhouse] w[i]th halffe ho[o]kes'.[133] The Yorkshire rebels of 1549 were moved by 'a blind and a fantasticall prophesie ... that there should no king reigne in England, the noblemen and gentlemen to be destroied'.[134] Although we will see in the next chapter that the target of plebeian hostilities changed in the later sixteenth century, in some respects, the anger felt by mid-sixteenth-century labouring people towards their rulers communicated itself to later generations. Ralph Watson of Dover was alleged to have said in 1584 that

This is a very evill land to lyve in except yt be for a man that hath a very good occupacion. I wold yt were warre. I knowe a great many richemen in the land; I wold have some of ther money yf yt were so come to passe

Ten years later, Thomas Delman allegedly remarked that 'he did hope to see the riche churles pulled out of there houses and to see them together by the eares in England before Candlemas daye nexte'. A prophecy circulating in Kent in 1568 foretold how 'he that lifeth untyll Whitsontyd comyth shalbe a twelvemonth or Bartholmewtyde following at the firthest shall nott see one gent[leman] in England but shalbe kyll[e]d and spoyl[e]d'.[135]

This angry language of class, which does not sit easily with characterisations of the 1549 rebellions as disciplined, limited demonstrations, was founded upon a polarised vision of society which defined a sharp conflict between a poor, oppressed commons and a rapacious, corrupt, violent, greedy, covetous and treacherous gentry. Thus, the inhabitants of Kelling and Salthouse described themselves as 'very poore and nedye folke', in contrast to their lords, who were 'men of gret possessione and substaunce and well frended and alied within ... Northefolke'.[136] Poor people routinely used such terminology in description of their gentry opponents: one group of plebeians described their lord as 'a man of greate myght substaunce and power', who intended 'theire utter empov[er]ishmente & undoing forev[er]'; another spoke of their lord as 'a man of covetouse and gredy mynde'. Yet another group of tenants noted the 'greate power and authority' of their lord, and their inability to 'stande in contencon of syte with him'.[137] Notably, in Norfolk, labouring people spoke not only of the 'covetous' mentality of their

[133] PRO, SP10/8/55(1).   [134] Holinshed, 985.
[135] Cockburn (ed.), *Kent indictments*, nos. 422, 429, 1322, 2228.   [136] PRO, STAC3/3/42.
[137] PRO, C1/1187/15–17; PRO, C2/Eliz/P12/48. For other examples, see PRO, STAC3/3/80; PRO, STAC3/6/30; PRO, REQ2/18/114.

governors, but also addressed the connections between the economic power of the gentry and their political authority: hence, one group of tenants emphasised the local authority wielded by their gentry opponents: whereas they were 'poore men & strangers unknowen and w[i]t[h]out Frends in ... Norff[olk]', the gentry were 'men of greete substaunce & Riches and greetly alyed and Frended in ... Norff[olk]'.[138]

In some contexts, therefore, the bitter experience of class could be disempowering, defining individual labouring people in terms of their lack of agency. Hence, as William Cowper, a Norwich cooper, put it in the aftermath of Kett's rebellion: 'as shepe or lambes are a praye to the woulfe or Lyon so are the poore men to the Riche men or gentylmen'. Likewise, one fifteenth-century bill described how 'the pore pepyll levyng in dystress ... be oppressed in all maner of thyng'.[139] In such formulations, social polarities were plotted in terms of disparities in power. In other contexts, however, the collective experience of social conflict could define plebeian community. Thus, one spreader of seditious stories in Bungay in 1537 assumed an opposition between (on the one hand) the 'gentillmen' and (on the other hand) 'the people', the 'gudd fellowes', the 'pore people' and 'the pore men'. Earlier that year, one of the rebel bills in Westmoreland identified an opposition between 'the commons' and the 'gentyllmen'. Likewise, the Walsingham plotters spoke of a conflict which pitted 'the pore pepyll and comy[n]s' against the 'gentyllmen'.[140] This perception of society as characterised by overt class conflict could produce a strong sense of social solidarity. One rebel bill in Westmoreland in January 1537 opened with the proclamation 'All comons styk ye together'.[141] Ominously, a song of 1434 told of how 'If thou art pore, than art thou fre / If thou be riche, than woo is the.'[142]

Given the leading role played by the 'honest men' – that is, wealthy yeomen farmers – in the organisation of rebel politics, it should be unsurprising to find that the Mousehold articles articulated the interests of landed groups within village society, rather than those of the landless wage labourer.[143] Similarly, the Suffolk rebel petition spoke on behalf of those who distributed charity to the poor, rather than the poor themselves.[144] It is therefore possible to read rebel petitions as evidence of the domination of insurrection by the wealthier 'honest men', and the slight role accorded to the poor.

---

[138] PRO, STAC3/6/13; PRO, STAC3/4/53.
[139] NRO, NCR/12A/1(a), fols. 11v–12r; Wright (ed.), *Political poems*, 286.
[140] PRO, SP1/120, fols. 100r–104v; PRO, SP1/114, fol. 227r; PRO, SP1/119, fols. 33r, 37r.
[141] PRO, SP1/114, fol. 228r.   [142] Dobson, *Peasants' revolt*, 385.
[143] Greenwood, 'A study of the rebel petitions', 292–3 and Whittle, *Development of agrarian capitalism*, 298 both make this point. Although note that the Kentish rebels demanded 'the augmenting [of] the price of day labour'. Clark, *Provincial society*, 423.
[144] Hatfield House, Cecil Papers, 201, fol. 60r.

Certainly, assessments of rebel politics have tended to emphasise the leading role played by village elites in organising and articulating protest. In attempting to stage a rebellion, it was important to have the 'honest men' on the side of the rebels. In Kendal, in 1537, the bailiff sought to tone down protest and to prevent rebellion. The language he employed in describing the confrontation within the town was significant: he described how rebellion had originated with 'certain of the lewde p[er]sons', but how it had been opposed by the 'honest men', who attempted to calm the 'tumulte'.[145] Likewise, the attempted rebellions and seditious mutterings in Norfolk in 1537 were initially suppressed by the village constables; rebellion in the county was described in that year as the province of 'Idell people'.[146] The Walsingham rebels' plan revealed the importance of having local office-holders involved in the organisation of rebellion, and also the conflicts between the poor and the 'honest men': the rebels intended to capture the head constables of all the hundreds in Norfolk 'and compelle than to call the underconstabills of e[ve]ry Town to reyse the pepull and so to go throw all the contr[i]e'.[147]

It is revealing that the rebels assumed that the office-holders would need to be forced into this leadership role. Certainly, the gentry recognised the pivotal role played by the 'honest men' in popular politics, seeing that they were capable of either stopping or leading rebellion. Hence, when the Lord Admiral was accused of attempting to organise a rising, it was stated that he intended first of all to win the support of the head yeomen of his estate. Likewise, in Wyatt's rebellion, it was intended that the Kentish yeomen would recruit those 'downward'.[148] Once rebellion was underway, the 'honest men' could play a central role in persuading rebels to return home. Thus, Edward VI noted how the spring rebellions of 1549 had been 'appeased . . . by fair purswasions, partly of honestmen among them selfes and partly by gentlemen'.[149] Likewise, the 'honest men' were often looked to by the gentry to maintain order in the aftermath of rebellion. In July 1549, Lord Grey ordered that the 'moost honest Inhabytants' should maintain nightly watch in the Thames Valley for signs of insurrection amongst the 'Light p[er]sones'. In the same vein, Sir Thomas Smith advised in the same month that order should be maintained by 'the gentleme[n] & other hed & grave yomen ho[u]sehold[e]rs'.[150]

The allegiances of the honest men were therefore critical to the organisation and maintenance of popular protest. But the evidence also demonstrates that in a number of situations, initial leadership of rebellion came not from

[145] PRO, E36/115, fol. 249r; PRO, E36/119, fols. 128v–129r.
[146] PRO, SP1/119, fol. 51r–v; PRO, SP1/120, fols. 101r, 102r; PRO, SP1/121, fol. 173r.
[147] PRO, SP1/119, fol. 30r.   [148] PRO, SP10/6/7, 12–13; PRO, SP11/3/18(I).
[149] Nichols, *Literary remains*, 226–7.   [150] PRO, SP10/8/9; PRO, SP10/8/33.

the honest men, but instead from the village poor; that the honest men joined
with poorer rebels in order to control their actions; and that significant
tensions thereafter sometimes manifested themselves between leaders and
led. Accounts of the rising at Beverley (Yorkshire) drew a distinction between
the actions of 'the comons' or 'the people' and 'the honest men'. It was
observed that it was the 'wilde people' who led the insurrection at
Beverley. Similarly, the origins of the rising of Louth, which provided the
spark for the Lincolnshire rebellion of 1536, lay with 'vi persones . . . of small
reputacion'. It was the 'pore men' of Louth who spread rumours that the
Crown intended to seize the church goods; in a direct statement of the
tensions between rich and poor, the 'pore men' threatened to hang the rich
at their own doors unless they joined in the rebellion. One eyewitness alluded
to the worries of the 'honnest men' for the safety of their property following
an act of theft by some rebels: the 'honnest men' decided to take part in the
rebellion, worrying that 'ells they shulde be robbed them selfs'. Once the
rebellion was underway, the honest men imposed order, on one occasion
punishing a thief 'by thadvice of manny honnest men'.[151] A report on the
popular mood in the north in January 1537 observed a similar tension
between the honest men and the poor. The correspondent observed that
the people were in

very good quyetnes and none of the honest sorte that had anything to lose desiring the
contrary except suche as having nothing of their owne wolde be glad to have such a
worlde as whereby they might have opportunyte to robbe and spoyle them that have
and that generally is the opynyon of all men in these p[ar]ts. For undoubtedly the
honest sorte of men through out all of this contrey do gretely desyre quyetnes.[152]

Reports to central government from the north in the aftermath of the defeat
of the Pilgrimage of Grace continued to focus upon the loyalties of 'the
honest men'. Interestingly, one correspondent noted a significant social
distinction in allegiances, observing that although some 'Light mys[or]derly
p[er]sonnes' remained seditious, 'the moste parte of the honest men' were
now loyal.[153] In other rebellions, initial leadership came from the poor.
Holinshed reported that the Evil Mayday rising of 1517 was the initiative
of 'light & ydle persones', while it was the 'substanciall persons' who
remained loyal to the Crown.[154] The rebellious crowd at Lavenham in
1525 was comprised of weavers and labourers, while it was a loyal clothier
who removed the bell from the parish church, thereby impeding the demonstrators' ability to signal the beginning of rebellion.[155] Again, both in 1525

[151] PRO, E36/118, fols. 77r, 81r; PRO, SP1/110, fols. 157r–162v.
[152] BL, Cotton MS, Caligula B II, fols. 361r–363v.
[153] PRO, SP1/115, fols. 82r, 175r; PRO, SP1/114, fols. 251r–253r.
[154] Holinshed, 590.   [155] HMC, *Welsh*, I, iii–v.

and during trouble in 1528, it was the clothiers who acted as middlemen, communicating between the Crown and the discontented commons.[156]

Very similar patterns in the initial leadership of rebellion can be observed during the commotion time of 1549. In Devon, leadership came at first from the poor. The rising at Sampford Courtenay was stoked by a tailor and a labourer, later to be joined by a fisherman and a shoemaker. Holinshed described these men as 'the reffuse, the scumme, and the rascals of the whole countrie'; Hooker called them 'the worst men & the refuse of all others'. Notably, Hooker also observed how, within a few days of the rebellion, these poor men were displaced from their leadership role by some gentlemen 'and yeomen of good countenance and credyt'.[157] Similarly, in the Yorkshire rising of 1549, the rebels planned to begin 'with the rudest and poorest sort, such as they thought were pricked with povertie'.[158] We find an identical pattern in Norfolk. In Norwich, popular support for the rising came from the 'scum of the City'; wealthier citizens opposed the rising.[159] In Buckenham, the commotioners 'sette div[er]se of the better sorte ... in the stocks & greatly threat[e]ned them'.[160] Similar evidence of internal conflicts amongst the commons in the early stages of the commotion time can be found in Aylsham, where a power struggle took place between the village constable and the rebels. Here, Edmund Chosell argued with the constable, who was collecting names to serve with Sir Edmund Wyndham against the rebels, crying out 'thow arte Wyndhams man & hast imbylled me to be a soldier, put me out of thy booke or I shall knock thye hede'. This preceded earlier conflict between the manor court jurors and some of the inhabitants, and disputes over the enclosure of common land.[161] Even in the opening stages of Kett's rebellion, apparently the outstanding example of yeomen-led popular protest, it took a few days before Robert Kett assumed control of the rebellion in Wymondham, and even then, only once his own property was threatened. Taking the evidence of early and mid-sixteenth-century popular rebellion as a whole, it therefore appears clear that in many cases men such as Robert Kett stepped into the leadership of insurrection out of a motive to control poorer, angrier and more violent rebels.

Rebel languages of class were multifarious and heterogeneous. As Michael Bush has observed, the 1536 rebels used a variety of terms to define their social constituency: 'within the jargon of the revolt, "the commons" and "poverty" were interchangeable terms and the "estate of poverty" was equivalent to "the commonalty"'.[162] So it was for the 1549 rebels. Just as

---

[156] Holinshed, 745–6.   [157] *Ibid.*, 939, 944, 948; Hooker, 67.
[158] Dickens, 'Some popular reactions', 164.   [159] Neville/Woods, sig. B4r.
[160] PRO, E134/38Eliz/Hil24.   [161] NRO, NRS 12131/27/B4.
[162] Bush, *Pilgrimage of Grace*, 285.

the Northern rebels in 1536–7 claimed to be led by Captain Poverty, so, as we have seen, Captain Commonwealth led the commotioners in Sussex, Surrey and Kent.[163] Whereas some of the mid-sixteenth-century rebels claimed to stand for the 'commons', others described their social constituency simply as the 'poverty' – an equivalent collective noun, but one loaded with more of an outraged sense of immiseration.[164] Within such formulations, social antagonisms drew labouring people together within a nexus of neighbourhood, community and class.

An organising problematic in social theory has long set 'class' in opposition to 'community'.[165] But in the language of late medieval and early modern popular protest, these concepts were conjoined: hence, the interests of the 'poorality' were synonymous with those of the 'commonwealth': one letter sent into Yorkshire by the Lincolnshire rebels in 1536 explained that 'the poorality of your realm be unrelieved, the which we think is great hurt for the commonwealth'. As in so many other respects, the mid-Tudor rebels spoke in the authentic language of late medieval popular protest. The monastic chronicler Walsingham observed of the 1381 rebels that 'they judged no name more honourable than the name *communitas*'. Similarly, Knighton's chronicle reported that the rebels fought in the name of what they called the '*communis utilitatis*'.[166] In this terminology we see the intersection of class, neighbourhood and community: Richard Wade, one of the leaders of the Suffolk commotioners, announced in the Ipswich town court that the insurrection stemmed from the 'small favour shewyd to the pore neybores'. Making a similar association between communal responsibility and political agency, but proffering a sharper sense of social antagonism, one of the rebel bills of 1537 observed how the 'gentylmen of our Cuntr[i]e' opposed the 'bretheren & neghbors'.[167] In some sources, a clear sense is given of how collective identity was fixed to a particular locality: hence, in 1536, the rebels at Horncastle (Lincolnshire) were at first sworn not to the 'true commons', but instead 'to be trewe to horn castill and them'. Communal interests therefore defined both senses of place and social identity: asked as to the reason for his participation in the 1548 near-insurrection in Hertfordshire, the Cheshunt labourer Henry Dellow explained that 'he sayeth the right of the comon & neighbour[hoo]d was the course of his being ther'. Giving an

---

[163] For a letter from Captain Poverty, see PRO, SP1/114, fol. 202r.
[164] For references to the 'poverty', see PRO, STAC3/4/89; Lamond (ed.), *A discourse*, lxiii; PRO, STAC10/16, fols. 152v–154r.
[165] See, for instance, C. J. Calhoun, *The question of class struggle: social foundations of popular radicalism during the industrial revolution* (Oxford, 1982).
[166] Bush, *Pilgrimage of Grace*, 18–19; Justice, *Writing and rebellion*, 172.
[167] MacCulloch, 'Kett's rebellion', 47; PRO, SP1/114, fol. 202r.

account of the same events, James Butler recalled how demonstrators 'came to ... doo as ther Naybors dyd'.[168]

Like the German rebels who claimed to be standing for *gemeinde*, Yorkshire rebels of 1392 sang of how 'will we stand and stoure / mayntayn our neighbour / with all our might'. This discourse was promiscuous. Jumbling together some of the keywords of late medieval popular politics, one rebel bill of 1536 called upon its subscribers to 'Tayke the owthe of the comowns to be sworn to be trewe to God and holl[y]e kyrk & to the kyngse & for the comon welth off the comownet[i]e'.[169] This bill highlights an outstanding aspect of the rebellions of 1536–7 and 1549: the willingness of rebels to perceive of social change, political conflict and religious transformation as intertwined. Importantly, the gentry's involvement in the Reformation was linked into popular complaint: mid-sixteenth-century labouring people often interpreted the Reformation in material terms, as yet another plot by the gentry to impoverish the commons and destroy the commonwealth. This view of the Reformation has significant implications for the way in which historians have understood the confessional politics of 1549. It is to that subject that we now turn.

IV THE RELIGIOUS POLITICS OF THE 1549 REBELLIONS

This section will challenge some conventional interpretations of the religious politics of the 1549 rebellions. It will suggest that both in terms of their confessional politics and in terms of their ideological content, distinctions between the Western rebellion and those in eastern and south-eastern England have been overdrawn. Whereas the Western rebellion is usually seen as concerned with religious issues, Kett's rebellion is often presented as motivated by economic complaint. In contrast, this section will argue that economics and religion should not be seen as separate categories, but were instead intertwined in rebel attitudes to the Reformation. The section begins by rethinking the confessional politics of Kett's rebellion.

As the most perceptive contemporary historian of the 1549 rebellions, Diarmaid MacCulloch's account of the confessional politics of Kett's rebellion has enjoyed considerable influence.[170] Like others, MacCulloch draws a clear distinction between religious loyalties of the Western rebels and those on Mousehold Heath. 'The further east one goes', he has argued, 'the more

---

[168] PRO, SP1/106, fol. 252r; PRO, STAC10/16, fols. 143v–145r, 168r–172r.
[169] Scribner and Benecke (eds.), *German Peasant War*, 174; Dobson, *Peasants' revolt*, 383; PRO, SP1/137, fol. 101Ar.
[170] See, for instance the account of the confessional politics of 1549 offered in Shagan, *Popular politics*. For an earlier statement of the 'Protestant' character of Kett's rebellion, see Zagorin, *Rebels and rulers*, 211.

positive enthusiasm for the new religion one finds amongst the camps.'[171] Whereas MacCulloch rightly presents the Western rebels as diehard opponents of the Edwardian Reformation, he claims that 'the East Anglian "rebels" showed little sign of religious discontent and a good deal of approval of the evangelical programme'.[172] He argues that both in the south-east and in East Anglia the rebels 'looked for further reformation of the Church ... were happy to use the new Prayer Book, and ... used the religious buzzwords familiar to Somerset's governing circle'.[173]

MacCulloch's characterisation of Kett's rebellion as pro-Reformation rests upon two pieces of evidence. Firstly, he points to the presence of three evangelical preachers, Robert Watson, Thomas Conyers and Matthew Parker, upon Mousehold Heath.[174] Conyers, the minister of the Norwich parish of St Martin at Palace, read to the rebels from the recently published vernacular Prayer Book. Watson, who held a prebend at Norwich Cathedral, had some unspecified role on the rebel council. Matthew Parker preached to the Mousehold rebels on the sins of rebellion. But this evidence can be read in different ways. Drawing a comparison between Parker and the activities of another evangelical preacher, Richard Turner, who 'preached twice in the camp at Canterbury', MacCulloch notes that 'the [Kentish] rebels would have hanged [Turner]'.[175] Matthew Parker received a similarly abusive response from the Norfolk rebels, facing angry denunciation as a 'hireling Doctor ... procured for his hire by the Gentlemen', and being poked with spears.[176] These two incidents hardly suggest a positive response on the part of the Kentish and Norfolk rebels to evangelical sermonising.

Secondly, and perhaps more significantly, MacCulloch makes much of the pro-evangelical tone of the Mousehold articles. These called for a preaching ministry, the election of ministers by parishioners and the involvement of ministers in the education of parishioners' children. MacCulloch is certainly right to identify the Mousehold articles as evidence of support for the evangelical programme; conceivably, Watson had some role in drawing them up.[177] But MacCulloch makes too much of this document, which he takes as evidence that 'there is no question of the Protestant tone of the

---

[171] MacCulloch, *Cranmer*, 432.
[172] D. MacCulloch, 'The Reformation in the balance: power struggles in the diocese of Norwich, 1533–1553', in C. Rawcliffe, R. Virgoe and R. Wilson (eds.), *Counties and communities: essays on East Anglian history presented to Hassell Smith* (Norwich, 1996), 108.
[173] MacCulloch, *Tudor church militant*, 121.
[174] MacCulloch, *Cranmer*, 433; Fletcher and MacCulloch, *Tudor rebellions*, 86–7; Shagan, *Popular politics*, 283.
[175] MacCulloch, *Cranmer*, 433.   [176] Neville/Woods, sigs. C4r–v; Holinshed, 967.
[177] Fletcher and MacCulloch, *Tudor rebellions*, 86. See also Shagan, *Popular politics*, 284.

Mousehold camp'. In particular, he describes the evangelical tone of the Mousehold articles as 'explicit and whole-hearted'.[178]

There are two reasons for suggesting that MacCulloch has overstated the importance of the Mousehold articles as evidence of the evangelical loyalties of the Norfolk rebels. Firstly, the government was itself sceptical about such declarations of support for its religious programme – Somerset wrote to the Essex rebels suggesting that their 'p[ro]fessinge christ's doctrine' was tactical and half-hearted.[179] Somerset's response is reminiscent of Peter Martyr's 'stinging sermon against the rebellious commons', in which he attacked them for 'pretending a zeal ... in their lips, and not in their hearts, counterfeiting godliness in name but not in deed'.[180] Secondly, MacCulloch places too much interpretive burden upon the Mousehold articles. It may possibly have been the case that the authors of the articles were indeed convinced evangelicals. But this should not be read as definite proof that *all* of the Norfolk rebels shared their leaders' religious loyalties. We have already seen that there existed significant tensions between the rebel leadership and the rank-and-file commotioners over other matters. And as we shall see in this section, there is good evidence to suggest that the religious loyalties of the Norfolk rebels were more heterogeneous than MacCulloch suggests.[181] As Eamon Duffy has put it:

The notion that rural Norfolk and Suffolk by 1549 were populated by tens of thousands of peasant Protestants contradicts almost everything else we know about the religion of the region in the 1540s. Protestantism certainly played a part in the formation of the official programme of the East Anglian commotions, but it would be naive to conclude that therefore all or most of those participating were convinced evangelicals.[182]

Some important scraps of evidence suggest that some Norfolk rebels harboured doubts about the Edwardian Reformation. In a tantalisingly obscure incident, Robert Kett's own religious loyalties are shown to have been more complicated than MacCulloch suggests. Two letters of 9 September 1549 indicate that, during the rebellion, Kett had drawn the conservative Bishop of Norwich, William Rugge, into his circle. The first letter stated unambiguously that Rugge had been indicted for treason 'for the comfortyng of the traytors of Norffolk'. The second letter provided more detail, describing how

---

[178] Fletcher and MacCulloch, *Tudor rebellions*, 85, 86.
[179] Shagan, 'Protector Somerset', 62. MacCulloch reads this letter differently: see his *Tudor church militant*, 122.
[180] Shagan, *Popular politics*, 271. For tactical shifts in the religious loyalties of one Hertfordshire rebel, see PRO, STAC3/7/53.
[181] For differing responses in Norwich and Yarmouth to the Edwardian and Henrician Reformations, see NRO, NCR/16A/6, p. 60; NRO, NCR/16A/5, pp. 374, 502; NRO, NCR/16A/4, fols. 54v, 59v; NRO, NQS C/S3/7, fol. 130.
[182] Duffy, *Voices of Morebath*, 130.

upon Keyttes sendyng for the . . . Busshop, eyther to come to the campe or elles to the towne of Norwhich . . . [Bishop Rugge] immedyately obeyd his commaundement and came to . . . [Norwich] long before my lord of Warrwickes comyng thyther, wheare he remayned with owt my lord knowyng of it untyll the morrowe after the Battell . . . it was proued by ffyve of the Busshoppes servauntes that Keytt had ben thryes yn the Busshoppes bedd chambor, they twoo alone, and also that the Busshopp had both vytaled the camp and ayded them with money.[183]

Other Norfolk rebels appear to have been explicit in their rejection of the Edwardian Reformation. Sir John Chaundler, who had taken part in the Castle Rising camp, left an unambiguously conservative will.[184] The rebels on Mousehold Heath, when confronted with one royal herald, mocked his 'gaie coate', which they said was 'patched togither of vestments and church-stuffe'. The reference was clear: it alluded to the belief that, in the Reformation-sanctioned seizure of goods out of parish churches, the Crown and the gentry had committed a giant act of theft.[185] It will be recalled how Robert Burnam, whom we encountered in Chapter Three, believed that 'If the gentylmen might have the higher hande styll the poore commons shulde be trodden under Foote; and destroye the Realme.' It is worth returning to Burnam's alleged words. He went on to link his critique of the gentry with the Crown's recent confiscation of church goods: 'be godds wounds', he exclaimed as he neared his parish church of St Gregory, 'he wolde have some of the Churche goodes for he was a parissheoner and his frendes gave things to it'. As parish clerk, Burnam was well placed to hide away the church's paraphernalia before it was confiscated. Evidently he did so, for the churchwardens can later be found demanding 'certeyn ornaments' from him. Interestingly, despite his evident hostility to this aspect of the Edwardian Reformation, Burnam had picked up some of the language of religious radicalism, describing the Mayor and aldermen as 'scribes and pharisees' who 'seke innocents bloude'.[186] Two years after Burnam's angry critique, the sadler William Bolton likewise found himself in trouble for his opinion that 'their are a sorte of Chorles that have the church goodes in their

---

[183] Brigden (ed.), 'The letters of Richard Scudamore', 90, 91. MacCulloch is too good a historian entirely to ignore evidence which contradicts his thesis, but he fails to integrate that evidence into his reading of the confessional politics of 1549. For MacCulloch's citation of the Scudamore letters, see MacCulloch, *Cranmer*, 437, 451–2; MacCulloch, 'The Reformation in the balance', 108. Rugge received a pardon on 1 January 1550: see *CPR, Edward VI*, III, 163.

[184] See N. Tyacke, *Aspects of English Protestantism, c. 1530–1700* (Manchester, 2001), 48.

[185] Holinshed, 978.

[186] NRO, NCR/12A/1(a), fol. 8v; NRO, NCR/16A/6, pp. 1, 2. In 1537, some parishioners of Aylsham, a village which was also caught up in Kett's rebellion, sold the church goods before they could be confiscated: see PRO, SP1/120, fol. 247v.

handes; that the poore can have noon. And I wolbe one of them that shall pluk it from them one Whitson Sondaye.'[187]

Kett's rebellion has often been seen as driven by economic concerns. Thus, Palliser has remarked that the Norfolk rebellion 'had almost purely economic motives'. Similarly, McClendon has observed that 'the grievances that led to Kett's rebellion were largely economic in nature . . . religious issues did not play a major role in motivating Kett's rebels'.[188] This is to apply an ahistorical, modern separation between 'belief' and 'economics'. As Oberman remarks, 'so-called "religious factors" . . . embraced a much larger range of experience than applies the most of us today'.[189] Again, Duffy puts it well:

There has been a tendency for historians to try to assign either religious or secular motives for Tudor rebellions, as if they could be neatly separated . . . But there was no such thing in Tudor England as 'religious causes alone', for religion was inextricably woven into the social fabric.[190]

The junction between religious language and economic complaint is perhaps at its clearest in the Mousehold articles' rejection of serfdom: 'We pray thatt all bonde men may be made fre for god made all fre with his precious blode sheddyng.' The local context of the article is to be found in a growing hostility to the maintenance of serfdom upon the estates of the attainted Duke of Norfolk, and upon those held by the Duchy of Lancaster. This local contextualisation of the article against the background of agrarian complaint in mid-sixteenth-century Norfolk, where on some manors serfdom remained a live issue, has been employed to dismiss comparisons with the critique of bondage deployed in the 1525 Swabian rebel articles, suggesting that the phrase had more to do with very localised struggles, and nothing to do with any connection to the German rebellions of 1525.[191] This interpretation of the Mousehold articles' critique of bondage has the great advantage of locating that otherwise obscure passage within the precise setting of mid-sixteenth-century Norfolk. But in pinning its subject down so neatly, this argument risks losing sight of another important aspect of the passage: that

---

[187] NRO, NCR/12A/1(a), fol. 29r. As Shagan notes: 'The idea that the goods of the church belonged to the commons was an old one in England and had played a role in many riots and rebellions, most significantly the 1381 peasants' revolt.' Shagan, *Popular politics*, 138.

[188] D. M. Palliser, 'Popular reactions to the Reformation during the years of uncertainty, 1530–70', in F. Heal and R. O'Day (eds.), *Church and society in England, Henry VIII to James I* (Basingstoke, 1977), 41; McClendon, *The quiet Reformation*, 4, 142–3.

[189] H. A. Oberman, 'The gospel of social unrest', in Scribner and Benecke, *German Peasant War*, 50.

[190] Duffy, *Voices of Morebath*, 141.

[191] MacCulloch, 'Kett's rebellion', 55–6. For the violence involved in the maintenance of bondage in sixteenth-century Norfolk, see PRO, STAC2/24/270; PRO, STAC2/19/141.

is, its striking similarity to earlier critiques of bondage. In a pleading to a royal court in 1310, a group of serfs argued that 'In the beginning every man in the world was free and the law is so favourable to liberty that he who is once found free and of free estate in court that there is record shall be held free forever.' We need not necessarily agree with Rodney Hilton that this passage discloses 'the doctrines of the radical Christian tradition' to see that there is an important continuity here with the language of the 1549 articles.[192] Prior to the 1381 rising, John Ball had allegedly asked 'What have we deserved, or why should we be kept thus in servage? We be all come from one father and mother, Adam and Eve.' Famously, John Ball expanded on his theme in his sermon on Blackheath in 1381: 'Whan Adam dalf, and Eve span / W[h]o was thane a gentilman?' The radical connotations of manumission also found their way into the austere language of the legal system: when Henry VII manumitted some of his serfs in 1485, he explained that this was 'because in the beginning nature made all men free and afterwards the law of nations reduced some under the yoke of servitude'. They also find their way, of course, across the North Sea: the Hallenser articles of 6 May 1525 observed that Christ had freely proclaimed the gospel and had 'made us free to know it'.[193] It is not proposed here that a *deliberate* religious radicalism was at work in the Mousehold articles. But this evidence does suggest, firstly, that the Mousehold articles need to be read not only within their precise geographical and historical setting, but also as the manifestation of a generic language of late medieval anti-seigneurialism; and, secondly, it highlights the difficulty of drawing clear distinctions between economics and religion in mid-sixteenth-century Europe. The institution of bondage may strike the materialist mind as a fundamental element in the feudal mode of production; but contemporaries were more likely to interpret it in spiritual terms – as an insult to Christ's sufferings upon the cross.

Certainly, the Reformation could be perceived in socio-economic terms, as part of a gentry plot to destroy the commons. John Palmer, a Sussex esquire, was accused by his tenants at Star Chamber of having claimed that the recent dissolution of monastic houses had presented him with the opportunity to dispossess them. In their complaint, they accused Palmer of 'being a man of great power', who had seized their land and driven them from their homes 'by force and violence'. Asked by one of his tenants, Margaret Benett, 'Jesu, in the Name of God, what do you mean thus extremely to handle us poor people?', Palmer answered: 'Doo ye not knowe that the Kinge's Grace hath

---

[192] Hilton, *Class conflict*, 148. See also J. H. Arnold, *Belief and unbelief in medieval Europe* (London, 2005), 211.

[193] Dobson, *Peasants' revolt*, 371, 374, 375; Eiden, 'Joint action', 30; Oberman, 'Gospel of social unrest', 43.

putt downe all the howses of monkes, fryers, and nunnes, thierfor now is the time come that we gentlemen will pull down the howses of such poor knaves as ye be?'[194] As always with such documentation, the complaint itself may well have been exaggerated; but nonetheless, it gives some insight into popular anxieties concerning the Reformation. Equally indicative of such anxieties was the complaint of the inhabitants of West Somerton against their lord, Sir John Clere, in 1546. They accused him of attempting to destroy the parish church 'of his covetous appetyt and ungoddly disposicon'. The parishioners claimed that Clere had taken the lead from the roof and seized the parish ornaments, 'intending utterly to deface & pul down the ... p[ar]isshe churche'. In all of this, they detected an intention to drive them from their homes. Notably, in an echo of the official proceedings of the Henrician and Edwardian Reformations, they alleged that he had commanded his servants to take an inventory of all the goods and ornaments

belongyng to the said towne & churche ... and hath takyn from the churchwardeyns ... the keyes of the ... churche and have unlawfully carried away the pyxe w[i]t[h] the holy sacrament of the aulter ... and will nott p[er]mitt or suffre any prest to mynistre the sacraments or to selebratt any dyvyne s[er]vyce ... to the grett [de]mynysshement of the s[er]vce of godd discomfort of yor ... ten[a]nts and inhabitants ... to the desolatyng & utter decaye of [the] ... town infeblynge of yor ... realme and to the most detestable ... example to all other covetous and ungodly peple and to the gret decay of the doctryne of the church catholyk.[195]

Social conflict was here fused with the language of religious complaint. In seeking to destroy their parish church, the West Somerton inhabitants claimed, Sir John Clere sought also the destruction of the little commonwealth of their village. As in other respects, this suggests that the politics of 1549 was not that dissimilar from 1536, when the rebels had detected an intention on the part of the King's advisers 'utt[er]lye to undo bothe the churche & the comynaltye'.[196] After all, any witness to the surveys conducted of church possessions in the Henrician and Edwardian Reformations might conclude that those responsible for such surveys, and for the subsequent seizure of church goods, were also the beneficiaries of that process; in this respect, the gentlemen had indeed 'seized the church goods'.[197]

---

[194] PRO, STAC2/6/181–2.
[195] PRO, STAC2/32/30. For similar cases, see PRO, STAC4/3/8; PRO, STAC2/21/93; PRO, STAC3/3/42.
[196] PRO, SP1/107, fol. 137r. See also PRO, SP1/108, fol. 186r.
[197] See, for instance, the lists of Norfolk gentlemen empowered to conduct such surveys; many were known as enclosers, oppressive landlords, and great sheep farmers: *L&P*, XII (1), 455. Subsequent grants of former church possessions were often made to such people. See *CPR, Edward VI*, I, 272–4; II, 112–18, 308–11; III, 334–5; IV, 29–31.

All of this helps to make sense of the vehemence with which the physical symbols of the Reformation were attacked in Norfolk in 1549. The dove-house and mansion house constructed from the former hospital dedicated to St Mary Magdalene, which was owned by the landowner and city oligarch John Corbet, was destroyed by the rebels on their way to Mousehold Heath. Similarly, the Great Hospital which had recently been re-established by Norwich's governors following its dissolution was attacked and partially burnt during the initial attack on the city.[198] Likewise, the new harbour at Great Yarmouth, built with the proceeds from the sale of church goods, was destroyed by the rebels.

If the religious politics of Kett's rebellion therefore emerges as rather more complicated than has been suggested, so the motives and behaviour of the Western rebels were influenced by a similar concoction of religious and social complaint. Holinshed's *Chronicles* began their account of the Western rebellion by claiming that the Cornish and Devon rebels were engaged in a 'religious quarrell' which set them apart from the other commotioners. Yet Holinshed swiftly contradicts this bald statement with the observation that although 'The priests ever harped upon one string, to bring the Bishop of Rome into England againe', the rebels were divided as to their aims, and that for some amongst them, social conflict was more important than religious change: 'some would have no justices, some no state of gentlemen'. This observation is given further weight by Holinshed's claim that the Western rising was initially inspired by rumours that the Crown intended to impose new taxes, stating that the priests 'contrived to raise . . . feined rumors, giving it out, that the people should be constreined to paie a ratable taske for their sheepe and cattell, and an excise for everie thing that they should eate or drinke'. Just as in Kett's rebellion, and just as in the Lincolnshire rising of 1536, in Devon the initial leadership of insurrection came from the lower orders: a tailor and a labourer, men whom Holinshed described as 'the woorst men and the reffuse of all others'. Moreover, as elsewhere in 1549, the Devon rebellion was spread by rumours that the gentry intended the destruction of the commons: on the outbreak of rebellion at Clyst St Mary, 'the common people . . . spread it abroad, that the gentlemen were altogither bent to over-run, spoile, and destroie them'.[199] Economics and religion, then, enjoyed a closer proximity than the modern mind might imagine.

---

[198] Holinshed, 965; C. Rawcliffe, *Medicine for the soul: the life, death and resurrection of an English medieval hospital* (Stroud, 1999), 229–33.
[199] Holinshed, 917, 918, 924, 939, 942, 944; for more on Clyst St Mary, see Wood, *Riot, rebellion and popular politics*, 58–9.

Part III

Consequences

5

The decline of insurrection in later sixteenth- and early seventeenth-century England

One may apply to the concept of passive revolution ... the interpretive criterion of molecular changes which in fact progressively modify the pre-existing composition of forces, and hence become the matrix of new changes. (Hoare and Nowell Smith, *Prison notebooks of Antonio Gramsci*, 109.)

I 'BASE EXCREMENTS OF THE COMMONWEALTH': SOCIAL AND CULTURAL CHANGE IN SOUTHERN AND EASTERN ENGLAND

In the later sixteenth century, facing the severe strain of demographic and economic pressure, wealthier, landed inhabitants in southern and eastern England turned on their poorer neighbours. Significantly, it was from amongst this 'better sort' of people that the leaders of rebellion in 1549 had been drawn. Benefiting from the increased prosperity which marked out their class, wealthier people increasingly came to see the poor as a dangerous burden. Keith Wrightson, one of the earliest historians of this phenomenon, has noted

the realignment of the vitally important middling group in rural communities, the yeomanry and minor gentry, the cocks of the parish. As the beneficiaries of economic change they had become increasingly distanced in their interests from their poor neighbours. As the officers and representatives of their communities they had learnt to identify themselves, albeit selectively, with the programme of order and social discipline with which the Elizabethan and Stuart state had attempted to contain, dampen and defuse the pressing problems of socio-economic change.[1]

As William Pfaff suggests in another context, 'Once the worker has won a position of basic economic security and reasonable expectations he has considerably more reason to be conservative on social issues ... for the workingman, everything could be jeopardised by radical change.'[2]

---

[1] Wrightson, *English society*, 181.
[2] Quoted in R. Sennett and J. Cobb, *The hidden injuries of class* (New York, 1972), 4–5.

In the last decades of the sixteenth century, the profound legitimation crisis that had been opened up by the early Reformation was resolved through the incorporation of wealthier social fractions, via the medium of office-holding, into state structures which, while open to the 'better sort', remained closed to the poor. What emerged from this process was a relatively inclusive, participatory state which relied for its legitimacy and functioning upon local elites drawn from beyond the parameters of the gentry. This section will survey processes of social change in southern and eastern England in the later sixteenth and early seventeenth centuries; the next section will look at the relationship between those changes and the growth of governance within later Tudor and early Stuart England; the final section will analyse the changing character of social conflict in southern and eastern England.

Perhaps the most notable social change of the later sixteenth century was the polarisation of rural communities, as the poor increased in number, while the living standards of their richer neighbours improved. For all that it was deplored by contemporary moralists, this combination of social polarisation and social mobility overturned earlier characterisations of the polity, which had assumed the existence of a fixed, immutable social structure. Thus, back in 1509, Edmund Dudley had warned that the commonalty should not 'presume above ther owne degree, nor any of them pretend or conterfete the state of his Better'.[3] It was doubtful whether Dudley's formulation related very closely to the real distribution of wealth and power in early Tudor England; certainly, it failed to describe the fluidity of social structure in the later sixteenth century.

The mobility of the Elizabethan period was anticipated by the commonwealth writers of the mid-sixteenth century. In one of the dialogues in Raphe Robynson's translation of *Utopia*, it was decided that rather than levy excessive taxes, it was better for the monarch to rule a kingdom comprised of wealthy households. Such a regime, it was assumed, would be built upon firmer foundations than one in which the monarch was wealthy, but the people poor.[4] In his approach to social mobility, as on so many other subjects, Robert Crowley managed to be both emphatic and contradictory. On the one hand, echoing the standard social theory articulated by Dudley, he denounced mobility as corrosive of a divinely ordained hierarchy.[5] On the other, like Robynson's translation of *Utopia*, Crowley proposed that a society characterised by a broader distribution of wealth would be better able to resist rebellion, writing in his discussion 'Of Commotionars' that 'When the swerde wyl not helpe / in the common wealthe / To purge it of

---

[3] Brodie (ed.), *Tree of commonwealth*, 45–6. [4] More/Robynson, 37–40.
[5] Crowley, *Select works*, 63–4, 89.

commotionars ... then must discrete counsell / fynde wayes to kyll / The power of those rebelles ... When these men, through cherishing / do growe and be stronge / Then can no Commotionars / continew long.'[6] Crowley envisaged a polity in which upward mobility conjoined with reformation. As he put it, the 'power' of commotioners lay in 'the people ignoraunte'. The answer to the threat posed by rebellion therefore lay in a cultural offensive, in which the commons would be reconciled to the exercise of authority via education and persuasion. The active consent of the governed would therefore be secured through a combination of material advancement and cultural hegemony.[7]

For Crowley, the success of this programme of cultural, educational and economic reformation depended upon the transformation of the gentry's attitude to the commons. Summarising the gentry's interpretation of the causes of the 1549 rebellions, Crowley wrote of how they believed that 'The paisant knaves [that is, the commons] be to welthy, provender pricketh them! ... Thei would not have us masters of that which is our owne! ... Thei wil have the law in their own handes! ... We wyll tech them to know theyr betters. And because they wold have al commone, we wil leave them nothing. And if they once stirre againe, or do but once cluster togither, we wil hang them at their owne dores!'[8] This vengeful spirit, Crowley argued, was not conducive to a settled state. Instead, he advised the gentry 'Grudge not to se the people growe in wealth under you, neither [should] you invent waies to kepe them bare.' In Crowley's analysis, this approach was sanctioned by biblical precedent, which demonstrated that social stability depended upon the broad distribution of wealth. Moreover, he argued that if the gentry wished to prevent future disorders, they should not only accept the growing prosperity of the better sort of people, but should also embrace godly religion.[9] Crowley's approach was typical of that of the commonwealth writers: Hugh Latimer was famously proud of his humble origins. 'By yeomen's sons the faith of Christ is and hath been maintained chiefly,' he preached. For Latimer, social stability was also built upon the wide distribution of wealth: 'if the Kings honour, as some men say, standeth in the great multitude of people; then these graziers, inclosers, and rent-rearers are hinderers of the Kings honour'.[10] In a sermon preached to Edward VI in 1552, Bernard Gilpin spoke of how the 'mightie men and gentlemen' dislike to see 'the comonaltie live to wel at ease' and believed that the commons 'grow everie day to be gentlemen'. The gentry therefore sought to prevent such social mobility through raising rents and other forms of oppression.[11]

---

[6] *Ibid.*, 21–3.   [7] *Ibid.*, 23.   [8] *Ibid.*, 142–3.   [9] *Ibid.*, 147–8.
[10] Latimer, *Sermons*, 100–2.   [11] Gilpin, *A godly sermon*, 64.

The commonwealth writers' new approach to social mobility did not result in a universal shift in gentry attitudes to the newly wealthy better sort. Thus, the Elizabethan Suffolk gentleman Sir John Tyrell complained of how the living standards of his tenants had risen 'farre above the degrees of their Auncestors'. In Tyrell's analysis, it was this increased prosperity that had stimulated these 'comminers and meane tenauntes' to oppose him; if allowed to succeed, he believed that the result would be to bring 'the astate of gentlemen and men of worship ... to suche ruyne as the cyvill and quyett governement of the common welthe shulde therebie be moche hindered'.[12] But within Elizabethan government circles, the commonwealth writers' earlier analysis held increasing sway. Thus, Sir Thomas Smith felt that a wider distribution of economic and political power would prevent rebellion. In his discussion of the yeomanry, he stated unambiguously that 'These be these which olde Cato calleth *Aratores* and *optimos cives in Republica*: and such as the writers of common wealthes praise to have manie in it.'[13] Francis Bacon agreed. In his discussion of 'seditions and troubles', he demonstrated a keen awareness of the importance of providing a material basis to social stability. He drew a comparison between England and France, arguing that the true martial strength of England had a material determinant, claiming that 'the middle people of England make good soldiers, which the peasants of France do not'.[14] Mervyn James has identified the decline of feudal links between lord and tenant as one of the reasons for the failure of the 1569 Northern rebellion.[15] The frustration of the commons at the failure of the gentry and nobility to fulfil the roles expected of them was also a cause of contemporary comment in East Anglia. In Norfolk in 1570, the husbandman William Shuckforth wished for a gentry-led rising to restore Catholicism; but he expressed doubts that such a rebellion would gain much support because the gentry 'are so extreme to poore men'.[16] Elizabethan policy therefore sought to exploit such divisions in order to undercut the nobility's capacity to oppose state power. Certainly, historians have identified the late sixteenth century as a period in which central courts afforded significant support to copyholders' rights.[17] Whether the gentry liked it or not, the increased

---

[12] MacCulloch, *Suffolk and the Tudors*, 331.

[13] T. Smith, *De republica Anglorum* (1583; Cambridge, 1982), 75.

[14] F. Bacon, *Essays civil and moral* (1612; London, 1892), 21–5, 46–51.

[15] M. E. James, 'The concept of order and the Northern rising', in M. E. James, *Society, politics and culture: studies in early modern England* (Cambridge, 1986), 270–307.

[16] *CPR, Elizabeth* I, V, *1569–72*, no. 1817.

[17] R. Hoyle, 'Tenure and the land market in early modern England: or, a late contribution to the Brenner Debate', *Economic History Review*, 2nd ser., 43 (1990), 5; R. C. Allen, *Enclosure and the yeoman: the agricultural development of the south Midlands, 1450–1850* (Oxford, 1988), 68.

wealth of the yeomanry, coupled with social mobility, became a defining characteristic of early modern English society.

In the countryside, the increased prosperity of the social fraction whom Bacon labelled 'the middle people' depended upon the enclosure of common land; stinting arrangements which marginalised or obliterated the common rights of the poor; the engrossing of farms; and the increased productivity of farming enterprises, achieved through a combination of agricultural improvement and decreases in wages paid to agricultural labourers. All of this occurred at the same time as the sharpening of social polarisation, felt through the decreasing number of middle-sized farms held by husbandmen, the increasing acreage of farm holdings maintained by wealthier yeomen, and the growth in the number of landless, poverty-stricken agricultural wage labourers.[18]

The key decades in this process were the 1580s and 1590s, years which saw recurrent harvest failures and resultant dearth in foodstuffs. William Hunt has argued that in Essex, 'the crisis that culminated in the 1590s, brought to a peak by the conjuncture of climatic disaster and military expenditure, left social perceptions and public policy decisively altered'.[19] Steve Hindle concurs with Hunt's assessment, identifying the 1590s as the decade which saw the forging of a 'culture of discipline' marked by a peculiar intensity, a wide range, a sharp severity and substantial statutory backing. In all these respects, Hindle argues, the disciplinary drive of the 1590s set itself apart from earlier attempts at the reformation of manners. The poor were the target of these new disciplinary regimes, their lives increasingly hedged in through discriminatory systems of poor relief and harsh social discipline.[20] The crisis years of the late sixteenth century fundamentally altered the structure of the agrarian economy of southern and eastern England. As Keith Wrightson notes, from the later sixteenth century, there occurred 'a growing divergence in the living standards of rich and poor, and a redistribution of income towards the upper ranks of society' such that 'by the end of the sixteenth century ... a permanent proletariat had emerged, collectively designated "the poor"'.[21] These structural changes had cultural consequences. Wrightson identifies the growing usage, from the later

---

[18] On changes in land-ownership, see M. Spufford, *Contrasting communities: English villagers in the sixteenth and seventeenth centuries* (Cambridge, 1974), 46–58.

[19] W. Hunt, *The puritan moment: the coming of revolution to an English county* (Cambridge, MA, 1983), 64.

[20] Hindle, *State and social change*, 177. On the 1590s in towns, see P. Clark, 'A crisis contained? The condition of English towns in the 1590s', in P. Clark (ed.), *The European crisis of the 1590s: essays in comparative history* (London, 1985), 44–66; M. Power, 'London and the control of the crisis of the 1590s', *History*, 70 (1985), 371–85.

[21] Wrightson, *English society*, 140, 141.

sixteenth century, of a 'language of sorts' which distinguished between a wealthier, office-holding, literate and powerful 'better sort of people', and their marginal, poorer neighbours, variously labelled the 'poorer sort'; the 'worse sort'; or the 'vulgar sort'.[22] Steve Hindle sees this labelling process as indicative of 'both immediate social tensions and the longer-term reconstruction of social identities'.[23]

The emergence of new modes of social and cultural discrimination was given added velocity by significant cultural, educational and linguistic changes in the later sixteenth and early seventeenth centuries.[24] The later sixteenth century witnessed a substantial overall rise in literacy rates. Again, it is notable that this was especially marked in East Anglia, the cockpit of rebellion in 1549. Yet that increase in literacy was socially specific – primarily, it was the children of the 'better sort' who benefited from the educational improvements of the age.[25] An important hegemonic purpose underlay this increase in literacy. As Fletcher and Stevenson have observed, 'Tudor and Stuart schools were just as much concerned to inculcate religion, civility, good behaviour and obedience as academic learning.'[26] Especially important in this regard was the teaching of history; we will see in Chapter Six how, from the later sixteenth century, the representation of the 1549 rebellions in historical and polemical writing contributed to the dissemination of notions of authority and hierarchy.

Increased literacy amongst middling social groups also contributed to an important linguistic shift: the increasing standardisation of spoken English amongst propertied groups, such that south-eastern English came to be regarded as the appropriate accent which educated people should use. As Adam Fox has observed, schooling was seen as a key means by which this standard English could be inculcated, in order to 'homogenise the speech of the social elite and in organising a self-conscious attempt to distance the language of the learned gentility from that of the lower orders'. Thus, at Bury St Edmunds (Suffolk), the schoolmaster Edmund Coote ordered his pupils to avoid 'imitating the barbarous speech of your countrie people'. By the later sixteenth century, 'alternative and subordinate strains of the language' had

---

[22] Wrightson, 'Sorts of people'; K. E. Wrightson, 'Estates, degrees and sorts: changing perceptions of society in Tudor and Stuart England', in P. Corfield (ed.), *Language, history and class* (Oxford, 1991), 30–52. See also H. French, 'The search for the "middle sort of people" in England, 1600–1800', *Historical Journal*, 43 (2000), 277–93.

[23] Hindle, *State and social change*, 49.

[24] For a powerful assessment of these modes, see D. Rollison, *The local origins of modern society: Gloucestershire, 1500–1800* (London, 1992).

[25] Wrightson, *English society*, 191; D. Cressy, *Literacy and the social order: reading and writing in Tudor and Stuart England* (Cambridge, 1980), 142–74.

[26] A. Fletcher and J. Stevenson, 'Introduction', in Fletcher and Stevenson (eds.), *Order and disorder*, 35.

come to be characterised as 'dialects'. Moreover, as with the teaching of history, this linguistic shift was closely related to the strengthening of cultural hegemony in Elizabethan England: Fox observes that 'in this period, to a much greater extent than ever before, language came to underpin social hierarchies', providing 'a vehicle for status differentiation', and helping 'to ratify and confirm' the social order 'in new and subtly pervasive ways'.[27]

Perhaps those most affected by this linguistic shift were the 'better sort' of people: the yeomanry of the countryside and the wealthier artisans of towns. Thus, in answer to the proposition that 'the base people [are] ... uncivill, rude, untowarde, discurteous, rough, savage', one conduct book advised that gentlemen should distinguish between the speech of 'labourers and rustikes' and those who 'ought to bee put in the middest between Gentleman and clownes'.[28] Likewise, writing in 1618, the Suffolk man Robert Reyce identified the wealthier classes of his locality with 'the best speach and pronunciation', and contrasted this with the 'honest country toyling villager'. He also noted a distinction between the speech of 'the ruder sort' and 'the artificer of the good townes', who instead 'prideth in the counterfitt imitation of the best source of language'. A tract of 1598 which offered advice to those yeomen's sons who aspired to become gentlemen's servants suggested that together with altering their appearance and manners, they should 'as well as [they] can, make satisfaction for the queenes currant English'.[29] Notably, it has been observed that distinctions between 'class-based speech' emerged at the same time as 'a growing discourse that linked disordered language and social disorder'.[30] This coincidence, it has been argued, was more than accidental. In the later sixteenth century just as elite contemporaries regarded the civility of property groups as articulated through their use of the 'queenes currant English', so the barbarous character of plebeian speech patterns identified the poor as a threatening social group.

The material changes of the late sixteenth century stimulated significant shifts in propertied perceptions of the poor. Back in 1552, Ridley could still compare the poverty of Christ with the lot of the urban poor.[31] Such formulations made decreasing sense to the governing classes of later sixteenth-century England, by which time the poor were more likely to be considered as marginal, dangerous and diseased. As Mike Braddick observes, 'measures to deal with poverty were closely associated with campaigns

---

[27] Fox, *Oral and literate culture*, 52, 53, 60, 100.   [28] Guazzo, *Civile conversation*, I, 175.
[29] Fox, *Oral and literate culture*, 101, 103, 104.
[30] J. M. Williams, '"O! When degree is shak'd": sixteenth-century anticipations of some modern attitudes toward usage', in T. W. Machan and C. T. Scott (eds.), *English and its social contacts: essays in historical sociolinguistics* (New York, 1992), 71.
[31] Tawney and Power (eds.), *Tudor economic documents*, II, 312.

against sin and disease'.[32] Thus, the 1571 Norwich orders for the poor described how the 'Fleshe' of beggars 'was eaton with vermyne and corrupte diseases grewe upon them'. Paul Griffiths has noted 'A recurring rant against excess linked begging and bingeing with icy indifference'. According to the orders for the government of the poor passed by the governors of Norwich in 1571, the diseased condition of the poor had four causes: idleness; gluttony; drunkenness; and ungodliness. The 'crewes' of beggars that begged at the doors of the citizenry of Norwich were condemned, for 'in ther pottes they abused the holy name of God with swearinge, pratinge and lyeinge'.[33] The city fathers responded to such ungodliness by drawing up a code which rewarded begging with a flogging, prohibited informal alms-giving, established a Bridewell for the punishment of beggars, and appointed officers responsible for the prevention of begging and the surveillance of the poor. Throughout, reference was made to how the 'commonwealth' would enjoy 'reformation' through the provision of the articles. The articles concluded by proudly noting that Matthew Parker, the Archbishop of Canterbury, had written to the aldermen asking for an account of the orders; all of this was to 'the citie[s] great commendacion'.[34] The settled poor were therefore relabelled as a burden, and the transient poor as a threat. One clergyman argued that 'if the poor man was idle and untoward "it is alms to whip him". Such persons were "scabs, filth and vermin", "base excrements of the commonwealth". "He that helpeth one of these steady beggars to the stocks and the whip and the house of correction not only deserveth better of the commonwealth, but doth a work of great charity in the sight of God, than he that helpeth him with meat and money and lodging."'[35]

J. A. Sharpe has identified a process by which the poor were criminalised in this period. Customary-use rights, such as gleaning or gathering firewood, were redefined as acts of theft; vagrants identified as thieves; and labourers and paupers labelled as a criminal class.[36] The poor were therefore regarded with increasing suspicion by the 'better sort', their numbers watched by their governors, and their composition and activities monitored. Thus, the vestries of early seventeenth-century Finchingfield and Braintree agreed 'to keep a close eye on the poor'. All of this had fundamental implications for social relations. In 1629, for instance, the godly minister John Rogers observed

---

[32] Braddick, State formation, 55.
[33] P. Griffiths, 'Inhabitants', in C. Rawcliffe and R. Wilson (eds.), Norwich since 1550 (London, 2004), 64; Tawney and Power (eds.), Tudor economic documents, II, 317.
[34] Tawney and Power (eds.), Tudor economic documents, II, 316–26.
[35] C. Hill, Society and puritanism in pre-revolutionary England (London, 1964), 276.
[36] J. A. Sharpe, Crime in early modern England, 1550–1750 (1984; 2nd edn, Harlow, 1999), 128.

that many wealthier householders regarded the poor as 'ill-tongued' and 'thievish'.[37]

Again, this process of criminalisation finds its origins in the later sixteenth century. Thomas Tusser's *Five hundred pointes of good husbandrie* (1573–80), which was designed for a readership of yeomen farmers, warned its readers that 'The champion [that is, the commoner] robbeth by night / and prowleth and filcheth by day / Himselfe and his beast, out of sight / both spoileth and maketh away / Not onely thy grasse, but thy corne / both after, and er[e] it be shorne . . . In Bridewell a number be stript / lesse worthie than these to be whipt.'[38] Such 'champions' were more than mere thieves; they represented an impediment to agrarian improvement, condemned by their poverty, marginality, criminality and idleness: 'For commons these commoners crie / enclosing they may not abide / Yet some be not able to bie / a cow with hir calfe by hir side / Nor laie not to live by their wurke / but theevishlie loiter and lurke.' In Tusser's account, the rural poor therefore represented a fundamental threat to the social order: 'Where champions ruleth the ro[o]ste / there dailie disorder is moste.' In contrast, Tusser praised the virtues of a private property unthreatened by such criminal commoners: 'Againe what a [j]oie is it knowne / when men may be bold of theire owne!' He concluded by dismissing popular criticism of enclosure, linking its advance with the extension of order: 'The poore at enclosinge doo grutch / because of abuses that fall / Least some man have but too muche / and some againe nothing at all / If order might therein be found / wat were to the severall ground?'[39] By the later sixteenth century, therefore, in many parts of southern and eastern England, the 'better sort of people' had separated themselves from their poorer neighbours. This process of polarisation manifested itself in education, culture, language, social structure and social relations. It also, of course, showed itself in the increasingly unequal distribution of social power within communities. The cultural and linguistic separation of the 'better sort' was underwritten by their class authority, and that authority was increasingly vested within state structures.

II STATE FORMATION, OFFICE-HOLDING AND THE LAW

Recent histories of the early modern English state have been characterised by two approaches: a focus upon the relationship between the state and social change; and an interest in the micro-politics of state formation. This latter approach has led to the reconceptualisation of the state: instead of seeing it as a distant, centralising 'set of institutions', it has been argued that the early

---

[37] Hunt, *Puritan moment*, 82–3, 237.
[38] Tawney and Power (eds.), *Tudor economic documents*, III, 65. [39] *Ibid.*, 65–8.

modern English state comprised 'a network of power relations which [became] ... institutionalised to a greater or lesser extent over time'. Central to the operation of this dispersed state were two key features: firstly, its 'incorporative character', drawing as it did upon the participation of a wide range of unpaid, amateur officers; and secondly, its basis in consent.[40] Hence, for Mike Braddick, the early modern state existed as a 'coordinated and territorially bounded network of agencies exercising political power', autonomous of 'other political organisations within those bounds'. State power depended upon a process of 'legitimation [which] gave force to ideas whose generally understood meanings were not determined' by agents of the state alone. Thus, as Steve Hindle puts it, 'order and authority did not merely "trickle down" but "welled up" within society itself'.[41] The state was therefore about more than institutions and officers: it was also about *ideas*.

In order to operate effectively, dominating ideas had to do more than mechanically legitimate authority; they had to be capable of winning the active consent of the governed. One implication of this, as we saw in Chapter Four, was that some political keywords could become free-floating, capable of being claimed by a variety of competing groups. A shared political language between elite and plebeians did not, in other words, necessarily mean a shared politics. The overlap of political language meant that both social consensus and social conflict were accommodated within the same discursive framework. Within successfully integrated states, notions of authority had therefore to be broadly shared within society. As John Walter puts it, 'central ... to popular political culture was a set of expectations about the proper exercise of authority'.[42] Perhaps the most sensitive point in early modern popular politics lay at the juncture between custom, law and order. Popular legalism was manifested through a concern with customary law; participation in the administration of the criminal law; and litigation before a multiplicity of local, municipal, hundredal, county, assize and central courts. Popular legalism was not only deeply felt, but also highly tactical. Where communal litigation failed to correct a perceived injustice, labouring people might have recourse to riot. Even rebellion can be understood as a means by which plebeians could open a dialogue with their governors. But rebellion could also be the result of the failure of governing elites to listen to popular complaints. Thus, the 1537 Walsingham rebellion was inspired by the belief that 'if we shuld complain to the counsail it shuld not be h[e]ard'.[43] Over the course of the later sixteenth century, however, popular litigation before equity courts increased rapidly. The subject matter

---

[40] Hindle, *State and social change*, ix, 19, 132.
[41] Braddick, *State formation*, 9–10; Hindle, *State and social change*, 115.
[42] Walter, *Understanding popular violence*, 5.   [43] PRO, SP1/119, fol. 38v.

of such litigation often concerned local disputes which, earlier in the century, might have led to riot or even to rebellion.[44] Historians of the early modern state have interpreted this increase in litigation as 'an index of growth of government'. Thus it has been argued that 'over the course of the sixteenth century ... there was a transformation of role of the law: once merely "an independent component within the social and political structure", law became "constitutive of the state"'.[45]

Within the recent literature on state formation, the law emerges as both an institutional and an ideological resource in the process of state formation: providing a forum for the resolution of local disputes, while also allowing for the articulation of plebeian complaint, had the effect of strengthening the political centre. Perhaps nowhere was this most obvious than in East Anglia, where, in the years after 1549, the population acquired a notoriety for litigiousness. Thus, according to William Camden, Norfolk 'always has been reputed the most fruitful nursery of lawyers; and even among the common people you shall meet many who ... if they have no just quarrel, are able to raise it out of the very quirks and niceties of the law'. The people of Norfolk retained their reputation into the seventeenth century: John Aubrey observed of the Norfolk inhabitants that 'they are good clear wits, subtle, and the most litigious of England: they carry Littleton's Tenures at the plough tail'.[46] The inhabitants of the Cambridgeshire fens had an almost identical reputation: it was said of the wealthier inhabitants that 'of ancient custom' they made 'it a part of their recreation to discourse of legal cases'.[47] Such popular litigiousness not only set lord against tenants, but villager against villager: thus, one poem of 1595 remarked that 'Thro[ugh] commoning in moore or heath or shack / More suits in Norfolk arise in a yeare / Than matters all in shires ... Not only Lords and Tenants be at jarr / But commoners among themselves do war ... The rich as poor the commons overthrowe / And gaynful but to lawyers only be.'[48] In 1549, the legal-mindedness of East Anglians had contributed to the politics of rebellion; by the later sixteenth century, it fuelled the engines of state formation.

We have seen that local officers had often taken a leading part in the medieval and early Tudor rebellions. This role stemmed in part from the significant role they played in mediating between central authorities and

---

[44] On the increase in popular litigation at central courts, see C. W. Brooks, *Pettyfoggers and vipers of the Commonwealth: the 'lower branch' of the legal profession in early modern England* (Cambridge, 1986), 52–4.

[45] Hindle, *State and social change*, 13, 31, 89; see also Sharpe, 'The people and the law'.

[46] R. W. Ketton-Cremer, *Norfolk in the Civil War* (London, 1969), 20–1.

[47] W. Cunningham (ed.), 'Common rights at Cottenham and Stretham in Cambridgeshire', *Camden Miscellany*, XII (Camden Society, 3rd ser., XVIII, London, 1910), 177.

[48] J. P. Boileau, 'Old poem on Norfolk', *Norfolk Archaeology*, 5 (1859), 165–6.

local communities. In Tudor England, authority in the countryside had long depended upon 'grave and wise yeomen', a social fraction that was often referred to as the 'honest men', 'the gravest or beste sorte' or the 'moost substancyall men'.[49] The relationship between local office-holding and state power was deepened over the course of the sixteenth century.[50] In particular, the mid-sixteenth century represented a key watershed in this development and in the wider thrust of social policy. Arguably, this had much to do with the immediate impact of the 1549 rebellions. In May 1549, sensing imminent trouble, the aldermen of Norwich had ordered the establishment of a compulsory collection for the poor.[51] Hindle picks up on this example, pointing out that poor rates were enforced in Norwich from 1549, in York from 1550, in Cambridge, Colchester and Ipswich from 1556–7, and in 'various rural parishes in the south-east from the 1560s'. Was it any coincidence that, of the five towns cited, four had seen significant trouble in 1549? The mid-sixteenth century also saw an indicative change in the material display of political culture within the parish church: 'if Elizabethan vestries met in parish churches they did so in the presence of the royal arms, the "dragon and the dog" having replaced Christ crucified as *a*, if not *the*, central symbol in parochial political culture in the mid-sixteenth century'.[52]

Importantly given the lack of organised rebellion in London in 1549, the mid-sixteenth century has been identified as a key moment in the organisation of authority in the capital. Parochial oligarchies were reshaped at that time, and parish vestries seem to originate in the mid-sixteenth century.[53] Certainly, the London Bridewell, established in 1552, provided both the model and the name for similar institutions elsewhere in England. In London, the broad basis of office-holding and participation in civic, guild and parochial government has been presented as a key reason for the political stability of the city despite the economic, demographic and social transformation that the capital underwent between the later sixteenth and mid-seventeenth centuries.[54] Ian Archer therefore notes 'a process analogous to

---

[49] PRO, SP12/58/23; BL, Cotton MS, Titus B II, fol. 142r; BL, Add MS 34079, fol. 11r.

[50] Braddick, *State formation*, 75, 76, 79. See also K. E. Wrightson, 'Two concepts of order: justices, constables and jurymen in seventeenth-century England', in J. Brewer and J. Styles (eds.), *An ungovernable people: the English and their law in the seventeenth and eighteenth centuries* (London, 1980), 21–46; Wrightson, *English society*, 172–3.

[51] Hudson and Tingay (eds.), *Records*, II, 126.

[52] Hindle, *State and social change*, 147, 229.

[53] B. A. Kumin, *The shaping of a community: the rise and reformation of the English parish, c. 1400–1560* (Aldershot, 1996), 253.

[54] In London, the evidence seems to suggest a growing incorporation of the urban middling sort into the local structures of authority in the later sixteenth century: see V. Pearl, 'Change and stability in seventeenth-century London', in J. Barry (ed.), *The Tudor and Stuart town: a reader in English urban history, 1530–1688* (London, 1990), 139–65; S. Rappaport, *Worlds within worlds: structures of life in sixteenth-century London* (Cambridge, 1989), 174–5;

that observed by Keith Wrightson in rural England whereby the rulers of local society came to align themselves with the value system of the national elite'.[55] But, again, this process finds its origins earlier in the century: in 1549, the London authorities had been able to rely upon the 'most best cheifest and saddest' householders to maintain nightly watches for trouble. These individuals were not only responsible for order on the streets, but also for that within their households: the authorities ordered the citizens to 'loke to their [w]hole famylyes and men s[er]vants that they suffer none of them to be abrode owte of ther howses' during the night-time, in 'this tyme of unquyetnes'.[56]

The care with which the London authorities drew up their plans for the prevention of insurrection probably prevented the outbreak of disorder within the capital and forms a stark contrast to the inability of the Norwich magistrates to control rebel activity within their city. Notably, the London governors assumed that they were able to rely upon the widespread participation of householders in the assertion of authority. But it is important to recognise that not only was such participation class-specific – only ratepaying householders were entitled to vote in parochial meetings – but they were also defined by age and gender. Civic participation, in its ideal form, was patriarchal: largely excluding women, and wholly excluding apprentices, servants, non-householding families and the young. As in the countryside, therefore, the exercise of urban authority was rooted in class, gender, age and place; and it produced its own peculiar anxieties.

If London had formed the vanguard of social policy in the mid-sixteenth century, in Elizabeth's reign that leading role was passed to East Anglia, and to Norwich in particular. As Paul Griffiths has observed, the 1570 orders for the relief of the poor, and the subsequent census of the poor, provided a 'blueprint for similar schemes across the land'.[57] The social experiment in Norwich probably provided the model for the 1572 Act passed by parliament for the government of the poor. Paul Slack has pointed to the existence of a cluster of precocious municipalities 'engaged in social-welfare enterprises ... in East Anglia, between Norwich and Colchester, beginning in the 1570s'. Matthew Parker, a Norwich man who had witnessed Kett's rebellion at first hand, had by 1572 risen to become Archbishop of Canterbury; he took a personal interest in the city's social reforms, and was involved in drawing up the Poor Law Act of that year. Importantly, this drive for the reformation of the poor was connected to puritan demands for further

---

I. Archer, *The pursuit of stability: social relations in Elizabethan London* (Cambridge, 1991), 19, 31–2; K. Lindley, 'The maintenance of stability in early modern London', *Historical Journal*, 34, 4 (1991), 985–90.

[55] Archer, *Pursuit of stability*, 258.   [56] CLRO, Journal 16, fols. 15v, 17v.

[57] Griffiths, 'Inhabitants', 63. See also Slack, *From reformation to improvement*, 45.

doctrinal reformation. As Slack puts it, in the 1570s, Norwich was on the way to 'becoming a renowned puritan citadel'.[58] The Norwich experiment was paralleled by a similar vigour elsewhere within East Anglia. In 1574, 'certen gentlemen and chief yomen' established a Bridewell in Acle, anticipating the Act which empowered magistrates to establish houses of correction by two years.[59] In 1588, a house of correction was established at Bury St Edmunds (Suffolk).[60] Other studies confirm the precocity of East Anglia as a centre for social reform: parish vestries were most likely to be found in the south and the east of England.[61] Within industrial towns, such as those located along the Thames Valley which had seen such trouble in 1549, governors were well aware of the potential fragility of their authority, observing the 'shomakers, Tailers, weavers and [other] ... lighte p[er]sones' that clustered within their communities; such people might be 'easilie moved to muyteny'. The incorporation of textile towns was often designed to solidify the existent distribution of power: thus, in 1596, Newbury (Berkshire) was granted a charter which strengthened oligarchical forces within the corporation; the following year, the corporation made illegal any unauthorised assembly of 'all persons of an inferior sort, freemen, journeymen and apprentices'.[62]

Although urban social reforms tended to be earlier and more focused, similar moves were underway within rural areas. Central to the reorganisation of social power in the countryside were the poor laws of 1598 and 1601, which both situated the administration of the relief of the poor within the civil parish and located responsibility for the maintenance of the poor amongst wealthier parishioners. This legislation connected with social polarisation, ensuring that within many parishes the administration of the new laws deepened the authority of parochial oligarchies. Thus, various contemporary luminaries suggested that constables should be assisted by 'the most substantial and discreetest yeomen'; and that overseers should be chosen from amongst the 'most substantiall' parishioners. In 1598, the Essex justices ordered that Overseers of the Poor were to be selected from amongst 'the most discreet and principal persons'. Settlement entitlements should be decided by two local magistrates and six of 'the most substancialest men' of the township. Hence, in one village in the early seventeenth century, power was held by 'the better sort of the parishioners'; in another, it was held by 'the ancientest and better sort of the parish', who opposed themselves to 'the inferior and meaner sort'. All of this confirmed the contemporary belief that

[58] Slack, *Poverty and policy*, 124, 149, 150.
[59] H. Ellis, 'Letter from secretary Walsingham to the Lord Treasurer', *Norfolk Archaeology*, 2 (1849), 92–6.
[60] F. M. Eden, *The state of the poor*, 3 vols. (London, 1797), I, cxxxvi–cxlvi.
[61] Hindle, *State and social change*, 211.
[62] PRO, SP12/58/19; Kegl, *Rhetoric of concealment*, 148.

the 'very rich and sufficient man' should 'do the king and countrey service' as a parish officer, such that he stood as a 'great governor' within his locality. Thus, parochial power passed into the hands of a social fraction which was defined in 1635 as the 'midle people, [those] betweene Cottagers and gentlemen'.[63]

All of this suggests a growing connection between social and institutional power: in many parishes, wealthier inhabitants monopolised the key offices through which their communities were governed. The most influential examination of this phenomenon has been conducted by Keith Wrightson and David Levine, in their study of the Essex village of Terling. Wrightson and Levine point to a coincidence between wealth, literacy, office-holding and puritanism amongst the 'better sort' of this increasingly polarised village. Most notably, the governing elite of Terling sought to prevent the in-migration of paupers, and to regulate the lives of the settled 'poorer sort' of the village.[64] Similar examples of this phenomenon have been found elsewhere: again, mostly in the south and east of the country.[65] The Essex preacher John Rogers pithily summed up the growing connection between social power and the monopolisation of parochial office-holding: 'In a town, when chief men hold together, what evil can stand against them? What good may they not affect?'[66]

The monopolisation of power by wealthier inhabitants helped to solidify social demarcations: hence, in 1619, a clear distinction was drawn between the 'townsmen' of Braintree (Essex) and the 'cottagers'. It also generated lasting social tensions. Parochial governors spoke routinely about their anxieties concerning the unruliness of the poor: one group of vestrymen described the 'great confusion' which would arise 'if the whole parish should be electors'; this would be 'popular, and excite the ruder sort to extreme liberty'. In particular, they feared that 'the inferior and meaner sort of the multitude of the inhabitants, being greater in number' would undermine 'the good proceedings for the benefit of the Church and parish'. The village elites

---

[63] Hindle, *State and social change*, 151, 154, 159, 204, 207, 213; Hunt, *Puritan moment*, 66.

[64] K. E. Wrightson and D. Levine, *Poverty and piety in an English village: Terling, 1525–1700* (1979; 2nd edn, Cambridge, 1995).

[65] Hunt, *Puritan moment*, 71–3, 143; S. Hindle, 'The problem of pauper marriage in seventeenth-century England', *Transactions of the Royal Historical Society*, 6th ser., 8 (1998), 71–89. For studies of village government, see J. R. Kent, *The English village constable 1580–1642: a social and administrative study* (Oxford, 1986), 82–122; R. von Friedeburg, 'Reformation of manners and the social composition of offenders in an East Anglian cloth village: Earls Colne, Essex, 1531–1642', *Journal of British Studies*, 29 (1990), 347–85; J. Pitman, 'Tradition and exclusion: parochial officeholding in early modern England, a case study from north Norfolk, 1580–1640', *Rural History*, 15, 1 (2004), 27–45. More research needs to be conducted into local variations in the relationship between office-holding and social change.

[66] Hunt, *Puritan moment*, 143.

of some communities could seem outrageously arrogant to their poorer neighbours: one poor man from Mildenhall (Suffolk) recalled being told by one of the parish governors 'that the xxiiii of mildenhall had as good power to make lawes … as the p[ar]lament might do'. In some villages, local conflicts could be complicated, situating the minister alongside the 'poorer sort': in 1613 the minister of Great Totham (Essex) compared the 'cheifest parishioners' to the sinners of Sodom and Gomorrah, singling them out for their 'pride fullness of bread idleness not strengtheninge the hand of the needye And they thinke to rule the minister and the whole parishe'. In many communities, however, the village minister was in the pocket of the wealthier inhabitants. Thus, in Tibenham in 1586, the preacher was main-tained by the profits of lands which had hitherto been held by the parochial guilds. Those funds also paid for taxes and subsidies, and for the relief of the poor. The similarity to the demands for integrated, autonomous local gov-ernment outlined in the Mousehold articles should be obvious.[67]

III 'YF POORE MEN RISE AND HOLD TOGUITHER': CHANGING PATTERNS OF SOCIAL CONFLICT IN THE LATE SIXTEENTH AND EARLY SEVENTEENTH CENTURIES

Early in the summer of 1594, two Essex labourers, William Barbor and Peter Francys, found themselves in serious trouble. As they explained in their sub-sequent confession to the assizes, the two men had given voice to some of the most dangerous opinions to be entertained by early modern labouring people. William Barbor admitted that, on 17 July 1594, he had remarked that

Corne wilbe dere … I know wher ther are fower shipps in the water laden with corne … I wilbe one of them that shall ryse and gather a company of eight or nyne skore togeyther and will go fetch yt owt wher yt is to be had; I can bringe them wher corne enowgh is to be had. And yf we were such a company gathered togeyther, who can withstand us.

Peter Francys admitted that on the following day he had repeated some of William's words, adding some of his own:

'Corne wilbe deare, and rather then I will storve I wilbe one of them that shall rise and gather a companie of eight skore or nyne skore toguither and will go and fetche yt owt wher yt is to be had. I can brynge them wher corne inoughe is to be had, and yf wee were such a companie gathered toguither, who cann withstand us?' And being asked,

---

[67] *Ibid.*, 72; Hill, *Society and puritanism*, 420; BL, Harl MS 98, fols. 124r–127r; L. Gowing, *Domestic dangers: women, words and sex in early modern London* (Oxford, 1996), 55; PRO, E133/4/667.

'what can poore men do against riche men?' he replid, 'what can riche men do against poore men yf poore men rise and hold toguither?'[68]

What, in the crisis years of the 1590s, could rich men do if poor men rose and held together? This section will explore some of the reasons why, during the late sixteenth and early seventeenth centuries, across southern and eastern England, poor men and women did not display such solidarity. It will focus upon three issues: the changing parameters of social conflict; the increasingly antagonistic language used by poor people about their richer neighbours; and the changing geography of enclosure rioting.

We have already seen how, as the sixteenth century drew to its close, social changes in agrarian regions increasingly divided rich from poor. The consequence of this was to fracture the social alliance upon which the tradition of late medieval popular rebellion had rested. Wealthier villagers had increasingly little in common with the social complaints of their poorer neighbours; indeed, in some communities, they became the target of popular opprobrium. This increasing internalisation of social conflict *within* the village community was strengthened by the withdrawal, in some villages, of lords from the conflicts that had led to rebellion in 1549. This was most obvious where lords concluded long-running disputes by dividing common land between themselves and their tenants. Such agreements were often negotiated by 'the best sorte' of the village. As with the grant of political autonomy to urban communities, such arrangements had close similarities to the rebel programme articulated in the Mousehold articles, in which a separation of the agrarian economy was imagined, whereby lords would retain certain rights in return for separating themselves from the village. As one lord put it, the effect was to 'exclude him selfe' from the economic affairs of his tenants.[69]

The changing character of land use in agrarian regions, in particular the stinting of common rights and the enclosure of common land, increasingly marginalised or even obliterated the customary entitlements of poorer villagers. In many respects, the 'better sort' of southern and eastern England were better placed to push through changes to the village economy than were the gentry. Wealthier villagers were not only the employers of poor labourers; they also acted as village constables, overseers of the poor rates and as vestrymen. They were therefore in a good position to stifle popular criticism of the economic changes of which they were beneficiaries. Thus, land in

[68] Cockburn (ed.), *Essex indictments*, 2579–80.
[69] PRO, STAC4/3/17. For more examples, see BL, M485/85/2017; E. Kerridge, *Agrarian problems in the sixteenth century and after* (London, 1969), 174–6; A. Hassell Smith and G. M. Baker (eds.), *The papers of Nathaniel Bacon of Stiffkey*, vol. III: *1586–1595* (Norwich, 1990), 256–7; Cunningham, 'Common rights', 257–8.

Brandon (Suffolk) which had once been 'sowen to the poore mens uses' was enclosed 'by the consent of the Auncyentest & Chiefeste Inhabitants' in the 1570s; this enclosure was carried out because 'the poore men were afraid' to oppose it.[70]

In Brandon, the enclosure of the 'poore mens' lands may have been greeted with bitten lips amongst the local poor; but elsewhere in southern and eastern England, the economic and social changes of the later sixteenth century inspired angry words. This period saw a significant shift in the terms of plebeian seditious conversation. Whereas in the middle of the century such speech had tended to identify the gentry as the 'enemies' of the commons, seditious speech in the later Elizabethan period tended to define the 'enemies' of the poor as a rather more vague social group: the 'rich men'.[71] Sometimes, those articulating seditious speech were more precise, identifying rich farmers or merchants as their leading opponents. The attempted rebellion in Suffolk in 1569 seems to represent a junction between the language of 1549 and that more commonly spoken in the 1580s and 1590s. In that year, one would-be Suffolk rebel identified his enemies as 'the riche churles' and 'such as be newe comme uppe'. In contrast, 'suche as be gentlemen of olde contynuance they shall not be hurte'.[72]

By the 1580s and 1590s, it was the 'rich men' and the 'farmers' who had become the enemies of the poor. In 1596 the Lord Treasurer was warned that the poor believed that 'the rich men have gotten all into their hands, and will starve the poor'.[73] Would-be rebels in Hampshire in 1586 identified themselves as 'of the porer sort', and stated that it had been their intention to 'have gotten some wh[e]at from the wealthyer sorte'.[74] One Essex man in 1591 was of the opinion that England was governed by a social alliance from which the poor were excluded, arguing that 'the noblemen and gentelmen were all one and the gentellmen and fermers wold hold togeyther one with another so that poore men cold gett nothinge amonge them'.[75] Three years later, the drama *A knack to know a knave* perhaps spoke for many when its character the Farmer confessed that 'I have raised the markets, and opprest the poore / And made a thousand goe from dore to dore.' Of the Farmer, it was said that 'he that lives must still increase his store / for he that hath most

---

[70] PRO, E134/39Eliz/East8. For one poor man's opposition to stinting, see W. Paley (ed.), *Les reportes del cases in Camera Stellata, 1593 to 1609, from the original Ms. of John Hawarde* (London, 1894), 176.

[71] For an exception, see J. Walter 'A "rising of the people"? The Oxfordshire rising of 1596', *P&P*, 107 (1985), 90–143.

[72] BL, Cotton MS, Titus B II, fols. 487r–492v; *CPR, Elizabeth I*, V, 1569–72, no. 1818.

[73] J. Strype (ed.), *Annals of the Reformation and establishment of religion and other various occurrences in the Church of England during Queen Elizabeth's happy reign*, 4 vols. (Oxford, 1824), 407.

[74] White, 'A Hampshire plot'.   [75] Cockburn (ed.), *Essex indictments*, no. 2245.

wealth of all desireth more'. Towards the end of the play, the poor indicted the Farmer for treason, litigiousness, withholding grain from sale so 'that the poore can buy no corne' and expelling 'poore Piers Plowman' from his cottage. All of this was taken to demonstrate that the Farmer had become 'one that feeds upon the poore commons'.[76]

Certainly, the fragmentary evidence points towards growing criticism of the 'farmers' by the poor. Thus, in 1596, twenty men of Hearn Hill (Kent), who described themselves as 'the poore men' of that village, made a plot 'to ryse for Corne' and 'to pull the farmers owte of their howses by the ears'.[77] Likewise, the Kentish weaver Thomas Bird 'intended to hang up the rich farmers which had corn at their own doors'.[78] In November 1596, Henry Went of Ardleigh (Essex), allegedly exclaimed that 'it would never be better untill men did rise & seeke thereby an amendment and wished in his harte a hundred men would rise and he would be there captayn to cut the throtes of the rich churles and the Rich cornemongers'.[79] A year earlier, the Essex blacksmith Thomas Bynder found himself in trouble for his altercation in an alehouse with one of the wealthy farmers of his parish, William Thrustell. On that occasion, he had accused men like Thrustell of having responsibility for the high price of grain, warning that he and others would rise and hang the farmers at their gates.[80]

Wealthier men such as William Thrustell were often protected from such criticism by their position as employers or as holders of the parish purse strings. As Keith Wrightson has observed, for much of the time the poor laws proved 'a powerful reinforcement of habits of deference and subordination'.[81] But sparks of plebeian anger at the suppression of begging and the deportation of the transient poor can still be glimpsed. Thus, John Jenkyns stood indicted in May 1598 for his opinion that 'yf the Queene did putt downe begginge she is worse than Nan Bennett [meaning Agnes Bennett, widow, lately executed for witchcraft], which forsooke God and all the world'. Two months earlier, Henry Danyell had allegedly said 'that he hoped to see such warre in this Realme to afflicte the rich men of this countrye to requite their hardnes of hart towards the poore', and that chief amongst this was the local parish constable, adding 'that they had made such lawes for the sendinge of poore people into ther countryes where they were

---

[76] Anon., *A knacke to knowe a knave*, lines 308–9, 316–17, 1222, 1263–72.
[77] K. S. Martin (ed.), *Records of Maidstone: being selections from documents in the possession of the Corporation* (Maidstone, 1928), 263–5.
[78] P. Clark, 'Popular protest and disturbance in Kent, 1558–1640', *Economic History Review*, 2nd ser., 29, 3 (1976), 367.
[79] ERO (Chelmsford), Q/SR 136/111.   [80] ERO (Chelmsford), Q/SR 131/34–6.
[81] Wrightson, *English society*, 181. On pauper deference, see S. Hindle, *On the parish? The micro-politics of poor relief in rural England, c. 1550–1750* (Oxford, 2004), 387–90.

borne that they that had made them would repent once within the yeare'.[82] Likewise, labourers could sometimes explode in fury at their employers: in the course of an argument with a Norfolk farmer, John Chibocke warned him that 'if a thowsaund such myssers were deade we poore men shoulde farre the better'.[83]

The evidence of seditious-speech prosecutions therefore implies that, within East Anglia and south-eastern England, the social basis for large-scale, united action on the scale of Kett's rebellion had, by the late sixteenth century, dissolved. The same conclusion is also suggested by the changing pattern of the prosecution of enclosure riot cases before the Court of Star Chamber. Roger Manning has calculated that whereas the East Anglian region had produced 12 per cent of enclosure riot cases heard before that institution during the reigns of Henry VIII and Edward VI, during that of James I this proportion dropped to a mere 3 per cent.[84] Manning's evidence is far from watertight: his sense of the geography of East Anglia is open to question; he appears to have missed a number of important cases; finally, crowd action over agrarian issues concerned a wider array of matters than enclosure alone.[85] Nonetheless, his insight remains revealing.

The contrast between Star Chamber litigation concerning enclosure rioting in the early sixteenth century and that of the early seventeenth century, is all the more stark when it is borne in mind that the large majority of East Anglian enclosure riot cases heard by the Jacobean Star Chamber were drawn from the fenland region of Cambridgeshire. During the early seventeenth century, this area was subject to massive drainage operations which

---

[82] Cockburn (ed.), *Kent indictments*, nos. 2573, 2589.

[83] NRO, NQS C/S3/13A, examination of Roger Wells and William Seaborne of Wicklewood, 7 March 1600 [i.e. 1601].

[84] R. B. Manning, *Village revolts: social protest and popular disturbances in England, 1509–1640* (Oxford, 1988), 323, 327.

[85] Manning defines 'East Anglia' as comprising the counties of Norfolk, Suffolk, Essex and Cambridgeshire. The poor survival of Star Chamber records for the earlier period renders any precise qualitative analysis difficult. My own scrutiny of the Star Chamber records for James I's reign produces a rather larger number of East Anglian enclosure riot cases than Manning's four. Concentrating on the four counties which Manning defines as comprising East Anglia, I have found some sixteen cases of enclosure riot heard by the Jacobean Star Chamber. These are PRO, STAC8/17/11; PRO, STAC8/73/19; PRO, STAC8/69/16; PRO, STAC8/98/7; PRO, STAC8/295/14; PRO, STAC8/5/2; PRO, STAC8/27/8; PRO, STAC8/5/21; PRO, STAC8/43/8; PRO, STAC8/203/30; PRO, STAC8/226/24; PRO, STAC8/227/21; PRO, STAC8/191/25; PRO, STAC8/189/9; PRO, STAC8/193/10; PRO, STAC8/311/30. Including the fenland areas of Huntingdonshire and Lincolnshire within the definition of 'East Anglia' yields a few more cases: PRO, STAC8/205/23; PRO, STAC8/7/3; PRO, STAC8/18/19; PRO, STAC8/42/11; PRO, STAC8/61/9; PRO, STAC8/129/13 (supplemented by PRO, STAC8/113/11); PRO, STAC8/145/20; PRO, STAC8/125/3; PRO, STAC8/265/7; PRO, STAC8/159/8; PRO, STAC8/15/13; PRO, STAC8/308/13; PRO, STAC8/296/10. Manning's view of the regional economies of early modern England obviously depends upon administrative divisions between counties rather than contemporary economic and cultural geography.

threatened to disrupt the rural economy upon which thousands of poor cottagers depended.[86] The Jacobean fenlands therefore faced a unique threat, which inspired large-scale rioting, and hence significant litigation before Star Chamber. In contrast, the fens were one of the few areas of East Anglia which appear not to have experienced rebellion in 1549.

Furthermore, whereas Norfolk contributed a large number of enclosure riot cases to Star Chamber during the reigns of Henry VIII and Edward VI, during the reign of James I the county was the location of a mere five such cases.[87] It appears, therefore, to be the case that the farmers of Wiveton were not alone in finding that, when they turned to the 'poorer sorte' and 'poore people' of their village for support in their dispute against their lord, they were refused help.[88] For, as we have seen, the yeomen elite of communities like Wiveton had long ago distanced themselves from the interests of their poorer neighbours. All that the 'poorer sorte' did at Wiveton was to return the compliment. Driven by a combination of social anxiety and economic opportunity, the 'better sort of people' now stood for a very different set of principles from the 'honest men' who, between 1381 and 1549, had formed the public leadership of popular insurrection.

---

[86] See K. Lindley, *Fenland riots and the English Revolution* (London, 1982) and C. Holmes, 'Drainers and fenmen: the problem of popular political consciousness in the seventeenth century', in Fletcher and Stevenson (eds.), *Order and disorder*, 166–95.

[87] For these cases, see PRO, STAC8/295/14; PRO, STAC8/73/19; PRO, STAC8/98/7; PRO, STAC8/17/11; PRO, STAC8/69/16.

[88] PRO, STAC8/17/11.

6

Memory, myth and representation: the later meanings of the 1549 rebellions

A creatively effective past, determining the present, produces in conjunction with the present a particular direction for the future, and, to a certain degree, predetermines the future. (M. M. Bakhtin, *Speech genres and other late essays* (Austin, TX, 1986), 34.)

I 'WHEN WE WERE YONDER EATING OF MUTTON': IMMEDIATE RECOLLECTIONS OF THE 1549 REBELLIONS

Within a few weeks of the rebel defeat at Dussindale, the meaning of the commotion time had already become contested. Considered as a piece of rhetoric rather than simply as a legalistic formula, the indictment proffered against Robert Kett represented the first attempt to organise the story of the Norfolk insurrection into a chronological narrative. In order to initiate the trial of the Kett brothers, in November 1549 the Crown's lawyers drew up a brief outline of the case against the men. This indictment encapsulated the earliest 'instant history' of Kett's rebellion. Robert Kett was alleged to have assembled a rebel host on 20 July 1549 and to have maintained the camp for the ensuing six weeks. The indictment described rebel weaponry, making mention of the 'banners unfurled, swords, shields, clubs, cannon, halberts, lances, bows, arrows, breast-plates, coats of mail, caps, helmets and other arms offensive and defensive, armed and arrayed in warlike manner' and highlighted the use of 'writings and bills' written in the King's name 'to excite and procure' the Crown's subjects 'to levy open war'. It claimed that the rallying cry of this rebel host had been 'Kyll the Gentlemen'. Evidence of their murderous intent was to be found in the rebels having 'traitorously despoil[ed]' the gentry 'of their goods and chattels'. Only the arrival of 'the most noble John Earl of Warwick', and his defeat of 'Robert Kete and the traitors aforesaid ... by the favour of God ... at Dussingesdale ... on the 27th. Day of August' had saved the gentry. The indictment concluded by

208

contrasting the 'conduct of the same Earl of Warwick' with that of 'Robert Kete', who had 'feloniously and traitorously' fled the field of battle. The same narrative, focusing upon the violent intent of the rebels, their maintenance of the Mousehold camp and the royal victory at Dussindale, was also laid out in the indictment of William Kett at the King's Bench and of lesser rebel leaders before the county quarter sessions. The indictments did more than spell out the legal case against the Kett brothers; they also formulated the template for later official accounts of the Norfolk insurrection. Although these grew ever more elaborate with time, their ideological meaning did not change from that laid out in the indictments. All concurred in their assessment of the rebellions: that they were inspired by a desire to destroy the gentry; that rebel conduct during the insurrections had revealed the incapacity of labouring people to exercise authority; and that the triumph of the Earl of Warwick at Dussindale had received 'the favour of God'.[1]

In contrast to the ideological uniformity of official accounts to the commotion time, the inhabitants of post-rebellion Norwich were divided in their responses to the traumatic recent events. The evidence of prosecutions for seditious speech heard before the Norwich magistracy in the aftermath of the rebellion suggests that many labouring people retained passionate feelings about the recent insurrection and that their recollections of it could provide an opportunity for a restatement of old rebel loyalties. But that evidence also hints at a different set of popular reactions to the commotion time: that prevalent amongst accusers. Whereas former rebels harked back to the commotion time, valorised their condemned leader or suggested alternative strategies for a new insurrection, their neighbours, workmates and drinking partners sometimes expressed a desire to forget the commotion time.

This section will assess these conflicting responses to the commotion time. Some popular memories enabled political organisation to proceed from a critical assessment of the 'last rising'; others kept popular politics alive, providing historical examples of treachery of the gentry and of the capacity of labouring people to organise politically. In contrast, other labouring people wished to escape implication in the events of 1549 by silencing conversation about those events; while still others expressed a clear hostility to the rebellion. The people of post-rebellion Norwich were caught in a contradiction. For some, 'Memory . . . was an encounter with a reality they would rather have forgotten.'[2] But we shall also see how the authorities' attempts to mould popular senses of the past were contested. Positive

---

[1] For the indictments of Robert and William Kett, see Russell, *Kett's rebellion*, 220–6. For the quarter sessions indictments, see NRO, NQS C/S3/8, fols. 132, 133.

[2] Quoting M. Richards, *A time of silence: civil war and the culture of repression in Franco's Spain, 1936–1945* (Cambridge, 1998), 28, 40.

memories of the 1549 rebellions endured, providing labouring people with a historical context within which to make sense of contemporary power relations, and thereby to legitimate resistance in the present.

Shortly after the rebel defeat, the clerk of the Norwich Mayor's Court acquired a new volume in which to record the proceedings of that body. Over the next few months, the book started to fill up with accounts of conversations that were taking place in the houses, courtyards, fields, streets, alleyways and porches of the city. A constant theme of these conversations concerned the fate, personality and motives of Robert Kett.[3] One of the first dialogues to find its way into the clerk's book occurred on 30 September 1549. A group of servants explained to the court how they had met Edmund Johnson, a Norwich labourer, 'at the late chappell in the felde', on the west side of Norwich. One of the servants called Boswell 'channced ... [to] saye That Robert Kette shulde be hanged'. In response Johnson 'sayed no, Whereunto the saide Bosewell sayed That he shulde be hanged without any doubte', at which Johnson threatened 'That it shulde coste a thousande mens lyves firste'.[4] Whereas for some Norwich people, such as Boswell the servant, mention of Kett's name inspired declarations of hostility to the rebellion or of loyalty to the established regime, for others, such as Edmund Johnson, Kett's name called forth rebellious words. In November 1549, the clerk recorded the testimony of Thomas Woolman, who explained how a man named Claxton had remarked to him 'that he did well in keping in ketts campe and so he wolde saye'. Woolman asked Claxton 'what he did think by kette'. Claxton responded 'nothing but well that he knewe ... he trusted to se[e] a newe day for suche men as I was'.[5] Kett's name therefore invoked controversy, highlighting the diversity of popular politics: while some labouring people were convinced that the late rebel leader had personified the finest values of their class, others were more sceptical. Hence, James Stotter of Randworth landed himself in trouble in May 1551 for his alehouse opinion 'That suche as were slayn & dyd upon mushold in the commocyon tyme wer honest men'. On being admonished by his fellow drinkers, he warmed to his theme, exclaiming 'That Robert kette was an honest man'.

In the immediate aftermath of the rebellion, the defeated rebels of Norfolk dreamt of having a second chance. John Rooke had a festive date in mind for the rerun of the commotion time, telling Marian Lelly how 'Excepte the mercy of god before Christmas; ye shall se[e] as greate a Campe uppon

---

[3] The commotion time was fairly immediately lodged in memory: for examples of individuals dating time according to the rebellion or Kett's execution, see NRO, NCR/12A/1(a), fols. 60v–61r; NRO, DN/DEP/6/5b, fol. 88r.
[4] NRO, NCR/16A/6, p. 2.   [5] NRO, NCR/16A/6, p. 3.

mushold as ever was. And if it be not thenne It shalbe in the Spring of the yere.'[6] Others suggested midsummer as a good time at which to start a new insurrection. Young John Oldman found himself in trouble in January 1550 for having allegedly suggested to his drinking mates that they should organise a second rising, but that this time they 'wolde have no more lieng [i.e. stationary] campe but a ronnyng [mobile] Campe'.[7] Robert Burnam, a former rebel whom we encountered in Chapter Three, agreed with young John Oldman that rebel strategy had been flawed in 1549. His fellow watchmen explained to the city authorities how, despite their warnings, he had consistently reiterated his view that 'If the Campe had taken [Sir Richard Southwell, Sir Thomas Woodhouse, Mr Roger Woodhouse and Mr Corbett] they wolde never have foughte on[e] strooke ... Mr Southwell and the woodhouses and Mr Corbet were theves, and if the campe men coulde have taken them fowre they woulde not have foughte a strooke.'[8] Perhaps next time, Burnam and Oldman suggested, things would turn out differently.

Robert Burnam and John Oldman's reported speech is reminiscent of the findings of the oral historian Alessandro Portelli, who argues that aged militants whose causes have been defeated look back on their younger selves and imagine what Portelli calls a 'uchronia', that is, an imagined counterfactual world in which they always took the right turning. For Portelli, uchronia comprises 'that amazing scene in which the author imagines what would have happened if a certain historical event had not taken place'. Thus 'the uchronic hypothesis allows the narrator to "transcend" reality as given and to refuse to identify himself and be satisfied with the existing order'. This inversion of the past therefore represents both a vision of the future, and a view upon the possibility of popular agency in the present: 'through uchronia, these speakers say that the most desirable of possible worlds ... could be created someday, if the right chances are seized'.[9] Similarly, within Burnam's and Oldman's uchronia, the experience of defeat in 1549 was not allowed to negate future possibilities. Instead, they mobilised an imagined version of the past in order to articulate agency in the present.

Proposing a repeat of the commotion time formed another way of remembering the rebellion. In the week before Pentecost 1550, the Norwich weaver John White was to be found at Wroxham, where he was working at the loom he hired from Robert Ederych. According to the story which Ederych subsequently told to the Norwich quarter sessions, White tried to open a

---

[6] *Ibid.*   [7] NRO, NCR/12A/1(a), fol. 81r.   [8] NRO, NCR/12A/1(a), fols. 8r–9r.
[9] A. Portelli, 'Uchronic dreams: working-class memory and possible worlds', in R. Samuel and P. Thompson (eds.), *The myths we live by* (London, 1990), 150. In an earlier piece, I somehow managed to misspell this important term: see Wood, '"Poore men woll speke one daye"', 80.

conversation with the tempting remark that 'he coulde tell him tydings'. Ederych took the bait, asking 'what that was', and White answered 'That by the masse we shall have as hoote a somere as ever was . . . this somer shulde be as evell and busy as the last somer was'.[10] Like so many other individuals who presented such evidence, Robert Ederych was at pains to distinguish his own loyal opinions from the seditious speech of the accused, explaining how he tried to terminate the conversation by answering that White should 'attende to his worke and meddell witt no suche matter', and by reminding the magistrates of White's reputation: 'John White is a very slanderous creature.' Once again, then, popular loyalism was counterposed to positive memories of 1549.

When the summer of 1550 arrived, John Warde the shoemaker was to be found informing his apprentice of the disappointing news that the rebellion had been deferred:

the Gentylmen watch now very faste, and they have not so muche nede to watch nowe, but to watch all the dayes of their lief aswell as nowe, For they have not had so good a skorge of late amonges[t] them. But it is not unlike they shall have as greate a plage as they had before, and excepte god be mercyfull unto them, they shall have suche a plage as they have not had before, allthough it be not this yere, the tyme woll come it shall so fall.

In such outbursts, the recent past and an imagined bloody future became mingled. Historians ought to take such speech more seriously; elite contemporaries certainly did. The record of the Norwich courts for the early 1550s shows how the magistracy dealt with recurrent talk of new insurrections against a background of periodic riots, seditious muttering, the dissemination of anonymous, threatening letters and the attempted organisation of petitioning campaigns. From the scantier evidence available for the rest of East Anglia and southern England, it would seem that Norfolk was not exceptional in this: reading such reports, midsummer loomed large in the magisterial mind as the likely date for the next insurrection. But the record of seditious speech suggests that Norfolk dissidents were especially likely to cite their earlier experience of insurrection and to call upon the name of Robert Kett.

So far, we have heard some former rebels wish for a direct repeat of the commotion time, and others propose alterations to the strategy pursued by the rebel council: that next time there should be 'a ronnyng Campe'; or that 'the campe men' had been insufficiently aggressive towards the gentry. Another reaction was to suggest a fantastic explanation for the whereabouts of dead rebels and thereby to imagine away the rebel defeat. Margaret

[10] NRO, NCR/12A/1(a), fol. 5r.

Adams found herself at the house of Edmunde Allen, a gentleman of the village of Earlham, in February 1550. Here she found Mistress Allen in conversation with John Petybon, a tailor of Norwich, concerning a legal case in which her husband was the defendant. Somehow, Margaret Adams worked their talk around to the commotion time of the previous summer. She told them that she had recently been in a house in Norwich, where she had heard how 'there are v.C [i.e. 500] of musholdmen are gon[e] to the great Turke [i.e. the Turkish Sultan] and to the dolphyn [i.e. the French Dauphin] and wilbe here agayne bye mydsomere'. In repeating the tale, she appears to have expanded upon it, adding her wishful belief that 'That the kings Majestie had p[ar]doned all them so that they came in by a day'.[11] But Robert Kett and the Mousehold men were not returning, and under the Duke of Northumberland the state rewarded insurrection with repression.

Most redolent of the spirit of the camping time was the alleged speech of a poor fisherman. In June 1550 'uppon Tuysday or wedensday before Mydsomer nowe last past', at about 5 o'clock in the morning, John Oldman was repairing his nets in the street in Conesford, in the south of Norwich alongside the river Wensum, when Thomas Mauclerke, the servant of one of his neighbours, leaned out of the door of a nearby house. Looking across the river to Thorpe Wood, where the rebels had camped in the previous year and where the rebel council had administered justice from under the Oak of Reformation, Oldman remarked wistfully that 'It was a mery world when we were yonder eating of mutton, meaning therby the woode.' Mauclerke's master overheard this exchange from his bedroom and subsequently recalled its content in his evidence to the city's magistrates. The servant differed slightly from his master in his account of Oldman's words. Thomas Mauclerke recalled that Oldman had said 'Mauclerke It was a mery worlde when we eate roste meate yonder.' Another neighbour, John Wortes, reported that he was getting dressed at the same time, and had heard some part of the conversation. He therefore 'demanded of his wief what was spoken there'. The semi-anonymous wife of John Wortes (we do not learn her first name) told her husband what Oldman's words had been, adding her own commentary upon them: 'woo [with] that worlde I pray god we have no more any suche worlde'.[12]

There are a number of possible ways of interpreting the reports of John Oldman's speech. Firstly, if this was indeed what Oldman had said (and all three deponents were consistent in their accounts of its context and meaning, differing only in whether he had wished for mutton or for 'roste meate'), we are presented with another rebel memory of the camping time. This time, the

[11] NRO, NCR/16A/6, p. 40.   [12] NRO, NCR/12A/1(a), fols. 9v–10r.

tone of the reported speech is nostalgic rather than bitter – how often did a mid-sixteenth-century labourer eat roast meat? – but its implication remains transparent. Secondly, we could read the documents as further evidence of the agitated condition of the Norwich magistracy as the threatening mid-summer of 1550 loomed. Thirdly, the depositions of Oldman's male neigh-bours point once again to the willingness of labouring people to reveal one another's words to the authorities: motivated perhaps by loyalty to the established regime, or alternatively out of fear of the consequences of keep-ing such speech secret. Finally, the reported speech of John Wortes' wife hints at another response to the memory of 1549: the desire to forget the commo-tion time.

Social historians, social anthropologists and sociologists have all argued that memory has a politics. For a subordinated group to assert itself as a collective political agent in the present, it is argued, that group must have a sense of its own past. How the past is encoded and recalled, therefore, provides a source of social solidarity and a cornerstone of collective iden-tity.[13] Similarly, successful ruling elites are often understood as governing through the manipulation of memory, as some aspects of the past are high-lighted while others are quietly suppressed. The conclusion of Keith Wrightson and David Levine's history of the mining village of Whickham (County Durham) encapsulates this approach to the politics of the past. They open this conclusion by quoting Milan Kundera: 'The struggle of man against power is the struggle of memory against forgetting.'[14] In drawing attention to Kundera's remark, Wrightson and Levine make an important interpretive contribution to the study of social memory. But historians of memory must not lose sight of those moments in which the exercise of ruling-class power was so heavy as to crush the capacity of subordinates to com-municate, and so collectively to retain, empowering images of the past. The past therefore emerges as a field of conflict in which the struggle of humanity against power has sometimes entailed a degree of necessary forgetfulness in its own interest.

For many working people, the 1549 rebellions represented a personal catastrophe that was best wished away. In 1551, Johanne Ryches was picked up by the Norwich magistrates. It was not long before she was identified as the widow of Robert Ryches of Stokesby, who had been 'slayn in the comocyon tyme'. At first, it was recorded 'that she denyth that she was marryed to him', but eventually she gave in. Johanne then presented the

---

[13] J. Fentress and C. Whickham, *Social memory* (Oxford, 1992); M. Halbwachs, *The collective memory* (1950; Eng. trans., New York, 1980).

[14] D. Levine and K. Wrightson, *The making of an industrial society: Whickham, 1560–1765* (Oxford, 1991), 428.

Norwich magistracy with an account of her doings after Robert's death: 'that she had a chylde and the same was buryed at Wymondham, where she late dwelled uppon shrostyde tuysday last past', but that, increasingly desperate, she had moved to Norwich to find work. It was scarcely surprising that Johanne Ryches wished to forget the commotion time.[15] In May 1553, Cecylye Barthford also distanced herself from the memory of the commotion time. Some men had come into her alehouse, calling for a pot of ale. Inspired by a new rumour that Edward VI had sanctioned the destruction of enclo-sures, the men began to talk about breaking down the fences that had recently been re-erected upon the city's common land at Town Close. In her testimony to the city quarter sessions, Cecylye claimed that she had gone to the men and said 'I pray the good fellow have no such talke here for we had of suche busynes late ynoughe,' and that she had departed from them.[16] John Wortes' wife was not, therefore, alone in 'pray[ing to] god [that] we have no more' of the camping time. Unlike those of their neighbours who recalled the rebellions in terms of liberty and lost opportunity, both Cecylye Barthford and John Wortes' wife distanced themselves both from any impli-cation in seditious speech and also from the memory of Robert Kett.

Ironically, the need to distance oneself from the memory of 1549 could also create a kind of resistance: in this case, in which the label of rebel was rejected. On 14 June 1553, Johanne Bray was gaoled at the order of the Norwich Mayor's Court after her husband's sword was found on Mousehold Heath – proof, in other words, that he had once been a part of Kett's rebel force. It was recorded in the court book 'That she defyed Mr Mayor and all them that shuld saye her husbands sword was founden on the heath'. The sheriff's sergeant deposed that he rebuked her for these words, but that she repeated them, saying 'twycs or thrycs I defy Mr Mayor'. In the end, Johanne was released after her husband, Thomas, entered into a recognisance for her future good behaviour. Whatever the truth of the allegation against Thomas Braye, in defying the sheriff's sergeant Johanne had done her best to save her husband's reputation and perhaps much more.[17] Perhaps Johanne Braye was wise to resist so vehemently her husband's categorisation as a rebel. Certainly, we saw in Chapter Three how some of those, like Robert Burnam, who did articulate critical views in the aftermath of the commotion time not only endured humiliating judicial punishment, but also the ridicule of their neighbours. It is notable that after Burnam lost his ears at the pillory, he made no further appearances in the city's criminal courts. Albeit in different ways, therefore, social power pressed heavily upon Robert Burnam and Johanne Braye. In the immediate aftermath of the commotion time, the

---

[15] NRO, NCR/16A/6, p. 127.   [16] NRO, NCR/12A/1(a), fol. 123r.
[17] NRO, NCR/16A/6, p. 254.

governors of Norwich wished to crush those labouring people who continued to identify themselves with Robert Kett. In so doing, they sought to
extinguish the possibility that Kett's name might carry with it any implication other than that of a rank traitor. But that did not mean that they wished
to forget Robert Kett: on the contrary, as we shall see in the succeeding two
sections, the governing class of early modern England reiterated his name for
centuries to come. The history of Kett's rebellion therefore became an
ideological battlefield: for, as we shall see, other memories of the commotion
time survived, enduring almost unnoticed over the generations, yet holding
within them a powerful, positive memory of the rebellions of 1549.

II 'TO SEE THE THING IN ORDER': IMPOSING IDEOLOGY
ON KETT'S REBELLION

In the introduction to his translation of Alexander Neville's history of Kett's
rebellion, Richard Woods admitted to conflicted feelings. Reflecting upon
his motives in offering Neville's detailed narrative to an English-reading
audience, Woods felt two opposing urges. He wanted simultaneously to
represent and to suppress the history of the Norfolk rising. Woods explained
how one part of him wished that his subject might be forgotten:

I would have wished verily, that those populous stirres, & seditious stormes, where-
with our Country, in the dayes of King Edward the sixt[h] was smitten and afflicted by
the villainy and the treachery of beastly men, had either never hapned, or (if it could
be) the remembrance of them were utterly rooted out of the minds of all men.

Opposing Woods' desire for collective amnesia was his injured civic pride:

because things past cannot be altered, or changed, and this staine of treason, branded
in the forehead of our Countrey by pernicious Citizens setteth deeper in the name of
the people of Norfolke (to the perpetual remembrance of that wickednesse) then can
be utterly blotted out, or altogether taken away.[18]

In any case, the story of Kett's rebellion had entered into oral tradition,
and was therefore likely to prove difficult to root 'out of the minds of all
men'. A powerful friction existed between the 'official' version of 1549 and
those more fragmentary recollections that became lodged within local memory. Despite this conflict, oral and printed histories of 1549 became intermixed. We will see later in this chapter how the detailed printed Elizabethan
accounts of Kett's rebellion helped both to preserve and to standardise
memories of the Norfolk rebellion, at the same time as memories of
the insurrections elsewhere within England were beginning to die out. But

[18] Neville/Woods, sig. B1r.

the distinction between oral and literate cultures should not be overstated. Just as local memory was structured by print, so oral tradition helped to generate products of literate culture: like elite and plebeian political languages, oral and literate worlds were conjoined.[19] Thus, Richard Woods explained how, before he had set eyes on Neville's 1575 Latin history of rebellion, 'receiving many strange things from the report of others', he had learnt much of the story of Kett's rebellion by word of mouth.[20] The fragmentary tales that Woods heard seemed tantalisingly disordered. The realist within Woods, knowing that 'things past cannot be altered', therefore combined with the storyteller to find in Neville's work an account of the rebellion that was both ordered and compelling. Finally, the Neville/Woods narrative was set within two overlapping sites: an ideological image of order; and a physical landscape.

The Neville/Woods narrative provides a detailed account of the encounters, negotiations, speeches and battles that took place within and around Norwich, all of it set within an intimately known environment. Importantly, Woods was a local man. The detailed specificity of his account of the 1549 rebellions grew from his own dense local knowledge of the places within which these events unfolded. Although many incidental details in the Neville/Woods narrative can be confirmed from archival evidence, what mattered to the power of the narrative was not so much its literal truth so much as its air of authenticity. In this respect, the consistency with which the story's physical location was evoked helped both to authenticate the narrative and to render it comprehensible. Key events within Woods' story were precisely located within specific sites: a walled city of gates, streets, lanes, parish churches, open spaces and fields, overlooked by the half-encompassing, threatening mass of Mousehold Heath. The physical topography of Norwich was therefore recast as the backdrop to a powerful, unfolding narrative.

In contrast to such local specificities, Woods' second theme concerned transcendent hierarchies and overarching socio-political certainties. His book presented Kett's rebellion as a morality tale designed to convey the sin of rebellion, the authority of magistrates, the inevitability of divine justice and the legitimacy of the established order. To emphasise these points, Woods drifted from local to comparative history, explaining how Robert Kett's defiance of properly constituted authority found its near-contemporary reflection in the Catholic plots against Elizabeth I and James I.[21] The specific

---

[19] For this interrelationship, see Fox, *Oral and literate culture*.   [20] Neville/Woods, sig. A2r.
[21] Neville/Woods, sigs. A2v–3r. Similarly, William Hacket's attempted rising was compared with the rebellions of 'Cade, Taylor [i.e. Wat Tyler] and them of Norfolke'. See HMC, *Kenyon*, 609.

causes of rebellion were irrelevant to Woods' analysis; instead, his account was built upon an opposition between the sin of insurrection and the divine sanction enjoyed by lawful authority. Underlying the finely textured detail of Woods' narrative, therefore, were the vast certainties of social authoritarianism. Woods explained his motives as author and translator to his readers:

be valiant, my good Countrymen, & fight with your God, for his worship, for your Country, your King, your selves, your wives, your children, & Inheritances, & make use of this Booke, where you shall see the truth prevaile, & Rebels receive their just hire. And now you Malecontents, which desire a change or disturbance of States, & watch for such opportunities, that you might bee rifling, & invert all order, thinking thereby to become Lords, & to make the Noble & Honourable vile, & care not what come, or who come, so you might be scuffling: settle yourselves in some honest calling, that you may live by the sweat of your owne browes, being blessed of God. For you that now promise yourselves golden hills, shall (as you may perceive in this History) find that you are but in golden dreame, drenched in all filthinesse. And you that covet to flie so high, with Icarus shall fall shamefully by an hempen string: & take heed lest (as you may finde here by experience) being contrived of an idle hope & the vaine promises of some, you bind not your selves aforehand, or enter too far: for you cannot get out when you would.[22]

Woods felt it necessary to explain the need for an English edition of Neville's 1575 pamphlet. He described how,

when in the house of my friend, among other Bookes I found ... this Treatise written in Latine, now more than twenty years since by one Alexander Nevil an English man: The very Title of the Booke drew mee into a farther desire of looking into the matter: the rather because lying at that time, and in that place, where these Furies were committed, I beheld something with my young eyes.

Frustrated by the apparent inconsistency of the 'strange ... report of others' concerning the events of 1549, Woods found in Neville's Latin work a narrative and an interpretive structure which enabled him to make sense of oral tradition:

I desired, and was glad to see the thing in order: which when I entred upon, The elegancie of the Phrase, together with the Argument, promised me a double fruit, viz. not only to knowe the Storie in order, but also to revive and sharpen my poore skill in that Tongue ... Wherefore reading it over now once, and againe, and communing with divers of my friends about the matters therein contained: I found a generall desire in them all to have it in English.[23]

In publishing his translation of Neville's work, Woods believed that he was making a contribution to the stock of local historical knowledge, while also providing a detailed case-study of the necessity of obedience to authority, such that

---

[22] Neville/Woods, sigs. A4r–v.   [23] Neville/Woods, sigs. A1v–2r.

all men may perceive from what beginning these so great tumults did arise; and by what meanes at the length they were suppressed, and may perfectly understand those wounds, and seditious villainies, to have bin brought upon our country, not by good and valiant persons, but printed upon her by the routs of most desperate, and ungracious men.[24]

The Neville/Woods narrative should not be read as a simple, straightforward description of the events of 1549. Although it was more than mere propaganda – their pamphlets provide the most detailed single source of information about the Norfolk rebellion and, until the publication of Diarmaid MacCulloch's article of 1979, have dominated the historiography of the 1549 insurrections – the narrative was intended to fulfil a didactic as well as a historiographical function. The density of the narrative added to its persuasive force. A rich ideological vein lay embedded within the thickly plotted local detail of the chronological narrative. An analysis of the Neville/Woods narrative is therefore instructive not only of the historiography of 1549 but also presents an important example of how historical writing was deployed in the later Tudor and early Stuart periods in order to persuade readers to submit to authority.

One constant theme in the Neville/Woods narrative concerned the failure of the rebels to recognise the force of providence. Thus, God's wrath was evident in the terrible weather that was inflicted on Norwich during the summer of 1549. The unseasonal hailstorms that afflicted the rebel camp in July were 'as a signe from heave[n]'. The 'just judgement of God' was also manifest in the poor marksmanship of rebels in battle; the heavy rains that extinguished the fires lit by rebels within the city; and the safe return of most of the captive gentry from the battle of Dussindale. The judicial retribution exacted upon named rebels in the wake of the rebellion was accorded special attention. For instance, the execution of Fulke the butcher, the man who had killed Lord Sheffield, was presented as 'the just judgement of God ... a just recompence for so great villany'. Woods took a special care to observe how frequently the rebels were warned by authority figures – Mayor Codd, the York Herald, Matthew Parker – of how God would punish them if they maintained their insurrection. Holinshed's *Chronicles*, heavily influenced by Neville's 1575 account, developed the same theme, describing how Parker's sermon on Mousehold Heath against rebellion, in which he gave them prior warning of God's wrath, was ignored by the rebels to their cost: 'who despising his wholesome admonitions, did afterwards by Gods just judgement prove his words to be most true'.[25]

---

[24] Neville/Woods, sig. B1r.
[25] Neville/Woods, sigs. D4r, G4r, K2r, G1r, G3v; Holinshed, 968.

Holinshed, Neville and Woods therefore invoked providence to condemn the rebels. If God made His presence felt in the defeat of the rebels, so the rebels' inspiration for their march to Dussindale was taken as evidence of their diabolic inspiration. The earliest narrative account of the rebellion, that written by Sotherton, insisted that the starving rebel host gathered on Mousehold Heath was persuaded to move to their defeat at Dussindale not (as Somerset was to explain in his letter to the English ambassadors) as a consequence of the disruption of their supply lines by Warwick's superior forces but as a result of the passage of a prophecy amongst their ranks, which foretold a great battle at Dussindale. Whereas Sotherton's earlier account made no reference to diabolic inspiration, but merely observed that the prophecy had been 'phantastically devisid', the later printed accounts were unanimous in explaining the disastrous prophecy as evidence that the Devil had been at work on Mousehold Heath.

In claiming that the commotioners had been motivated by diabolic forces, the historical accounts of Kett's rebellion reiterated the claims made in the original indictment of William and Robert Kett before the King's Bench, which stated that the rebel strategy had been guided by the Devil. By 1615, it seemed plain to Richard Woods that the rebels, having forsaken 'the good and mighty God . . . gave over themselves bondslaves to the Devil'. Holinshed's *Chronicles* concurred: the rebels were led to Dussindale 'through the divels procurement, that had nourished and pricked them forward all this while in their wicked proceedings'. Once again, Woods detected the hand of providence in the rebel defeat. Having failed to recognise 'the anger and vengeance of God', the rebels 'swelling with raging cruelty and obstinacy' put their faith in 'the blind illusions of Soothsayers' who had been inspired by Satan:

So great a mist of darknesse undoubtedly is Satan wont to bring upon the mindes of men, as oft as he findeth them drowned in mischiefe . . . the Devill infused such poyson into the minds of these most wretched men, as they decreed to commit their hope of good successe to a doubtfull event of a false place.

Holinshed drew a similar conclusion from the *Chronicles'* brief discussion of the Yorkshire rebellion in 1549. Like the fatal decision to march to Dussindale, the rebels in Yorkshire were influenced by 'a blind and a fantasticall prophesie', described as a 'traitorous divelish devise'.[26]

There was a profound significance to the allegation that the 1549 rebels had been inspired by the Devil. The proposition formed the inverse of the equally powerful claim that God had preferred the gentry's cause over that of

---

[26] Sotherton, 97–8; Holinshed, 981, 985; Neville/Woods, sig. K1r; Russell, *Kett's rebellion*, 220–6.

the rebels. In both cases, these claims need to be understood within the emergent early modern world-view which saw the material world as a theatre within which struggled contending forces of good and evil. This Manichean perspective underwrote both social authoritarianism, which presented the social order as divinely ordained, and the religious confrontations of the period, in which both Catholic and Protestant polemicists identified their opponents as inspired by the Devil. The contemporary historiography of Kett's rebellion therefore takes us into some of the fundamental organising principles of the early modern world-view.[27]

III 'REBELS, IN HELL, WITH SATAN': PROPAGANDA, PATRIARCHY AND PERSUASION

One constant theme running through the narrative accounts of Kett's rebellion concerned the unhappy fate of the citizenry of Norwich. This is significant, because it will be argued here that, in terms of both perspective and assumed readership, the narrative accounts display a strong urban bias. Although rural complaint finds an occasional voice within the narratives, the reader is expected to sympathise with the dangerous position of the prosperous, urban householder. This perspective is at its clearest in descriptions of the purported rebel atrocities which occurred in the wake of Northampton's defeat. The Neville/Woods narrative provides a lurid account of how, during the fight with Northampton's army,

the Rebels entred the houses of the rich men in the citie, and rifled them; and after they had emptied them, set some of them on fire, & committed so great and sundry examples of cursed cruelty, as every wher it seemed at this time, not men endued with reason were entred the citie, but wilde beasts under the shape of men.

Having put the royal army to flight, the rebels then 'utterly robbed ... the Citizens' of 'all that ever they had', justifying their plunder 'under pretence of seeking the Earle of Northampton'. In order to placate the enraged rebels, the citizens agreed to deliver 'to the furious multitude, bread and drinke, and all kind of victuall; whereby it came to passe, that the miserable and hungry people being pacified, they were somewhat stayed from the rage of spoyling'.[28] The Neville/Woods narrative drew attention to the lasting harm which the citizens' forced charity did to their household economies:

very many ... sustained great losse and injury; and were so overcharged with such great expenses, that ever after while they lived (and many live at this day) in their houshold affaires, fared the worse.

---

[27] S. Clark, 'Inversion, misrule and the meaning of witchcraft', *P&P*, 87 (1980), 98–127.
[28] Neville/Woods, sig. G4r.

Not to be outdone, Holinshed's *Chronicles* both abbreviated and exaggerated Neville's account of the same events, describing how

> The rebels entering into the houses of such as were knowne to be wealthie men, despoiled and bare awaie all that might be found of anie value . . . There was shooting, howling, and wringing among them, weeping, and crieng out of women and children. To be short, the state of the citie at that present was most miserable.

Although the Neville/Woods narrative briefly acknowledges that only the houses of certain gentlemen were singled out for attack, this recognition of rebel selectivity stood in opposition to the fundamental message conveyed in all of the narratives: that the insurgents' assault upon property, and their transgression of domestic space, showed that the rebels were 'not men endued with reason . . . but wilde beasts under the shape of men'.[29]

In emphasising rebel excesses, the narrative accounts of the rebellion dwelt upon one of the most notable anxieties of contemporary householders: the fear of domestic invasion. The functioning of early modern communities depended upon mutual trust. The label of 'thief' represented the reverse of the moral values of the street, village and marketplace; and the act of theft transgressed the sensitive boundary between public and private space. Forced intrusions into the house were therefore understood as disruptive of both domestic safety and household authority. Precisely the same logic was pursued in the narratives of the rebellions. The aggressive, bestial rebels were presented as an anarchic, senseless, violent force, destructive not only of the public order of the realm and the city, but also of the private harmony of the prosperous urban household.

The historical representation of the 1549 rebellions therefore provided a harsh contemporary example of the paternal certainties articulated in that classic statement of social authoritarianism, the Homily on Obedience, which warned that

> Where there is no right order their reigneth all abuse, carnal liberty, enormity, sin and babylonical confusion. Take away kings, princes, rulers, magistrates, judges and such states of God's order, no man shall ride or go by the highway unrobbed, no man shall sleep in his own house or bed unkilled, no man shall keep his wife, children and possessions in quietness; all things shall be common and there must needs follow all mischief and utter destruction.[30]

The Homily on Obedience represented an attempt to convey the blunt precepts of social authoritarianism into popular consciousness. Within the homily, divinely sanctioned and lawfully constituted authority was opposed to the inevitable chaos of popular politics. A similar contrast between

---

[29] Neville/Woods, sig. H1r; Holinshed, 975.
[30] G. R. Elton, *The Tudor constitution: documents and commentary* (Cambridge, 1960), 15.

authority and disorder was developed by Sir John Cheke in his work *The hurt of sedition*. Although Cheke's work opened with a brief denunciation of the Western rebellion, the bulk of his book was directed against 'The other rable of Norffolke rebels'. This work was first published in 1549 and was republished in the same year. Notably, *The hurt of sedition* was reprinted in 1569 and in 1641, two other moments at which the Crown faced insurrectionary challenge, and was reproduced verbatim in the second edition of Holinshed's *Chronicles*.[31] The work therefore enjoyed a long life, spanning the commotion time and the English Revolution, and helped to communicate a distorted memory of the 1549 rebellions into the collective historical consciousness of the English gentry and nobility.[32]

Cheke's *Hurt of sedition* was more than a simple statement of social authoritarianism. It can be read as an attempt to rid wealthier plebeian men, through appeals to their social and patriarchal interests, of their habit of rebellion. Like almost every mid-sixteenth-century printed text concerned with authority, Cheke described the socio-political order as a static structure: 'in countries some must rule, some must obeie . . . everie man is not like wise . . . though all be parts of one common-wealth, yet all be not like worthie parts'.[33] Similarly, his condemnation of rebellion was highly formulaic. Following the conventions of other writers, he cited the divine sanction enjoyed by established authority, implied that the 1549 rebels had been led into the 'witchcraft of sedition' by 'the divell' and called upon history to demonstrate the inevitable failure of rebellion: 'Have not examples aforetimes both told the end of rebels, and the wickednesse of rebellion it selfe?'[34] But Cheke's work amounted to much more than another negative refutation of popular politics. Instead, he attempted to *persuade* potential rebels of the positive material and political benefits which flowed from obedience.

Although Cheke denounced the Norfolk rebels as 'frantike beasts', he undermined this cliché by committing much of his text to an attempt to appeal to the 'conscience' of those commotioners.[35] Notably, like the commonwealth writers, Cheke assumed that the commons of Tudor England possessed a legitimate place within the polity, including the right to petition. He argued that by taking part in rebellion, the commons had undermined this position: 'Now the gentlemen be more in trust' with the monarch 'bicause the commons be untrustie.'[36] Most importantly, Cheke assumed that he was

---

[31] Holinshed, 987–1011.
[32] For more journalistic Elizabethan mentions of Kett's rebellion, see B. Googe, *Eglogs, epytaphes and sonettes*, ed. E. Arber (London, 1871), 69–70; W. Warner, *Albion's England: the third time augmented and corrected, continuing an history of the same countrey and kingdome* (London, 1592), 173.
[33] Holinshed, 989, 1006.   [34] Holinshed, 988, 989, 991, 993, 998, 1009.
[35] Holinshed, 991, 993.   [36] Holinshed, 1003, 1006.

addressing a male, propertied, socially mobile householder: 'If there should
be such equalitie, then ye take awaie all hope from yours to come to anie
better estate than now you leave them.'[37] Working upon the classic patriar-
chial analogy between the social authority of the gentleman and the domestic
authority of the male householder, he warned that if rebellion prevailed, not
only would magistrates, laws and 'degrees of men' be ignored, but also
'maisters' should 'no longer [be] well served, nor parents truelie reverenced,
nor lords remembered of their tenants . . . what reason would yee be obeied of
yours as servants, if yee will not obeie the King as subjects?'

Such passages were intended to touch sensitive spots within the collective
psyche of propertied male householders. In Chapter Four we saw how
tensions between the rebel council on Mousehold Heath and some of the
rank-and-file commotioners reflected fundamental antagonisms within village society which set younger, landless, wage-dependent villagers in opposition to their older, established, propertied employers. It is therefore
significant that the lazy and the poor were presented in Cheke's account as
the sole beneficiaries of rebellion. He denounced the waste committed at
rebel camps by 'vagabonds and loitering beggers' and the economic impact
of the rebellion upon 'honest and true dealing men' who due to the rebels'
'crueltie and abhorred insurrections [have] lost their goods, their cattell, their
harvest'.[38] Expanding upon this point, Cheke argued that rebellion had
impeded both wealth creation and social mobility, producing a commonwealth in which the 'people' would be less likely to 'growe to wealth'.[39]
Repeatedly, Cheke insisted upon the sanctity of property, assuming that his
readership had experience of passing sentence as criminal court jurors upon
village thieves: 'if the besetting but of one house to rob it, be justlie deemed
worthie death; what shall we thinke of them that besieged whole cities the
desire of spoile?'[40]

The argument was clearly directed to the literate property-holder: precisely the group from which the leadership of the revolts had sprung. In a
perceptive comment on *The hurt of sedition*, J. A. Sharpe has observed that
Cheke 'sought to remind the natural leaders of peasant society, that stratum
of peasants who had played a key role in 1549 . . . that if they disobeyed those
placed above them in the social hierarchy, how could they expect their own
social inferiors, their servants and families, to obey them'. Writers like Sir
John Cheke worked upon the positive political allegiances of this group,
hoping to persuade them into obedience not 'for feare . . . but for conscience

---

[37] Holinshed, 990. Like Cheke, government propagandists in 1536 directed their attentions to
the leaders of rebellion, warning them of the 'rude rusticalles' whom they led. See Zeeveld,
Foundations, 171.
[38] Holinshed, 990, 993–4, 1000–2.   [39] Holinshed, 1003.   [40] Holinshed, 994, 996, 997.

state like Christians'. In the long run, Sharpe argues, this hegemonic project proved ultimately successful. Exploiting pre-existent divisions within the village economy, propagandists for the early modern state helped to convince wealthier, office-holding villagers to distance themselves from their poorer neighbours and to relocate their allegiances within the central state.[41] The consequence was a broader, more socially inclusive and more stable polity. Via the printing press, the pulpit, the homily and the catechism, the changing material interests of propertied male villagers were given new meanings which simultaneously bolstered state authority and drew the 'better sort of people' into an enlarged circle of ruling ideas.

Historical writing was therefore mobilised to legitimate authority. Key texts designed to call upon the loyalties of the commons presented history as a storehouse of examples of the sinfulness and failure of rebellion and of the violent chaos that was popular politics. Catechisms, sermons, homilies, conduct books, histories and drama were all used to convey this message. Thus, Grafton's *Chronicle* of 1569 stated its intention to inspire 'high and lowe [to] ... shone rebellions by their dreadfull effectes, and beware how they attempt against right, how unable soever the person be that beareth it'.[42] Likewise, the 1571 homily against disobedience and wilful rebellion enjoined subjects to

Turne over and reade the histories of all nations, looke over the chronicles of our owne countrey, call to mynde so many rebellions of olde tyme and yet some yet freshe in memorie, ye shall not finde that God ever prospered any rebellion against their naturall and lawfull prince, but conrarywyse that the rebelles were overthrowen and slaine, and such as were taken prisoners were dreadfully executed.

The homily lavished the same attention upon the rituals of execution as we find in Holinshed's *Chronicles*: rebels were 'rewarded with shamefull deathes, their heads and carcasses set upon poles, or hanged in chains, eaten with kites and crows, judged unworthy the honour of buriall'. The lessons of history were bolstered by divine authority: as the homily put it, 'eternall dampnation [was] ... prepared for rebels, in hell, with Satan'.[43]

Cranmer had made similar points in his sermon against rebellion, preached at St Paul's Cathedral at the height of the commotion time. Like Cheke, he scarcely mentioned the Western rebels, concentrating instead on the commotioners of southern and eastern England. He denounced their

---

[41] J. A. Sharpe, 'The law, law enforcement, state formation and national integration in late medieval and early modern England', in X. Rousseaux and R. Lévy (eds.), *Le pénal dans tous ses états: justice, états et sociétés en Europe (XIIe–XXe siècles)* (Brussels, 1997), 76–7; Holinshed, 988, 996, 1001.

[42] F. Smith Fussner, *Tudor history and the historians* (New York, 1970), 256.

[43] Bond (ed.), *Certain sermons*, 227, 229, 233, 234, 235.

insurrections as ungodly, citing both biblical and historical examples of the failure of popular rebellion. Cranmer drew upon the classical instances of 'Catiline, Cethegus and Manlius' alongside 'Jack Straw, Jack Cade, the blacksmith, Captain Aske ... who have suffered just punishment after their deserving'.[44] This appeal to the past rapidly worked its way into the magisterial mind. Writing to the Privy Council in 1554, the magistrates of Kent, keen to demonstrate their ostentatious loyalty at a time of Protestant insurrection within their county, emphasised the historical basis of their appeals to popular opinion, explaining how they had

publyshe[d] unto the people on the m[ar]kett daye ... [and] made an oracion unto the people of obedyaunce due to the Crowne and what meschyf punysshment and over throwe hathe in all cronacles and all ages happened to rebells & traytors.[45]

History, then, was mobilised to serve a very obvious purpose: that of reminding subjects of their duties to the Crown, and warning them of the horrible fate which awaited rebels. The overall effectiveness of the Tudor historiographers' reiteration of the failure of rebellion is impossible to chart; but in at least one recorded instance, their appeals to duty and threats of protracted execution had a discernible effect on one potential rebel. In the hungry year of 1586, the tailor Richard Vassinger came under pressure from his neighbours to join them in a rebellion which would 'amend' the 'hardnes of the worlde and dearthe of all things ... for ere longe the pore people wolde ryse'. He later told his interrogators that his reply had been that

yt were a better waye to redresse the dearth, by supplycacon ... that yt was not lyke that smale number of poore men were lyke to doe anye good in this enterprise and that he never harde any lyke attempte come to good.[46]

Over the course of the sixteenth century, governors sought to strengthen authority through appeals to the historical past. This political priority had a decisive influence upon the emerging tradition of historical writing. The media for the projection of this politicised interpretation of history included the pulpit, the catechism, the homily and popular historical work. Given the importance of the written word to this project, it is important that the later sixteenth century saw a significant expansion of literacy amongst the English population. In particular within rural East Anglia, the capacity of wealthier yeomen to sign their own name increased significantly during this period. Once again, the exact effects of this phenomenon can only be guessed at. What *is* possible to demonstrate is that key products of Tudor historical scholarship were sanctioned by the authorities for wide distribution.[47] One

---

[44] Cox (ed.), *Miscellaneous writings*, 196.   [45] PRO, SP11/2/27.
[46] BL, Cotton MS, Vespasian F IX, fol. 148r.   [47] Cressy, *Literacy and the social order*.

such work which received the sponsorship of the authorities was a 1582 collection of tracts which, importantly, included Alexander Neville's Latin history of Kett's rebellion. The volume was dedicated to Queen Elizabeth, carried her arms and opened with a copy of a letter from the High Commission which praised the work, and ordered bishops to see that it be used 'for the publike reading & teaching within their Dioceses'.[48] The wide dissemination of Neville's tract helped to rewrite memories of the commotion time, presenting the insurrections as violent, senseless assaults upon the established order. His work also had a determining influence over the early modern historiographical representation of the rebellions. Most obviously, Neville's work obscured the history of the rebellions outside Norfolk and thereby invented Kett's rebellion as a phenomenon independent from national politics. It will be argued in the next section that one effect of this shift in geographical emphasis was to simplify the complicated history of the 1549 rebellions, and thereby to strengthen hostile depictions of popular politics.

IV 'SOE MANY CADES AND KETTS': THE INVENTION
OF KETT'S REBELLION

Both Alexander Neville's account of Kett's rebellion and its stunted derivative in Holinshed's *Chronicles* were published a generation after the events they describe. These two accounts provided both the narrative structure and the interpretive template for later histories of the insurrection. Neville's pamphlet of 1575, its translation by Woods in 1615, and the account offered by Holinshed in 1577 and 1586 need to be understood as products of the specific historical periods in which they were produced. Placed within the social context of the early modern city, the printed descriptions of this last large-scale popular uprising in English history had an obvious relevance to the contemporary anxieties of wealthier urban householders. This was especially true of Elizabethan Norwich. The 'most vagrand and vacabond persons' whom Sotherton identified as the social basis of rebel support within Norwich did not vanish from the city's streets after 1549; but the authorities did ensure their closer surveillance and supervision. Similarly, as Carole Rawcliffe has recently emphasised, civic schemes for charity and welfare provision were driven by a combination of Christian duty, ideals of social reciprocity, fear of disorder and desire for social control. The consequence was a city which seemed to one early seventeenth-century visitor 'to be another Utopia ... The people are so orderly, the streets kept so cleanly, the tradesmen, young and old, so industrious, the better sort so provident and withal so charitable, that it is rare to meet a beggar.'[49]

[48] Ocland, *Anglorum praelia.*   [49] Sotherton, 88; Rawcliffe, *Medicine for the soul*, 239.

Understanding that those who failed to learn the lessons of history were doomed to repeat them, the magistracy of mid-Tudor Norwich ensured that the memory of Kett's rebellion was seared into civic consciousness. With much of Norwich still lying in ruins, the authorities decreed in 1550 that 27 August, the anniversary of Kett's defeat at Dussindale, should 'from hensfurth for ever' be kept as a commemorative holiday. The constables of every ward in the city were instructed that

> they shall gyve warning to every inhabitant within their wardes to ... shutte in their shoppes; and that both man and woman and childe Repayre to their parisshe Churches after they have Rong in at the howres of Seven of the Clokke, in the morning, And there to Remayn in supplication and prayors to god; hering the divine servyce of the churche that shalbe there song or sayed; and to gyve humble thanks to god, and praye for the preservation of the kings majestie hartely for the delyverey of this Cittie from the greate perill and daunger it was in.

In order that future inhabitants should 'have the same day allwayes in [their] Remembraunces for ever', it was further ordered that at the end of divine service, 'every parisshe [should] Ring a solemn peall with all there belles, to the ... prayse of god and the greate rejoysing of the peopull for ever'. The clamour of church bells, which in the countryside in 1549 had rallied commotioners, became after 1550 the auditory expression of civic hostility to popular insurrection. All parish churches maintained the tradition until the death of Queen Elizabeth, and thereafter the bells of the wealthiest church in the city, St Peter Mancroft, marked 'Kett's Day' until at least 1667, while the sheriffs, aldermen and Mayor processed to the cathedral 'to give God thanks for the deliverance of the city from Ket's rebellion'. Moreover, for a century after 1549, the city paid for annual lectures on 'Kett's Day' in the main parish churches and in the cathedral on the sins of rebellion.[50]

The authors of the main accounts of Kett's rebellion concluded their narratives with expressions of approval for the civic remembrance of the insurrection. Holinshed described how 'the citizens' agreed 'to give thanks to God for the deliverance at that daie'. Likewise, Richard Woods noted both the establishment of the 'solemne custome' of bellringing, and the presentation of sermons 'at the common place' of the city, 'to the which al the Citizens should resort'. Ronald Hutton and David Cressy have argued that the Protestant Reformation was advanced, in part, through the deliberate reconstruction of the ritual year. Both have shown how a sense of Protestant national consciousness was articulated through official commemorations of events such as the accession of Queen Elizabeth, the defeat of the

---

[50] NRO, NCR/16D/2, fol. 239r; Russell, *Kett's rebellion*, 155–6; R. Hutton, *The rise and fall of merry England: the ritual year, 1400–1700* (Oxford, 1994), 153–4.

Spanish Armada and the discovery of the Gunpowder Plot.[51] The civic celebration of Kett's defeat must be understood in similar terms. In both the creation of a national Protestant calendar, and the civic remembrance of Kett's rebellion, elites consciously invented public commemorations, politicised the calendrical year and disseminated print propaganda in order to project a distinct interpretation of recent history. In this version of history, certain aspects of the past were exaggerated, others were minimised and some suppressed altogether.

The governors of later Elizabethan and early Stuart Norwich were to project an image of their city as solidly, even fervently, Protestant. Yet as we saw in Chapter Four, popular religious opinion in the region was rather more diverse than such a simple picture suggested. This rather muddled story of the early Reformation was conveniently simplified in subsequent projections of the history of the city, especially treatments of the Marian period. As elsewhere in England, the wide dissemination of Foxe's *Acts and monuments*, with its detailed accounts of Protestant martyrdom, smoothed the reconstruction of recent religious history into both popular folklore and printed local histories. Just as the history of early Reformation Norwich was more complicated than was later appreciated, so it is necessary to distinguish between the historical actuality of the 'commotion time' and its historical representation. For this reason, a convenient distinction will here be drawn between the 'commotion time' – that is, the events of 1549 themselves – and 'Kett's rebellion', which henceforth will be understood as referring to the later construction placed upon those events. It is in this respect that Kett's rebellion is understood to have been 'invented' as a discrete historical 'event', specific only to Norfolk and Norwich, and separated from the broader history of the commotion time.

After 1575, historical accounts of the 1549 rebellions concentrated upon events in Norfolk and in Devon and Cornwall, to the near-exclusion of the risings within the rest of the country. This narrowing of the geography of insurrection in 1549, although it stemmed accidentally from the special treatment accorded to the Western and Norfolk rebellions by Holinshed's *Chronicles*, and from the publication of Neville's account of Kett's rebellion, proved useful to elite interests. It helped to obscure certain aspects of the events of 1549: in particular, the history of the negotiations between the Crown and the rebels; the disciplined, but less confrontational behaviour of rebels outside Norfolk and the West Country; and the subsequent execution of the leaders of those rebellions in the aftermath of the commotion time. The gradual

---

[51] Neville/Woods, sig. K4r; Holinshed, 984; Hutton, *The rise and fall of merry England*; D. Cressy, *Bonfires and bells: national memory and the Protestant calendar in Elizabethan and Stuart England* (Berkeley, 1989).

erasure of the memory of the rebellions elsewhere within England (outside the West Country) was enabled by the 'invention' of Kett's rebellion as a discrete event. This limiting of the geography of protest in 1549 aided the polemical deployment of Kett's rebellion as an instance of the evils of insurrection.

Despite their relative brevity, the earliest chronicle histories dealing with the reign of Edward VI gave proper recognition to the wide geography of rebellion in 1549. Stow's 1565 *Summarie*, for instance, devoted only one and a half paragraphs to the 'Commocion in Norwiche', followed by a brief mention of the execution of William and Robert Kett. It gave roughly the same space to the Cornish and Devonshire risings, and also made mention of Lord Grey's depredations around Oxfordshire and Buckinghamshire. Although, like almost all accounts, it paid no attention to the disturbances of 1548, the 1565 *Summarie* recognised that the commotions had begun 'about Whitsontide, and [had continued] so foorthe untyll September'. This periodisation of the 'sundry insurrections and commotions' of 1549 encompassed, without privileging, the Norfolk rising. Finally, the *Summarie* recognised the contribution made by commoners of Suffolk to the commotion time. The work stated that those who had 'encamped them selves' on Mousehold Heath had come from both 'Norffolke and Suffolke', and gave as much attention to the execution on 5 February 1550 of Robert Bell of Gazeley, the leader of the Suffolk insurrection, as it spent upon the execution of William and Robert Kett. The geographical perspective developed upon the 1549 rebellions in the 1565 edition of Stow's *Summarie* was typical of early printed accounts of the commotion time. Although, prior to the publication of the first edition of Holinshed's *Chronicles* in 1577, such earlier works tended to be relatively diminutive they nonetheless presented a fuller sense of the geography and the national implications of the commotion time than that laid out in Holinshed's much more substantial work. Fuller coverage was granted in the early printed accounts to the rebellions in Suffolk, Essex, the south-east, Somerset, Wiltshire and the south Midlands. The extent of repression within many of these counties was assessed alongside the slaughter in Norfolk and in Devon and Cornwall. Somerset's negotiations with the rebels, while certainly not explored, were hinted at: in his 1565 *Summarie*, Stow recognised that the rebellions had been 'constrayned ... partely by power ... partly by promis of their pardo[n]'.[52]

---

[52] J. Stow, *A summarie of Englyshe chronicles* (London, 1565), fols. 210v–211v, 213r–214r. For Stow's treatment of the mid-sixteenth century, see B. L. Beer, 'John Stow and the English Reformation, 1547–1559', *Sixteenth Century Journal*, 16, 2 (1985), 257–71; B. L. Beer, 'John Stow and Tudor rebellions, 1549–1569', *Journal of British Studies*, 27 (1988), 352–74. Stow made extensive use of a mid-Tudor London manuscript chronicle, which accorded similar coverage to Kett's rebellion (described as the risings of the 'comons of Norfolke & Suffolke') and to the risings in the Midlands, Berkshire, Oxfordshire and the west. See Kingsford (ed.), 'Two London chronicles', 17–19.

In contrast to the wide geographical coverage of earlier accounts, the first edition of Holinshed's *Chronicles* was more selective in its treatment of the commotion time. Whereas it presented very full accounts of Kett's rebellion and of the Western rising, other aspects of the commotion time received little attention. Although Holinshed's account made only fleeting reference to the course of the risings elsewhere in the country, its description of Kett's rebellion – the initial rising at Wymondham, the march on Norwich, the camp at Mousehold, the defeat of Northampton, the struggle with Warwick and the final slaughter at Dussindale – was fulsome. With the exception of its detailed account of the Yorkshire insurrection, and brief mention of Lord Grey's brutal progress through Oxfordshire and Buckinghamshire, Holinshed obscured the geographical scale of the commotion time. Although the second edition of Holinshed's *Chronicles* added further detail, it did not expand its geography. By way of contrast, even after the publication of the first edition of Holinshed's *Chronicles*, the 1580 edition of Stow's rival *Chronicles* expanded its coverage of the commotions outside Norfolk and the far west, but repeated Stow's earlier cursory treatment of the Norfolk rising.[53]

The reason for the differing emphasis between Holinshed's *Chronicles* and the earlier printed accounts of the commotion time was simple. Whereas earlier chroniclers could not draw upon any detailed account of any single insurrection of 1549, the *Chronicles* absorbed the Norwich-centred account established in Neville's 1575 account. Thereafter, the combined influence of the *Chronicles* and of the Neville/Woods narrative was to establish Kett's rebellion as the central event in the commotion time; to downgrade the history of the Western rising to a secondary event; and to almost obliterate the risings elsewhere within the country. The contemporary coverage accorded to Kett's rebellion in Sir John Cheke's *Hurt of sedition* was also significant, especially given its history of republication between 1549 and 1641. Although Cheke claimed that his venom was directed against all rebels, only his first few paragraphs addressed those who would 'rise for religion' (by which he meant the rebels in the far west). The vast bulk of his text was instead directed at 'The other rable of Norffolke rebelles', those who would 'change [their] obedience from King to a Ket'.[54]

In some respects, it is unsurprising that Kett's rebellion should have commanded such historical attention. Even without the deliberate memorialisation

---

[53] J. Stow, *The chronicles of England from Brute unto this present yeare of Christ* (London, 1580), 1040–3, 1045, 1047. Ironically, John Stow was included amongst the new editorial team at work on the second edition of Holinshed's *Chronicles*, although individual responsibility for specific sections of the *Chronicles* remains contentious. See Patterson, *Reading Holinshed's Chronicles*, 10.

[54] Holinshed, 988–9.

of Kett's rebellion by the civic elite, the ferocity of the struggles within Norwich meant that it would be a long time before Kett's rebellion passed out of popular memory. A full generation later, housing lots remained vacant in King Street in Conesford Ward, testimony to the damage inflicted on the south of the city. Similarly, deponents in the 1590s possessed clear memories of the destruction wrought upon Holmstreet and the Great Hospital 'in Kett's commotion'. The ecological damage inflicted upon Mousehold Heath was still more severe. As local inhabitants were to recall, Thorpe Wood had been almost wholly destroyed by the rebels in 1549; what remained had been cut down by the Pastons immediately afterwards.[55] The dramatic events which had unfolded in Norwich left their scars upon the mental landscape as well: the creators of a 1589 map of Mousehold Heath found it impossible not to mention 'the Oke of Reformacon so-callyd by Kett the Rebel'.[56] Such visible and readily understood marks helped to inscribe the commotion time within local memory and laid the basis for the successful memorialisation of Kett's rebellion by the city's governors. The relative ease with which Kett's rebellions slipped into both local and national historical memory is therefore much easier to explain than the collective forgetting of the wider insurrections of 1549.

In contrast to the deliberate memorialisation of Kett's rebellion in Norwich, authorities elsewhere preferred to obscure the participation of their localities in the insurrections. The clearest contrast between the clarity with which Kett's rebellion was recalled in Norwich is to be found in Yarmouth. As we saw in Chapter One, support for the commotion had been strong in Yarmouth in the summer of 1549. For a brief period, the town was controlled by the rebels; moreover, there was a direct connection between the commotion of 1549 and earlier troubles in 1548. Yet after 1549, the town's support for the rebels was forgotten. In contrast, officially sanctioned histories of Yarmouth presented Kett's rebellion as an important moment in the history of the town, in which the malign intentions of rebel outsiders had been frustrated by the loyal inhabitants. This interpretation was articulated in two manuscript histories of the town, both written by men who were closely integrated into Yarmouth's governing elite. The earlier work was written in the later sixteenth century by Thomas Damet, a prominent man who served as bailiff and represented the borough in parliament. Damet's work was succeeded by that of Henry Manship, who occupied the

---

[55] For the extent of destruction after 1549, see M. Rodgers, M. Wallace and E. Rutledge (eds.), *Norwich landgable assessment, 1568–1570* (Norfolk Record Society, LXIII, Norwich, 1999), 4. For the damage on Holmstreet, see PRO, E134/43& 44Eliz/25. For the destruction of Thorpe Wood, see PRO, REQ2/18/106.

[56] PRO, MPC 2787; for the common rights dispute which led to the production of this map, see PRO, E178/7153.

office of town clerk between 1579 and 1585, and was a member of the Corporation until 1604. Upon the request of the Corporation, Manship compiled a report on the town archives in 1612, finishing his 'History of Great Yarmouth' seven years later. The Corporation celebrated the completion of Manship's work by rewarding him with £50 for the manuscript. Manship's remarkable work represented a small classic in the emergent tradition of local antiquarianism and traced the history of the town since its site had first emerged as a sandbank from the North Sea. Based upon extensive searches within the town's archives, both works represented the historiographical expression of a broader civic identity.[57]

Local history was important to the governors of early modern Yarmouth. Like the inhabitants of More's Utopia, the town burghers had long maintained their 'cronicles ... with all deligente circumspection'. Since at least 1542, the town's extensive archives had been held within a large chest, called the Hutch, the use of which was overseen by a 'Hutch committee'. In a clear attempt to broaden civic access to the archives, from the later sixteenth century many of the town's more important documents, such as its charters, were translated from Latin into English. The operation of the Hutch committee generated further documentation, in the form of the 'Hutch book', which lovingly recounted the use of the town's archives. The primary purpose of the Corporation's maintenance of the archives lay in their usefulness as a legal bulwark of the town's rights. A secondary result of their maintenance was to embed a legitimating sense of the past within civic identity. As Robert Tittler has stressed, the late sixteenth-century growth of this literate antiquarianism connected with other expressions of cultural and political assertion by urban ruling groups, such as the construction or extension of guildhalls and the elaboration of civic rituals.[58]

The preservation of town archives therefore projected a distinct image of urban identity: as literate and ordered, and as founded upon an authority that was sanctioned by royal charter. This ordering ideology crept into Manship's historical writing. In his 1612 report on the state of the archives, Manship noted how the

---

[57] Damet may be responsible for the 'Hutch Map', a later sixteenth-century map which purports to show the Yare estuary as it was in about AD 1000. Although listed in the NRO as Y/C37/1, the original is displayed in the Town Hall at Yarmouth. For Manship's work, see Ecclestone (ed.), *Henry Manship's Great Yarmouth*. Manship's account of Yarmouth's role in the 1549 rebellion has provided the template for all subsequent discussions. It is fully replicated in H. Swinden, *The history and antiquities of the ancient burgh of Great Yarmouth* (Norwich, 1772), 934–41, and is uncritically repeated in Beer, *Rebellion and riot*, 102–3. For Manship's report on the Yarmouth archives, see NRO, Y/C1/1.

[58] More/Robynson, 53; R. Tittler, 'Reformation, civic culture and collective memory in English provincial towns', *Urban History*, 24, 3 (1997), 283–300; R. Tittler, *Townspeople and nation: English urban experiences, 1540–1640* (Stanford, CA, 2001).

Charters Rolls and evidences w[hi]ch doo remayne in the vestry, Guildhall and other places doe lye not onely displ[er]sedly but also very disorderly and have not theise great nomber of yeres been p[er]used and read to the no little damage of the whole Incorporacon.

Manship's purpose in his 'reporte' was therefore twofold: to ensure the preservation and proper organisation of the town's archives; and to broaden their readership. With this in mind, he noted how in order that

> every one of the Comon assembly and every other good and well affected Townsmen may be further instructed wth knowledge whereby they may bee the better able to doe more good to the estate of this Township in future tyme.[59]

Manship's choice of language is instructive: he intended to impose order upon the 'very disorderly' archives. Manship's reorganised archive was intended to expand 'knowledge' of civic history, and thereby to strengthen 'the estate of this Township in future tyme'. This was, therefore, no simple empiricist exercise in local history: instead, Manship intended to strengthen the case for the town's legal rights and thereby to deepen its authority amongst its key constituents: the 'well affected Townsmen'.[60]

Manship's purpose recalls Annabel Patterson's suggestion that Holinshed's *Chronicles* were aimed at what she calls an urban 'middle-class' readership. The intention of the *Chronicles* was, Patterson argues, 'to construct a *textual* space ... in which the public's right to information could to some extent be satisfied'. Amongst the many divergent themes within the *Chronicles*, Patterson detects an intention to legitimate civic (and especially metropolitan) autonomy, to cast English history in a light favourable to 'middle-class' interests and periodically to disparage the arbitrary exercise of royal authority.[61] Although Patterson overstates her case, there is more than a germ of truth here: Manship and Holinshed presented their readers with versions of history, and with ordered compilations of contemporary documents, which emphasised civic autonomy and which assumed the existence of an educated, politically aware and historically literate readership. The fact that both works were so selective in their coverage of the history of the 1549 rebellions sheds some light on the changing historiographical representation of those insurrections.

Amongst the bundles of charters, legal papers and court rolls listed by Manship, the Yarmouth Hutch divulged an original 'l[ett]re of K[ing] Edward the Sixt of thanksgivings to the Towne for keeping the same agaynst the Rebell Kett'. The discovery of such documentation – other finds included a rebel warrant of July 1549, correspondence from the Council to the

---

[59] NRO, Y/C1/1.   [60] *Ibid.*
[61] Patterson, *Reading Holinshed's Chronicles*, ch. 1, passim, quoting 16, 21.

Yarmouth authorities and orders agreed by the bailiffs for the defence of the town – enabled Manship to construct an account of Yarmouth's role in the commotion time which, while empirically satisfying, obscured the real complexity of events within the town in 1549.[62] Backed by his readership of Neville's 1575 pamphlet, Manship distinguished 'the rebels' from 'the townsmen'. Hence, the rebels' destruction of the new harbour works was presented as their vindictive response to the town's loyalty to the Crown. Yet Manship's punctilious transcriptions sometimes undermined his case: in copying the orders made for the defence of Yarmouth against the rebels in August 1549, he included an item which instructed the constables to identify those Yarmouth householders who had joined the rebel camp. Nonetheless, Manship persisted in presenting the rebels as dangerous outsiders. Thus, describing the defeat of the first rebel attempt to seize Yarmouth, Manship wrote that 'The whole town thought they had seen the last of the rebels and thanked God for it.' Considering the rebels' next defeat, he wrote of how 'Again Yarmouth gave thanks to God, and celebrated its success with feasting and revelry.'[63]

All this is of more than merely antiquarian significance. The Yarmouth historians' account of the town's role in the commotion time was more subtle than any simple exercise in censorship. Instead, through manipulating some of the facts and suppressing others, Manship and Damet established a consistent narrative which presented the town's rulers with a useful historical example of their traditional loyalty to the Crown. In 1594, the Yarmouth town governors petitioned Elizabeth I for help in rebuilding their harbour. They justified this request with an account of how 'Kett with his rebelles' had intended 'to take [Yarmouth] for their hold, which the inhabitants of the towne would in no wise permit, or consent unto, but kept the towne for the kinges majesty according to their allegiance'. In revenge, the rebels 'did revenge upon ... Yermouth' by destroying the harbour works. Linking their defence of the established order with their loyalty to the Protestant religion, the petitioners went on to explain how during the reign of Mary I their predecessors had approached the Crown for help in reconstructing their harbour, but because 'the townsmen [were] not ... greatly favoured in those daies by reason of there religion had no such help at the said Queen Mary's handes', the Queen had refused them. Manship and Damet's version of events therefore established an authorised local narrative of the commotion time which proved convenient to the town's elite, and which would be echoed on subsequent occasions in their negotiations with the Crown.[64]

---

[62] NRO, Y/C1/1. [63] Ecclestone (ed.), *Henry Manship's Great Yarmouth*, 88–93.
[64] Swinden, *History and antiquities*, 401–2, 413, 446–9.

The authorised version of the events in Yarmouth in 1549 proceeded from the suppression of certain facts and the exaggeration of others. Most obviously, it supported a clear set of interests: the need to forget the complexity of the commotion time and the imperative to consolidate the relationship between the town elite and the Crown. In both cases, the removal of the broad geography of the commotion time from historical record and its replacement with the Norwich-centred story of Kett's rebellion was convenient, enabling the Yarmouth historians to depict the rebels as a disruptive, alien force. Whatever their motives, it was Neville and Woods who, unwittingly aided by Holinshed, invented Kett's rebellion as a distinct 'historical event', as distinct from elite politics as it was separate from the rebellions underway elsewhere. In contrast, until Neville wrote his history, Kett's rebellion had been understood alongside the other rebellions. This was as true of continuing local memories of the rebellions, as it was of their coverage within printed chronicles.

Court witnesses old enough to remember the Norfolk insurrections were most likely to refer to those events as the 'commotion time'.[65] Although the motives of Robert Kett were the subject of alehouse argument in post-rebellion Norwich, the insurrection he had led had been subsumed under the more general heading of the 'commotion time' or the 'camping time'. In Kent, the insurrections were still remembered in the 1580s as 'the tyme of rebellion of comon welth'.[66] In any case, all of these terms assumed that the insurrections of 1549 had covered a wide area and neither privileged the events in Norwich over those that had taken place elsewhere. But Woods' translation of Neville, combined with the deliberate attempts of the Norwich civic elite to memorialise the black legend of Robert Kett, helped to impose the more limited story of Kett's rebellion upon the complicated diversity of the 'commotion time', just at the very time as the events of 1549 were passing out of living memory. It was at this point that the 'commotion time', the 'camping time' and the 'rebellion of comon welth' started to vanish. Older people giving evidence to courts were still using those terms in the 1580s; but they were gone from the record by 1600.[67] In the place of the 'commotion time' came the term 'Kett's rebellion', bringing with it both the limitation of the geographical focus and political implications of the 1549 rebellions.

Whereas the 'commotion time' had covered a broad swathe of England, the story of Kett's rebellion concentrated upon Norwich. As those who

---

[65] For an early reference to 'Ketts Campe', see Cambridge University Library, EDR D/2/11, fol. 159v.
[66] PRO, E133/6/815; PRO, E134/30&31Eliz/Mich19.
[67] See, for instance, PRO, E178/7153.

retained immediate memories of the 'commotion time' passed away, so the memory and implications of its wide geography died with them. Likewise forgotten were the summertime executions in Cambridge, the apparent surrender of Colchester and Yarmouth to the rebels, the camps outside Canterbury and Salisbury, and the pitched-battle slaughter of rebels in Oxfordshire, Buckinghamshire and Wiltshire. Forgotten were the winter-time executions in Essex and Suffolk. Forgotten also was the fluidity of mid-Tudor politics: namely, the extensive negotiations between Crown and rebellious commons that had preceded the decision of the Suffolk and Essex rebels to disarm. The fact of negotiation between ruler and ruled within a polity which was meant to be closed to the popular voice threatened such standard conceptions of authority and obedience. The fuller story of the negotiations between Somerset and the rebels undermined that authoritarian vision of the Tudor polity. It is noteworthy that the only early modern historical work which delved into the record of those negotiations, that written by Sir John Hayward, was not published in his lifetime. Hayward had earlier burnt his fingers with his treatment of the reign of Henry IV. His publication of a book on the subject in 1599 had led to his imprisonment in the Tower of London and to his periodic interrogation by the Privy Council, concerned to learn whether he had intended to draw contemporary parallels from the rebellion which had placed Henry IV on the throne.[68] Equally problematic was the repression that followed those negotiations. The dark contrast between summertime negotiations and wintertime repression in Suffolk and Essex, even within the standard terms of elite political culture, did little to build confidence in the distribution of power within English society. The English state had traumatic memories of the 'commotion time' which needed to be buried.

In contrast, the story of Kett's rebellion was simpler, and fitted more conveniently into standard elite concepts of popular politics, authority and obedience. The Neville/Woods narrative told of how, in the early summer of 1549, a peasant rebellion had erupted in Norfolk. In this tale, the lower orders, released from the shackles of proper government, were allowed a brief, violent liberty in which the social order was inverted and the 'vulgar commons' once again demonstrated their incapacity for government. In particular, the violent excesses of the uncivilised rural commons within the ordered environment of Norwich, aided by what Neville/Woods called 'the

---

[68] For Hayward's treatment of the negotiations between Somserset and the rebels, see B. L. Beer (ed.), *The life and raigne of King Edward the sixth by John Hayward* (Kent, OH, 1993), 87–8. For Hayward's biography of Henry IV, see J. J. Manning (ed.), *The first and second parts of John Hayward's The life and raigne of King Henrie IIII* (Camden Society, 4th ser., XLII, London, 1991). For the record of his interrogation, see PRO, SP12/274/58–62.

scum of the City', were held up for condemnation.[69] Following military defeat at the hands of a Protestant hero, the status quo was re-established, rank-and-file rebels were pardoned and the leaders of insurrection were condemned to proper punishment. All of this fitted a standard pattern within Tudor historiography and could be conveyed in ways which were both intimidating to would-be rebels and reassuring to the proper subject. Within the genre of Tudor historical writing, an important place was always reserved in accounts of popular insurrection for detailed descriptions of the punishment of defeated rebels. The Neville/Woods narrative was no exception. The executions which followed in the wake of rebel defeat at Dussindale were gloated over with a pornographic enthusiasm:

> the Ringleaders, and principalls were hanged on the Oke: Called the Oke of Reformation, and many companions with them in these villanies, were hanged, and then presently cut downe, and falling upon the earth: (these are the Judgements of Traytors in our Country) first their privie parts are cut off, then their bowels pulled out alive, and cast into the fire, then there head is cut off, and their bodies quartered: the head set upon a Pole, and fixed on the tops of the Towers of the City, the rest of the body bestowed upon severall places, and set up to the terror of other.[70]

Public execution was intended to provide a dramatic, visual statement of the power of the established order. The printed accounts of the punishment which flowed from the defeat of Kett's rebellion, and of similar events elsewhere within English history, fulfilled the same function, but for a wider audience, regaling their readers with detailed descriptions of the evisceration of the opponents of proper authority. The printed historical narrative therefore formed a scaffold on which the opponents of authority were fated upon every reading, like Prometheus at his rock, to be ripped and torn over and over again.

Regular republication of Holinshed's *Chronicles* and Cheke's *Hurt of sedition*, coupled with Richard Woods' 1615 translation of Neville's narrative, together with the consistent plagiarism of the Neville/Woods narrative, guaranteed that Robert Kett's name came to rank alongside those of Wat Tyler, Jack Straw and Jack Cade as one of the terrifying personifications of popular disorder. Whereas the rebels of 1381 and 1450 remained distant to the gentry of early Stuart England, the insurrections of 1549 lay just on the cusp of living memory. It was therefore important that early modern representations of the 1381, 1450 and 1549 rebellions so often presented rural popular politics as a senseless terrifying continuum. I have argued elsewhere that this was most apparent in William Shakespeare's depiction of Jack Cade

---

[69] Neville/Woods, sig. B4r.
[70] Neville/Woods, sig. K3v. In its combination of repetition and bodily violation, this account may be thought of as pornographic.

in *Henry VI Part Two*. Shakespeare's Cade formed a dramatic personification of medieval and early Tudor rural insurrection.[71] In this respect, the slippage between quite distinct historical episodes – those of 1381, 1450 and 1549 – helped to dramatise contemporary social authoritarianism.

More historically discriminating accounts of 1549 also tended to view the events of that year within the context of contemporary concerns. When parliament met in the aftermath of large-scale enclosure rioting in the Midlands in 1607, one of the most pressing issues which faced legislators concerned the usefulness of new anti-enclosure legislation. The last such statute had been passed in 1597, in the wake of an attempted rising in Oxfordshire.[72] A manuscript was circulated amongst legislators which argued forcefully against such laws, questioning 'Whether the time be fit to give remedy, when such encouragement may move the people to seek redress by the like outrage, and therefore in Edward the sixth his time the remedy was not pursued until two years after the rebellion of Kett'. The document went on to describe common land as 'nurseries of beggars', and to advance arguments in favour of further enclosure. This was the first time that parliament had responded to popular insurrection by rejecting legislation against enclosures and the outcome of the debates represented an important victory for the pro-enclosure lobby. Ironically, Kett was invoked in justification of the proposal that the government withdraw from the regulation of agrarian change.[73]

At moments of crisis, early modern England's ruling class liked to remind themselves of some of their founder-myths. It was reassuring to rehearse the need for the unity of the educated and cultured gentry and equally worrying to be reminded of the violent chaos which seethed in the collective mind of the 'vulgar people'. Mention of Robert Kett was useful: as was citation of Jack Straw, Jack Cade, Wat Tyler, the German Peasants' War of 1525, or (for the classically minded) the social struggles within Republican Rome and democratic Athens. In early modern England, a substantial body of historical literature was dedicated to such depictions of popular politics, within which the work of Richard Woods, Alexander Neville and the Holinshed editorial team had their own special place. Ironically, the increased output of such work during the later sixteenth and early seventeenth centuries occurred at the same time as a gradual diminution in the scale and gravity of popular disorder. Nonetheless, citation of the dangerous names of Straw, Cade, Kett and Tyler seemed almost obligatory within contemporary discussions of the dangers of social disorder. Thus, scraping the barrel for arguments against proposed legislation intended to strengthen the rights of tenants on the northern border,

---

[71] Wood, *Riot, rebellion and popular politics*, 1–5.
[72] For which, see Walter, 'A "rising of the people"'.   [73] Kerridge, *Agrarian problems*, 200–3.

the gentry of the region warned the 1581 parliament of how, if the bill became law, the 'under-sort and tenants' would transform into the Tudor north's answer to Jack Straw and Wat Tyler. Similarly, writing in 1628 at a time of food and enclosure rioting, Ralph Knevet fretted over of how 'The rude multitude', if led by 'some daring Ket', was always ready to mutiny.[74]

Long after his execution, therefore, the ghost of Robert Kett continued to haunt the early modern gentry, a reminder always to stand on their guard against the hideous evil of 'popularity'. Kett's name was expected to stimulate two linked responses in the gentry: the fear of popular chaos coupled with a desire for maximum elite unity. On the eve of the English Civil War, Royalist propagandists hoped to stimulate this Pavlovian response by damning the leaders of the parliament as the creatures of a plebeian mob. Thus, the Earl of Dorset made sense of the riots and demonstrations of 1641–2 through his reading of the past, wishing that 'my children had never been borne, to live under the dominion of so many Cades and Ketts, as threaten by their multitudes and insurrections to drowne all memory of monarchy, nobility, gentry, in this land'. Royalist propaganda exploited such images to their full, reminding the gentry of the depredations of 'Wat Tyler, Jack Cade and Kett the Tanner': horrid rebels whose shades seemed to move amongst the crowds that flocked outside Westminster Hall in December 1641.[75] The editor of the 1641 version of Sir John Cheke's *Hurt of sedition* perceived the same historical parallels. He observed how although Cheke's work had not been

intended by the Author as a Prophecy for any future times . . . yet there is a continuall recurrence of the same Pageants . . . consult the storie of those times under EDWARD the VI and you shall meet with insolent demands from some rebellious subjects against the forme of religion then established by Act of Parliament: others you shall finde sitting under their Oake of Reformation upon the life and death of all civility and learning.

Comparisons between 1549 and the crisis of 1641–2 seemed obvious to Royalists:

may it not be feared that an Anabaptisticall parity as well in State as Church sounds too plausibly in the eares of the multitude? Consult our Chronicles, see what the aymes and ends of those rude companies under Jack Straw and Wat Tyler . . . look upon Kets demands and Ombles Prophecy [that is, the prophecy that motivated the Yorkshire rebels in 1549] under Edward VI. Doe not they all amount to this Summe, they would have no Noble men, no Gentlemen, no Lawyers, no Justices, as well as no Bishops?[76]

---

[74] S. J. Watts, *From border to middle shire: Northumberland, 1586–1625* (Leicester, 1975), 31; Hill, 'The many-headed monster', 186.

[75] Walter, *Understanding popular violence*, 19.

[76] J. Cheke, *The true subject to the rebell, or the hurt of sedition, how greivous it is to a commonwealth* (Oxford, 1641), sigs. A2r–v, 63r.

Parliamentarian propagandists, cannily aware that history usually bears more than one reading, answered by highlighting the popularity of the Royalist cause in Cornwall as evidence of the same religious conservatism that the Cornish had last exhibited back in 1549.[77] But the damage was done to the parliamentary cause. The collective memory of the early modern gentry was filled with such partial but nonetheless terrifying images of popular politics. Such anxieties influenced both social relations and political events. When, after the First Civil War, organised radical movements began to emerge within London and the New Model Army, their opponents rendered them comprehensible by identifying them as the ideological descendants of earlier rebels. The early modern gentry had long ago built 1549 into their collective memory, remembering that year as a terrible catastrophe, proof of the levelling instincts which lurked amongst the lower orders. Years before the radicals of the late 1640s had emerged as an organised force, they had therefore been invented as categories of the political imagination.

V 'THE MORE WAS AN HAWLTER': REMEMBERING REBELLION IN EARLY MODERN ENGLAND

How should the history of popular memory be written? For the early modern historian, the task lies at the limits of feasible research. The personal and collective memories of working people have usually left only the faintest of documentary imprints. This must be especially true of societies such as sixteenth- and seventeenth-century England, in which few working people left autobiographical writings. Records of positive popular memories of the 1549 rebellions are therefore minimal. The dangers of remembering the commotion time contrast with the freedom with which the lower classes recorded other aspects of social memory: most notably, issues concerning customary law.[78] Nonetheless, if interpreted with sufficient boldness, and taken together with some deafening silences, the few tantalising traces of positive memories of 1549 allow us to guess at how some early modern labouring people might have remembered the commotion time.

We have already seen how, in the immediate aftermath of Kett's rebellion, the authorities established their own version of events in 1549. This presented the commotion time as a class war, waged by diabolically inspired peasants (in its class character, as we suggested in Chapter One, this enjoyed some basis in truth). This authorised narrative was enforced through the prosecution of those who presented alternative accounts. Hence, articulation

---

[77] M. J. Stoyle, 'Pagans or paragons?: Images of the Cornish during the English Civil War', *English Historical Review*, 111 (1996), 302–4.
[78] A subject about which I intend to write more fully elsewhere.

of some uncomfortable aspects of the 1549 rebellions might carry with it an appalling peril. One such uncomfortable aspect concerned events in Suffolk, where the rebels had first been persuaded to disarm, only later to face the execution of their leaders. Within the authorised history of the rebellions, which presented the rebels as distant from state politics, hostile to the gentry and deserving of proper punishment, the events in Suffolk in 1549 were somewhat inconvenient. But popular memories of the commotion time could not be so easily reconstructed. For some generations, direct reminiscences of the commotion time continued to colour local senses of the past. As we saw in later sixteenth-century Norwich, some such memories connected with the deliberate memorialisation of the commotion time by the authorities. But elsewhere, that past weighed like a nightmare on the minds of the living.

The most powerful surviving plebeian memory of the insurrections comes, appropriately enough, from the town of Lavenham (Suffolk). Early Tudor Lavenham provides a strong example of continuity in local traditions of popular protest. In 1525, and again in 1549, the weavers and farmers of the Lavenham area rose in armed rebellion. In the spring of 1525, thousands of local people had gathered in the town in order to demonstrate against Cardinal Wolsey's Amicable Grant. Confronted by a force that had been hastily assembled by the Dukes of Norfolk and Suffolk, demonstration nearly turned into open warfare. The would-be rebels had agreed to rise upon the sounding of the great bell of Lavenham, but were frustrated at the last moment by the removal of the bell's clapper by a loyal clothier. In the end, the rebels agreed to disband in return for the Dukes' representation of their grievances to Wolsey.[79] In the summer of 1549, the Suffolk commotioners were once again persuaded to disband. This time, the rebels went home in return for the consideration of their grievances. The subsequent execution of the leaders of the Suffolk rebels concluded Lavenham's role in the commotion time. Memories of that betrayal lingered within the town. Twenty years later, a Lavenham man named James Fuller admitted to plotting a new rising with John Porter. The target of their insurrection was to be the 'riche churles' and 'heardemen' of the locality, whom they intended to kill. Seeking a pardon in 1571, Fuller explained how he and Porter intended to make use of the bells of Lavenham church:

I have agreed with the sexten of La[ve]nham Churche that he shall delyver unto me the keys of the saide churche dore uppon Sondaye nexte. And then abowte tenne of the clocke in the nighte I and others shall mete at a place called the Gravell Pittes nere to La[ve]nham and from thence we will goe to the towne of Brente Illeigh and rayse uppe the people in that towne, and from thence to Preston and there to rayse uppe the

---

[79] HMC, *Welsh*, I, ii–v; Holinshed, 709–10; Hall, *Chronicle*, 696–702.

people in that towne, and from thens to La[ve]nham and there to rynge the bells awake.[80]

The geography of Porter and Fuller's planned insurrection was built upon a tradition of popular protest: in 1525 and 1549, these villages had risen together in rebellion.[81] Porter and Fuller's insurrectionary plans also drew upon their reading of the events of 1549. Fuller admitted that he had warned how

we wyll not be deceyved as we were at the laste rysinge, for then we were promised ynoughe and more than ynoughe. But the more was an hawlter.

Fuller's speech brimmed with bitter symbolism. The 'hawlter' evoked social subordination: 'hawlters' were worn by beasts of burden, pulling ploughs in the field. But Fuller's remark also alluded to a continuing local knowledge of the events of 1549, illuminating how the commons of Lavenham had been promised much by the 'rich churles' in the negotiations that year, but had only been placed more firmly under the 'hawlter'. Finally, the phrase held another possible meaning. As we saw in Chapter Two, the suppression of the commotion time in Suffolk had entailed hangings. It might be, therefore, that after 1549 the halter was remembered in Lavenham as a noose. Notably, Fuller dwelt heavily upon the imagery of public execution in the revenge fantasy which he reconstructed in his admission of guilt:

But nowe *we* wyll appoynte them that shall take the riche churls and sett *them* on *theyre* horsebacks under a tree, whereupon *we* wyll hange a wythe and putte it aboute *theire* neckes and then dryve *theire* horses from under *them* and so lett *them* hange.[82]

Fuller's plan might be read as a uchronic reversal of the 1549 executions: the 'riche churls' are set on '*theire* horses' and hanged with their own halters. Fuller's inversion of the symbolism of authority and of the local history of the 1549 rebellions remained unfulfilled. But it reminds us that, at least for a couple of generations, some labouring people continued to cling to their black memories of 1549, and to find in the past a message for the future.

James Fuller was not alone in remembering the broad geography and dark history of the commotion time. Plotting a rising in 1566, four Colchester weavers debated their strategy. One of their number, Roger Morrell, proposed that they should 'gett a madde knave and sett hym on horsebacke' and raise the commons in the weaving villages about Colchester before descending upon the town, where they would 'crye they are up, they are up, and the people to gett to the churches and to rynge awake'. His comrade John Broke

---

[80] *CPR, Elizabeth* I, V, *1569–72*, no. 1818.
[81] MacCulloch, 'Kett's rebellion', 49–50; MacCulloch, *Suffolk and the Tudors*, 296–7.
[82] *CPR, Elizabeth* I, V, *1569–72*, no. 1818. My emphasis.

saw in the early stages of the commotion time a template for a successful insurrection, suggesting an amendment to Morrell's geography by arguing that their 'rising' should be 'at mydsomer next for that wylbe the best tyme for at that tyme beganne the last commotion'.[83] Like the Essex weavers of 1566, at least one Elizabethan Norfolk labourer perceived of the camping time as a model for future insurrections. In 1597, Thomas Veare of Fakenham landed himself before the county's quarter sessions for his proposal that 'ther shold be a campe at wessonsett, meaning suche as ketts campe was, & ther men shold fytt for corne'. In what looks like a clampdown on critics of the village authorities, Veare's presentment was placed alongside that of other Fakenham inhabitants 'for complayninge of the towne of Fakenham w[i]t[h]out cause & ... for unfit & contemptius speches in the open market'.[84] His appearance before the Bench also fitted into a broader, national pattern of muttered criticism and open riot against the authorities at a time of spiralling food prices, hard winters and foreign war.

The hard conditions of the mid-1590s also reminded the Oxfordshire carpenter Bartholomew Steer of the bitter stories he had heard about the commotion time. In the autumn of 1596, stimulated by his conversations with his neighbour Richard Bradshawe about the high price of food, Bartholomew proposed to the people of Hampton Gay and Yarnton (Oxfordshire) that there should be a 'rising of the people' on Enslow Hill.[85] Steer later confessed that he and Bradshawe

> first thought yt fytt that the rising should be at Enslowe hill ... And confesseth he hadd heard that in former time there was a rising of people at Enslowe hill, And this Exam[inant] told Symonds [another conspirator] that then the people that there did rise were p[er]swaded to goe home, and were after hanged like doggs. But this Exam[inant] said that yf they were once up, that they would never yeelde but goe through wth yt.[86]

Roger Symonds remembered Bartholomew's speech as follows:

> That at the last rising or rebellion w[hi]ch was at Enselowe hill, how those w[hi]ch then did rise, weare intreated to give ov[er] But Stere said ... we will not nowe be made such fooles and therfore we will goe thorowe wth the matter.[87]

The invocation of this deep social memory helped to legitimate Bartholomew Steer's social analysis. Like his neighbours, Steer believed that the dearth of food was caused by enclosure and depopulation by the local gentry. He later explained that, since he was 'a single man, and therefore stoode in no neede,

---

[83] Cockburn (ed.), *Essex indictments*, nos. 288–91.
[84] NRO, NQS C/S3/12A, Presentment of Gallow hundred.
[85] An incident brilliantly discussed in Walter, 'A "rising of the people"'. [86] PRO, SP12/262/4.
[87] PRO, SP12/261/27. See also Symonds' examination in PRO, SP12/262/4.

he want to have risen to have helpen his poore frendes, and other poore people that lyved in miserie'. Bartholomew therefore proposed that popular hunger should be assuaged through direct action, arguing 'that hit would nev[er] be well untill some of the gentlemen were knockt downe'. Bartholomew and his conspirators expected to be met upon Enslow Hill by an armed crowd of 'good fellowes' from the nearby town of Witney, with whom they would tour the immediate district, slaughtering leading gentlemen. In fact, on the intended night of the insurrection, only Steer and two other men turned up on Enslow Hill. Their conspiracy was betrayed; Steer died in gaol and his supporters were executed.

In his examination of this incident, John Walter has made a strong case for identifying Steer's reference to an earlier 'mutiny' with the Buckinghamshire and Oxfordshire rebellions of 1549: Lord Grey's clash with the rebels had led to large-scale bloodshed in the county; moreover, Bartholomew Steer planned to murder his former master, Lord Norris of Rycote, for whom he had worked as a carpenter, and whom he labelled as one of the leading oppressors of the commons. Walter notes that Rycote stood at 'the centre of an area with the considerable history of the population and enclosure for sheep' which in 1549 'had attracted the attention of the Edwardian rebels'.[88] Steer's strategy seems therefore to have developed from his own experience of social conflict and harvest failure, and to have been legitimated within a local memory of rebellion and betrayal.

Despite the fragmentary nature of the surviving evidence, the recorded speech of James Fuller of Lavenham, Thomas Veare of Fakenham, Bartholomew Steer of Hampton Gay and the Colchester weavers of 1566 reveals much about continuing popular memories of the 1549 rebellions. This is especially true of James Fuller's analysis of the events in Lavenham in 1549, which amongst the often laconic archives of the early modern legal system retains a remarkable richness. Notably, all presumed that their intended audiences were familiar with the course of local events in 1549. Thus, the Colchester weavers had only to hint at the history of 'the last commotion'; James Fuller assumed a continuing knowledge of the execution of the Suffolk rebel leaders 'at the laste rysinge'; Thomas Veare knew that those listening to him would know what 'ketts campe' was; Bartholomew Steer was confident that the sanguine events upon Enslow Hill in 1549 remained common knowledge in north Oxfordshire in 1596. All four of these sources imply the endurance of a shared body of local knowledge concerning the commotion time. This tiny archive therefore suggests that,

---

[88] Walter, 'A "rising of the people"', 100, 107, 114; A. Vere Woodman, 'The Buckinghamshire and Oxfordshire rising of 1549', *Oxoniensia*, 22 (1957), 80; Kingsford (ed.), 'Two London chronicles', 18.

despite the best efforts of the early modern state to inculcate its own version of the commotion time into popular consciousness, alternative memories of those events endured.[89]

This conflict over the meaning of the commotion time reflects a wider confrontation between ruling ideology and popular memory. For Neville, Woods and Holinshed, the 1549 rebellions represented a violent onslaught by wicked plebeians upon authority. In contrast, James Fuller and Bartholomew Steer understood the history of the 1549 rebellions as a tale of betrayal and lost opportunity. Unlike Fuller and Steer's emphasis upon bloodshed and failure, Thomas Veare and the Colchester weavers saw the commotion time as a model for successful insurrection. There was some sense to this view, which focused more upon the organisation and early success of the insurrections, than upon their final outcome: the 1549 rebellions had followed a similar organisational pattern as other Tudor risings, its organisation had been concealed from the authorities, and in its earliest stages the rebellions had been highly successful. Finally, in all four cases, memories of the commotion time operated within a close local context. The Colchester weavers imagined their insurrection as expanding from the poor textile villages that neighboured their town, following the pattern established in 'the last commotion'. James Fuller and Bartholomew Steer both deployed specific, local memories of the rebellions in order to prove a wider point: that the 'riche churls' could not be trusted. Thomas Veare's understanding of the camping time was also located within his locality; but his recollection of the rebellion differed in important respects from the other three surviving traces. Most significantly, his speech suggests something of how the collective memory of the commotion time was shifting during the last decade of the sixteenth century. When Thomas proposed that 'ther shold be a campe ... meaning suche as ketts campe was', he proposed the nearby village of Whissonsett as the venue. Although Whissonsett had witnessed the spread of seditious rumour in the aftermath of the commotion time, there is no evidence that it had been the site of a rebel camp in 1549.[90] Unlike recollections of rebellion in Colchester, Lavenham and Enslow Hill, Thomas Veare was not recalling an actual event, but was rather *imagining* the appearance of 'ketts campe' within his locality. Moreover, the inspiration for Thomas' seditious speech came from the high food prices prevailing in 1597. In contrast, although 1549 had also been a time of harvest failure, the Mousehold articles were more concerned with seigneurial oppression and village government than with food supplies. Thomas Veare did not,

---

[89] For three further examples of popular memories of the rebellions, see PRO, E178/2244; Jones, "'Commotion time'", 130–5.
[90] APC, II, 385.

therefore, propose a rerun of Kett's rebellion, so much as its modification to the specific circumstances facing the rural poor in 1597. Unlike the other three examples, Thomas Veare's words reflect not the precise memorialisation of the events of 1549, but instead a willingness to invoke the rebellion as evidence of the *possibility* of plebeian resistance.

We have seen how, over the later sixteenth and early seventeenth centuries, the complexities and broad geography of the commotion time were simplified to produce the tale of Kett's rebellion. The invention of Kett's rebellion was intended to blacken popular politics, through its personification in Robert Kett. One effect of this representation was to erode memories of the commotion time elsewhere; another was to provide an exaggerated hostile image of Kett's rebellion. And yet, just as the memory of the commotion time remained a field of conflict, so it was possible for plebeian dissidents to take this negative characterisation of Kett's rebellion and to turn it on its head. As with Thomas Veare's speech in Fakenham in 1597, the effect might be to highlight earlier examples of popular resistance and so to legitimate lower-class agency.

Alternatively, Robert Kett's name could be deployed as a kind of threat. The sharpest example of the use of Robert's name in this way came from the angry words spoken by a basketmaker called John Kettle in the council chamber of the guildhall in Norwich in December 1627. As early as 1617, John Kettle had been in trouble for refusing to obey orders from the Mayor's Court. Between 1622 and 1627, he refused to pay a variety of taxes, rates and subsidies due to his parish, the city and to the Crown. His vocal opposition to Charles I's fiscal demands appears to have resonated amongst other Norwich people. He was also enraged by the city's attempts to force him to contribute to the traditional feast held for the civic elite. On a number of occasions John Kettle raged 'in calumpnious & slanderous manner', giving out 'many outragious speeches' within the guildhall against his powerful opponents. On one occasion, Kettle was recorded as having bluntly (if repetitively) told the Mayor and aldermen to their face 'that they doe make bylawes to oppresse the poore And againe said that they make bylawes to oppresse poore Comoners'. The city authorities prosecuted him for this speech, and bound him to his good behaviour. The magistracy therefore had reason to be alarmed when, supported by what they called 'a great multitude of mecanicall men and other Citizens of meanest quality [who] had Combined themselves together by wagers p[ro]mises and p[ro]testations', John Kettle presented himself as a candidate for the office of Sheriff. After the magistrates denounced Kettle to the Privy Council, he was interrogated in London before being returned to Norwich where he was instructed to submit himself to the Mayor and required to pay a crippling £40 fine. Perhaps thanks to the similarity of Kettle's surname to that of Robert Kett, some common talk in

Norwich identified him as a rebel: thus, in response to statements 'that John Kettle was as honest a man as mr Lane [one of the Subsidy Commissioners for the Crown and John Kettle's opponent in the election for the shrievalty]', one Norwich man remarked 'that John Kettle was a Rebbell ... [who] had shewed himselfe rebellious against the gov[er]nement of the City'. But it was Kettle himself who spelled out the association most clearly. When he appeared in the council chamber in December 1627 to 'make humble submission & acknowledgemt of his said offences with promise of his future conformity and obedyence', it was recorded that

after many allegations & undue speeches by him uttered did at last make his submission ... But the said John Kettle when he was moved to make his submission saide in the hearinge of Mr Alderman Remyngton if he would have made a mutiny or a second ketts Campe it would never have come to this.[91]

The state-authorised presentation of Kett's rebellion might therefore be open to subversion. It is impossible to say whether John Kettle's knowledge of 'ketts Campe' grew from an oral tradition that reached back to 1549, or whether he became acquainted with Kett's rebellion from some other source: a city-sponsored 'Kett's Day' sermon, for example, or a printed history of Kett's rebellion. Indeed, the rendering of such distinctions is facile. By the time at which John Kettle apparently suggested the need for a 'second ketts Campe', there could scarcely have been many living witnesses to the events of 1549. Oral traditions, of course, are communicated from one generation to the next. But, especially where such traditions are perceived to represent class interests (in this case, the possibilities of plebeian resistance), their intergenerational transmission tends to result in simplification. Given that by 1627, Norwich had for several generations commemorated Kett's rebellion, it should scarcely be surprising to find that Robert Kett's name provided a meaningful reference point for lower-class dissidents. As with Wat Tyler and Jack Cade, the early modern authorities' obsessive reiteration of the history of Kett's rebellion might have helped to legitimate popular politics, validating resistance with reference to a local hero.[92]

Throughout this book, the 1549 rebellions have provided an interpretive lens for the scrutiny of the formation of the early modern social order. One key theme which has reared its head has concerned those moments at which hitherto subordinated people acquire a political voice. It has been argued, following James C. Scott, that such moments of popular assertiveness grow

---

[91] NRO, NCR/16A/15, fols. 141v, 144v; NRO, NCR/16A/16, fols. 6v, 16r, 82v, 84r, 109r, 148v, 160r, 161r, 169r–170r; PRO, SP16/78/53; PRO, SP16/79/38. For more on the remarkable John Kettle, see College of Arms, Curia Militaris, 3/41, 3/42, 13/1b, 14/1d.

[92] See, for instance, PRO, STAC8/100/18.5, a libel of 1604 criticising the minister of a Shropshire village, signed by 'Thy very good frend, Jack Straw'.

from the collective maintenance of semi-public spaces within which critiques of the dominant social order can be voiced and in which tactics for resistance can be developed. An important part of this hegemonic contest frequently takes the form of struggles over memory and the past. Scott therefore points to the significance of autonomous 'codes, myths, heroes, and social standards' within plebeian communal identities.[93] For some early modern labouring people, Robert Kett represented one such hero. The origins of their knowledge of the rebellions – whether it arrived from pure oral tradition, from hostile printed histories and their derivative effects in sermons and catechisms, or (most likely) from the interface between tradition and propaganda – is less important than its function and meaning within popular political culture.

In their comparative history of social memory, James Fentress and Chris Wickham argue that 'social memory identifies a group, giving it a sense of its past and defining its aspirations for the future ... it also provides the group with material for conscious reflection'.[94] Early modern labouring people certainly reflected upon the experience of the commotion time. We saw how the Colchester weavers used their memory of the rebellions as an example of an insurrection that had begun well; in contrast, we also saw how James Fuller presented the commotion time as a catastrophe from which lessons had to be drawn. It is upon the maintenance of such memories that conscious popular political traditions depend. And yet, since the survival and protection of such traditions often requires that they be cloaked in semi-secrecy, their existence can frequently slip past the eye of the historian: as Scott puts it, 'Short of actual rebellion, the great bulk of public events, and hence the great bulk of the archives, is consecrated to the official transcript [of elite power relations].'[95]

Momentarily, we catch fleeting glimpses of how, in certain localities, memories of earlier rebellions cascaded upon one another, producing an ideological consistency amongst labouring people. It is this consistency which provides the basis for the formation and maintenance of political traditions. James Fuller's 1569 plot suggests that some key aspects of the tradition of political protest in Lavenham remained lodged within the minds of some Elizabethan labouring people. Such consistencies are detectable elsewhere. The Cornish village of St Keverne contributed a significant number of rebels to the 1549 Western rising. A year earlier, the parish priest of St Keverne had been responsible for the murder of William Body at Helston, the events which had sparked the 1548 Cornish rising. In 1537, some of the parishioners had proposed to make a banner depicting the Five Wounds of

---

[93] Scott, *Domination*, 135.   [94] Fentress and Wickham, *Social memory*, 25–6.
[95] Scott, *Domination*, 87.

Christ, the same standard as that under which the Northern rebels of 1536 had marched. Back in 1497, St Keverne had been the home village of Michael Joseph An Gof, the leader of the Cornish rising of that year. Without evidence such as that provided by James Fuller's plea for a pardon, we can only guess at the possible connections between these events.[96]

It is unlikely that the rebellious history of St Keverne was mere coincidence; just as Robert Kett enjoyed an afterlife in the collective memory of the East Anglian commons, so it is quite possible that the memory of Michael Joseph An Gof lived on in St Keverne, sustaining the knowledge that the commons had once exerted a collective political agency and so could do again. Another such example suggests something of how Kentish working people maintained long-term memories of earlier insurrections. In 1452, with the bloody aftermath of Jack Cade's revolt still fresh in their minds, a group of Kentish labourers met to plan a new rising. The plotters drew up a list of those gentlemen whom they intended to slaughter; they planned to place upon the bodies of their victims a note explaining that they had been so killed because this was how things had been done in the time of Jack Straw.[97] If a conscious memory of the 1381 rebellions provided these mid-fifteenth-century insurrectionaries with a useful organisational model, might it not be that memories of Jack Cade's rising in 1450 provided a similar template for Kentish commotioners in 1549? Certainly, this helps to explain the marked similarities in tactics, organisation and language that linked the 1549 rebellions to earlier political traditions, and the tendency for the Kentish villages that had risen for Cade in 1450 to rise in the 'rebellion of comon welth' of 1549. If so, this legitimates the suggestion in Chapter Five that something very important happened to those traditions after 1549.

In Fentress and Wickham's account, the social organisation of social memory provides the bedrock for the political culture of subordinated groups, helping to maintain 'the stability of a set of collectively held ideas'. In particular, ideological cohesion amongst the ruled is guaranteed through the inhibition of oral tradition. When an event is integrated into social memory, it undergoes a process of simplification, resulting in a more stable and uniform version of that event. Thus, 'Once memory has been conceptualised into a story, the process of change and of factual loss naturally slows down.' Memory therefore emerges as more than the neutral bearer of past knowledge into the present; instead, it constructs a particular version of the past in order to serve interests in the present. As Fentress and Wickham put it, 'memory ... is not a passive receptacle, but instead a process of

---

[96] Fletcher and MacCulloch, *Tudor rebellions*, 50, 120; Beer, *Rebellion and riot*, 43–4, 48; Rose-Troup, *Western rebellion*, 76, 93; PRO, SP1/118, fol. 248r.
[97] Harvey, *Jack Cade's rebellion*, 166–7.

active restructuring, in which elements may be retained, reordered, or suppressed'.[98]

Our fragmentary evidence suggests something like this seems to have occurred in popular memories of the 1549 rebellions: specifically, that key aspects of the commotion time were exaggerated. These included the following propositions: that the gentry could not be trusted; that organised resistance could be both feasible and effective; and that it was possible for labouring people to advance political claims. Similarly, the print narratives of the Elizabethan era produced an enduring conceptualisation of the 1549 risings, albeit one opposed to the positive stories embedded within oral tradition. But, as the generations that had experienced the 1549 rebellions passed away, as the force of literacy deepened within popular culture and as the basic message of the print narratives was disseminated through education, catechism, sermons and the printing press, those oral traditions were both diminished by and fused with the more narrow tale told in the print narratives. As Fentress and Wickham point out: 'Writing ... transforms memory, by fixing it.'[99] As we have seen, however, this fixing of the narrative of Kett's rebellion, although it originated from state propaganda, could not always nail down the meaning of that story. Rather, some labouring people took the depiction of the rebellion in the authorised narrative, inverted it and turned the rebels into heroes.

This suggests that such examples of costly plebeian assertiveness should not be seen as a preordained fact of popular political culture but rather represented a costly achievement. Fentress and Wickham's view that 'community defiance does tend to be remembered by peasants ... with more insistence than many other forms of historical event' ought therefore to strike us as unnecessarily optimistic.[100] We have already seen how state power was mobilised in the immediate aftermath of the commotion time to crush the positive memory of those events. The use of such force did not end with the accession of Elizabeth I. Rather, the speech of James Fuller, Thomas Veare, Bartholomew Steer and the Colchester weavers only found its way into the written record because they were prosecuted under the sedition and treason laws.

Our search for popular memories of the commotion time seems, therefore, to have produced a binary opposition between the bitter memories of isolated individuals and the collective silence of the majority. The former seems to speak of a failing attempt to sustain earlier traditions of popular protest in the face of economic and cultural change; the latter appears to suggest that memories of the commotion time were drowned under the steady wash of

---

[98] Fentress and Wickham, *Social memory*, 39–40, 58, 59, 74.   [99] *Ibid.*, 97.
[100] *Ibid.*, 114.

collective amnesia. There is, however, a third way of conceptualising popular memories of the commotion time. Rather than emphasising simply a blunt confrontation between plebeian agency and state power we might instead explore the care with which labouring people could negotiate authority and so discover how popular memories of the commotion time might be partially imprinted within the written record.[101]

As we saw at the beginning of this chapter, some important aspects of early modern social memory are surprisingly well documented. Labouring people were encouraged to speak about their memories of local customary law to commissions of gentlemen empowered by central courts to hear evidence in disputes concerning issues such as tenure, common rights, enclosure and rents. Other legal bodies also assembled such evidence: much of the business of church courts concerned disputes over tithe rights. Landlords or their estate stewards occasionally persuaded older tenants to speak of their memories of customary law, which would then be transcribed and entered into the corpus of estate papers. Similarly, parish ministers sometimes retained such documents within the parish chest. The thousands of bundles of depositions concerning such matters are scarcely neutral reflections of collective memory. Although historians have sometimes been tempted to treat them as though they represented transcriptions in the oral history of a locality, in fact they were heavily scripted. Most obviously, depositions were produced in answer to specific questions within written interrogatories. Deponents' answers to these questions were recorded by an educated gentleman, acting as the clerk of the commission. This scribal authority strongly influenced the recorded deposition, in that most clerks appear to have been interested solely in transcribing material which they considered relevant to the case in hand. Nonetheless, occasional examples survive where deponents were allowed to wander from the interrogatory, producing answers that were sometimes irrelevant to the matter in hand, but which (for the historian) shed bright light upon otherwise obscure issues. Less obviously, it is also significant that deponents were rarely disinterested in the outcome of the matter in question. Both sides in a dispute sought to validate their case with reference to the local memories provided by deponents. In this respect, the equity court deposition represents a peculiar textual product of the early modern legal system, simultaneously homogenising individual testimonies within the 'common voice' of a locality while also validating working people's articulation of their own histories. Such histories were scripted not only by the interrogatory and the ordering hand of the clerk, but also by the interests and agency of the deponents.

---

[101] For this emphasis in a different context, see Braddick and Walter 'Introduction'.

It was in the interests of deponents to present their local rights as sanctioned by custom: that is, of long and unbroken continuance; as granted by legitimate authority; and as articulated in the 'common voice'. The collective memory of the commotion time, which as we have seen continued to live within many localities, did not help to maintain such claims. It is therefore unsurprising to find that only a very few Elizabethan deponents in southern and eastern England made any mention of the 1549 rebellions. In some cases, such silence was deafening. In the early 1590s, for instance, the aged inhabitants of Wymondham were called upon by two commissions of the Court of Exchequer to answer questions concerning disputes over the lands formerly held by the Abbey of Wymondham. It will be recalled that the Neville/ Woods narrative identified the disputes between Robert Kett and John Flowerdew over these lands as the spark that ignited the insurrection in Wymondham. Although deponents on both sides articulated their sharp memories of the Abbey and its estates, none made any reference to Kett's rebellion.[102]

Presumably, despite their conflicts, the inhabitants of late Elizabethan Wymondham felt too compromised by their infamous involvement with the insurrection to risk any mention of it to the commissioners of the Exchequer Court. In contrast, the aged inhabitants of New Buckenham delighted in labelling the villagers of the neighbouring settlement of Carleton as rebels. In the course of Exchequer litigation of the 1580s and 1590s over a boundary dispute, the New Buckenham inhabitants presented their neighbours as deeply implicated in Kett's rebellion. This depiction contrasted sharply with the recorded involvement of the New Buckenham villagers in Kett's rebellion: Sir Edmund Knyvett, the lord of New Buckenham, had been besieged by rebels.[103] No mention of this siege was made in the evidence presented by the New Buckenham people to the Court of Exchequer in September 1594. Some lost Knyvett estate papers, apparently including an account of the bounds between the two villages, were important to the outcome of the case. New Buckenham deponents explained how 'In anncyent tyme ... before the comocyon at norw[i]ch' the inhabitants of New Buckenham would begin their perambulation of their village bounds at the neighbouring village of Old Buckenham. From there, they would proceed to the garden of Buckenham Castle, 'and there drinkinge' continue with their perambulation. Kett's rebellion marked a discontinuity in this custom: 'For some tyme after the Comocyon at Norwch the towneshippe

---

[102] PRO, E134/35&36Eliz/Mich12; PRO, E134/35&36Eliz/Mich5. See also depositions concerning the warrening rights of Castle Rising from 1591, which omit any reference to the rebel camp there in 1549: PRO, E134/34&35Eliz/Mich16.
[103] Holinshed, 969.

of newe Buckenham did discontinue the use of their ... p[er]ambulacon.'
Thomas Rutland, aged sixty-eight, explained how the decline of the custom
of perambulation coincided with the loss of the

evidences remayninge in the castle at Buckenham [which] were rifled and imbeaseled
by the rebelles at ketts rising at norwiche and that yt was sayd that some of the then
townesmen of Carleton were doers therein.

Another deponent, the sixty-five-year-old John Roberts, added that 'one of
the town of Carleton did strike the first deere that was then kylled by the
Rebells in Buckenham parke at that tyme wch this deponent did see'.[104]

The New Buckenham deponents of 1594 introduced Kett's rebellion into
their account of their conflict with Carleton in order to blacken their opponents as rebels and to implicate them in the loss of the Knyvett manorial
archive. But it is difficult to take this story at face value. It is hard to imagine
that the New Buckenham inhabitants stood aside as the Carleton tenants
slaughtered the Knyvetts' deer and plundered the castle's archives. The story
recorded by the Exchequer commissioners was at best a partial one, presenting Buckenham Castle as the location of a vanished communal ritual. The
self-censorship of the 1594 deponents enabled them to communicate a
detailed local history of the commotion time to the commissioners of the
Court of Exchequer. In this case, the memory of the commotion time fulfilled
a useful function: Kett's rebellion was invoked in order to strengthen the
New Buckenham tenants' case against their neighbours. As such, the people
of New Buckenham both (improbably) distanced themselves from the old
rebel cause, and provided testimony of its continued remembrance.

In a 1588 case involving the rights of the tenants of the Cambridgeshire
village of Soham over the neighbouring fen, the seventy-year-old William
Yaxley explained to commissioners of the Duchy Court how he remembered
willows growing upon the disputed fen being 'cutt downe in the tyme of
Kett's campe by certaine rebellious p[er]sons'.[105] Once again, it is difficult to
believe that the villagers of Soham did not take the opportunity afforded by
the camping time to remove these willows themselves. Yet Yaxley establishes
a further distance between the people of Soham and these anonymous
'rebellious p[er]sons' by mentioning the distant 'Kett's campe' at Norwich
while avoiding any reference to the nearby rebel camp at Thetford. In both

---

[104] The depositions illuminating the Carleton villagers' involvement are in NRO, PD254/171,
which the New Buckenham inhabitants retained in their parish chest. For another mention of
the commotion time in New Buckenham, see PRO, E134/38Eliz/Hil24. For the full history of
the disputes between New Buckenham and Carleton, see PRO, E134/37&38Eliz/Mich62;
PRO, E134/34Eliz/Hil11; PRO, E134/42Eliz/Hil15.

[105] PRO, DL4/30/17. For another account of rebel depredations in 1549, in which the rebels are
identified as outsiders, see PRO, DL3/56/G1k–g.

cases, popular memory of the commotion time strayed into what Scott calls the 'public transcript' of the court testimony. Yet it did so without danger. The memories recorded in equity court depositions were therefore partial, their contents influenced both by the nature of the legal case in question and by the danger of providing unblemished accounts of local traditions concerning the insurrection. We have good reason, therefore, to be sceptical about the precise truth of the stories told in such evidence. Clearly, just as deponents had an interest in identifying their opponents as former rebels, they had no interest in so identifying themselves. But the partiality of this evidence should not obscure its significance: at the very least, it should be clear that both in Soham and in Buckenham, memories of the collapse of authority during the commotion time survived. The fact that late sixteenth-century deponents recognised the dangers of publicly recording their participation in the camping time does not mean that in private, beyond the written record, they did not articulate more positive recollections of the rebellion. It is possible to gain some insight into the hidden implications of such carefully modulated memories through one court testimony recorded in 1593.

In that year, Thomas Gunthorpe, a fifty-two-year-old yeoman of Holkham, gave evidence to a commission of the Duchy Court concerning some land transactions on the estates of Sir James Boleyn 'about the third yeare of Edwarde the sixt'. Thomas explained to the commissioners how in 1549 his grandfather, Henry Gunthorpe, had acquired a favourable lease of two foldcourses on Holkham common from the lord of the manor, Sir James Boleyn. Boleyn apparently awarded this lease to Henry Gunthorpe as thanks for 'some pleasure that he [that is, Gunthorpe] did Sr James Bullen', during the 'Comosion Tyme in Norff[olk]'. These foldcourses were transferred to Henry 'about the third yeare of Edwarde the sixt' and a lease was accordingly drawn up but never sealed, for afterwards 'Sir James Bullins mynd altered' and instead leased them to a local gentleman. Thomas Gunthorpe explained that his father had told him this story some thirty years ago, instructing him 'to set downe in writinge for better memory ... least any matter afterwards should arise or be brought in question conc[ern]inge the said manor fould-courses'. The history of land transactions upon Holkham common was further documented by an 'auncient field booke wch was one masons of holch[a]m' which Thomas had in his possession.[106]

Thomas Gunthorpe's deposition raises some intriguing questions concerning the relationship between his grandfather and Sir James Boleyn, while also implying something of how the 'Comosion Tyme' was remembered in

---

[106] PRO, DL4/35/8; for other recollections of Sir James Boleyn's difficulties during the camping time, see PRO, DL4/63/23.

Holkham. There are two possible explanations for Boleyn's initially favourable treatment of Henry Gunthorpe. Possibly, the story which his grandson told in 1594 was accurate, and Henry had indeed performed some unspecified act of kindness towards Sir James – maybe hiding him from rebels or protecting his property. Alternatively, it could be that, during the rebellion, Henry Gunthorpe had intimidated Boleyn into signing his name to a lease of the Holkham foldcourses and that, after the rebellion, Boleyn had refused to recognise the agreement. Either way, we are presented with another local memory of 1549 which emphasises both popular agency – the sudden dependence of Sir James Boleyn upon the lowly Henry Gunthorpe – and gentry betrayal. In his grandson's story, Henry Gunthorpe's loyalty to his lord (whether fictional or not) was not repaid once the balance of power shifted back to Boleyn. Significantly, the story was not only passed down from father to son, but the son instructed the grandson to set it into writing. Like the distant memories which it encodes, Thomas Gunthorpe's transliteration of his grandfather's story fulfilled two functions within local culture. Like the 'auncient field booke' in his possession, it added to the stock of written documentation deployed by the tenants of Holkham in order to contextualise their legal claims to customary rights; but it also provided testimony, beyond the reach of oral memory, of a time at which the gentry were without power and of how a tenant's (apparent) loyalty was repaid.

Memories of 1549, therefore, survived. Where they were not written down, they endured for up to three generations after the events they described. As we have seen, oral traditions contributed to the written accounts of Kett's rebellion. The only source cited in Sotherton's account, after all, was oral testimony: that 'reported to mee by divers persons that uppon enquery did gett the understanding thereof'.[107] But gradually, as the generations that had witnessed the events of 1549 passed away and as the powerful, authorised story of Kett's rebellion began to impose itself over the complicated diversity of the commotion time, so direct popular memories of the camping time began to lose their authority. As we have seen, the story of Kett's rebellion remained ripe for subversion. The early modern gentry's obsessive need to reiterate the names of their long-dead opponents – Wat Tyler, Jack Cade and Robert Kett – provided seditious basketmakers like John Kettle, and radicals like the Levellers, with an opportunity to contextualise their own struggles. Nonetheless, for the first two and half centuries following Robert Kett's defeat at Dussindale, the authorised narrative established by Holinshed, Neville and Woods maintained its ideological domination over the events of 1549.

[107] Sotherton, 80.

VI UNDER ANOTHER NAME: RADICALISM, SOCIALISM AND THE REINVENTION OF KETT'S REBELLION

Regular republication of Woods' translation of Neville throughout the eighteenth century, coupled with the repetition of its basic message in popular works of history, ensured that Robert Kett's name was kept alive as an example of senseless rustic violence. Eighteenth-century print interpretations of Kett's rebellion were uniformly hostile, focusing upon the linked themes of the rebel violence and the 'mischief' done to Norwich. The Norfolk historian Blomefield summed up the standard approach taken to the rebellion by contemporary writers, denouncing the rebels as a 'tumultuous rabble' who had 'thoroughly imbibed the wicked notions of the ancient levellers [that is, the rebels of 1381] ... in religion, and in levelling all men to an equality of fortunes, &c.'.[108] As in earlier years, Kett's name was invoked at moments of social tension: in 1725, following enclosure riots in the Broadland village of Stokesby, the reporter for *Mist's weekly journal* worried that 'Such a beginning had Kett's rebellion.'[109]

The authorised narrative of the later sixteenth century continued to make sense two centuries later. As in the 1640s, the radical challenges of the years that followed the French Revolution were stereotyped as the equivalents of Kett's rebellion. Thus, in the 1790s, as the long tradition of Norwich radicalism fused with French revolutionary republicanism, one loyalist satire depicted the people of Norwich celebrating how 'Since the days of old Kett, the Republican Tanner / Faction has always seen us lost under her Banner / From our country's best Interests we've ever dissented / In War

---

[108] Blomefield, III, 222–3. For eighteenth-century printed treatments of Kett's rebellion, see, for instance, Anon., *A compleat history of the famous city of Norwich from the earliest account, to the present year 1728* (Norwich, 1728); Anon., *An appendix to the chronological history of the famous city of Norwich* (Norwich, 1728); Anon., *The history of the city and county of Norwich from the earliest account to the present time* (Norwich, 1768), 188–215. For eighteenth-century republications of Neville/Woods, see A. Neville, *The history of the city of Norwich. Containing a description of that city ... To which is added, Norfolk's furies: or, a view of Kett's camp* (Norwich, 1718); *The history (as related by A. Neville) of the rebellion in Norfolk in the year 1549, which was conducted by R. Kett, etc.* (Norwich, 1750?); Anon., *The history of the rebellion in Norfolk, in the year 1549; which was conducted by Rob. Kett, etc.* (Norwich, 1751). For an abridged addition, see Anon., *Norfolk's furies: or, a view of Kett's camp* (Norwich, n.d. (1728?)). For eighteenth-century manuscript histories of the rebellion, which owe much to the Neville/Woods narrative, see NRO, COL/9/117; NRO, NNAS Frere, Safe II 1a–b, Benamin Mackerell's MS History of Norwich, vol. II, fols. 745r–772v.

[109] E. P. Thompson, *Customs in common* (London, 1991), 117; on the context of the 1725 Stokesby riots, see T. Williamson, *The Norfolk Broads: a landscape history* (Manchester, 1997), 99.

we're disloyal; in Peace discontented.'[110] As Norwich emerged as one of the leading centres of organised radicalism during the French Revolutionary Wars, Kett's name therefore became a means by which the civic elite could contextualise the new political challenges they faced. By 1815, the middle classes of Norwich could sit down in the Theatre Royal to watch a performance of *The rebellion, or Norwich in 1549*. The play dwelt upon parallels between Kett's rebellion and the radicalism of early nineteenth-century Norwich workers, emphasising that

The subject chosen was strictly apposite, and afforded an opportunity of throwing in certain touches which might, through implication – like the sympathetic tones which are heard to vibrate from one instrument, when the same notes are struck from another – influence the chords of modern times.[111]

During the nineteenth century, however, the meanings that were attributed to Kett's rebellion were transformed. In earlier centuries, Kett's name had been deployed as an emblem of plebeian disorder. Thereafter, it was to be utilised by radicals and socialists in legitimation of their own struggles.[112] Gradually, the effect was to transform both Robert Kett's reputation and the meanings attributed to his rebellion. From being a reviled symbol of rustic violence, Kett came to be seen within Norfolk as a local hero who had stood for the rights of the common people.

This reinvention of Kett's rebellion represented a local twist upon an important strain of working-class radical politics. Fundamental to what Edward Thompson identified as the 'making' of the English working class was the creation of a radical counterculture which prized autonomy, discipline, education, assertiveness and a sometimes bookish autodidacticism. One element of this counterculture comprised a distinct interpretation of English history. Within radical narratives, post-conquest history was presented as a story of conflict between 'the people' and the ancestors of Old Corruption – namely, the Crown, the Church and the nobility.[113] This transcendent conflict took place over land and resources and over political organisation, religious belief and self-expression. This narrative enabled

---

[110] M. D. George (ed.), *Catalogue of prints and drawings in the British Museum*, 12 vols. (London, 1942), VII, 55, no. 8617.

[111] G. P. Bromley, *The rebellion; or Norwich in 1549: a drama, interspersed with music* (Norwich, 1815), vii.

[112] For late examples of negative depictions of Kett's rebellion, see H. Neele, *The romance of history: England*, 3 vols. (London, 1828), III, 149–84; J. Stacy, *A topographical and historical account of the city and county of Norwich* (London, 1819), 10–16.

[113] This represents an important corrective to Peter Mandler's claim that early nineteenth-century depictions of Tudor England presented that period as the epitome of 'Merry England'; see P. Mandler, '"In the olden time": romantic history and English national identity, 1820–50', in L. Brockliss and D. Eastwood (eds.), *A union of multiple identities: the British Isles, c. 1750–1850* (Manchester, 1997), 82.

radicals to conduct their war against Old Corruption on a new front: that of the legitimating terrain of history. Thus, contemporary radicalism was understood as the bequest of an 'illustrious dead ... who by their acts and deeds have contributed to the cause of liberty' and whose numbers included Wat Tyler, John Ball and Robert Kett. The radicals' rereading of English history was both powerful and dangerous: it eliminated the landed classes' claim to rule as the natural governing elite. Like Gerrard Winstanley before them, Chartists traced the origins of Old Corruption back to 'the aristocracy of the country, founded by that tyrant, William the Robber'. One Chartist's account of early Tudor history presented the delightful opportunity of taunting Lord John Russell with his family's history, highlighting how Russell's ancestors 'had benefited, at the expense of the poor, from the plunder of the church during Henry VIII's reign'.[114]

Social historians have sometimes made the mistake of treating the rarefied political culture of radicalism as though it reflected the everyday practice of life within working-class communities, rather than the political project of a politicised and articulate minority. In fact, the radical political movements of the early nineteenth century were sometimes as much at war with working-class culture as they were with Old Corruption. But at least within Norfolk, one small victory for this emergent tradition lay in the popularisation of the radicals' version of their county's history in the mid-Tudor period.

The consequence of this rewriting of history was that even conservative writers tended to replace their view of Kett's rebels with a certain sympathy. The dominant approach to the rebellions was informed by an increasingly intense identification with the rebel cause.[115] Importantly for Kett's reputation, the changing meanings given to his insurrection coincided with a dramatic improvement in the quality of the historical research devoted to the subject. In an anonymous work of *c.* 1843, the objectivity of the Neville/Woods narrative was questioned for the first time. The author distanced her or himself from Neville, who was described as 'violently prejudiced against the rebels'. Instead, the intention was to provide a sympathetic account of the causes of rebellion, which were defined as an assault by 'sundry lords and gentlemen' upon 'the long recognised rights of the poor ... their just and lawful heritage'.[116]

This work influenced Reverend F. W. Russell's magisterial study of 1859, which provided the standard for future research into Kett's rebellion. In his

---

[114] R. G. Hall, 'Creating a people's history: political identity and history in Chartism, 1832–1848', in O. Ashton, R. Fyson and S. Roberts (eds.), *The Chartist legacy* (Rendlesham, 1989), 232–54.

[115] See, for instance, the diary of one mid-nineteenth-century Norwich radical: NRO, MC93/1–2.

[116] Anon., *History of Kett's rebellion*, 3, 123–36.

preface, Russell suggested that it was 'Kett's great misfortune ... to live before his time ... his efforts ... had been directed ... against the feudal system, with its manifold extortions'. Russell concluded that 'though Kett is commonly considered a rebel, yet the cause he advocated was so just, that one cannot but feel he deserved a better name and a better fate'. Russell suggested that the use of biblical teaching to justify class authority had been met with 'the steady common sense of ... Norfolk people' who 'refused to accept any such interpretation of Scripture, as warranted the few in oppressing the many, as sanctioned man's holding his fellow-men in slavery'.[117] It is difficult not to interpret Russell's comments in their contemporary context. Mid-Victorian rural England was racked by conflict over land rights, wages, working conditions and rights of union organisation. This was especially true of Norfolk. Historians of nineteenth-century rural society have argued that, anxious about the relationship between radicalism and Methodism, rural Anglican clergymen often took the side of the landlords.[118] It is therefore ironic that Reverend Russell's 1859 work should accord so directly with the radicals' version of history.[119]

The land question remained a source of constant conflict throughout the later nineteenth and early twentieth centuries, focusing a broader antagonism amongst radicals to the gentry and nobility. This period coincided with the emergence of the study of history as a distinct discipline, and with the increasing professionalisation of historical research within universities. Some of the early fruits of that professionalisation, such as Tawney's 1912 study of rural conflict in Tudor England and the Hammonds' multi-volume work on class struggle in the early Industrial Revolution, were intended to provide detailed empirical validation of the radical interpretation of English history.[120] The later nineteenth-century republication of the Leveller and Digger tracts was motivated by a similar desire to document the early history of radicalism, republicanism and popular agitation over land rights.[121] The purpose underlying this politicised interest in the past was twofold: to

---

[117] Russell, *Kett's rebellion*, viii. For another Victorian Norfolk clergyman's assessment of Kett's rebellion, see NRO, PD209/479.

[118] A. Howkins, *Reshaping rural England: a social history 1850–1925* (London, 1991).

[119] This is not to say that Russell necessarily sympathised with rural radicalism; but his work certainly illustrates how the radical paradigm had come to dominate contemporary interpretations of Kett's rebellion. For another sympathetic mid-nineteenth-century account of Kett's rebellion, see Anon., *Robert Ket: the Wyndham tanner. A poem* (London, 1869).

[120] Tawney, *Agrarian problem*; J. L. Hammond and B. Hammond, *The skilled labourer* (London, 1919); J. L. Hammond and B. Hammond, *The town labourer* (London, 1919); J. L. Hammond and B. Hammond, *The village labourer* (London, 1911).

[121] T. Prasch, 'The making of an English working past, the rediscovery of Gerrard Winstanley, and late Victorian English radicalism', *Wordsworth Circle*, 25, 3 (1994), 166–72; C. Steedman, *The radical soldier's tale: John Pearman, 1819–1908* (London, 1988).

contextualise contemporary struggles; and to undermine conservative claims that socialism represented an alien ideology, foreign to the English instinct. Thus, H. M. Hyndman, one of the leading figures in the Social Democratic Federation, observed (with more than a touch of xenophobia) that

> It is well to show that the idea of socialism is no foreign importation into England. Tyler, Cade, Ball, Kett, More, Bellers, Spence, Owen read to me like sound English names: not a foreigner in the whole batch. They all held opinions which our capitalist-landlord House of Commons would denounce as direct plagiarisms from 'continental revolutionists'. We islanders have been revolutionists however, and will be again, ignorant as our capitalists are of the history of the people.[122]

For Victorian and Edwardian radicals, the opportunity to deploy Robert Kett's name in the intense contemporary struggles over land rights was irresistible. Opponents of the attempted conversion of Mousehold Heath into building land and ordered civic parkland, many of them poor labourers who made a living from brickmaking on the Heath, received support from the urban radicals of Norwich who 'invoked the historic memory of Kett's rebellion' against the transformation of Mousehold. Similarly, Joseph Clayton's 1912 study of Kett's rebellion was dedicated to the formerly radical Member of Parliament John Burns, 'always a large-hearted lover of the common people'; Clayton ended the dedication by citing the 'memory of a joint pilgrimage to the scenes of the Norfolk rising'.[123] Six years earlier, there had been an especially bitter General Election, where at least one observer felt that the deep conflict between the farm labourers and the landed interest reached back into the distant past. Watching the election at North Walsham (the site of the defeat of Geoffrey Lister's peasant rebels in 1381), one observer remarked how the labourers

> poured into the booth, recorded their 'wut', and streamed off to the lesser public houses. There was no stopping them. Something influenced them for a few hours, something left over from Litester's Rebellion and Kett's Rebellion ... [they] recorded their 'wut' and felt they had got back at all the rest of the world, for all the pheasants they had not poached, all the beer they had not drunk, all the money they had not spent.[124]

Kett's rebellion, then, became a way in which socialists and radicals could explain contemporary struggles over land, rights and resources. In 1926, the newspaper *Labour weekly* ran an article entitled 'A war that has lasted 400

---

[122] H. M. Hyndman, *The historical basis of socialism in England* (London, 1883), 4.

[123] N. MacMaster, 'The battle for Mousehold Heath, 1857–1884: "popular politics" and the Victorian public park', *P&P*, 127 (1990), 117–54; Clayton, *Robert Kett*. See also F. C. Tansley, *For Kett and countryside* (London, 1910).

[124] A. Howkins, *Poor labouring men: rural radicalism in Norfolk, 1870–1923* (London, 1985), 85–6.

years' making the case for the nationalisation of the land. Kett's name was invoked in order to provide historical support for the proposal; the article climaxed with the stirring statement that 'Kett's body rotted on the Norwich castle walls, but the progress towards the use of the land to meet the people's needs still goes marching on.'[125] Labour's victory in the 1945 General Election was likewise understood by one leading Norwich socialist as a forward step in a march which reached back to 1549.

By 1948, when he rose in the council chamber of the city of Norwich to propose the erection of a monument commemorating Robert Kett's rebellion, Alderman Fred Henderson had long been integrated into the city's political establishment. But he had a more radical past. In 1885, Henderson had been imprisoned in Norwich Castle for his role in food rioting; shortly after, he was elected to the city council as its first socialist member. He had long held an interest in history. Keir Hardie had written to him in 1898, suggesting that he write some sketches of radical historical figures for the Independent Labour Party newspaper, *Labour leader*, and proposing that he should 'stick to home patriots ... why not take some of the levellers of the Cromwellian period'. Later in his life, Henderson prized his ownership of 'the green cap of honour worn by Daniel O'Connell the liberator'.

Henderson's council chamber speech in favour of erecting a monument to Robert Kett opened by asking for 'a new appraisement of the [1549] revolt and the men who were active in it'. He noted that 'during the [past] 4 centuries ... stigma has remained upon their name', and that 'most of the contemporary records of the facts come to us from Enemy sources'. In contrast to this representation, Henderson argued that the rebels had exhibited a notable self-discipline, and had articulated a cogent ideology within 'two documents: 1. The Rebels complaint (a general statement of their aspirations) 2. The 29 detailed requests'. By 'The Rebels complaint', Henderson referred to the rebel complaints at the beginning of the Neville/Woods narrative; his '29 detailed requests', of course, were the Mousehold articles. Both texts had been transcribed in a recent socialist history of Kett's rebellion written by Reg Groves and it is possible that it was this work that drew Henderson's attention to these sources. Groves' work argued that Kett's rebellion formed

one episode in the age-long battle of our people for a commonwealth of fellowship and equality ... the rising of 1549 stands high in the annals of the fight for a good

---

[125] *Labour weekly*, 11 December 1926, 10. See also G. Colman Green's manuscript filmscript of 1923, which concludes with Kett's ghost prophesying that 'the time shall come when Britain will be free and every true man will be a king unto himself'. The manuscript is in the Norfolk Heritage Centre, the Norwich Millennium Library.

society. Let us hope we in our time will do as well and as much and earn the right to stand with Kett and his men in the great fellowships of rebels of all ages.

Henderson's speech pursued a similar interpretation. No longer a hot-headed young activist, Alderman Henderson emphasised the orderly nature of rebel politics in 1549, observing that the Mousehold articles did not articulate 'the voice of a rabble of rogues & vagabonds'. Fred Henderson was intrigued by the distance between the mid-Tudor period and his own world, arguing that 'The plain fact about the character of the revolt is that it took place at a period when the common people of England had no voice in government and no other way than revolt for seeking the redress of grievances.' Yet, for Henderson, 'While in all the details of their immediate requests theirs was another world than ours, none the less their struggle has a deep significance for us.' Significantly, in the decade which saw the greatest achievements of British social democracy, Henderson remarked that the rebels' struggle grew from 'that urge in the spirit of the people of this land, whatever the special circumstances of their times might be, to seek for freedom and the establishment of just conditions'. For Henderson, the past was stitched into the present. In his analysis, the rebels' demands of 1549 had, by 1948, been largely achieved:

Practically everything they could have thought of as the essentials of freedom is now the established procedure of life for us. There is no longer any class or section shut out from sharing fully & equally the power to remedy anything whatever we feel to be unjust.

Defeating a Conservative amendment to remove any hint of apology from the wording of the monument to Robert Kett, the Labour majority on the city council therefore voted through a resolution

that ... the proposed Memorial to Robert Kett do take the form of a stone plaque engraved with the following inscription:– 'In 1549 A.D., Robert Kett, yeoman farmer of Wymondham, was executed by hanging in this Castle, after the defeat of the Norfolk Rebellion, of which he was the leader. In 1949 A.D. – four hundred years later – this Memorial was placed here by the citizens of Norwich in reparation and honour to the memory of a notable leader in the long struggle of the common people of England to escape from a servile life into the freedom of just conditions.'[126]

Originally, Henderson had proposed the erection of a statue of Robert Kett. In the austere conditions of the post-war period, however, the funds did not exist for such a project. Instead, in 1949, a stone plaque bearing Henderson's proposed wording was attached to the wall of Norwich Castle, alongside the

---

[126] NRO, MS 4265, MC4/HEN43/26, 40; NRO, MS 21525, MC4/HEN8; Groves, *Rebels' oak*, 99, 101–5.

entrance through which Robert Kett had been led to his death 500 years earlier. In one sense, a kind of victory had been achieved.

But of course, all of this represented a new form of myth-making. Just as, in the early modern period, Kett had been invoked in order to blacken popular politics, so modern radicals and socialists deployed his name in order to validate their own struggles. Professional historians are trained to hold up their hands at such politicised uses of the past. Yet charting the representations of Kett's rebellion highlights not only how history can be deployed for partisan purposes; it also emphasises the passions that the past can inspire in later generations. Such emotional readings of history need not always be inaccurate. Were the gentry of early modern England so foolish to perceive of Kett's rebellion as a dangerous assault upon their authority? Were Reg Groves and Fred Henderson so wrong to see the Norfolk insurrection as part of a long struggle on the part of labouring people for 'a good society', rising 'from a servile life into the freedom of just conditions'?

Let us return to the distant past. The power structures that arose in the aftermath of Kett's rebellion bore little resemblance to any kind of socialism. Groves' and Henderson's optimistic analysis misses one of the defining concerns of this book: the significance of rebel divisions in the formation of early modern social identities. Popular hostility to the gentry in 1549 had concealed a fundamental tension within the rebel camp, that between order and disorder. Robert Kett personified one of those polarities; he was, after all, a wealthy yeoman on the borders of gentle status. Antagonistic towards the restrictions of seigneurial authority, in 1381 and in 1549 such people had joined with the poor against a common enemy. But, over the course of the later sixteenth and early seventeenth centuries, as the gentry withdrew from village conflicts, the descendants of Robert Kett stepped into their place. The social configurations that resulted were not those that had been anticipated in 1549. Lines of division within many communities now pitted rich farmer against poor neighbour, landed against landless, literate against illiterate, godly against the seemingly godless. Class society could not be wished away; instead, one form of power replaced another.

I pondered ... how men fight and lose the battle, and the thing that they fought for comes about in spite of their defeat, and when it comes turns out not to be what they [had] meant, and other men have to fight for what they meant under another name. (William Morris, 'A dream of John Ball'.)

BIBLIOGRAPHY

MANUSCRIPT MATERIAL
Bodleian Library, Oxford

Tanner MSS

British Library, London

Additional MSS
Cotton MSS
Harleian MSS
Lansdowne MSS
Salisbury MSS (microfilm M485/39)
Stowe MSS

Cambridge University Library

EDR D/2   Ely Diocesan Records, Consistory Court depositions

Cambridgeshire Record Office, Cambridge

CCA Cambridge Corporation Archives

College of Arms, London

Curia Militaris

Corporation of London Records Office, London

Repertory Books
Journals

Essex Record Office, Chelmsford

Q/SR   Quarter Sessions Records

Essex Record Office, Colchester

D/35/R2   Red Paper Book of Colchester

Hatfield House, Hertfordshire

Cecil Papers

Inner Temple Library, London

Petyt MSS

Longleat House, Wiltshire

Thynne Papers

National Archives, Public Record Office, London

C1   Chancery, Early Proceedings, Richard II to Philip and Mary
C2   Chancery Proceedings, 1558–, series one
C3   Chancery Proceedings, 1558–, series two

DL1   Duchy of Lancaster, bills and answers
DL3   Duchy of Lancaster, depositions, Henry VIII to Mary
DL4   Duchy of Lancaster, depositions, Elizabeth I to Victoria
DL5   Duchy of Lancaster, entry book of decrees and orders

E36   Exchequer, Treasury of the Receipt: miscellaneous books
E133   Exchequer, depositions before the Barons (Elizabeth I to Victoria)
E134   Exchequer, depositions taken by Commission (Elizabeth I to George II)
E163   Miscellanea of the Exchequer
E178   Exchequer, Special Commissions of Inquiry
E315   Court of Augmentations, miscellaneous books
E321   Court of Augmentations and Court of General Surveyors: legal
            proceedings
E351   Exchequer, Declared Accounts (Pipe Office)
E368   Exchequer, Memoranda Rolls (Pipe Office)

MPC   Maps, plans and charts

REQ2   Requests, proceedings

SP1   State Papers, Henry VIII
SP6   Theological Tracts: Henry VIII
SP10   State Papers, Domestic, Edward VI
SP11   State Papers, Domestic, Mary
SP12   State Papers, Domestic, Elizabeth
SP14   State Papers, Domestic, James I
SP15   State Papers, Domestic, Addenda, Edward VI to James I

SP16   State Papers, Domestic, Charles I
SP68   State Papers, Foreign, Edward VI

STAC2   Star Chamber, Henry VIII
STAC3   Star Chamber, Edward VI
STAC4   Star Chamber, Philip and Mary
STAC5   Star Chamber, Elizabeth I
STAC8   Star Chamber, James I
STAC10   Star Chamber, Miscellanea

Norfolk Heritage Centre, the Norwich Millennium Library

G. Colman Green, manuscript filmscript of Kett's rebellion, 1923.

Norfolk Record Office, Norwich

COL   Colman Collection
DN/ACT   Diocese of Norwich Consistory Court act books
DN/DEP   Diocese of Norwich Consistory Court deposition books
KL/C7   King's Lynn Hall books
MS 4265, MC4/HEN   Papers of J. F. Henderson
MS 21525, MC4/HEN   Papers of J. F. Henderson
NCR/12A   Norwich Quarter Sessions files (interrogations and depositions)
NCR/16A   Norwich Mayor's Court books
NCR/16D   Norwich Proceedings of the Municipal Assembly
NCR/17B   Norwich 'Liber Albus'
NCR/18A   Norwich Chamberlain's accounts
NCR/20A   Norwich Quarter Sessions minute book
NCR/26B   Norwich miscellaneous collection
NNAS Frere   Frere Collection
NQS C/S3   Norfolk Quarter Sessions, sessions rolls
NRS 12131/27   Aylsham manor court rolls
PD209   North Elmham parish documents
PD254   New Buckenham parish documents
Y/C1/1   Yarmouth 'sumary reporte' on town archives by Henry Manship
Y/C4   Yarmouth Borough court rolls
Y/C18/1   Yarmouth book of charters
Y/C19   Yarmouth Borough Assembly minute book
Y/C20/1   Yarmouth Proceedings of the Hutch Committee

Oxburgh Hall, Norfolk

Muniments

Parker Library, Corpus Christi College, Cambridge

MS 128   Depositions concerning Anabaptists in Kent, 1542
XXV   Landbeach estate documents

CONTEMPORARY PRINTED BOOKS

Anon., *A ruful complaynt of the publyke weale to Englande* (London, 1550).

Anon., *A most pleasant and merie new comedie, intutled, a knacke to knowe a knave* (London, 1594).

Anon., *A compleat history of the famous city of Norwich from the earliest account, to the present year 1728* (Norwich, 1728).

Anon., *An appendix to the chronological history of the famous city of Norwich* (Norwich, 1728).

Anon., *The history of the city and county of Norwich from the earliest account to the present time* (Norwich, 1768).

Anon., *The history (as related by A. Neville) of the rebellion in Norfolk in the year 1549, which was conducted by R. Kett, etc.* (Norwich, 1750?).

Anon., *The history of the rebellion in Norfolk, in the year 1549; which was conducted by Rob. Kett, etc.* (Norwich, 1751).

Anon., *Norfolk's furies: or, a view of Kett's camp* (Norwich, n.d. (1728?)).

Bible in English (London, 1549).

Bromley, G. P., *The rebellion; or Norwich in 1549: a drama, interspersed with music* (Norwich, 1815).

Cheke, J., *The true subject to the rebell, or the hurt of sedition, how greivous it is to a commonwealth* (Oxford, 1641).

Crowley, R., *The vision of Pierce Plowman, nowe the seconde time imprinted* (London, 1550).

Faret, N., *The honest man* (London, 1632).

Gilpin, B., *A godly sermon preached in the court at Greenwich the firste Sonday after the Epiphanie ... 1552* (London, 1581).

Morison, R., *A remedy for sedition* (London, 1536).

Neville, A., *De furoribus Norfolciensium* (London, 1575).

Neville, A., *The history of the city of Norwich. Containing a description of that city ... To which is added, Norfolk's furies: or, a view of Kett's camp* (Norwich, 1718).

Ocland, C., *Anglorum praelia* (London, 1582).

Perkins, W., *A direction for the governmente of the tongue* (Edinburgh, 1593).

Stow, J., *A summarie of Englyshe chronicles* (London, 1565).

Stow, J., *The chronicles of England from Brute unto this present yeare of Christ* (London, 1580).

Warner, W., *Albion's England: the third time augmented and corrected, continuing an history of the same countrey and kingdome* (London, 1592).

Wilson, T., *The arte of rhetorique, for the use of all suche as are studious of eloquence* (London, 1553).

Woods, R., *Norfolke furies and their foyle* (London, 1615).

Wright, T., *The passions of the mind* (1604; London, 1630 edn).

EDITIONS OF MANUSCRIPTS AND CONTEMPORARY
PRINTED WORKS AND CALENDARS

Bacon, F., *Essays civil and moral* (1612; London, 1892).

Bateson, M., 'Aske's examination', *English Historical Review*, 5 (1890), 550–73.

Bateson, M., 'Ballad on the Pilgrimage of Grace', *English Historical Review*, 5 (1890), 344.

Bateson, M., 'The Pilgrimage of Grace', *English Historical Review*, 5 (1890), 331–43.

Bateson, M. (ed.), *Records of the Borough of Leicester, 1509–1603*, 3 vols. (Cambridge, 1905).

Beer, B. L. (ed.), 'A critique of the Protectorate: an unpublished letter of Sir William Paget to the Duke of Somerset', *Huntington Library Quarterly*, 34 (1971), 277–83.

Beer, B. L. (ed.), 'The commosyon in Norfolk, 1549', *Journal of Medieval and Renaissance Studies*, 6, 1 (1976), 73–99.

Beer, B. L. (ed.), *The life and raigne of King Edward the sixth by John Hayward* (Kent, OH, 1993).

Beer, B. L. and Jack, S. M. (eds.), 'The letters of William Lord Paget of Beaudesert, 1547–63', *Camden Miscellany*, XXV (Camden Society, 4th ser., XIII, London, 1974), 1–135.

Boileau, J. P., 'Old poem on Norfolk', *Norfolk Archaeology*, 5 (1859), 161–7.

Bond, R. B. (ed.), *Certain sermons or homilies (1547) and A homily against disobedience and wilful rebellion (1570): a critical edition* (Toronto, 1987).

Brigden, S. (ed.), 'The letters of Richard Scudamore to Sir Philip Hoby, September 1549–March 1555', *Camden Miscellany*, XXX (Camden Society, 4th ser., XXXIX, London, 1990).

Brodie, D. M. (ed.), *The tree of commonwealth: a treatise* (Cambridge, 1948).

Bryn Davies, M., 'Boulogne and Calais from 1545 to 1550', *Bulletin of the Faculty of Arts, Fouad I University, Cairo*, 12, 1 (1950), 1–90.

Calendar of the patent rolls preserved in the Public Record Office: Edward VI, 5 vols. (London, 1926).

Calendar of the patent rolls preserved in the Public Record Office: Philip and Mary, 4 vols. (London, 1939).

Calendar of the patent rolls preserved in the Public Record Office: Elizabeth I, 9 vols. (London, 1939–86).

Carthew, G. A., 'Extracts from papers in the church chest of Wymondham', *Norfolk Archaeology*, 55 (1884), 121–52.

Cockburn, J. S. (ed.), *Calendar of assize records: Essex indictments, Elizabeth I* (London, 1978).

Cockburn, J. S. (ed.), *Calendar of assize records: Kent indictments, Elizabeth I* (London, 1979).

Cooper, C. H., *Annals of Cambridge*, 4 vols. (Cambridge, 1843–5).

Corrie, G. E. (ed.), *Sermons of Hugh Latimer, sometime Bishop of Worcester, Martyr, 1555*, Parker Society, 22 (Cambridge, 1844).

Cox, J. E. (ed.), *Miscellaneous writings and letters of Thomas Cranmer*, Parker Society, 18 (Cambridge, 1846).

Cunningham, W. (ed.), 'Common rights at Cottenham and Stretham in Cambridgeshire', *Camden Miscellany*, XII (Camden Society, 3rd ser., XVIII, London, 1910), 173–289.

Dasent, J. R. *et al.* (eds.), *Acts of the Privy Council, 1542–1631*, new ser., 46 vols. (London, 1890–1964).

Davis, N. (ed.), *Paston letters and papers of the fifteenth century*, 3 vols. (Oxford, 1976).

Ecclestone, A. W. (ed.), *Henry Manship's Great Yarmouth* (Great Yarmouth, 1971).

Eden, F. M., *The state of the poor*, 3 vols. (London, 1797).

Ellis, H., 'Letter from secretary Walsingham to the Lord Treasurer', *Norfolk Archaeology*, 2 (1849), 92–6.

Elyot, T., *The book named the governor* (1531; London, 1962).

Fortescue, J., *On the laws and governance of England*, ed. S. Lockwood (Cambridge, 1997).

Foxe, J., *Acts and monuments*, 8 vols. (London, 1837–41).

George, M. D. (ed.), *Catalogue of prints and drawings in the British Museum*, 12 vols. (London, 1942).

Goitein, H. (ed.), *Utopia, translated by Ralph Robinson, 1551; The new Atlantis, 1622* (London, 1925).

Googe, B., *Eglogs, epytaphes and sonettes*, ed. E. Arber (London, 1871).

Grosart, A. B. (ed.), *Nicholas Breton: the works in verse and prose* (1879; repr. Darmstadt, 1969).

Guazzo, S., *The civile conversation*, 2 vols. (1581–6; London, 1925).

Hall, E., *Hall's chronicle; containing the history of England during the reign of Henry the Fourth and the succeeding monarchs, to the end of the reign of Henry the Eighth* (London, 1809).

Halliwell, J. O. (ed.), *A chronicle of the first thirteen years of the reign of King Edward the fourth* (Camden Society, 1st ser., X, London, 1839).

Hamilton, W. D. (ed.), *A chronicle of England during the reigns of the Tudors* (Camden Society, new ser., XX, London, 1877).

Harte, W. J., Schopp, J. W. and Tapley-Soker, H. (eds.), *The description of the citie of Excester by John Vowell alias Hoker*, 3 vols. (Exeter, 1919).

Hassell Smith, A. and Baker, G. M. (eds.), *The papers of Nathaniel Bacon of Stiffkey*, vol. III: *1586–1595* (Norwich, 1990).

Historical Manuscripts Commission, *The manuscripts of His Grace the Duke of Rutland, G. C. B., preserved at Belvoir Castle*, 4 vols. (London, 1888–96).

Historical Manuscripts Commission, *14th Report, Appx. IV, The manuscripts of Lord Kenyon* (London, 1894).

Historical Manuscripts Commission, *Report on manuscripts in the Welsh language*, 3 vols. (London, 1898–1905).

Historical Manuscripts Commission, *Calendar of the manuscripts of the Marquis of Bath preserved at Longleat, Wiltshire*, 5 vols. (London, 1904–80).

Holinshed, R., *Chronicles of England, Scotland and Ireland*, 6 vols. (1577 & 1586; new edn, London, 1808).

Hope Robbins, R. (ed.), *Historical poems of the fourteenth and fifteenth centuries* (New York, 1959).

Hudson, W. and Tingay, J. C. (eds.), *The records of the city of Norwich*, 2 vols. (Norwich, 1906–10).

Hughes, P. L. and Larkin, J. F. (eds.), *Tudor Royal Proclamations*, 3 vols. (New Haven, CT, 1964–9).

Hume, M. A. S. (ed.), *Calendar of letters and state papers relating to English affairs, preserved principally in the Archives of Simancas*, 4 vols. (London, 1892–9).

Kingsford, C. L. (ed.), 'Two London chronicles from the collections of John Stow', *Camden Miscellany*, XII (Camden Society, 3rd ser., XVIII, London, 1910).

Lamond, E. (ed.), *A discourse on the commonweal of this realm of England* (Cambridge, 1893).

Letters and papers, foreign and domestic, of the reign of Henry VIII: preserved in the Public Record Office, the British Museum and elsewhere in England, 21 vols. (London, 1880–91).

Lloyd, C. (ed.), *Formularies of faith put forth by authority during the reign of Henry VIII* (Oxford, 1856).

Macray, W. D. (ed.), *The history of Grisild the Second: a narrative, in verse, of the divorce of Queen Katherine of Arragon. Written by William Forrest* (London, 1875).

Manning, J. J. (ed.), *The first and second parts of John Hayward's The life and raigne of King Henrie IIII* (Camden Society, 4th ser., XLII, London, 1991).

Martin, K. S. (ed.), *Records of Maidstone: being selections from documents in the possession of the Corporation* (Maidstone, 1928).

Meadows Cowper, J. (ed.), *A supplicacyon for the beggers, with A supplycacion to our moste soveraigne lord Kynge Henry the Eyght, A supplication of the poore commons, The decaye of England by the great multitude of shepe* (Early English Text Society, extra ser., 18 London, 1871).

Meadows Cowper, J. (ed.), *The select works of Robert Crowley* (Early English Text Society, extra ser., 15, London, 1872).

Meadows Cowper, J. (ed.), *Henry Brinklow's complaynt of Roderyck Mors; and, The lamentacyon of a Christen agaynst the cytye of London* (Early English Text Society, extra ser., 22, London, 1874).

Nichols, J. G. (ed.), *The diary of Henry Machyn, citizen and merchant-taylor of London, from AD 1550 to AD 1563* (Camden Society, 1st ser., XLII, London, 1848).

Nichols, J. G. (ed.), *Literary remains of Edward the sixth*, 2 vols. (London, 1857).

Nichols, J. G. (ed.), *Narratives of the days of the Reformation* (Camden Society, 1st ser., LXXVII, London 1859).

Page, W. (ed.), *The certificates of the commissioners appointed to survey the chantries, guilds, hospitals, etc., in the County of York*, 2 vols. (Surtees Society, 91, Durham, 1894).

Paley, W. (ed.), *Les reportes del cases in Camera Stellata, 1593 to 1609, from the original Ms. of John Hawarde* (London, 1894).

Percy, T. (ed.), *Reliques of ancient English poetry: consisting of old heroic ballads, songs, and other pieces of our earlier poets*, 3 vols. (London, 1889).

Pocock, N. (ed.), *Troubles connected with the Prayer Book of 1549* (Camden Society, 2nd ser., XXXVII, London, 1884).

Rawcliffe, C., *Sources for the history of medicine in late medieval England* (Kalamazoo, MI, 1995).

Ringler, W. A. and Flachmann, M. (eds.), *Beware the cat, by William Baldwin: the first English novel* (San Marino, CA, 1988).

Robinson, H. (ed.), *Original letters relative to the English Reformation* (Parker Society, XXVI, Cambridge, 1846).

Rodgers, M., Wallace, M. and Rutledge, E. (eds.), *Norwich landgable assessment, 1568–1570* (Norfolk Record Society, LXIII, Norwich, 1999).

Sharp Hume, M. A., *Chronicle of King Henry VIII of England* (London, 1889).

Smith, T., *De republica Anglorum* (1583; Cambridge, 1982).

Statutes of the realm, 11 vols. (London, 1810–24).

Stevenson, J. (ed.), *The life of Jane Dormer, Duchess of Feria by Henry Clifford. Transcribed from an ancient manuscript in the possession of the Lord Dormer* (London, 1887).

Strype, J. (ed.), *Ecclesiastical memorials relating chiefly to religion and the reformation of it and the emergencies of the Church of England under King Henry VIII, King Edward VI and Queen Mary I*, 4 vols. (Oxford, 1822).

Strype, J. (ed.), *Annals of the Reformation and establishment of religion and other various occurrences in the Church of England during Queen Elizabeth's happy reign*, 4 vols. (Oxford, 1824).
Tawney, R. H. and Power, E. (eds.), *Tudor economic documents: being select documents illustrating the economic and social history of Tudor England* (London, 1924).
White, B. (ed.), *The vulgaria of John Stanbridge and the vulgaria of Robert Whittinton* (Early English Text Society, 187, London, 1932).
Williams, J. F. (ed.), *Bishop Redman's visitation, 1597: presentments in the archdeaconries of Norwich, Norfolk, and Suffolk* (Norfolk Record Society, Norwich, 1946).
Wright, T. (ed.), *Political poems and songs relating to English history, composed during the period from the accession of Edw. III to that of Ric. III*, 2 vols. (London, 1859–61).

SECONDARY WORKS

Alford, S., 'Politics and political history in the Tudor century', *Historical Journal*, 42, 2 (1999), 535–48.
Allen, R. C., *Enclosure and the yeoman: the agricultural development of the south Midlands, 1450–1850* (Oxford, 1988).
Alsop, J. D., 'Latimer, the "Commonwealth of Kent" and the 1549 rebellions', *Historical Journal*, 28, 2 (1985), 379–83.
Anon., *The history of Kett's rebellion in Norwich in the reign of Edward the sixth* (Norwich, c. 1843).
Anon., *Robert Ket: the Wyndham tanner. A poem* (London, 1869).
Apps, L. and Gow, A., *Male witches in early modern Europe* (Manchester, 2003).
Archer, I., *The pursuit of stability: social relations in Elizabethan London* (Cambridge, 1991).
Arnold, J. H., *Inquisition and power: Catharism and the confessing subject in medieval Languedoc* (Philadelphia, 2001).
Arnold, J. H., *Belief and unbelief in medieval Europe* (London, 2005).
Arriaza, A., 'Mousnier and Barber: the theoretical underpinning of the "society of orders" in early modern Europe', *P&P*, 89 (1980), 39–57.
Arthurson, I., 'Fear and loathing in west Cornwall: seven new letters on the 1548 rising', *Royal Institution of Cornwall*, 3, 4 (2000), 68–96.
Austin, J. L., *How to do things with words* (Cambridge, MA, 1975).
Bakhtin, M. M., *Speech genres and other late essays* (Austin, TX, 1986).
Beer, B. L., *Northumberland: the political career of John Dudley, Earl of Warwick and Duke of Northumberland* (Kent, OH, 1973).
Beer, B. L., *Rebellion and riot: popular disorder in England during the reign of Edward VI* (Kent, OH, 1982).
Beer, B. L., 'John Stow and the English Reformation, 1547–1559', *Sixteenth Century Journal*, 16, 2 (1985), 257–71.
Beer, B. L., 'John Stow and Tudor rebellions, 1549–1569', *Journal of British Studies*, 27 (1988), 352–74.
Beer, B. L. and Nash, R. J., 'Hugh Latimer and the lusty knave of Kent: the Commonwealth movement of 1549', *Bulletin of the Institute of Historical Research*, 52 (1979), 175–8.
Beetham, D., *The legitimation of power* (Basingstoke, 1991).

Bellamy, J., *The Tudor law of treason: an introduction* (London, 1979).
Belsey, C., *The subject of tragedy: identity and difference in Renaissance drama* (London, 1985).
Bensly, W. T., 'St Leonard's Priory, Norwich', *Norfolk Archaeology*, 12 (1895), 190–228.
Bernard, G. W., *War, taxation and rebellion in early Tudor England: Henry VIII, Wolsey and the Amicable Grant of 1525* (Hassocks, 1986).
Bevington, D., *Tudor drama and politics: a critical approach to topical meaning* (Cambridge, MA, 1968).
Bindoff, S. T., *Ket's rebellion, 1549* (London, 1949).
Blickle, P. (ed.), *Resistance, representation and community* (Oxford, 1997).
Bloch, M., 'Introduction', in M. Bloch (ed.), *Political language and oratory in traditional society* (London, 1975), 1–28.
Blomefield, F., *An essay towards a topographical history of the county of Norfolk* (1739–75; 2nd edn, London, 1805–10, 11 vols.).
Bohna, M., 'Armed force and civic legitimacy in Jack Cade's revolt, 1450', *English Historical Review*, 118, 477 (2003), 563–82.
Braddick, M. J., *State formation in early modern England, c. 1550–1700* (Cambridge, 2000).
Braddick, M. J. and Walter, J., 'Introduction. Grids of power: order, hierarchy and subordination in early modern society', in Braddick and Walter (eds.), *Negotiating power*, 1–42.
Braddick, M. J. and Walter, J. (eds.), *Negotiating power in early modern society: order, hierarchy and subordination in Britain and Ireland* (Cambridge, 2001).
Brigden, S., *London and the Reformation* (Oxford, 1989).
Brooks, C. W., *Pettyfoggers and vipers of the Commonwealth: the 'lower branch' of the legal profession in early modern England* (Cambridge, 1986).
Burke, P., 'Introduction', in P. Burke and R. Porter (eds.), *The social history of language* (Cambridge, 1987), 1–20.
Bush, M. L., 'Protector Somerset and requests', *Historical Journal*, 18, 3 (1974), 451–64.
Bush, M. L., *The government policy of Protector Somerset* (London, 1975).
Bush, M. L., 'Tax reform and rebellion in early Tudor England', *History*, 76 (1991), 379–400.
Bush, M. L., *The Pilgrimage of Grace: a study of the rebel armies of October 1536* (Manchester, 1996).
Bush, M. L., 'The risings of the commons, 1381–1549', in J. H. Denton (ed.), *Orders and hierarchies in late medieval and renaissance Europe* (London, 1999), 109–25.
Bush, M. L., 'The Pilgrimage of Grace and the pilgrim tradition of holy war', in C. Morris and P. Roberts (eds.), *Pilgrimage: the English experience from Becket to Bunyan* (Cambridge, 2002), 178–98.
Buszello, H., 'The common man's view of the state in the German Peasant War', in Scribner and Benecke (eds.), *German Peasant War*, 109–22.
Calhoun, C. J., *The question of class struggle: social foundations of popular radicalism during the industrial revolution* (Oxford, 1982).
Camporesi, P., *Bread of dreams: food and fantasy in early modern Europe* (1980; Eng. trans., Oxford, 1989).
Carter, A., 'The site of Dussindale', *Norfolk Archaeology*, 39 (1987), 54–62.
Champion, M., 'Kett's rebellion 1549: a Dussindale eyewitness?', *Norfolk Archaeology*, 43 (2001), 642–5.

Chomsky, N., *Language and responsibility* (Hassocks, 1979).

Clark, P., 'Popular protest and disturbance in Kent, 1558–1640', *Economic History Review*, 2nd ser., 29, 3 (1976), 365–82.

Clark, P., *English provincial society from the Reformation to the Revolution: religion, politics and society in Kent, 1500–1640* (Hassocks, 1977).

Clark, P., 'A crisis contained? The condition of English towns in the 1590s', in P. Clark (ed.), *The European crisis of the 1590s: essays in comparative history* (London, 1985), 44–66.

Clark, S., 'Inversion, misrule and the meaning of witchcraft', *P&P*, 87 (1980), 98–127.

Clayton, J., *Robert Kett and the Norfolk rising* (London, 1912).

Clopper, L. M., *Drama, play, and game: English festive culture in the medieval and early modern period* (Chicago, 2001).

Collinson, P., *Godly people: essays on English Protestantism and puritanism* (London, 1982).

Collinson, P., *Elizabethan essays* (London, 1994).

Cooper, J. P. D., *Propaganda and the Tudor state: political culture in the Westcountry* (Oxford, 2003).

Corbin, A., *Village bells: sound and meaning in the nineteenth-century French countryside* (New York, 1998).

Cornwall, J., *Revolt of the peasantry, 1549* (London, 1977).

Cressy, D., *Literacy and the social order: reading and writing in Tudor and Stuart England* (Cambridge, 1980).

Cressy, D., *Bonfires and bells: national memory and the Protestant calendar in Elizabethan and Stuart England* (Berkeley, 1989).

Curry, P., 'Towards a post-Marxist social history: Thompson, Clark and beyond', in A. Wilson (ed.), *Rethinking social history: English society, 1570–1920 and its interpretation* (Manchester, 1993), 158–200.

Dickens, A. G., 'Some popular reactions to the Edwardian Reformation in Yorkshire', *Yorkshire Archaeological Journal*, 34 (1939), 151–69.

Dobson, R. B., *The peasants' revolt of 1381* (Basingstoke, 1970).

Duby, G., *The three orders: feudal society imagined* (1978; Eng. trans., Chicago, 1980).

Duffy, E., *The voices of Morebath: reformation and rebellion in an English village* (New Haven, CT, 2001).

Dyer, C., 'The rising of 1381 in Suffolk: its origins and participants', in C. Dyer, *Everyday life in medieval England* (London, 1994), 221–39.

Dyer, C., 'The political life of the fifteenth-century English village', in L. Clark and C. Carpenter (eds.), *The fifteenth century, IV: Political culture in late medieval Britain* (Woodbridge, 2004), 135–58.

Dymond, D., 'A lost social institution : the camping close', *Rural History*, 1 (1990), 165–92.

Eiden, H., 'Joint action against "bad" lordship: the peasants' revolt in Essex and Norfolk', *History*, 83, 269 (1998), 5–30.

Eiland, H. and Jennings, M. W. (eds.), *Walter Benjamin: selected writings*, 4 vols. (Cambridge, MA, 2003).

Elton, G. R., *The Tudor constitution: documents and commentary* (Cambridge, 1960).

Elton, G. R., *Policy and police: the enforcement of the Reformation in the age of Thomas Cromwell* (Cambridge, 1972).

Elton, G. R., 'Reform and the "Commonwealth-men" of Edward VI's reign', in P. Clark, A. G. R. Smith and N. Tyacke (eds.), *The English Commonwealth: essays in politics presented to Joel Hurstfield* (Leicester, 1979), 23–38.

Epstein, J., *Radical expression: political language, ritual and symbolism in England, 1790–1850* (Oxford, 1994).

Epstein, J., '"Our real constitution": trial defence and radical memory in the age of revolution', in J. Vernon (ed.), *Rereading the constitution: new narratives in the political history of England's long nineteenth century* (Cambridge, 1996), 22–51.

Epstein, J., *In practice: studies in the language and culture of popular politics in modern Britain* (Stanford, CA, 2003).

Ertman, T., *Birth of the leviathan: building states and regimes in medieval and early modern Europe* (Cambridge, 1997).

Fairclough, N., *Language and power* (Harlow, 1989).

Fentress, J. and Wickham, C., *Social memory* (Oxford, 1992).

Figes, O. and Kolonitskii, B., *Interpreting the Russian Revolution: the language and symbols of 1917* (New Haven, CT, 1999).

Fletcher, A. and MacCulloch, D., *Tudor rebellions* (1968; 5th edn, 2004).

Fletcher, A. and Stevenson, J., 'Introduction', in Fletcher and Stevenson (eds.), *Order and disorder*, 1–40.

Fletcher, A. and Stevenson, J. (eds.), *Order and disorder in early modern England* (Cambridge, 1985).

Fox, A., *Oral and literate culture in England, 1500–1700* (Oxford, 2000).

Freedman, P., *Images of the medieval peasant* (Stanford, CA, 1999).

French, H., 'The search for the "middle sort of people" in England, 1600–1800', *Historical Journal*, 43 (2000), 277–93.

French, H. and Barry, J. (eds.), *Identity and agency in England, 1500–1800* (Basingstoke, 2004).

Friedeburg, R. von, 'Reformation of manners and the social composition of offenders in an East Anglian cloth village: Earls Colne, Essex, 1531–1642', *Journal of British Studies*, 29 (1990), 347–85.

Giddens, A., *Capitalism and modern social theory: an analysis of the writings of Marx, Durkheim and Max Weber* (Cambridge, 1971).

Ginzburg, C., *The cheese and the worms: the cosmos of a sixteenth-century miller* (1976; Eng. trans., London, 1980).

Ginzburg, C., *Myths, emblems, clues* (1986; Eng. trans., London, 1990).

Goheen, R. B., 'Peasant politics? Village community and the Crown in fifteenth-century England', *American Historical Review*, 96, 1 (1991), 42–62.

Gowing, L., *Domestic dangers: women, words and sex in early modern London* (Oxford, 1996).

Griffiths, P., *Youth and authority: formative experiences in England, 1560–1640* (Oxford, 1996).

Griffiths, P., 'Inhabitants', in C. Rawcliffe and R. Wilson (eds.), *Norwich since 1550* (London, 2004), 63–88.

Grillo, R., 'Anthropology, language, politics', in R. Grillo (ed.), *Social anthropology and the politics of language* (London, 1989), 1–24.

Groves, R., *Rebels' oak: the great rebellion of 1549* (London, 1947).

Gunther, K. and Shagan, E., 'Protestant radicalism and political thought in the reign of Henry VIII', *P&P* forthcoming.

Guy, J., *Tudor England* (Oxford, 1988).

Guy, J., *The Tudor monarchy* (London, 1997).

Habermas, J., *Legitimation crisis* (1973; Eng. trans., London, 1976).

Halbwachs, M., *The collective memory* (1950; Eng. trans., New York, 1980).

Hall, R. G., 'Creating a people's history: political identity and history in Chartism, 1832–1848', in O. Ashton, R. Fyson and S. Roberts (eds.), *The Chartist legacy* (Rendlesham, 1989), 232–54.

Hammond, J. L. and Hammond, B., *The skilled labourer* (London, 1919).

Hammond, J. L. and Hammond, B., *The town labourer* (London, 1919).

Hammond, J. L. and Hammond, B., *The village labourer* (London, 1911).

Harris, T., 'Problematising popular culture', in T. Harris (ed.), *Popular culture in England, c. 1500–1850* (Basingstoke, 1995), 1–27.

Harris, T., 'Perceptions of the crowd in later Stuart London', in J. F. Merritt (ed.), *Imagining early modern London: perceptions and portrayals of the City from Stow to Strype, 1598–1720* (Cambridge, 2001), 250–72.

Harris, T. (ed.), *The politics of the excluded, c. 1500–1850* (Basingstoke, 2001).

Harriss, G. L., 'Introduction: the exemplar of kingship', in G. L. Harriss (ed.), *Henry V: the practice of kingship* (Oxford, 1985), 1–29.

Harvey, I. M. W., *Jack Cade's rebellion of 1450* (Oxford, 1991).

Harvey, I. M. W., 'Was there popular politics in fifteenth-century England?', in R. H. Britnell and A. J. Pollard (eds.), *The McFarlane legacy: studies in late medieval politics and society* (Stroud, 1995), 155–74.

Hay, D., 'Property, authority and the criminal law', in D. Hay, P. Linebaugh and E. P. Thompson (eds.), *Albion's fatal tree: crime and society in eighteenth-century England* (London, 1975), 17–64.

Hicks, M. A., 'The Yorkshire rebellion of 1489 reconsidered', *Northern History*, 22 (1986), 39–62.

Hill, C., *Society and puritanism in pre-revolutionary England* (London, 1964).

Hill, C., *The world turned upside down: radical ideas in the English Revolution* (London, 1972).

Hill, C., 'The many-headed monster', in C. Hill, *Change and continuity in seventeenth-century England* (1974; 2nd edn, New Haven, CT, 1991), 181–204.

Hillen, H. J., *History of the Borough of King's Lynn*, 2 vols. (Norwich, 1907).

Hilton, R., *Class conflict and the crisis of feudalism: essays in medieval social history* (London, 1985).

Hindle, S., 'The shaming of Margaret Knowsley: gossip, gender and the experience of authority in early modern England', *Continuity and Change*, 9 (1994), 391–419.

Hindle, S., 'The problem of pauper marriage in seventeenth-century England', *Transactions of the Royal Historical Society*, 6th ser., 8 (1998), 71–89.

Hindle, S., 'Communication: hierarchy and community in the Elizabethan parish: the Swallowfield articles of 1596', *Historical Journal*, 42, 3 (1999), 835–51.

Hindle, S., *The state and social change in early modern England, c. 1550–1640* (Basingstoke, 2000).

Hindle, S., 'Exhortation and entitlement: negotiating inequality in English rural communities, 1550–1650', in Braddick and Walter (eds.), *Negotiating power*, 102–22.

Hindle, S., *On the parish? The micro-politics of poor relief in rural England, c. 1550–1750* (Oxford, 2004).

Hoak, D. (ed.), *Tudor political culture* (Cambridge, 1995).

Hoare, C. M., *The history of an East Anglian soke: studies in original documents* (Bedford, 1918).

Hoare, Q. and Nowell Smith, G. (eds.), *Selections from the prison notebooks of Antonio Gramsci* (London, 1971).

Hoare, R. C., *The modern history of Wiltshire*, 6 vols. (London, 1843).

Holmes, C., 'Drainers and fenmen: the problem of popular political consciousness in the seventeenth century', in Fletcher and Stevenson (eds.), *Order and disorder*, 166–95.

Holstun, J., 'The spider, the fly and the commonwealth: merrie John Heywood and the agrarian class struggle', *English Literary History*, 71 (2004), 53–88.

Howkins, A., *Poor labouring men: rural radicalism in Norfolk, 1870–1923* (London, 1985).

Howkins, A., *Reshaping rural England: a social history 1850–1925* (London, 1991).

Hoyle, R., 'Tenure and the land market in early modern England: or, a late contribution to the Brenner Debate', *Economic History Review*, 2nd ser., 43 (1990), 1–20.

Hoyle, R., 'Communication: agrarian agitation in mid-sixteenth-century Norfolk: a petition of 1553', *Historical Journal*, 44, 1 (2001), 223–38.

Hoyle, R., *The Pilgrimage of Grace and the politics of the 1530s* (Oxford, 2001).

Hoyle, R., 'Petitioning as popular politics in early sixteenth-century England', *Historical Research*, 75, 190 (2002), 365–89.

Hunt, W., *The puritan moment: the coming of revolution to an English county* (Cambridge, MA, 1983).

Hunt, W., 'Spectral origins of the English Revolution: legitimation crisis in early Stuart England', in G. Eley and W. Hunt (eds.), *Reviving the English Revolution: reflections and elaborations on the work of Christopher Hill* (London, 1988), 305–32.

Hutton, R., *The rise and fall of merry England: the ritual year, 1400–1700* (Oxford, 1994).

Hymes, D., 'Models of the interaction of language and social life', in J. J. Gumperz and D. Hymes (eds.), *Directions in sociolinguistics: the ethnography of communication* (New York, 1972), 35–71.

Hyndman, H. M., *The historical basis of socialism in England* (London, 1883).

Ingram, M., '"Scolding women cucked or washed": a crisis in gender relations in early modern England?', in J. Kermode and G. M. Walker (eds.), *Women, crime and the courts in early modern England* (London, 1994), 48–80.

Izzo, A., 'Legitimation and society: a critical review', *Current Sociology*, 35, 2 (1987), 41–56.

James, M. E., 'The concept of order and the Northern rising', in M. E. James, *Society, politics and culture: studies in early modern England* (Cambridge, 1986), 270–307.

Jordan, W. K., *Edward VI, the young king: the Protectorship of the Duke of Somerset* (London, 1968).

Joyce, P., *Democratic subjects: the self and the social in nineteenth-century England* (Cambridge, 1994).

Justice, S., *Writing and rebellion: England in 1381* (Berkeley, 1994).

Kamensky, J., *Governing the tongue: the politics of speech in early New England* (Oxford, 1997).

Kegl, R., *The rhetoric of concealment: figuring class and gender in Renaissance literature* (Ithaca, NY, 1994).

Kekewich, M. L., Richmond, C., Sutton, A. F., Visser-Fuchs, L. and Watts, J. L. (eds.), *The politics of fifteenth-century England: John Vale's book* (Stroud, 1995).

Kent, J. R., *The English village constable 1580–1642: a social and administrative study* (Oxford, 1986).

Kerridge, E., *Agrarian problems in the sixteenth century and after* (London, 1969).

Kesselring, K. J., *Mercy, authority and the Tudor state* (Cambridge, 2003).

Ketton-Cremer, R. W., *Norfolk in the Civil War* (London, 1969).
Kirk, N., 'History, language, ideas and post-modernism: a materialist view', *Social History*, 19, 2 (1994), 221–40.
Kumin, B. A., *The shaping of a community: the rise and reformation of the English parish, c. 1400–1560* (Aldershot, 1996).
Land, S. K., *Kett's rebellion: the Norfolk rising of 1549* (London, 1977).
Le Roy Ladurie, E., *Montaillou: Cathars and Catholics in a French village, 1294–1324* (1978; Eng. trans., London, 1978).
Levine, D. and Wrightson, K., *The making of an industrial society: Whickham, 1560–1765* (Oxford, 1991).
Lindley, K., *Fenland riots and the English Revolution* (London, 1982).
Lindley, K., 'The maintenance of stability in early modern London', *Historical Journal*, 34, 4 (1991), 985–90.
Loades, D., *John Dudley: Duke of Northumberland, 1504–1553* (Oxford, 1996).
McClendon, M. C., *The quiet Reformation: magistrates and the emergence of Protestantism in Tudor Norwich* (Stanford, CA, 1999).
MacCulloch, D., 'Kett's rebellion in context', *P&P*, 84 (1979), 36–59.
MacCulloch, D., *Suffolk and the Tudors: politics and religion in an English county, 1500–1600* (Oxford, 1986).
MacCulloch, D., 'Bondmen under the Tudors', in C. Cross, D. Loades and J. J. Scarisbruck (eds.), *Law and government under the Tudors* (Cambridge, 1988), 91–109.
MacCulloch, D., 'The Reformation in the balance: power struggles in the diocese of Norwich, 1533–1553', in C. Rawcliffe, R. Virgoe and R. Wilson (eds.), *Counties and communities: essays on East Anglian history presented to Hassell Smith* (Norwich, 1996), 97–114.
MacCulloch, D., *Thomas Cranmer: a life* (New Haven, CT, 1996).
MacCulloch, D., *Tudor church militant: Edward VI and the Protestant Reformation* (London, 1999).
MacMaster, N., 'The battle for Mousehold Heath, 1857–1884: "popular politics" and the Victorian public park', *P&P*, 127 (1990), 117–54.
Mandler, P., '"In the olden time": romantic history and English national identity, 1820–50', in L. Brockliss and D. Eastwood (eds.), *A union of multiple identities: the British Isles, c. 1750–1850* (Manchester, 1997), 78–91.
Manning, R. B., 'The origins of the doctrine of sedition', *Journal of British Studies*, 12, 2 (1980), 99–121.
Manning, R. B., *Village revolts: social protest and popular disturbances in England, 1509–1640* (Oxford, 1988).
Mansueto, A., 'Religion, solidarity and class struggle: Marx, Durkheim and Gramsci on the religious question', *Social Compass*, 35 (1988), 261–77.
Marx, K., *Capital: a critique of political economy*, 3 vols. (Chicago, 1926).
Marx, K. and Engels, F., *Collected works*, 37 vols. (London, 1975–98).
Miller, B., *Narratives of guilt and compliance in unified Germany: Stasi informers and their impact on society* (London, 1999).
Moreton, C. E., 'The Walsingham conspiracy of 1537', *Historical Research*, 63 (1990), 29–43.
Moreton, C. E., 'Mid-Tudor trespass: a break-in at Norwich, 1549', *English Historical Review*, 108 (1993), 387–98.
Mousnier, R., *Social hierarchies* (1969; Eng. trans., London, 1973).

Myers, F. R. and Brenneis, D. L., 'Introduction: language and politics in the Pacific', in F. R. Myers and D. L. Brenneis (eds.), *Dangerous words: language and politics in the Pacific* (New York, 1984), 1–29.

Neele, H., *The romance of history: England*, 3 vols. (London, 1828).

Newton, K. C. and McIntosh, M. K., 'Leet jurisdiction in Essex manor courts during the Elizabethan period', *Essex Archaeology and History*, 3rd ser., 13 (1981), 13–14.

Oberman, H. A., 'The gospel of social unrest', in Scribner and Benecke (eds.), *German Peasant War*, 39–51.

Palliser, D. M., 'Popular reactions to the Reformation during the years of uncertainty, 1530–70', in F. Heal and R. O'Day (eds.), *Church and society in England, Henry VIII to James I* (Basingstoke, 1977), 35–56.

Patterson, A., *Shakespeare and the popular voice* (Oxford, 1989).

Patterson, A., *Reading Holinshed's Chronicles* (Chicago, 1994).

Pearl, V., 'Change and stability in seventeenth-century London', in J. Barry (ed.), *The Tudor and Stuart town: a reader in English urban history, 1530–1688* (London, 1990), 139–65.

Pettit, T., '"Here comes I, Jack Straw": English folk drama and social revolts', *Folklore*, 95, 1 (1984), 3–20.

Pickering, P. A., 'Class without words: symbolic communication in the Chartist movement', *P&P*, 112 (1986), 144–62.

Pitman, J., 'Tradition and exclusion: parochial officeholding in early modern England, a case study from north Norfolk, 1580–1640', *Rural History*, 15, 1 (2004), 27–45.

Pocock, J. G. A. 'The concept of a language and the *métier d'historien*: some considerations on practice', in A. Pagden (ed.), *The languages of political theory in early-modern Europe* (Cambridge, 1987), 19–38.

Pollard, A. F., *England under Protector Somerset: an essay* (London, 1900).

Portelli, A., 'Uchronic dreams: working-class memory and possible worlds', in R. Samuel and P. Thompson (eds.), *The myths we live by* (London, 1990), 143–60.

Power, M., 'London and the control of the crisis of the 1590s', *History*, 70 (1985), 371–85.

Prasch, T., 'The making of an English working past, the rediscovery of Gerrard Winstanley, and late Victorian English radicalism', *Wordsworth Circle*, 25, 3 (1994), 166–72.

Rappaport, S., *Worlds within worlds: structures of life in sixteenth-century London* (Cambridge, 1989).

Ravensdale, J. R., 'Landbeach in 1549: Ket's rebellion in miniature', in L. M. Munby (ed.), *East Anglian Studies* (Cambridge, 1968), 94–116.

Rawcliffe, C., *Medicine for the soul: the life, death and resurrection of an English medieval hospital* (Stroud, 1999).

Reay, B., *Popular cultures in England, 1550–1750* (London, 1998).

Richards, M., *A time of silence: civil war and the culture of repression in Franco's Spain, 1936–1945* (Cambridge, 1998).

Rollison, D., *The local origins of modern society: Gloucestershire, 1500–1800* (London, 1992).

Rollison, D., 'Discourse and class struggle: the politics of industry in early modern England', *Social History*, 26, 2 (2001), 166–89.

Rollison, D., 'Conceits and capacities of the vulgar sort: the social history of English as a language of politics', *Cultural and Social History*, 2, 2 (2005), 141–64.

Rollison, D., 'The specter of the commonalty: class struggle and the commonweal in England before the Atlantic World', *William and Mary Quarterly*, 3rd ser., 63, 2 (2006), 221–52.

Roper, L., '"The common man", "the common good", "common women": gender and meaning in the German Reformation commune', *Social History*, 12, 1 (1987), 1–21.

Rose-Troup, F., *The Western rebellion of 1549* (London, 1913).

Rushton, P., 'Texts of authority: witchcraft accusations and the demonstration of truth in early modern England', in S. Clark (ed.), *Languages of witchcraft: narrative, ideology and meaning in early modern culture* (Basingstoke, 2001), 21–39.

Russell, F. W., *Kett's rebellion in Norfolk* (London, 1859).

Sassoon, D., *One hundred years of socialism: the West European left in the twentieth century* (London, 1996).

Scase, W., '"Strange and wonderful bills": bill-casting and political discourse in late medieval England', *New Medieval Literatures*, 2 (1998), 225–47.

Scott, J. C., *Domination and the arts of resistance: hidden transcripts* (New Haven, CT, 1990).

Scribner, R. W. and Benecke, G. (eds.), *The German Peasant War of 1525, new viewpoints* (London, 1979).

Sennett, R. and Cobb, J., *The hidden injuries of class* (New York, 1972).

Sewell, W. H., *Work and revolution in France: the language of labor from the Old Regime to 1848* (Cambridge, 1980).

Shagan, E., 'Protector Somerset and the 1549 rebellions: new sources and new perspectives', *English Historical Review*, 114, 455 (1999), 34–63.

Shagan, E., 'Rumours and popular politics in the reign of Henry VIII', in T. Harris (ed.), *The politics of the excluded, c. 1500–1850* (Basingstoke, 2001).

Shagan, E., *Popular politics and the English Reformation* (Cambridge, 2003).

Sharpe, J. A., *Crime in early modern England, 1550–1750* (1984; 2nd edn, Harlow, 1999).

Sharpe, J. A., '"Last dying speeches": religion, ideology and public execution in seventeenth-century England', *P&P*, 107 (1985), 144–67.

Sharpe, J. A., 'The people and the law', in B. Reay (ed.), *Popular culture in seventeenth-century England* (London, 1985), 244–70.

Sharpe, J. A., *Early modern England: a social history, 1550–1760* (1987; 2nd edn, London, 1997).

Sharpe, J. A., 'The law, law enforcement, state formation and national integration in late medieval and early modern England', in X. Rousseaux and R. Lévy (eds.), *Le pénal dans tous ses états: justice, états et sociétés en Europe (XIIe–XXe siècles)* (Brussels, 1997), 65–80.

Shepard, A., *Meanings of manhood in early modern England* (Oxford, 2003).

Shrank, C., 'Civil tongues: language, law and reformation', in J. Richards (ed.), *Early modern civil discourses* (Basingstoke, 2003), 19–34.

Simons, J., *Foucault and the political* (London, 1995).

Slack, P., *Poverty and policy in Tudor and Stuart England* (Harlow, 1988).

Slack, P., *From reformation to improvement: public welfare in early modern England* (Oxford, 1998).

Smith Fussner, F., *Tudor history and the historians* (New York, 1970).

Spufford, M., *Contrasting communities: English villagers in the sixteenth and seventeenth centuries* (Cambridge, 1974).

Stacy, J., *A topographical and historical account of the city and county of Norwich* (London, 1819).

Stallybrass, P. and White, A., *The politics and poetics of transgression* (London, 1986).

Steedman, C., *The radical soldier's tale: John Pearman, 1819–1908* (London, 1988).

Stone, L., 'Patriarchy and paternalism in Tudor England: the Earl of Arundel and the peasants' revolt of 1549', *Journal of British Studies*, 13 (1974), 19–23.

Stone, L., 'Lawrence Stone – as seen by himself', in A. L. Beier, D. Cannadine and J. M. Rosenheim (eds.), *The first modern society: essays in English history in honour of Lawrence Stone* (Cambridge, 1989), 575–95.

Stoyle, M., 'Pagans or paragons?: Images of the Cornish during the English Civil War', *English Historical Review*, 111 (1996), 299–323.

Stoyle, M., *Circled with stone: Exeter's city walls, 1485–1660* (Exeter, 2003).

Strohm, P., *Hochon's arrow: the social imagination of fourteenth-century texts* (Princeton, 1992).

Swinden, H., *The history and antiquities of the ancient burgh of Great Yarmouth* (Norwich, 1772).

Tansley, F. C., *For Kett and countryside* (London, 1910).

Tawney, R. H., *The agrarian problem in the sixteenth century* (London, 1912).

Therborn, G., *What does the ruling class do when it rules? State apparatuses and state power under feudalism, capitalism and socialism* (London, 1978).

Thomas, K., 'The place of laughter in Tudor and Stuart England', *Times Literary Supplement*, 21 (January, 1977), 76–83.

Thompson, E. P., *The making of the English working class* (London, 1963).

Thompson, E. P., *Customs in common* (London, 1991).

Tittler, R., 'Political culture and the built environment of the English country town, c. 1540–1620', in Hoak (ed.), *Tudor political culture*, 133–56.

Tittler, R., 'Reformation, civic culture and collective memory in English provincial towns', *Urban History*, 24, 3 (1997), 283–300.

Tittler, R., *Townspeople and nation: English urban experiences, 1540–1640* (Stanford, CA, 2001).

Tittler, R. and Battley, S. L., 'The local community and the Crown in 1553: the accession of Mary Tudor revisited', *Bulletin of the Institute of Historical Research*, 57 (1984), 131–9.

Tyacke, N., *Aspects of English Protestantism, c. 1530–1700* (Manchester, 2001).

Underdown, D. E., 'The taming of the scold: the enforcement of patriarchal authority in early modern England', in Fletcher and Stevenson (eds.), *Order and disorder*, 92–115.

Vere Woodman, A., 'The Buckinghamshire and Oxfordshire rising of 1549', *Oxoniensia*, 22 (1957), 78–84.

Voloshinov, V. N., *Marxism and the philosophy of language* (Cambridge, MA, 1986).

Walker, G., *Crime, gender and social order in early modern England* (Cambridge, 2003).

Walker, G., 'Just stories: telling tales of infant death in early modern England', in M. Mikesell and A. Seeff (eds.), *Culture and change: attending to early modern women* (Newark, DE, 2003), 98–115.

Walker, S., 'Rumour, sedition and popular protest in the reign of Henry IV', *P&P*, 166 (2000), 31–65.

Walter, J., 'A "rising of the people"? The Oxfordshire rising of 1596', *P&P*, 107 (1985), 90–143.

Walter, J., *Understanding popular violence in the English revolution: the Colchester plunderers* (Cambridge, 1999).

Walter, J. and Wrightson, K., 'Dearth and the social order in early modern England', *P&P*, 71 (1976), 22–42.

Watts, J., *Henry VI and the politics of kingship* (Cambridge, 1996).

Watts, J., 'The pressure of the public on later medieval politics', in L. Clark and C. Carpenter (eds.), *The fifteenth century, IV: Political culture in late medieval Britain* (Woodbridge, 2004), 159–80.

Watts, S. J., *From border to middle shire: Northumberland, 1586–1625* (Leicester, 1975).

Weil Baker, D., *Divulging utopia: radical humanism in sixteenth-century England* (Amherst, MA, 1999).

White, H. T., 'A Hampshire plot', *Papers and Proceedings of the Hampshire Field Club and Archaeological Society*, 12 (1934), 54–60.

Whittle, J., *The development of agrarian capitalism: land and labour in Norfolk, 1440–1580* (Oxford, 2000).

Williams, J. M., '"O! When degree is shak'd": sixteenth-century anticipations of some modern attitudes toward usage', in T. W. Machan and C. T. Scott (eds.), *English and its social contacts: essays in historical sociolinguistics* (New York, 1992), 69–101.

Williams, R., *Marxism and literature* (Oxford, 1977).

Williamson, T., *The Norfolk Broads: a landscape history* (Manchester, 1997).

Withington, P., 'Two renaissances: urban political culture in post-Reformation England reconsidered', *Historical Journal*, 44, 1 (2001), 239–67.

Wood, A., *The politics of social conflict: the Peak Country, 1520–1770* (Cambridge, 1999).

Wood, A., '"Poore men woll speke one daye": plebeian languages of deference and defiance in England, c. 1520–1640', in Harris (ed.), *Politics of the excluded*, 67–98.

Wood, A., *Riot, rebellion and popular politics in early modern England* (Basingstoke, 2002).

Wood, A., 'Kett's rebellion', in C. Rawcliffe and R. Wilson (eds.), *Medieval Norwich* (London, 2004), 277–300.

Wood, A., 'Fear, hatred and the hidden injuries of class in early modern England', *Journal of Social History*, 39, 3 (2006), 803–26.

Wright, T., 'On the municipal archives of the City of Canterbury', *Archaeologia*, 31 (1846), 198–211.

Wrightson, K. E., 'Two concepts of order: justices, constables and jurymen in seventeenth-century England', in J. Brewer and J. Styles (eds.), *An ungovernable people: the English and their law in the seventeenth and eighteenth centuries* (London, 1980), 21–46.

Wrightson, K. E., *English society, 1580–1680* (London, 1982).

Wrightson, K. E., 'Estates, degrees and sorts: changing perceptions of society in Tudor and Stuart England', in P. Corfield (ed.), *Language, history and class* (Oxford, 1991), 30–52.

Wrightson, K. E., 'Sorts of people in Tudor and Stuart England', in J. Barry (ed.), *The middling sort of people: culture, society and politics in England, 1550–1800* (Basingstoke, 1994), 28–51.

Wrightson, K. E., 'The politics of the parish in early modern England', in P. Griffiths, A. Fox and S. Hindle (eds.), *The experience of authority in early modern England* (Basingstoke, 1996), 10–46.

Wrightson, K. E., *Earthly necessities: economic lives in early modern Britain* (New Haven, CT, 2000).

Wrightson, K. E. and Levine, D., *Poverty and piety in an English village: Terling, 1525–1700* (1979; 2nd edn, Cambridge, 1995).

Wunder, H., 'The mentality of rebellious peasants: the Samland peasant rebellion of 1525', in Scribner and Benecke (eds.), *German Peasant War*, 144–59.

Zagorin, P., *Rebels and rulers 1500–1660*, vol. I: *Society, states and early modern revolution: agrarian and urban rebellions* (Cambridge, 1982).

Zeeveld, W. G., *Foundations of Tudor policy* (Cambridge, MA, 1948).

UNPUBLISHED DISSERTATIONS

Evans, S., 'Gentlemen clothiers in sixteenth century Norfolk', MA dissertation, Centre of East Anglian Studies, University of East Anglia (1999).

Greenwood, A., 'A study of the rebel petitions of 1549', PhD dissertation, Manchester University (1990).

Hammond, R. J., 'The social and economic circumstances of Ket's rebellion', MA dissertation, London University (1933).

Jones, A., '"Commotion time": the English risings of 1549', PhD thesis, University of Warwick (2003).

INDEX

Titles in the series

*Images and Cultures of Law in Early Modern England: Justice and Political Power,
1558–1660*
PAUL RAFFIELD

Print Culture and the Early Quakers
KATE PETERS

*Ireland and the English Reformation: State Reform and Clerical Resistance in the
Diocese of Dublin, 1534–1590*
JAMES MURRAY

London and the Restoration, 1659–1683
GARY S. DE KREY

Defining the Jacobean Church: The Politics of Religious Controversy, 1603–1625
CHARLES W. A. PRIOR

Queenship and Political Discourse in the Elizabethan Realms
NATALIE MEARS

John Locke, Toleration and Early Enlightenment Culture
JOHN MARSHALL

The Devil in Early Modern England
NATHAN JOHNSTONE

Georgian Monarchy: Politics and Culture, 1714–1760
HANNAH SMITH

*Catholicism and Community in Early Modern England: Politics, Aristocratic
Patronage and Religion, c.1550–1640*
MICHAEL C. QUESTIER

*The Reconstruction of the Church of Ireland: Bishop Bramhall and the Laudian
Reforms, 1633–1641*
JOHN McCAFFERTY

Europe and the Making of England, 1660–1760
TONY CLAYDON

Parliaments and Politics during the Cromwellian Protectorate
PATRICK LITTLE, DAVID L. SMITH

*Also published as a paperback